AI-Powered Augmented Reality for Public Administration

Jan Vrba
https://orcid.org/0000-0002-8404-5091
Akademia Jagiellonska w Toruniu, Poland

Thi Ngoc Quynh Huynh
https://orcid.org/0000-0002-6772-7621
Akademia Jagiellonska w Toruniu, Poland

Oldřich Hájek
https://orcid.org/0009-0003-5400-1420
University of ss. Cyril and Methodius, Slovakia

IGI Global
Scientific Publishing
Publishing Tomorrow's Research Today

Vice President of Editorial	Melissa Wagner
Director of Acquisitions	Mikaela Felty
Director of Book Development	Jocelynn Hessler
Production Manager	Mike Brehm
Cover Design	Jose Rosado

Published in the United States of America by
IGI Global Scientific Publishing
701 East Chocolate Avenue
Hershey, PA, 17033, USA
Tel: 717-533-8845 | Fax: 717-533-7115
Website: https://www.igi-global.com E-mail: cust@igi-global.com

Library of Congress Cataloging-in-Publication Data

LCCN: 2026002854 (CIP Data Pending)
ISBN13: 979-8-3373-7804-6
Isbn13Softcover: 979-8-3373-7805-3
EISBN13: 979-8-3373-7806-0

British Cataloguing in Publication Data
A Cataloguing in Publication record for this book is available from the British Library.

Table of Contents

Detailed Table of Contents

This chapter examines the transformative potential of AI-powered augmented reality (AI-AR) in advancing inclusive local governance, particularly for marginalized communities. Despite growing digitalization in public administration, structural inequalities continue to limit meaningful participation, transparency, and access to public services for disadvantaged groups. The chapter explores how the integration of artificial intelligence with augmented reality can enhance citizen engagement, simplify administrative processes, improve service delivery, and strengthen accountability at the local level. Drawing on concepts from inclusive governance, digital public administration, and social justice, the chapter analyzes applications of AI-AR in participatory planning, welfare delivery, grievance redressal, and capacity building of local institutions. It also critically examines ethical, legal, and implementation challenges, offering policy-oriented recommendations for responsible and equitable adoption of immersive technologies in local governance systems.

This chapter proposes an AI-enabled participatory governance model to strengthen sustainable urban service delivery through citizen feedback. The web-based system enables residents to report neighbourhood problems by uploading an image with a short text description. NLP estimates urgency and ranks severity, while image classification assigns each complaint to a relevant category. This dual-AI pipeline improves triage efficiency, reduces manual workload, and supports municipal decision-making by prioritising issues with higher social or environmental impact. The chapter also shows how real-time dashboards, geospatial mapping, and automated workflow routing help governments identify citywide patterns. Longitudinal analytics further enable tracking recurring issues, detecting seasonal trends, and evaluating intervention outcomes over time. Overall, the work demonstrates how data-driven participation platforms can operationalise sustainability as a continuous improvement cycle rather than a one-time intervention.

Smart cities have become a central frame of reference for contemporary urban governance. Public administrations are increasingly using artificial intelligence to analyse complex data environments and support administrative decision making processes. At the same time, augmented reality is opening up new forms of visualisation by embedding analytical results directly in spatial and administrative contexts. Both technologies are changing how information is generated, interpreted and used in public decision-making processes. This chapter analyses AI-supported augmented reality applications in smart cities from an administrative science and governance-oriented perspective. The focus is not on technical performance characteristics, but on institutional adaptation processes within public organisations. Based on a comparative qualitative case study analysis, three internationally established smart cities are analysed: Singapore, Barcelona and Amsterdam. These cases represent different governance models and administrative logics that characterise the use of AI-based and immersive systems.

This study examines the relationship between AI policy and data privacy in Indonesia, focusing on social media, public services, and electronic government systems. Using a Regulatory Impact Assessment (RIA) approach with normative legal and public policy analysis, the study draws on national surveys, policy documents, and academic literature. Privacy Calculus Theory and Social Exchange Theory are applied to explain personal data sharing behavior in digital environments. The findings indicate that high internet and social media use, particularly among individuals aged 15–34, is not supported by adequate digital security literacy, encouraging oversharing and increasing risks of online fraud, identity theft, and account hacking. Furthermore, the implementation of the Personal Data Protection Law remains limited in regulating AI-based data processing, especially regarding algorithm transparency, accountability of automated decision-making, and oversight mechanisms.

Use of artificial intelligence and augmented reality in the governance system is reforming the process of immigration to support the administration, decision-making and participation by the population. Even though these technologies are expected to bring greater efficiency, transparency and innovativeness in public services, they equally present a considerable ethical and legal dilemma. The chapter analyzes ethical standards and the law that regulates AI and AR use in governance, and specifically issues of accountability, data privacy, algorithmic bias, surveillance and democratic values. It examines regulatory loopholes, cross-jurisdictional issues and endangers to civil liberties, boasting of the necessity of transparency, fairness and humanism in governance models. The chapter gives a full background to responsible deployment of AI and AR in the governance of the people by critically analyzing the existing practices and the emerging policy approaches.

The combination of AI algorithms and extensive augmented reality technologies, is revolutionizing the service delivery in the occupational sector in the form of intelligent, immersive, and citizen-driven digital ecosystems. The government is able to process vast quantities of data automatically, predict the needs of the society and automate its operations through AI, and use AR to engage more people through superimposing real-time, context-driven information onto the environment of the user involved. Collectively, the technologies will aid in responsive and accountable governance in the sector of healthcare, urban governance, transport, education, and emergency services. Their intersection enhances transparency, efficiency, and accessibility and it also allows to engage citizens and government systems more intuitively. These opportunities, however, have their share of challenges associated with privacy, capacity of the infrastructure, digital equity, and regulation.

This chapter examines the integration of Artificial Intelligence (AI) and Augmented Reality (AR) in public service delivery, highlighting their combined potential to improve efficiency, decision-making, and citizen engagement. AI provides analytical intelligence for automation, prediction, and data processing, while AR enhances visualization and real-time interaction within physical environments. The chapter explores applications across healthcare, administration, urban planning, and emergency response, as well as challenges related to ethics, infrastructure, and governance. It concludes that AI–AR synergy offers a transformative pathway toward smarter, more responsive, and citizen-centered public services.

AI and AR in the combination form a radical change in how governments imagine the conceptualization and provision of public services, which allows customers to experience immersive, context-dependent, and personalized experiences. The human-centered design of the public services also incorporates technology in a design that has a responsible grasp in the needs, accessibility challenges and environmental limitations of the citizens so as to have meaningful participation. The AI-assisted AR applications will contribute to the improvement of transparency, reduction of the time spent working through the bureaucratics, real-time multilingual communication, or visual overlay of the features allowing civilians to learn more about their city, react to crises, access healthcare, and interact with the government. This chapter will look at the design architectures, application paradigms, and guidelines on governance needed to safely, equitably.

The integration of Artificial Intelligence (AI) and Augmented Reality (AR) is redefining digital governance by shifting e-government toward immersive, context-aware, and predictive public services. AI enables decision intelligence through adaptive policies, behavioral insights, and proactive interventions, while AR enhances citizen interaction with spatial, real-time information. This chapter reviews the foundations, technological enablers, challenges, and applications of AI and AR in smart cities, public safety, healthcare, and participatory platforms. It also highlights ethical and regulatory concerns including fairness, accountability, surveillance risks, and institutional readiness. A conceptual framework outlines the architecture and organizational alignment required for effective deployment, followed by future directions stressing interoperability, ethical safeguards, and adaptive policy design.

The rise of Artificial Intelligence (AI)-powered governance marks a profound transformation in the way public services are delivered, managed, and experienced, ushering in a new era of efficiency, transparency, and citizen-centric administration. As governments worldwide face growing complexities—including rapidly expanding populations, socio-economic inequalities, climate challenges, and heightened expectations for accountability—AI has emerged as a strategic enabler capable of supporting smarter decision-making and seamless service delivery across the public sector. AI-powered governance leverages technologies such as machine learning, natural language processing, predictive analytics, and autonomous systems to modernize public administration by automating bureaucratic operations, enhancing data-driven policymaking, and improving accessibility and responsiveness in citizen-

However, challenges related to ethics, privacy, and digital inequality persist, necessitating a human-centered governance framework. This study concludes that AI-AR integration can advance smart, resilient, and inclusive cities when guided by transparency, sustainability, and cross-sector collaboration.

Preface

Public administration is undergoing a profound transformation as governments across the world confront increasing complexity, rising citizen expectations, and rapid technological change. Artificial intelligence (AI) and augmented reality (AR) have emerged as two of the most promising technologies shaping this transformation. When combined, they offer powerful new ways to reimagine governance, enhance transparency, improve service delivery, and foster more meaningful engagement between public institutions and citizens. This edited volume, *AI-Powered Augmented Reality for Public Administration*, is situated at the intersection of these developments.

The motivation for this book stems from a growing recognition that digital transformation in the public sector can no longer be addressed through isolated technological solutions. Instead, it requires integrated, interdisciplinary approaches that consider organizational structures, policy processes, ethical frameworks, and societal impacts. AI-powered AR systems—ranging from data-driven visualization tools and immersive decision-support platforms to citizen-facing applications—present unique opportunities to bridge information gaps, support evidence-based policymaking, and make public administration more accessible and responsive.

The primary objective of this book is to examine how AI and augmented reality can be effectively integrated within public administration frameworks. The chapters collectively highlight innovative applications that improve governance, accountability, and citizen participation, while also presenting empirical and case-based studies that demonstrate gains in administrative efficiency and policy implementation. Equally important, this volume addresses the ethical, legal, and societal implications of AI–AR adoption, acknowledging challenges related to privacy, bias, accountability, and inclusiveness. By doing so, the book aims not only to showcase technological potential but also to encourage responsible and sustainable use of these emerging tools.

This volume brings together contributions from scholars and practitioners across disciplines, reflecting the inherently interdisciplinary nature of AI-powered augmented reality in the public sector. The intended audience includes researchers in public administration, digital governance, and emerging technologies; policymakers and government officials tasked with implementing AI and AR solutions; IT professionals and system designers involved in public sector innovation; graduate students exploring digital transformation and smart governance; industry experts and consultants working in civic technology; and, more broadly, citizens interested in the future of governance.

As Editors, we hope this book will serve as a valuable reference for advancing research, informing policy, and guiding practice in the evolving landscape of digital governance. We also hope it will stimulate further dialogue and collaboration among academics, practitioners, and citizens, contributing to more transparent, inclusive, and effective public administration in the age of AI-powered augmented reality.

ORGANIZATION OF THE BOOK

Chapter 1: AI-Powered Augmented Reality for Inclusive Local Governance

Focusing on equity and social justice, this chapter explores how AI-powered augmented reality can advance inclusive local governance, particularly for marginalized and underserved communities. The authors examine applications of AI-AR in participatory planning, welfare delivery, grievance redressal, and institutional capacity building, demonstrating how immersive technologies can lower barriers to participation and enhance transparency. At the same time, the chapter critically addresses ethical, legal, and implementation challenges, offering policy-oriented recommendations to ensure responsible and equitable adoption of AI-AR solutions at the local governance level.

Chapter 2: AI-Enabled Participatory Governance for Sustainable Urban Problem Reporting

This chapter presents an applied, data-driven model for participatory governance that leverages artificial intelligence to improve urban service delivery. By integrating natural language processing and image classification, the proposed system enables citizens to report neighborhood issues efficiently while supporting municipal decision-making through automated prioritization and severity assessment. The chapter further demonstrates how dashboards, geospatial mapping, and longitudinal analytics can transform citizen feedback into a continuous sustainability improvement cycle, reinforcing the role of AI-enabled participation in smart and responsive urban governance.

Chapter 3: AI-Supported Augmented Reality in Smart Cities: Administration Between Innovation and Institutional Adaptation

Drawing on comparative case studies from Singapore, Barcelona, and Amsterdam, this chapter examines how AI-supported augmented reality is reshaping administrative practices within smart cities. Rather than focusing on technical performance, the authors adopt an administrative science perspective to analyze institutional adaptation processes and governance logics. The chapter highlights how different political-administrative contexts influence the adoption and use of immersive technologies, offering valuable insights into the organizational challenges and opportunities associated with AI-AR integration in public administration.

Chapter 4: AI Regulations and Policies for Data Privacy Protection in Indonesia

This chapter provides a focused regulatory and policy analysis of AI and data privacy in Indonesia, with particular attention to social media, public services, and e-government systems. Using a Regulatory Impact Assessment approach, the authors examine gaps between high levels of digital engagement and limited digital security literacy, especially among younger populations. The findings reveal critical shortcomings in the implementation of personal data protection laws, particularly in relation to algorithmic transparency and accountability, underscoring the need for stronger governance frameworks to manage AI-driven data processing in the public sector.

Chapter 5: Legal Challenges of AI and AR in Governance

Addressing the normative dimensions of technological adoption, this chapter examines the ethical and legal challenges posed by AI and augmented reality in governance. The authors analyze issues related to accountability, data privacy, algorithmic bias, surveillance, and democratic values, while also highlighting regulatory gaps and cross-jurisdictional complexities. By critically assessing existing legal frameworks and emerging policy approaches, the chapter provides a foundation for responsible, transparent, and human-centered deployment of AI-AR technologies in public administration.

Chapter 6: Fusion Technologies in Governance: From Algorithmic Intelligence to Augmented Reality

This chapter explores the convergence of AI and augmented reality as fusion technologies that are reshaping public service delivery into intelligent, immersive, and citizen-driven digital ecosystems. The authors examine applications across healthcare, urban governance, transportation, education, and emergency services, demonstrating how AI-driven analytics and AR-based visualization collectively enhance responsiveness, transparency, and accessibility. Alongside these opportunities, the chapter addresses challenges related to privacy, infrastructure capacity, digital equity, and regulation.

Chapter 7: AI Algorithms and Augmented Reality Integration with Public Services

Building on the theme of technological synergy, this chapter analyzes how the integration of AI algorithms and augmented reality can transform public service delivery. AI contributes automation, prediction, and data intelligence, while AR enhances visualization and real-time interaction within physical environments. Through examples from healthcare, administration, urban planning, and emergency response, the chapter highlights both the transformative potential and governance challenges of AI–AR integration, reinforcing the need for ethical and institutional readiness.

Chapter 8: Designing Human-Centered Public Services through AI-Driven Augmented Reality Systems

This chapter places human-centered design at the core of AI-driven augmented reality applications in public services. The authors discuss how immersive, personalized, and context-aware systems can reduce bureaucratic complexity, enhance transparency, and improve accessibility through features such as multilingual communication and real-time visual overlays. By examining design architectures and governance guidelines, the chapter emphasizes the importance of aligning technological innovation with citizen needs, equity considerations, and responsible public sector values.

Chapter 9: Enhancing Citizen Engagement and Transparency via Immersive Technologies

This chapter examines how AI and AR are redefining digital governance by moving beyond transactional e-government toward immersive, predictive, and context-aware public services. The authors review key technological enablers, applications, and challenges across smart cities, public safety, healthcare, and participatory platforms. A conceptual framework is proposed to align organizational structures and technological architectures, while ethical and regulatory concerns—such as fairness, accountability, and surveillance risks—are critically addressed.

Chapter 10: Future Trends and Innovations in Digital Public Administration

Focusing on emerging trajectories, this chapter explores future trends in AI-powered governance and their implications for public administration. The authors highlight how machine learning, natural language processing, predictive analytics, and autonomous systems are reshaping bureaucratic operations, policymaking, and citizen-facing services. By examining the growing use of intelligent virtual assistants and automated systems, the chapter provides a forward-looking perspective on how AI can support more efficient, transparent, and citizen-centric governance.

Chapter 11: Impact of Augmented Reality on Visual, Experiential, and Collaborative Learning in Early Education

This chapter extends the discussion of augmented reality into the education sector, examining its impact on early childhood and primary education. Through a synthesis of existing studies, the authors demonstrate how AR enhances visual, experiential, and collaborative learning by transforming abstract concepts into engaging, interactive representations. The chapter highlights improved learner engagement, concentration, and teamwork, illustrating how AR-supported learning contributes to broader public sector goals related to education and human capital development.

Chapter 12: Case Studies of AI-AR Applications in Urban Planning and Emergency Management

Using global case studies from Singapore, Japan, Barcelona, and Los Angeles, this chapter illustrates how AI-AR integration supports predictive, participatory, and sustainable urban governance and emergency management. The authors show how AI-driven analytics enhance forecasting and planning, while AR facilitates real-time visualization and public engagement during crises. The chapter also addresses persistent challenges related to ethics, privacy, and digital inequality, advocating for a human-centered and collaborative governance framework.

CONCLUSION

As this edited volume demonstrates, the convergence of artificial intelligence and augmented reality represents far more than a technological upgrade in public administration; it signals a fundamental rethinking of how governments design, deliver, and govern public services. Across diverse institutional contexts, policy domains, and levels of government, the chapters in this book collectively illustrate how AI-powered augmented reality can enhance administrative intelligence, improve transparency, and foster more meaningful and inclusive forms of citizen engagement. At the same time, they underscore that technological innovation must be accompanied by institutional adaptation, ethical reflection, and sound regulatory frameworks.

Taken together, the contributions reveal a dynamic landscape in which data-driven decision-making, immersive visualization, and participatory platforms are reshaping governance processes—from urban management and emergency response to education, healthcare, and local service delivery. The volume highlights both the promise and the complexity of AI–AR adoption, showing that while these technologies can increase efficiency and responsiveness, they also raise critical concerns related to privacy, accountability, algorithmic bias, digital equity, and democratic values. Addressing these challenges requires not only technical expertise but also interdisciplinary collaboration and human-centered design approaches that place citizens at the core of digital transformation.

As Editors, we view this book as a timely reference for scholars, practitioners, policymakers, and students seeking to understand and shape the future of digital governance. The insights offered here are intended to inform research agendas, guide policy development, and support responsible implementation of AI-powered augmented reality in the public sector. Ultimately, we hope this volume contributes to the ongoing global dialogue on building smarter, more transparent, and more inclusive public administrations—capable of harnessing emerging technologies while remaining firmly grounded in the principles of public value, trust, and social responsibility.

Chapter 1

AI-Powered Augmented Reality for Inclusive Local Governance:

Transforming Participation, Transparency, and Service Delivery for Marginalized Communities

A. Ranjithkumar
https://orcid.org/0000-0002-6744-7603
Vel Tech Rangarajan Dr. Sagunthala R&D Institute of Science and Technology, India

ABSTRACT

This chapter examines the transformative potential of AI-powered augmented reality (AI-AR) in advancing inclusive local governance, particularly for marginalized communities. Despite growing digitalization in public administration, structural inequalities continue to limit meaningful participation, transparency, and access to public services for disadvantaged groups. The chapter explores how the integration of artificial intelligence with augmented reality can enhance citizen engagement, simplify administrative processes, improve service delivery, and strengthen accountability at the local level. Drawing on concepts from inclusive governance, digital public administration, and social justice, the chapter analyzes applications of AI-AR in participatory planning, welfare delivery, grievance redressal, and capacity building of local institutions. It also critically examines ethical, legal, and implementation challenges, offering policy-oriented recommendations for responsible and equitable adoption of immersive technologies in local governance systems.

DOI: 10.4018/979-8-3373-7804-6.ch001

1. INTRODUCTION

1.1 Background and Problem Statement

Public administration digitization has become the main direction of enhancing the efficiency of governance, transparency, and citizen involvement in all parts of the world. National and subnational governments are progressively adopting e-governance platforms, digital service ports, mobile apps and information-driven decision-making services to transform the way they administer their businesses and deliver services to the population (Dunleavy et al., 2006; Margetts & Dunleavy, 2013). Digital governance initiatives are frequently advanced at the local level as a way of enhancing participatory democracy, as well as curbing bureaucracy and bringing the government nearer to the citizens.

Nevertheless, with these technological innovations, structural inequalities of local governance still exist mainly in societies that are characterized by highly socio-economic stratified societies. Empirical research suggests that technological changes do not solve existence of long-standing exclusions of poverty, caste, gender, disability, and geographic marginality (Heeks, 2018; Madon, 2020). Local governance institutions, such as Panchayati Raj Institutions locally and municipalities, still have unequal participation, lack of transparency, and unequal access to and delivery of public services, despite the implementation of digital platforms in many developing contexts, including India (Bhatnagar and Singh, 2019).

The marginalized populations, such as rural poor, Scheduled Castes, women, and persons with disabilities, and ethnic minorities, are often fraught with several and competing obstacles in using digital governance systems. Some of these obstacles are low digital literacy, unavailability of devices and internet connectivity, language barrier, and bureaucratic hurdles (van Dijk, 2020). Consequently, the process of involvement in the decision-making forums is still biased against socially and economically advantaged groups, whereas the mechanisms of transparency and the systems of service provision often cannot reach those who require them the most (UNDP, 2023). This digital expansion but social exclusion paradox poses essential questions concerning whether the modern local governance reforms are inclusive or not.

The closest contact point between the state and citizens is the local governance especially to marginalized communities that rely on the local institutions greatly in terms of welfare, dispute resolution, and provision of services to the communities. Local governance structures are much more entrenched in daily social relations than national-level digital systems and hence, they constitute a key place of inclusive and participatory digital change.

Table 1. Structural barriers to digital participation in local governance

Dimension	Marginalized Groups Affected	Evidence from Studies
Internet access	Rural poor, SC households	Lower rural connectivity
Digital literacy	Women, elderly	Skill gap persists
Language barriers	Ethnic minorities	English-dominated portals
Physical access	Disabled persons	Inaccessible interfaces

Source: UNDP, World Bank, National Sample Survey

Table 2. Digital exclusion in local governance: Key indicators (India)

Indicator	Marginalized Group	Evidence
Internet access	Rural households	~31%
Smartphone ownership	SC/ST households	~52%
Women using internet	Rural women	~33%
Access to e-services	Persons with disabilities	<25%
Gram Sabha participation	SC households	Lower than average

Sources: NSS, NFHS-5, UNDP India

1.2 Research Gap and Significance

The current literature related to the field of digital governance has mostly explored the themes of artificial intelligence (AI) and augmented reality (AR) as distinct technological spheres. The field of AI in public administration has been addressed in terms of automation, predictive analytics, welfare-targeting, and decision-support systems, with the idea of algorithms bias, accountability, and transparency also being raised (Wirtz et al., 2019; Sun & Medaglia, 2019). Equally, research on augmented reality has focused on its application in urban planning, smart cities, and visualization of the population, mainly in the urban environment that is highly technologically developed (Batty et al., 2019; Shirazi & Behzadan, 2015).

Nevertheless, the current literature has a significant gap on the use of AI-AR to apply inclusive local governance. The intersection of the analytic and adaptive features of AI and the immersive and visual interfaces of AR has not been explored further, especially on the lower governance level. More to the point, the marginalized community is seldom the focus of the immersive governance research, as efficiency, innovation, or urban smartness are often considered as its priority instead of equity and social justice (Eubanks, 2018; Kitchin, 2021).

Such a gap is also considerable since AI-enabled augmented reality could help resolve digital and social divides at the same time. Whereas AI is able to individualize information, translate it automatically and predict services, AR is able to make complicated administration processes transparent and interpretable by applying the use of complex and understandable overlays into the real world. AI-AR can also make the process less dependent on middlemen, more transparent, and allow meaningful engagement of citizens that cannot engage with the text-intensive or interface-rich digital space. Consequently, it is topical and needed to conduct a narrower study on AI-AR in the context of inclusive local governance.

This chapter expands the literature on the topic by incorporating the concept of artificial intelligence and augmented reality into an inclusive system of governance. It provides one of the initial policy-based, systematic analyses of AI-driven immersive technologies within the context of local governance, paying particular attention to marginalized communities in the developing environments. This chapter considers AI-enhanced augmented reality a supplementary governance tool that can assist democratic institutions, but not a technological alternative to political change.

1.3 Objectives and Research Questions

The central aim of the chapter is to review the way in which participation, transparency, and delivering services more publicly can change in marginalized communities in local governments through the use of AI-powered augmented reality. In order to pursue this goal, the chapter discusses the following research questions: 1. What role can AI-driven augmented reality play in improving citizen engagement of disadvantaged groups in local governance? 2. How can AI-AR enhance transparency and accountability of local institutions of governance? 3. What is the potential of AI-AR to reinvent socially and economically disadvantaged population access to the delivery of public services and access to welfare? 4. Which are the ethical, legal, and implementation issues of the AI-AR implementation in local governance cases? The chapter aims at being useful in emerging debates of digital public administration, inclusive governance, and responsible technology adoption by answering these questions.

1.4 Chapter Structure

The chapter is organized in the following way. Section 2 gives the conceptual and theoretical framework based on the inclusive governance theory, participatory democracy, literature of digital divide, justice-based technology frameworks, etc. Section 3 presents research methodology to be employed in the study. Section 4 conducts a literature review on the field of digital governance, artificial intelligence, and augmented reality and its inclusion implications. Section 5 is an analytical part where it is discussed how AI-based augmented reality can be used in citizen engagement, transparency, service provision, redressal of grievances, and capacity building accompanied by examples. Section 6 presents a critical analysis of the ethical, legal, and implementation issues related to the adoption of AI-AR. Section 7 will provide policy advice and a blueprint of responsible and inclusive implementation. Lastly, the chapter is rounded off by Section 8 that summarized main findings and plans of future research.

2. CONCEPTUAL AND THEORETICAL FRAMEWORK

The development of this chapter is based on an interdisciplinary conceptual and theoretical framework that incorporates the view of public administration, democratic theory, development studies, and science and technology studies. The framework allows conceptualizing the positioning of AI-powered augmented reality (AI-AR) as a tool of inclusive local governance and not just a technological breakthrough. The chapter places AI-AR in the context of further discussions about the role of participation, equity, and public value by incorporating ideas of inclusive governance, digital public administration, immersive technologies, and justice-oriented design.

2.1 Key Concepts

Inclusive Governance and Social Justice

Inclusive governance has been defined as the form of governance and decision making where all social groups are given equitable participation, representation and accessibility of government resources especially the historically sidelined groups (Graham, Amos, and Plumptre, 2003). It is not just a procedural inclusion, including the use of meetings or consultations, but substantive inclusion, which is about whether people and groups actually have an impact and can benefit through the public policies.

With regards to social justice, inclusive governance is aimed at structural inequalities that are based on caste, class, gender, disability, and ethnicity. Marginalized communities tend to be left out in the process of local governance because of the asymmetry of power, bureaucratic complexity, and information barriers. Thus, inclusive governance must have institutional mechanisms, which proactively reduce the thresholds of participation and redistribute power of decisions. This chapter theorizes AI-driven augmented reality as one of the potential facilitators of such mechanisms by opening up governance processes, making them more vulnerable, readable, and involveable.

Digital Public Administration and the Evolution of E-Governance

Digital public administration is the transformation of the old systems of bureaucracy into the use of information and communication technologies (ICTs). Initiatives on e-governance at the early stages were aimed at online digitization of the administrative procedures and better efficiency of the services provided by online portals and databases (Heeks, 2018). Recent trends are more user-focused, interoperable, data-driven, and increasingly known as digital-era governance or smart governance (Dunleavy et al., 2006; Margetts & Dunleavy, 2013).

Nevertheless, the history of the development of e-governance has demonstrated the long-standing disparities in access and use. Researchers maintain that digital government is often a reflection of social inequalities that exist in the real world and that privileges digitally literate and economically advantaged groups of people at the expense of marginalized persons (Madon, 2020). This chapter further develops this criticism by stating that immersive and adaptive technologies like AI-AR can transform digital public administration into more inclusive and participatory models of governance than transactional efficiency.

Artificial Intelligence in Public Administration

Artificial intelligence in public administration is the application of machine learning, natural language processing, predictive analytics, and automation in the context of helping people make decisions and delivering services. In government, AI could be used to target welfare, chatbots to provide services to citizens, fraud detection and prediction of policies (Wirtz, Weyerer, and Geyer, 2019). Advocates suggest AI has the potential to help make public administration more efficient, consistent, and responsive. Meanwhile, the critical scholarship presents the dangers posed by algorithmic bias, lack of transparency, and absence of responsibility, especially when the AIs use the past that is based on social discrimination (Eubanks, 2018; Kitchin, 2021). To marginalized people, AI systems may lessen or eliminate marginalization (by personalizing and reaching) or increase inequality because fairness and transparency are not mentioned. The chapter takes a somewhat optimistic, although skeptical, perspective on AI and stresses its possibilities when they are integrated into ethical and inclusive systems of governance.

Augmented Reality as an Immersive Governance Interface

Augmented reality (AR) is an immersive technology that superimposes digital data onto the physical world in order to enable one to engage with the virtual world in the real-world situation. In contrast to the conventional screen-based interfaces, AR offers spatial, visual, and contextualized information which can be useful in the context of understanding and interaction. AR was applied in visualization of urban planning, infrastructure monitoring, and public education programs in the context of the public sector (Batty et al., 2019). Being an interface to governance, AR is particularly promising to low-literate and digitally marginalized groups. AR can help to eliminate the use of textual content and intermediaries in the form of bureaucracy by visualizing budgets, infrastructure projects, and pathways of service in physical space. The conceptualization of AR in the chapter presents AR as the mediating layer that converts the complex administrative data into the more accessible, experiential forms and conveys them to the citizens.

Convergence of AI and AR (AI-Powered Augmented Reality)

The intersection of artificial intelligence and augmented reality creates AI-based AR systems that are adaptive, interactive and context-aware. The AI makes AR applications personalized, identify objects and locations, handle voice recognition and generate real-time insights, whereas AR gives the immersive interface in which all these features are seen (Billinghurst et al., 2015). In the governmental context, AI-enhanced AR could assist in real-time visualization of the projects in the community, individual guidance to reach the services, and predictive warning to administrators and citizens. This union would make AR more than a visualization tool since it can be a dynamic governance platform that has the potential to facilitate inclusive participation, transparency, and service delivery. In this chapter, AI-AR is seen as a socio-technical system whose benefit can be based on the institutional design, ethical protection, and inclusion of users.

2.2 Theoretical Foundations

Participatory Democracy: Arnstein's Ladder of Participation

The participatory democracy is a theory that focuses on the active participation of the citizens in making decisions that impact on their lives. The concept of Ladder of Citizen Participation suggested by Arnstein (1969) is a continuum of participation, where the opposite ends (non-participation in the form of manipulation and therapy), as well as intermediate forms (informing and consultation), and the final stage of participation (citizen power in the form of partnership, delegated power, and citizen control) are presented. In most local governance environments, the participation has been limited to tokenism especially to the marginalized groups. AI-based AR could shift the involvement to the higher levels of the ladder developed by Arnstein, as it allows informed communication, consultation, and co-creation. The AI-AR tools can strengthen collaborations between citizens and local governments instead of symbolic consultation by visualizing policy alternatives and allowing people to provide feedback in an interactive way.

Digital Divide Theory and the Capability Approach

The digital divide theory studies disparities in the access to, use of, and the benefits of digital technologies (van Dijk, 2020). Modern literature points to the fact that digital exclusion is not only the lack of physical access to technology but also a skill set, motivation, and the ability to transform digital tools into valuable services. The capability approach, created by Amartya Sen (1999) and extended by Martha Nussbaum (2011) is a normative theory explaining how much people can have actual autonomy to attain the treasured functioning. The capability approach in applied to digital governance gives more focus on human empowerment as opposed to technology provision. The capability perspective is incorporated in this chapter by considering the AI-AR technologies as ways of building the agency and capabilities of marginalized citizens, and not merely improving system efficiency.

Technology Acceptance Models for Marginalized Users

Technology Acceptance Models (TAM) and Unified Theory of Acceptance and Use of Technology (UTAUT) are models explaining technology adoption on the basis of perceived usefulness, ease of use, social influence and enabling conditions (Davis, 1989; Venkatesh et al., 2003). Although these models are commonly used in organizational and consumer contexts, they usually neglect structural inequalities that are experienced by marginalized users. This chapter transfers TAM and UTAUT to the local governance contexts by introducing the issues of literacy, accessibility to languages, trust towards the government and social power relations. The visual and voice-driven AR system, enhanced by AI, can become the tool that would enable more marginalized groups to perceive AR as easy to use and helpful enough to adopt, which will lead to higher adoption and engagement rates.

Justice-Oriented Technology and Responsible AI Frameworks

Technology justice systems believe that technological infrastructures ought to be created and regulated to promote equity, responsibility, and social accessibility (D'Ignazio and Klein, 2020). Responsible AI frameworks focus on the transparency, explainability, non-discrimination, privacy protection, and human oversight (Floridi et al., 2018). This chapter uses a viewpoint of justice to analyze AI-AR in local governance. Instead of considering ethics as a secondary concern, that framework incorporates the code of responsible AI in the creation and use of immersive governance technologies. This strategy will ensure that AI-AR systems will have an inclusive governance outcome and will not recreate or increase existing inequalities.

3. RESEARCH METHODOLOGY

The chapter is a qualitative, exploratory, and conceptual research design based on investigating the possibility of AI-powered augmented reality (AI-AR) to promote inclusive local governance. Due to the interdisciplinary and emerging nature of AI-ARs use in the government sector, a qualitative strategy will be suitable to consolidate theoretical knowledge, policy discussions, and initial implementation feedbacks (Creswell and Poth, 2018). The research unites the lenses of public administration, digital governance, science and technology research, and social justice research to create a comprehensive analysis approach. The chapter is not designed to test some preset hypotheses: instead, it is designed to generate conceptual clarity and insight into policy-relevant information on how immersive technologies can redefine participation, transparency, and service provision to marginalized communities. The analysis will be conducted solely relying on secondary sources, peer-reviewed journal articles published in the past years (2020-25), policy reports and governmental documents in India and at the global level and publications made by international organizations like the United Nations Development Programme (UNDP), the Organisation of Economic Co-operation and Development (OECD), and the World Bank. The thematic content analysis allowed analyzing these sources, and it was possible to identify common patterns, opportunities, and risks related to the adoption of AI-AR in the local governance. Besides, the chapter uses illustrative case examples, especially in Indian Panchayati Raj Institutions and Scheduled Caste welfare programs, to contextualize the theoretical argument. Although the generalizability would be restricted due to the lack of primary empirical data, the methodology is very appropriate to inform the designing of policies and be the baseline of other empirical and comparative studies.

Table 3. Research objectives, methods, and analytical outputs

Objective	Data Source	Method	Output
Study participation	Literature	Thematic analysis	Participation framework
Examine transparency	Policy reports	Content analysis	Governance indicators
Assess service delivery	Case documents	Comparative analysis	AI-AR use cases

Table 4. Secondary data sources used in the chapter

Source	Coverage	Used For
NSS	Digital access & social groups	Participation analysis
UNDP	Governance & inclusion	Equity lens
World Bank GovTech	Digital governance	Policy comparison
OECD AI reports	Responsible AI	Ethics framework
MoPR	Panchayats	Local governance

4. REVIEW OF LITERATURE

There is a swift growth in the digital governance, artificial intelligence, and immersive technologies literature in the previous decade. Nonetheless, there is unequal scholarship on the topic of local governance and marginalized communities. This part provides a critical review of the existing literature on four interconnected strands, which include digital tools in local governance, augmented reality in public services, artificial intelligence and inclusion, and emerging AI-AR applications. The review reports the major contributions and conceptual and empirical gaps that this chapter is aimed to cover..

4.1 Digital Tools in Local Governance

Digital tool Any digital tool is something that allows governmental services to be offered through online means so that people could access valuable information or services with the help of such gadgets as the Internet and smartphones. Digital tools have been advocated extensively as tools to enhance efficiency, transparency and accountability in local governance. The initial e-governance efforts aimed at digitalizing the administrative operations, including online service portals, e-record keeping, and digital payment systems, and the hope that the reform would help close corruption and enhance service delivery (Heeks, 2018; Bhatnagar, 2014).

Lately, local governments have adopted mobile governance (m-governance) and GIS-led planning tools to improve the outreach with citizens, spatial planning, and monitoring of development projects (Bertot, Estevez, and Janowski, 2016). In spite of these developments, a large literature body points out the narrow scope of digital governance instruments within the less privileged groups. Research indicates that the socio-economic status, education, gender, and geographic location tend to influence access to e-governance platforms and result in the unequal distribution of the benefits of digital reforms (Madon, 2020; van Dijk, 2020). According to local governance, rural residents, Scheduled Castes, women and persons with disabilities often experience the obstacles of low digital literacy, poor connectivity, language barrier, and reliance on the intermediaries (Kuriyan, Bailur, and Gigler, 2016). Consequently, the digital tools that are supposed to democratize governance can inadvertently build up ex-ante inequalities unless inclusion is made an explicit consideration in designing and implementation.

4.2 Augmented Reality in Public Services

AR is receiving more and more interest within the field of the research of the public sector, specifically, urban planning, smart cities, and public visualization. AR applications enable users to see proposed infrastructural projects and land-use changes, visualizing the effects of these changes on the real environment through superimposition of digital information (Batty et al., 2019). AR was found to boost comprehension, enable stakeholder interaction, and aid in collaborative decision-making in the context of the public planning process by making complicated technical data more accessible (Shirazi & Behzadan, 2015). However, in terms of public services, the entire world has a limited experience with AR in large urban areas with a high level of technological development. European, East Asian, and North American studies highlight its application in smart city dashboards, transport planning, disaster preparedness, and managing cultural heritage (Ratti and Claudel, 2016). Although these applications prove technical functionality and communicative capacity of AR, researchers mention that they tend to focus on innovation and visualization rather than social inclusion (Kitchin, 2021). Scarcity of the focus on the rural governance, low-literacy segments, and marginalized social groups imply that the prospects of AR in the role of an inclusive system of governance have not been explored fully.

4.3 Artificial Intelligence, Governance, and Inclusion

To generalize, artificial intelligence has been a paradigm-shifting technology in the field of public administration, which has been implemented in automated chatbots, predictive analytics, and welfare targeting to fraud detection (Wirtz et al., 2019). Artificial Intelligence-driven systems are becoming popular to facilitate service delivery, better policy forecasts, and administrative efficiency. Predictive models are also used to determine who is eligible to receive the benefits, predict demand in the service, and maximize resource distribution in the context of social welfare (Sun and Medaglia, 2019). Simultaneously, an increasing number of critical literature sources alert about the dangers of the use of AI in governance. Researchers bring up the issues of algorithmic bias, a lack of transparency, and the replication of structural inequalities, especially in the case of AI tools based on historical data influenced by social discrimination (Eubanks, 2018; Noble, 2018). The risks do not affect marginalized communities in the same ways since biased algorithms can deny them access to welfare or expose them to heightened monitoring. In turn, recent studies focus on the necessity of responsible artificial intelligence structures that anticipate fairness, accountability, explainability, and human control in the case of applications in the public sector (Floridi et al., 2018).

4.4 Emerging AI–AR Applications

Artificial intelligence and augmented reality intersect with each other and present a new direction in the study of digital governance. Pilots and experimental projects in early use AI-enabled AR systems in civic education, urban navigation, infrastructure surveillance, and immersive consultations with populations (Billinghurst et al., 2015). These applications imply that AI-AR has the potential to integrate the analytical intelligence with the intuitive visualization and allow real-time interaction between citizens, data and physical environments. Nevertheless, the available body of literature on AI-AR is still disjointed and exploratory in nature. Majority of the researches are centered on technical feasibility or user experience with little consideration of the governance outcomes, ethical issues, or social inclusion. More importantly, the lack of the research on the applications of AI-AR in the local governance context and their implication on marginalized communities is a considerable gap. Such issues as access, affordability, digital literacy, and institutional capacity are infrequently covered in detail. The chapter addresses these gaps by contextualizing AI-enhanced augmented reality in the context of inclusive local governance and the possibility of how it can revolutionize participation, transparency, and service provision among marginalized groups of people.

Table 5. Summary of literature on digital governance, AI, AR, and inclusion

Theme	Key Authors	Focus	Gap Identified
E-Governance	Heeks, Madon	Efficiency	Exclusion
AR in public sector	Batty et al.	Visualization	Urban bias
AI in welfare	Eubanks	Automation	Bias risk
AI-AR convergence	Billinghurst	Tech feasibility	Inclusion missing

5. APPLICATIONS OF AI-AR IN INCLUSIVE LOCAL GOVERNANCE

The adoption of artificial intelligence and augmented reality (AI-AR) presents both groundbreaking opportunities to local governance to tackle the old-time issues pertaining to participation, transparency, and service delivery. In contrast to traditional digital capabilities, AI-AR systems can integrate analytical intelligence with an immersive visualization where citizens can engage with the governance processes in sensitive and contextual manners. This section explores the main areas of its application when AI-AR can be useful to inclusive local governance with special consideration to the marginalized communities.

Table 6. Applications of AI-powered AR in local governance

Governance Function	AI Component	AR Component	Inclusion Outcome
Participation	NLP, analytics	Virtual town halls	Voice & visual access
Transparency	Fraud detection	Budget overlays	Social audits
Service delivery	Predictive models	Guided navigation	Easier access
Grievances	Classification	Visual tracking	Faster resolution

Table 7. Gaps in local service delivery affecting marginalized groups (India)

Area	Problem	Evidence
Welfare delivery	Eligible households excluded	20–30%
Grievance redressal	Delayed resolution	>40% pending
Public works	Low transparency	Weak monitoring
Participation	Low Gram Sabha attendance	SC & women underrepresented

5.1 Enhancing Citizen Participation

Citizen Participation is an inherent component of democratic local government yet participation systems tend to be inaccessible or ineffective to disadvantaged groups. The augmented reality facilitated by AI can be used to transform participatory spaces by reducing cognitive, linguistic, and procedural resistances to participation. AR-powered virtual town halls can make citizens engage in consultations remotely, which is especially useful to the rural population, women with care obligations, and people with disabilities. Translations with AI and voice interfaces make the process even more inclusive, as they allow engaging in multilingualism and lessen the use of literacy (UNDP, 2023). This can be simulated through such virtual forums simulating Gram Sabha or ward meetings where the citizens can visualize the agendas, proposals and the outcomes in real time.

Participatory planning that is facilitated by AR is another major innovation. With AR superimposition, people are able to see the proposed infrastructure project (like a road, sanitation facility, or housing) imposed on the real world. This visualization allows making informed decisions and valuable feedback and goes past consultatory stops and shops to collaborative decision-making (Batty et al., 2019). It is possible to use AI tools to analyze the inputs of citizens concurrently to identify patterns and priorities to aid in evidence-based planning. Moreover, AI-AR-based methods of gamified civic engagement can inspire young people and users with low literacy levels to take part. Through implementing game-like concepts, which include rewards, challenges, and visual narrative, governance processes become less confusing and frightening (Ratti and Claudel, 2016). These strategies are more applicable to disadvantaged groups who have generally been locked out of mainstream politics.

5.2 Improving Transparency and Accountability

The level of transparency and accountability is also central to establishing trust in local institutions of governance. The use of AI-AR technologies will be able to enrich these dimensions and make the administrative processes transparent, understandable, and accessible to the scrutiny of the citizens. Budgets and projects are AR visualized so that citizens can have access to financial and project information on-site. As an illustration, when a citizen observes a site of a public works with the help of a mobile device, its AR interface may show budgetary allocation, schedule, and contractor information. This openness of space minimizes the information asymmetry and gives citizens the power to keep track of development processes (Kitchin, 2021).

AI also enhances transparency by detecting fraud and anomalies. Machine learning algorithms are able to detect anomalies in procurement, welfare disbursement or project execution based on big administrative data (Wirtz et al., 2019). Combined with AR dashboards, these insights may be introduced in a convenient format that can be easily read by officials and citizens and perform a social audit and community control. AI-AR dashboards with features accessible to citizens would enable the real-time tracking of the indicators of service delivery, grievance state, and project progress. The democratizing of access to governance information and a decrease in reliance on intermediaries are especially significant in marginalized groups that usually do not have political connections (Madon, 2020). AI-AR systems can improve downward accountability and institutional responsiveness by facilitating the easy access of information.

5.3 Transforming Service Delivery and Welfare Access

Local delivery of public services is usually marked by cumbersome processes, disjointed information and bureaucratic whims, and largely the process disadvantages the marginalized groups. A service delivery that is personal, proactive, and accessible can be developed with AI-driven AR. Individualized AR instructions would help the citizens move around the welfare offices, comprehend the eligibility requirements and application procedures. As an example, AR overlays can be used to take users step-by-step through the points of services, and AI chatbots may explain everything in real time and in local languages. These systems decrease bureaucracies and decrease mistakes, which facilitates access to social protection initiatives (Heeks, 2018). In addition, the proactive outreach predictive analytics allow local government to see vulnerable households ahead of any crisis. AI models have the potential to act on socio-economic and demographic data to predict service needs, whereas AR interfaces can assist the frontline workers to visualize and prioritize interventions on the ground (Sun and Medaglia, 2019). Such a change in reactive to preventive service delivery is especially useful to Scheduled Castes and other disadvantaged groups which are often hindered by claiming entitlements.

5.4 Grievance Redressal and Capacity Building

Inclusive governance requires effective grievance redressal mechanisms, but marginalized communities often face problems with lodging complaints and following up on their results. The AI-AR technologies can support the grievance system making it more approachable and receptive. Multilingual voice-enabled AI-AR complaint systems permit citizens to file complaints through speech instead of text and transcend the limits of literacy and language. AR interfaces can visually assist users with the process of complaint categorization and update on the status of resolving the complaint in real time. It is also possible to classify and rank grievances by urgency and impact with the help of AI and increase the efficiency of administration (Bertot et al., 2016). AI-AR is also essential in capacity building amongst local officials, in addition to applications that are directed at citizens. AR training simulations allow the officials to train in dealing with issues like service delivery, rejection of emergency responses, and interaction with citizens in real life situations. The use of AI to assist in feedback mechanisms promotes continuous learning and skill acquisition and improves institutional capacity and professionalism (Dunleavy et al., 2006).

5.5 Case Studies and Illustrative Examples

The Indian context is also quite suitable in the context of studying AI-AR in local governance because of its size, institutionalized decentralization, and the ongoing socio-economic inequalities. The practical usefulness of AI-AR in the context of inclusive local governance is illustrated in the context of India and other international settings. In India, Panchayati Raj Institutions have been using digital technologies to deliver services and monitor them and established a base to implement AI-AR. Indicatively, AR interfaces can be added to digitized welfare databases and mobile monitoring systems to enhance transparency and citizen participation on a village level (Bhatnagar and Singh, 2019).

Using AI-AR systems to visualize entitlement and service pathways can be used to support targeted outreach, documentation support, and grievance redressal in the context of Scheduled Caste welfare delivery. The applications are used to overcome some typical challenges encountered by the SC households, such as information asymmetry and complexity of administration (UNDP, 2023). The range of applicability of AI-AR to various governance environments can be illustrated on the example of smart village projects in Southeast Asia and participatory planning efforts in Latin America. These examples differ in size and complexity but they highlight the potential of immersive technologies to enhance inclusive governance in case it is adjusted to local needs and institutional capabilities (OECD, 2021).

Table 8. Illustrative AI-AR use cases in Indian local governance

Context	Digital Base	Potential AI-AR Layer	Inclusion Benefit
Panchayats	e-Panchayat	AR project maps	Community monitoring
SC welfare	Digitized records	Eligibility overlays	Reduced exclusion
Grievances	Online portals	Voice AR filing	Literacy-neutral

Table 9. Existing digital foundations for AI-AR in India

Initiative	Existing Digital Layer	AI-AR Extension
e-Panchayat	Online records	AR project tracking
MGNREGA NMMS	Geo-tagged works	AR transparency
SC welfare portals	Digitized benefits	Eligibility visualization
Online grievances	Complaint databases	Voice-based AR filing

6. CHALLENGES AND CRITICAL ANALYSIS

Although AI-powered augmented reality (AI-AR) offers great prospects to improve the aspect of inclusive local governance, its use also comes with various ethical, legal, and implementation issues. Unless designed, regulated and institutionally prepared, AI-AR systems can replicate or even enhance inequalities. In this section critical analysis of these challenges will be offered to give a balanced and realistic evaluation of AI-AR in the context of governance.

6.1 Ethical Challenges

Privacy and Surveillance

AI-AR systems are primarily dependent on the data gathering, such as topographical data, biometric data, video footage, and behavioral statistics. These data practices become a big issue of concern in the context of local governance, especially within marginalized communities. Permanent surveillance of people and places is possible due to the immersiveness of AR and AI-based analytics, which may result in various types of surveillance that threatened civil liberties (Zuboff, 2019). Scheduled Castes, informal workers, and the occupants of low-income settlements are some of the groups that may be disproportionately impacted since they usually have little ability to challenge data misuse or withhold their consent to digital systems. Furthermore, AI-AR setting consent is usually implicit or ill-conceived particularly to users with low literacy levels. The scope and intent of data collection can be obscured by visual overlays and automatic prompts, casting doubts on the issue of informed consent and ownership of data (Floridi et al., 2018). The absence of strong principles concerning privacy-by-design and clear governance frameworks creates a threat to the erosion of trust between citizens and local institutions, as opposed to its reinforcement by AI-AR systems.

Algorithmic Bias and Discrimination

The issue of algorithmic bias is one of the key ethical issues of applying AI to governance systems. Artificial intelligence systems that are trained on past administrative records can reproduce the previous social prejudices based on caste, sex, physical handicap, or location (Eubanks, 2018; Noble, 2018). Such biases may lead to errors of exclusion or unequal prioritization or even discrimination in welfare delivery and grievance redressal systems. Under the circumstances that they are combined with AR interfaces, biased AI decisions can seem to be authoritative and unquestionable as they are presented in a visual and immersive manner. It is commonly known as the automation bias and may demoralize any critical questioning of the citizens and officials (Kitchin, 2021). This is a major threat to the marginalized communities; algorithmic decisions can embolden the process of exclusion under the pretext of being neutral to technology. Countering algorithmic bias thus needs unceasing auditing, disclosure as well as incorporation of human control measures.

Digital Exclusion and Unequal Access

Though AI-AR is typically a technology that is advertised as inclusive, it can contribute to digital exclusion under the pretext of neglecting to address access barriers. Applications of AR usually demand the use of a smartphone, a stable internet connection, and some basic knowledge of the digital world, which is not evenly distributed among individuals (van Dijk, 2020). The rural population, women, individuals with disabilities, and low-income households can be discriminated against when it comes to accessing and using AI-AR systems. Moreover, the interface of AI-AR processes is frequently designed with the presumptions regarding the abilities and the technical literacy of the users. Without being designed with accessibility features, including voice interaction, local language support, and the ability to operate with low bandwidth, systems can disenfranchise exactly the groups that the system is supposed to empower (Madon, 2020). Ethical use of AI-AR therefore requires a solid belief in universal access and inclusive design.

6.2 Legal and Regulatory Issues

Data Protection and Privacy Laws

The law of AI-AR systems is strictly connected with the laws of data protection and privacy. The General Data Protection Regulation (GDPR) introduced by the European Union sets up stringent demands concerning data minimalization, the consent, the transparency, and the right to clarification of the automated decision-making (European Union, 2016). The Digital Personal Data Protection (DPDP) act in India offers a legal framework in processing personal information with a focus on consent and accountability (Government of India, 2023). The implementation of these laws to AI-AR systems in local governance however is complicated. AR makes the line between the world life and personal space unclear and provokes the need to question legal data collection and proportionality. Besides that, most local governments do not have the institutional capacity to guarantee adherence to the emerging standards of data protection. Lose enforcement systems can expose the marginalized citizens to violation of their rights as well as misuse of their data.

Accountability and Liability for AI Decisions

The other important legal issue is the responsibility in decision-making or decision-making guided by AI systems. Under AI-AR-based governance, there is a possibility of automated recommendations or predictions in the decision-making process of welfare eligibility, prioritizing grievances, or distributing services. The question of accountability in the context of an error, discrimination, or harm is unclear in the law, especially when the AI systems are created by third-party sellers and implemented by governmental agencies (Wirtz et al., 2019). In the case of marginalized populations, ambiguous accountability frameworks may restrict the access to redress and justice. In case citizens cannot question AI-informed decisions or receive explanations, the authority of local institutions of governance can be compromised. Laws should hence specify the liability, require explainability and hold the decision-maker accountable in the human element.

6.3 Implementation Barriers

Cost and Infrastructure Constraints

The use of AI-AR systems comes along with the great investment in digital infrastructure, hardware, software development, and maintenance. A lot of the local governments, particularly in developing states, are under budgetary constraints and competing development priorities (OECD, 2021). Scalability and sustainability could be constrained by high prices of the AR devices, data storage and training AI models. There are also infrastructure deficiencies including poor electricity and internet connectivity, which limits implementation in countryside and remote regions. AI-AR projects will fail to reach beyond urban or other better-nourished areas, and without special purpose public investment and subsidies, will have to be limited to those areas, which will further enlarge spatial disparities.

Institutional Resistance and Capacity Deficits

Another major challenge to the adoption of AI-AR is the institutional resistance. Local authorities might be unhappy or lack technical expertise to seek interaction with new technologies, especially when they think that they will upset the status quo or hierarchies (Heeks, 2018). Resistance can also be based on the fear of greater scrutiny and accountability that transparent systems of data-driven systems can provide. The issue of the lack of capacity both technical and organizational can block the successful implementation. The fundamental components of an AI-AR involved are training programs, change management strategies and institutional support mechanisms that will help to make AI-AR tools part of daily governance practices instead of pilot projects with minimal impact.

Risk of Reinforcing Existing Inequalities

This is perhaps the most important issue, which is the danger that the AI-AR systems will only support the status quo in the event that they are implemented without being explicitly required to include everyone. Technologies launched under unequal social conditions tend to favor those who have already enjoyed it, which is what has been termed as the Matthew effect in the digital governance (van Dijk, 2020). Unless marginalized communities actively take part in the decision-making procedure of AI-AR systems, their requirements and limitations might be neglected. This danger highlights the significance of the justice-based and participatory methods of technology adoption. In the absence of these precautions, AI-AR can be another administrative stratum that privileges efficiency at the expense of equity. Other researchers warn that immersive governance technologies may lead to the process of adjustment to structural political reform to the technical one, but, as it is claimed in this chapter, AI-AR should be considered an addition to, but not a replacement of, the strengthening of democratic institutions. This chapter thus does not discuss AI-based augmented reality as a technocratic solution to governance failures, but an enabling factor whose success will be based on the quality of the democratic institutions, political goodwill, and social responsibility.

Table 10. Ethical, legal, and implementation risks of AI-AR

Risk	Description	Mitigation
Privacy	Surveillance	Data minimization
Bias	Algorithmic exclusion	Audits
Access	Digital divide	Kiosks, offline AR
Cost	Budget limits	Open-source tools

Table 11. Differential risk exposure among marginalized groups

Risk	Most Affected Group
Surveillance	Informal workers
Data misuse	SC households
Algorithmic bias	Women, disabled
Access exclusion	Rural poor

7. POLICY RECOMMENDATIONS AND WAY FORWARD

The successful implementation of AI-based augmented reality (AI-AR) into the local governance framework must be approached in a well-organized policy that will emphasize on inclusiveness, accountability, and sustainability over time. Although technological innovation can be used to improve the results of governance, its effectiveness may finally rely on the institutional design, ethical protection, and the ability of the public institutions to change. In this section, a list of policy recommendations/strategic directions is described that will facilitate the responsible adoption of AI-AR in inclusive local governance.

7.1 Responsible Adoption Framework

An inclusive and human-centered design framework should form the basis of a responsible adoption framework of AI-AR in local governance. Marginalized communities should be designed and not designed to use technologies, so that their experiences, needs, and limitations can shape the architecture of the system and user interfaces (D'Ignazio and Klein, 2020). The human-centered design focuses on accessibility, usability, and contextual relevance, which are especially relevant in an environment with low literacy, language variety, and minimal exposure to digital technology. The institution of community participation must be made across the technology life cycle such as in problem identification and design to implementation and evaluation. The use of participant co-design workshops, pilot testing with local populations and feedback systems can be used to make sure that AI-AR systems react to actual governance problems and not to theoretical technological opportunities (UNDP, 2023). The participatory techniques also improve trust and legitimacy, which is essential in adoption among the marginalized groups. Moreover, AI-AR governance principles should be incorporated in the policy frameworks. They are transparency, explainability, fairness, data minimalisation and human control (Floridi et al., 2018). The local governments ought to implement ethical principles that require the use of algorithmic audits, bias reduction policies, and responsibility frameworks. Policymakers can guarantee that innovation can promote social justice instead of worsening the inequality situation by incorporating the concept of responsible AI in immersive governance technologies.

7.2 Policy and Institutional Measures

In order to facilitate the implementation of AI-AR, governments should invest in interoperable, accessible, and resilient digital public infrastructure. This involves the proliferation of broadband provision, quality power distribution, and shared digital access centre like community kiosk at Panchayat or ward offices (OECD, 2021). The digital infrastructure in society must be viewed as a common good, and there should be specific investments to narrow the spatial and social inequality of access. Capacity building is also important both to the citizens and the officials in the government. The local government authorities should also be trained in ethical decision-making, data governance, and participatory technology management, as well as technical skills. In the case of citizens, the digital literacy programs are to be oriented at the practical interaction with AI-AR systems, with the focus on the rights awareness, grievance mechanisms, and service navigation (Heeks, 2018). This is necessary through such capacity-building efforts so that technology adoption is not a top-down or technocratic undertaking. In addition, the policymakers will need to encourage pilot projects that have in-built evaluation mechanisms. Pilot projects enable governments to experiment with AI-AR applications under controlled conditions and determine obstacles and correct designs before implementing them on large scales. To determine whether AI-AR systems truly increase inclusion and effectiveness in governance, impact evaluations based on quantitative indicators (e.g., the uptake of service, the time of grievance resolution) and qualitative feedback (e.g., the level of trust in the used system, its perceived accessibility) are required (Madon, 2020).

7.3 Scalability and Sustainability

To guarantee the scalability and sustainability of AI-AR endeavors, one should consider the cost, flexibility, and institutional alignment. The mobile-based AR solutions that are cost-effective are especially applicable in the local governance environment, since smartphones are more accessible as compared to specialized devices. The creation of AR applications that work on simple devices and with low-bandwidth opportunities can greatly expand the coverage of the marginalized groups (van Dijk, 2020). By promoting vendor lock-in, reducing costs, and promoting the creation of local innovation, the use of open-source platforms and interoperable systems can also increase sustainability. The open-source creates opportunities as well that enable governments and civil society organizations to tailor applications to the local requirements, language and governance bodies. The interoperability with current e-governance systems would guarantee AI-AR tools do not replace the current digital infrastructure. Lastly, strong monitoring and evaluation (M&E) systems are the key to success in the long run. The M&E systems must also follow technical performance in addition to social performance including equity, participation, and trust in the local institutions. Accountability and constant improvement should be encouraged through regular evaluation and public reporting so that AI-AR initiatives could be in line with the inclusive governance goals (OECD, 2021). AI-facilitated augmented reality can become a sustainable instrument of local governance that is inclusive through adaptive learning and policy modifications.

8. CONCLUSION

On the conceptual level, this chapter adds to the digital public administration literature by connecting the immersive technologies to the participatory and justice-oriented governance theories in a systematic manner. In practice, it provides a policy relevant roadmap to policy makers and local administrators who would wish to implement AI-powered augmented reality (AI-AR) in a decentralized government structure in a responsible manner. The chapter breaks the efficiency-based accounts of digital governance by preempting the ideas of equity, inclusion, and democratic engagement.

This chapter has explored the potential power of AI-AR in introducing changes in the functioning of local governance, especially concerning citizen engagement, transparency, and government service delivery to underserved populations. Although digitalization has broadened the efficiency of the administration and the scope of procedures, the analysis shows that it has not necessarily brought about outcomes of inclusive governance. The marginalized groups are still characterized by structural constraints that make them unable to meaningfully participate in governance activities and the availment of the services of the state. It is against this background that the fusion of artificial intelligence and augmented reality presents itself as one of the promising courses of action towards solving both digital and social exclusion.

Based on theoretical perspectives of the participatory democracy, capability approach, and justice-focused technology design, the chapter is used to show how AI-AR can redesign the interface between the citizen and state. The immersive and adaptable technologies can reduce the informational, linguistic, and procedural barriers and present the governance processes as visuals, personalize access to services, and provide multilingual and voice-activated interaction. The review of applications in the domains of participatory planning, transparency and accountability systems, welfare delivery, redressal of grievances, and administrative capacity building proves the fact that AI-AR can advance local governance out of the transactional e-governance to more deliberative, more accessible, and citizen-centric frameworks (Arnstein, 1969; Sen, 1999; Floridi et al., 2018).

In terms of public administration, the chapter contributes to the modern discussions on digital governance by making equity and inclusion major assessing principles of technological innovation. Instead of considering AI and immersive technologies as rather neutral or technical tools, the chapter highlights their socio-technical nature and the need to ensure ethical protection, institutional capacity, and participatory design. By so doing, it expands the field of digital governance by combining new technology with normative issues of social justice, accountability, and democracy participation (Heeks, 2018; Madon, 2020).

The chapter also highlights the importance of the fact that digital transformation made possible by AI-AR should be unequivocally equity-focused, otherwise, it will reproduce or exacerbate existing inequalities. Privacy, surveillance, and algorithmic bias ethical dilemmas, legal, infrastructural, and institutional limitations also need proactive and context-sensitive policy responses. The adoption models should be responsible, designed with inclusion, and proper regulatory control measures that will enable AI-AR systems to empower the marginalized communities instead of further marginalizing them. Digital transformation that is equity-based thus requires the use of not only technological innovation but also institutional change and a long-lasting political commitment.

Lastly, the chapter provides the main research directions of the future. Empirical field research which investigates the experience of AI-AR application by marginalized users in actual contexts of local governance is necessary. The longitudinal impact evaluation is needed to examine the long-term change in participation, service delivery, and trust in local institutions. Besides, comparative cross-country studies can provide insight into the role of the differences in the system of governance, regulatory frameworks, and socio-cultural factors in determining AI-AR adoption and performances. It will be essential to fill these research gaps to further evidence-based policymaking and to be certain that AI-driven augmented reality will lead some contribution to inclusive, responsible, and democratic local governance.

REFERENCES

Arnstein, S. R. (1969). A ladder of citizen participation. *Journal of the American Institute of Planners*, *35*(4), 216–224. DOI: 10.1080/01944366908977225

Batty, M., Hudson-Smith, A., Milton, R., & Crooks, A. (2019). *The computable city*. MIT Press.

Bertot, J. C., Jaeger, P. T., & Grimes, J. M. (2016). Using ICTs to create a culture of transparency: E-government and social media as openness and anti-corruption tools for societies. *Government Information Quarterly*, *33*(2), 264–271. DOI: 10.1016/j.giq.2015.12.001

Bhatnagar, S., & Singh, N. (2019). Assessing the impact of e-government: A study of projects in India. *Information Technologies and International Development*, *15*, 1–17.

Billinghurst, M., Clark, A., & Lee, G. (2015). A survey of augmented reality. *Foundations and Trends® in Human—Computer Interaction,* *8*(2-3), 73-272.

D'Ignazio, C., & Klein, L. F. (2020). *Data feminism*. MIT Press. DOI: 10.7551/mitpress/11805.001.0001

Dunleavy, P., Margetts, H., Bastow, S., & Tinkler, J. (2006). New public management is dead—Long live digital-era governance. *Journal of Public Administration: Research and Theory*, *16*(3), 467–494. DOI: 10.1093/jopart/mui057

Eubanks, V. (2018). *Automating inequality: How high-tech tools profile, police, and punish the poor*. St. Martin's Press.

European Union. (2016). *General Data Protection Regulation (GDPR)*. Official Journal of the European Union.

Floridi, L., Cowls, J., Beltrametti, M., Chatila, R., Chazerand, P., Dignum, V., Luetge, C., Madelin, R., Pagallo, U., Rossi, F., Schafer, B., Valcke, P., & Vayena, E. (2018). AI4People—An ethical framework for a good AI society. *Minds and Machines*, *28*(4), 689–707. DOI: 10.1007/s11023-018-9482-5

Government of India. (2023). *Digital Personal Data Protection Act, 2023*. Ministry of Law and Justice.

Heeks, R. (2018). *Information and communication technology for development (ICT4D). Routledge Handbook of Development Management*. Routledge.

Kitchin, R. (2021). Civil liberties or public good? Smart cities, surveillance, and privacy. *Journal of Urban Technology*, *28*(1–2), 3–19. DOI 10.1080/10630732.2020.1781567

Madon, S. (2020). Digital governance for development: A critical review of literature. *Information Polity, 25*(1), 5–20. DOI: 10.3233/IP-190146

Margetts, H., & Dunleavy, P. (2013). The second wave of digital-era governance: a quasi-paradigm for government on the Web. *Philosophical transactions of the royal society A: mathematical, physical and engineering sciences, 371*(1987), 20120382.

Noble, S. U. (2018). *Algorithms of oppression: How search engines reinforce racism*. NYU Press. DOI: 10.18574/nyu/9781479833641.001.0001

OECD. (2021). *The state of digital government*. OECD Publishing., DOI: 10.1787/4de9f5bb-

Ratti, C., & Claudel, M. (2016). *The city of tomorrow: Sensors, networks, hackers, and the future of urban life*. Yale University Press.

Sen, A. (1999). *Development as freedom*. Oxford University Press.

Shirazi, A., & Behzadan, A. H. (2015). Design and assessment of a mobile augmented reality-based information delivery tool for construction and civil engineering curriculum. *Journal of Professional Issues in Engineering Education and Practice, 141*(3), 04014012. DOI: 10.1061/(ASCE)EI.1943-5541.0000229

Sun, T. Q., & Medaglia, R. (2019). Mapping the challenges of artificial intelligence in the public sector. *Government Information Quarterly, 36*(2), 368–383. DOI: 10.1016/j.giq.2018.09.008

UNDP. (2023). *Human development report 2023–2024: Breaking the gridlock*. United Nations Development Programme.

van Dijk, J. (2020). *The digital divide*. Polity Press.

Wirtz, B. W., Weyerer, J. C., & Geyer, C. (2019). Artificial intelligence and the public sector—Applications and challenges. *International Journal of Public Administration, 42*(7), 596–615. DOI: 10.1080/01900692.2018.1498103

Zuboff, S. (2019). *The age of surveillance capitalism*. PublicAffairs.

Chapter 2
AI-Enabled Participatory Governance for Sustainable Urban Problem Reporting

Shivam Nikhra
https://orcid.org/0009-0005-1232-4354
Jaypee University of Engineering and Technology, Guna, India

Shubham Jaiswal
https://orcid.org/0009-0004-1742-6814
Jaypee University of Engineering and Technology, Guna, India

Shreshtha Tudha
https://orcid.org/0009-0006-3932-0652
Jaypee University of Engineering and Technology, Guna, India

Kunj Bihari Meena
https://orcid.org/0000-0001-8159-9024
Jaypee University of Engineering and Technology, Guna, India

Vipin Tyagi
https://orcid.org/0000-0003-4994-3686
Jaypee University of Engineering and Technology, Guna, India

ABSTRACT

This chapter proposes an AI-enabled participatory governance model to strengthen sustainable urban service delivery through citizen feedback. The web-based system enables residents to report neighbourhood problems by uploading an image with

DOI: 10.4018/979-8-3373-7804-6.ch002

a short text description. NLP estimates urgency and ranks severity, while image classification assigns each complaint to a relevant category. This dual-AI pipeline improves triage efficiency, reduces manual workload, and supports municipal decision-making by prioritising issues with higher social or environmental impact. The chapter also shows how real-time dashboards, geospatial mapping, and automated workflow routing help governments identify citywide patterns. Longitudinal analytics further enable tracking recurring issues, detecting seasonal trends, and evaluating intervention outcomes over time. Overall, the work demonstrates how data-driven participation platforms can operationalise sustainability as a continuous improvement cycle rather than a one-time intervention.

1. INTRODUCTION

India, being a developing nation, has gone through a massive transformation in recent years. People are migrating from smaller towns to bigger cities, municipal authorities and due to this migrations urban governance bodies are facing difficulty in managing urban issues. According to the United Nations (2025), India's urban population has reached 589 million in the year 2025. This number of population is creating high pressure on roads, drainage and other public utilities. Existing infrastructure is not able to handle this high number of people and therefore there is an increase in number of complaints by the citizens of these cities.

There is a need of finding effective solution to manage a wide range of issues… (e.g., potholes, garbage accumulation, malfunctioning streetlights, water supply problems); in this chapter, the prototype evaluation focuses on four visually identifiable classes for image classification, while the overall framework is intended to extend to additional civic issue categories. When citizens face such problems they start complaining more and more. A common way to report problems related to road conditions, waste management, water supply and street lights is through government department websites or mobile applications (Nam & Pardo, 2011; Ministry of Housing and Urban Affairs, 2017). According to recent research related to issue, effectiveness of such platforms can be increased by using artificial intelligence to classify, prioritize and route citizen complaints, ensuring that urgent issues like public safety hazards are addressed promptly (Heyik et al., 2025; Shin et al., 2024).

In 2015, the Government of India came with the concept of transforming cities into Smart Cities. This concept was having an aim of improving the quality of life for people living in these urban areas (Government of India, 2015). Focus of the Smart Cities Mission was on strengthening existing urban infrastructure while also developing new housing and roads for ease of citizens. It emphasized the use of technology to improve delivery of various services and support the government in managing cities more efficiently. Its primary goal of this mission is to ensure that the residents of the Smart Cities can access the basic services that are functional, like access to water, 24/7 power supply and efficient transport infrastructure. It also attempts to maintain clean and neat city streets. The others are to provide the local authorities and city administrations with a timely and appropriate response to needs and issues of the citizens. To fulfill these objectives, the Smart Cities Mission promotes the application of the information and communication technologies, including digital systems and online platforms, to ensure the efficiency and effectiveness of the urban management industry.

Nevertheless, lots of municipal institutions still have a number of challenges in terms of conducting their activity efficiently. The staff shortage is a problem in most urban areas and as a result, the municipal offices find it difficult to cope with their daily activities. Due to this factor, they tend to fail to manage the high number of complaints made by citizens in a manageable period Citizens complain about various road, sanitation and other public services related problems and municipal organizations cannot address all of them in a short period of time. This is the current issue of handling and addressing the complaints of the citizens that has been previously emphasized in the studies of Meijer and Rodríguez Bolívar (2016) and indicates that there should be more effective systems to overcome the challenges.

The earlier manual approach to handling complaints in India was generally unstructured and highly bureaucratic. This made it difficult for citizens to report and monitor issues within their cities. People were often required to complete extensive paperwork, make phone calls that rarely connected, or visit municipal offices in person. Such processes were frustrating and discouraged public participation in addressing city-related problems. The system did little to support individuals in reporting issues or ensuring timely resolution. Citizens often had to make repeated efforts before their grievances were even acknowledged. Once a complaint was submitted, verification procedures were slow and on-ground investigations took considerable time. As a result, it was common for people to wait weeks or even months before seeing any action taken on their complaints (Meijer & Rodríguez Bolívar, 2016). When individuals are forced to wait to be responded to, they begin to lose faith in the system and they will not engage in the process. This is particularly so when even simple matters such as services are not maintained over a long time. Indicatively, when a problem is reported like with a road, one should get a response in time.

Studies of the way cities deal with complaints indicate that there are usually numerous issues that cannot be solved immediately and nobody is aware of who is supposed to do it. Responsible people do not necessarily inform the people on what is happening with their complaints.

This situation becomes particularly critical, when it comes to such calamities as monsoons, the infrastructure of the city may often fail, leading to safety and health issues. It is through municipal systems of complaint that are important at such times. They should already be functioning properly so that individuals are able to complain and obtain assistance within a short period of time. Such systems of municipal complaints require improvement to ensure that people have confidence in such systems and obtain the assistance they require.

Existing systems used by citizens to report civic issues suffer from a major limitation. They do not provide an effective way to distinguish between minor concerns and serious problems that may pose risks to public safety. As a result, all complaints are treated in the same manner, regardless of their severity, urgency, or potential impact on a large number of people. These grievance platforms lack mechanisms for prioritizing issues and identifying which problems require immediate attention. Consequently, authorities are often unable to determine what should be addressed first. High-risk issues such as flooded roads, open sewage lines and damaged streets may remain unresolved for extended periods, just like less critical complaints. This delay can make cities unsafe for citizens, as such conditions can cause significant damage to people (Meijer & Rodríguez Bolívar, 2016). The failure to utilize data in deciding what to do by cities makes responding to the issues very slow. It also translates to the fact that cities do not utilize their resources in such a manner. This sometimes results in social unrest. The issue is particularly a problem in urban areas where many individuals are involved (Nam & Pardo, 2011).

One such promising alternative has been crowdsourcing-based civic engagement platforms whereby citizens can report urban issues by providing geotagged images, textual descriptions as well as interactive maps (Goodchild, 2007). These platforms make it easy to collect real time data and make a better situational awareness to the municipal authorities enabling them to respond quickly by directing complaints to the appropriate departments (Brabham, 2008). Previous research shows that digitally mediated grievance systems have a sweeping effect on response times and enhance transparency by offering a chance to track reported concerns end-to-end (Bertot et al., 2010).

The use of technology in civic reporting systems becomes more effective when supported by artificial intelligence. AI-based techniques can be used for automatic classification, assessment of urgency and data analysis (Janssen & Kuk, 2016). AI based systems can analyse large number of complaints and identify patterns related to location and timing of complaints (Batty et al., 2012). AI based systems can provide support in detection of areas experiencing a high number of issues and planning city authorities timely solution and address problems before situations worsens (Batty et al., 2012). It is observed that cities that apply AI in determining what is to be done and forecasting what will occur can react to problems faster and maintain people safer (Batty et al., 2012). AI based systems will provide good support as it will provide better services in cities. Due to high efficiency of AI-based civic reporting systems, there is a need of employing such systems (Meijer & Rodríguez Bolívar, 2016).

2. LITERATURE REVIEW

These days participatory governance in public participation has become a central concept. Participatory governance emphasizes on the involvement of its citizens in policy-making, service delivery and supervision of government actions. Traditional governance structure models are hierarchical in nature and mostly have limited citizen participation. Due to limited citizen participation, these traditional systems face criticism for their inability to address complex urban problems effectively (Fung, 2006). While participatory governance model promotes collaboration, openness and mutual trust by actively listening to citizens' views on administrative matters (Ansell & Gash, 2008). The main feature of participatory governance is that in this type of system, public opinions have importance and are included in decision making process.

Using advanced technologies have provided opportunities for citizen participation. Various applications such as E-government platforms, social media and mobile applications can be used to report issues, express their views and direct communication with officials. (Linders, 2012; Shayamunda & Bhanye, 2024). With the help of these tools citizens can provide feedback and report their problems quickly. This helps in strengthening direct communication between governments and citizens. By inclusion of citizen's input into decision making, public trust is increased and it enables governments to respond more effectively to societal needs (Porumbescu, 2015). According to research, participation alone is not sufficient unless citizen-provided data is actively analysed and required action is taken (Bovaird & Löffler, 2015).

In urban governance, the involvement of its citizens is very important. Cities are growing fast, population in cities is increasing and hence pressure on infrastructure and public services in cities is increasing. Urban residents are the first to observe issues such as potholes, waste accumulation and safety hazards (Goldsmith & Crawford, 2014). They can report the issue with accurate description and location. Therefore there is a need of systems, using which residents can report problems easily and engage with authorities. Participatory urban reporting systems now play a key role in solving everyday urban challenges and aligning governance with needs of citizens.

Increase in initiatives related to smart city shows growing efforts to use information and communication technologies to improve efficiency, sustainability and finally quality of life. Earlier focus of smart city projects was mainly on sensor deployment, automation and infrastructure optimisation (Harrison et al., 2010). Although this improved operational efficiency, but it was observed that technology-driven models often overlooked social dimensions and citizen needs (Hollands, 2008). More recent research highlights the value of citizen-reported data in complementing administrative datasets by offering detailed, context-rich insights into urban problems (Kitchin, 2014). However, analysis of large amount and diversity of citizen-generated data is difficult. Many participatory platforms still process complaint manually, which is generally slow, inconsistent and prone to bias (Janssen & Helbig, 2018). Governments are now moving towards adoption of digital grievance redressal systems to streamline complaint registration and resolution. Generally input to such platforms is text based description and photos of problems provided by citizens. (King & Brown, 2007). It has resulted in higher reporting rates and faster responses compared to traditional channels (Offenhuber, 2014).

Despite these benefits, most existing systems use basic classification methods and sequential complaint handling. Problems reported are not handled based on urgency or severity of the complaints. This results in critical problems being overlooked while less severe complaints receive attention as per the sequence. According to several research studies, conventional municipal systems are not having any effective prioritisation mechanisms, highlighting the need for more advanced approaches that can interpret citizen input more intelligently and support informed decision-making (Chatfield & Reddick, 2018).

Another related concern is inequality of citizens' participation. In general, a small group of highly active users may generate a disproportionate number of complaints, potentially skewing administrative attention (Peixoto & Fox, 2016). Engagement indicators e.g. comments and upvotes and comments can be used to measure broader community concern and reduce reporting bias. However, well defined techniques that integrate these metrics into administrative decision-making are very less.

An important tool used for analyzing large amount of unstructured data received from digital platforms is use of natural language processing. In the public sector, NLP techniques are increasingly used to analyze official documents and citizen-generated content to better understand public communication and policy-relevant concerns (Jurafsky & Martin, 2023; Tan et al., 2023). Sentiment analysis, in particular, helps in identifying emotions, opinions and apparent importance in textual data, enabling a structured understanding of public concerns.

It has been observed that sentiment analysis can be used to identify the level of dissatisfaction and urgency expressed in citizen complaints (Liu, 2012). However, interpretation of this communication is a big challenge due to use of informal language, sarcasm, mixed emotions and ambiguity in communication (Balahur & Turchi, 2014). To address these issues, machine learning and deep learning approaches are now being used that are able to capture complex linguistic patterns and improve classification accuracy (Kim, 2014).

It has been observed that perception of citizens related to a specific issue also changed with time. Initially, a person may report an issue in a very concise form. Later with time by further discussions, the same person may provide more detailed description having growing concern. Analysis of comments given by various users can be used by researchers to find progress of public sentiment and its intensity (Ceron et al., 2016). Although this information is valuable, but presently, this information is not used in making decisions related to priority of handling the issues by municipality. Therefore there is a need of development of techniques that can utilize citizen feedback into making urban governance more useful.

Collective problem solving is another important feature of a successful participatory governance. Related research work shows that participation of groups of citizens can provide better output in comparison to use of individuals when their inputs are properly structured and aggregated (Malone et al., 2010). Use of online platforms is helpful in facilitating large-scale participation, making shared priorities and patterns of concern visible. User interactions such as comments, shares and endorsements provide inputs related to importance of issues, thereby showing the relevance of collective intelligence in public decision-making (Muchnik et al., 2013).

Although considering opinion of citizens in solving problems enhances inclusiveness in the governance, converting public input into actionable decisions remains difficult (Nabatchi & Amsler, 2014). Sometimes concentrating on majority views may fail to notice critical issues raised by smaller groups (Gil-Garcia et al., 2016). Citizens expect from the government that urgency of their issues should be noticed. It has been observed that combining emotional intensity with the volume of discussion improves assessments of urgency, particularly in emergency situations (Imran et al., 2020). Analysis of large-scale user-generated content can reduce individual bias and provides more reliable indication of urgent issues (Vieweg et al., 2010).

According to recent research studies, iterative urgency scoring methods are useful that update issue rankings depending on inputs by the citizens. However, the application of such models in everyday urban governance is presently limited, especially outside crisis situations. Visual data submitted by citizens further enhances issue validation. Advances in computer vision, particularly convolutional neural networks, have enabled automated detection of infrastructure problems from images (Krizhevsky et al., 2012; Maeda et al., 2018). Mostly systems use image classification only for issue identification, without linking visual severity indicators to decision-making processes (Zheng et al., 2014). Integrating image analysis techniques with textual data improves classification accuracy and reduces dependence on manual inspection (Baltrušaitis et al., 2019). Addressing this limitation can improve the operational relevance of reporting systems.

Artificial intelligence is increasingly used in public administration to support prediction, classification and optimisation tasks, improving efficiency and reducing human error (Wirtz et al., 2019). However, concerns about transparency, accountability and fairness persist (Veale & Brass, 2019). AI systems are expected to support, not replace, human decision-makers by transforming citizen input into actionable insights while remaining explainable and contestable (Busuioc, 2021; World Bank, 2025).

According to research, AI models should be developed specifically for the public sector rather than adapted from commercial contexts (Sun & Medaglia, 2019). Urban issue reporting is a particularly promising area as multimodal citizen-generated data is accessible and operational decisions are clearly defined. By integrating NLP-based urgency assessment, community feedback aggregation and image classification, AI-enabled participatory systems is one of the emerging best practices in digital public administration.

Overall, existing research demonstrates the value of citizen-generated data, sentiment analysis, collective feedback and computer vision in urban governance. However, most current systems treat these elements in isolation and lack integrated frameworks that combine textual sentiment, community engagement and visual evidence for prioritisation. Continuous urgency assessment based on evolving citizen interaction remains underexplored in non-crisis urban contexts. This research addresses these gaps by proposing and evaluating an integrated AI-enabled participatory reporting framework that contributes to more effective and sustainable urban public administration, both theoretically and practically. Recent research proposes integrated AI-powered civic platforms that combine real-time reporting, urgency detection and image validation to support sustainable urban problem management, aligning with SDG 11 goals (Bosco et al., 2024; Motet Hansen & Dahiya, 2025).

3. PROPOSED METHOD

Work in this chapter proposes a structured, AI-based participatory reporting framework that address the limitations of existing civic grievance systems. Proposed framework integrates citizen reporting, automated issue analysis, community validation and continuous feedback and provides more effective urban governance system. The following steps describe the End-to-end workflow of the proposed system is described. These steps show that how citizen input and artificial intelligence are combined to improve identification of issues, their prioritisation and resolution.

Step 1: Citizen Issue Reporting

Citizens having internet access through computer or mobile can use the proposed system to complain about problems in their surrounding areas to city authorities. These issues may be related to garbage accumulation, potholes on roads, malfunctioning of streetlights and waterlogging; however, the experimental validation in this chapter evaluates the image classifier on four categories (potholes, garbage dumps, safety hazards, illegal parking) as a representative subset of visually grounded issues. The web application can be accessed by all residents through computer or mobile and supports the reporting of a wide range of civic issues within neighbourhoods. Using this platform, citizens can submit their complaints easily and bring local problems to the attention of municipal authorities.

Step 2: AI-Based Issue Processing

Artificial intelligence based techniques are very useful in improving the efficiency and accuracy of civic issue reporting systems. Advances in machine learning and deep learning have enabled the automation of many activities involved in public support services. Some prototypes have been developed by researchers that use AI techniques to enhance the identification, classification and analysis of urban problems.

AI-powered image analysis models, particularly based on convolutional neural networks, are widely used to analyse visual data submitted by citizens. These models can identify infrastructure issues such as potholes, road cracks, damaged sidewalks, garbage accumulation and waterlogging from images captured using mobile devices or vehicle-mounted cameras.

Although such systems are effective, but still they face challenges related to varying lighting conditions, weather changes and the need for large annotated datasets. The model first identifies the type of issue from the image and then estimates a visual severity score (S,0-1) representing the visible intensity/extent of the problem, normalised to a 0-1 scale for downstream prioritisation..

Key characteristics include training on large datasets of labelled civic issue images, detection of visual cues such as road damage and water accumulation and output of both issue type and a normalised visual severity score (S, 0–1). This automation improves reporting accuracy and enables more reliable characterisation of urban issues.

Text-based descriptions provided by citizens are analysed using natural language processing techniques. Models such as BERT and DistilBERT are used to extract relevant information from user descriptions and social media posts related to urban issues. The NLP module identifies keywords associated with issue type and urgency, standardises different expressions referring to the same problem and filters duplicate or spam reports. This ensures consistency in issue classification even when citizens describe the same problem in different ways.

Step 3: Crowd-Sourced Validation and Prioritisation

Once processed by the AI system, reported issues are displayed on a public issue feed and map interface. Citizens can view reported problems, comment on them and upvote issues they are also experiencing. Issues that receive higher numbers of upvotes are considered more significant, as they indicate wider community impact. This is used as an engagement signal (E) to weight priority, not as a direct substitute for urgency or severity.

Key participatory features include the ability for citizens to upvote issues they face personally and comment on reported problems. The system computes a priority score (P) by integrating visual severity (S), dynamic urgency (U_dyn) and engagement (E) to rank issues by overall importance; here, S is image-based impact (0–1), U_dyn is time-criticality inferred from the initial report and follow-up comment text (0–1) and E captures community validation (e.g., upvotes and comment volume, independent of comment text content). Combining technical severity assessment with community validation, the system ranks issues based on their overall importance.

Municipal authorities will receive a list of issues with priorities assigned. This will help authorities in solving problems which are high-impact problems that involve larger number of the citizens. Using this approach supports efficient resource allocation and ensures that critical issues are solved on priority.

In this chapter, severity (S) refers to visually estimated impact from images (0–1), dynamic urgency (U_dyn) refers to time-criticality inferred from the initial report text and subsequent comment text (0–1), engagement (E) refers to community validation signals (e.g., upvotes and comment volume) and priority (P) is the combined ranking score used for operational triage.

Step 4: Resolution Tracking and Feedback Loop

Action taken by authorities on reported issues is updated on the platform, such as problem solved or under process. This will bring transparency to the process. The update on resolutions will assure citizens that their concerns are being considered and action is being taken. After an issue is resolved, then there is facility of providing feedback on the resolution through comments. They can share their response on the quality of response and their satisfaction level. This feedback is used to improve system performance as well as for maintaining of records. These responses can be analyzed to identify strengths and areas for improvement, creating a continuous feedback loop that supports more responsive and accountable urban governance.

4. EXPERIMENTS AND RESULTS

In this section, details of experiments conducted to evaluate the effectiveness of the proposed AI-enabled participatory governance for sustainable urban problem reporting system is provided. Performance analysis of three main components (1) issue categorization using image classification model (2) urgency scoring using sentiment analysis model (3) dynamic urgency updating based on follow-up citizen comments (text), while upvotes and comment volume contribute to engagement (E) and are used in the priority score to reflect broader community impact in following sections. In this chapter, visual severity (S) denotes the image-based estimate of physical impact (normalised to 0–1), initial urgency (U_0) is inferred from the original complaint text, dynamic urgency (U_dyn) represents time-criticality updated from subsequent comment text (0-1), engagement (E) captures community validation signals such as upvotes and comment volume and priority (P) is the combined ranking score used for operational triage

4.1 Issue Categorization using Image Classification

A convolutional neural network (CNN) model was trained to classify images of urban issues into four categories such as street potholes, garbage dumps etc. These categories are based on common problems faced by citizens. Limiting the classification to four classes helps simplify the model and supports validation of the proposed approach.

The model was trained on a dataset of approximately twenty-six thousand images collected from various non-copyrighted online sources. This dataset contains images of four primary categories representing significant urban challenges. llegal Parking images come from the Car Parking Violation Detection dataset, which contains about 147 manually labeled examples of vehicles parked in violation across different street settings (Gari, 2025). The annotations specify violation types, making it useful for supervised learning and academic studies, though its small size suits exploratory work and method demonstrations (Gari, 2025; Himan, 2025). The Potholes category captures road damage such as cavities, cracks and uneven asphalt under varied lighting and environmental conditions (Maske et al., 2025). It supports research on road condition assessment and hazard detection for prioritizing repairs (Himan, 2025; Maske et al., 2025). The Garbage Dumps category shows uncollected waste, open dumping and littered public spaces in multiple contexts (Maske et al., 2025). It is relevant for sanitation monitoring, environmental management and citizen reporting systems (Himan, 2025; Maske et al., 2025). The Safety Hazards category includes damaged electricity poles and fallen or broken trees that create immediate public risks, such as leaning poles, exposed lines and obstructed roads or sidewalks

(Himan, 2025). It is useful for training systems that prioritize municipal response and improve urban resilience (Himan, 2025).

The dataset is split into training, validation and test sets. Training data is largest for Safety Hazards (15,754) and Potholes (6,143), with fewer images for Garbage (462) and Illegal Parking (57) (Himan, 2025). Validation contains 1,491 Safety Hazards, 1,352 Potholes, 132 Garbage and 3 Illegal Parking images. Testing includes 1,958 Safety Hazards, 436 Potholes, 66 Garbage and 7 Illegal Parking images. This imbalanced distribution mirrors real-world reporting and supports evaluation across both common and rare cases (Himan, 2025; Maske et al., 2025).

Data augmentation techniques were applied to address variations in image conditions that may occur in user-submitted photographs. 80 percent images from the dataset were used for training, 10 percent images for validation and 10 percent images for testing of the model. To prevent data leakage issue, each class was split independently. Performance was evaluated using standard metrics: precision, recall, F1 score and overall accuracy. After 15 training epochs, the model achieved a training accuracy of 97.17 percent. As shown in Figure 1, training accuracy increased steadily across epochs, suggesting that the model learned meaningful visual patterns from the images and did not show signs of overfitting.

Figure 1 illustrates the training and validation accuracy trends for the CNN-based issue classification model.

Figure 1. Training accuracy and validation accuracy of issue categorization using CNN

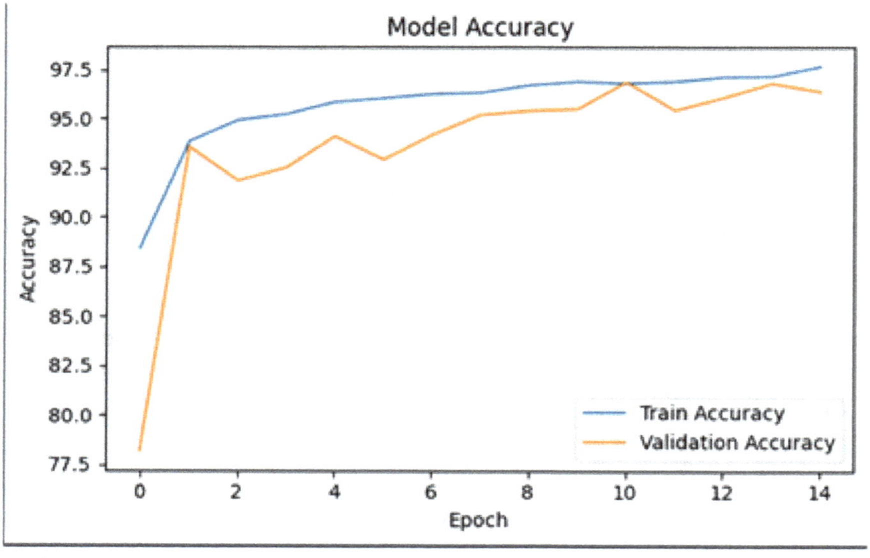

It is also observed that the validation accuracy also increased steadily, similar to the training accuracy. This shows that the model effectively learned generalisable patterns from the training data and performed well on unseen data. Results in Table 1 show that the proposed model achieved an overall classification accuracy of 96% on the test dataset.

Table 1. Classification accuracy of image classification using CNN

Issue Class	Precision	Recall	F1-score	Support(N)
Potholes	0.96	0.93	0.95	436
Garbage Dumps	0.78	0.21	0.33	66
Safety Hazards	0.96	0.99	0.97	1958
Illegal Parking	0.50	0.14	0.22	7

The results indicate that the safety hazards and potholes classes achieved the highest F1 score i.e. 0.97 and 0.95 respectively. This performance may be due to the larger number of training samples and the presence of distinct visual features in these categories. In contrast, the illegal parking class showed considerably lower performance, primarily due to the very small number of images available for training.

4.2 Urgency Scoring using Sentiment Analysis

Sentiment analysis of the descriptions provided by reporting citizens was used to generate a baseline initial urgency score (U_0). DistilBERT model, which is a smaller and faster variant of Bidirectional Encoder Representations from Transformers, was used for urgency scoring (Sanh et al., 2019).

The model was fine-tuned on a corpus of 3,000 urban complaint descriptions. These descriptions were generated using various large language models to simulate human-like reporting styles and were manually assigned urgency labels.

The model was trained to predict a normalised urgency score based on three classes: not urgent, urgent and critical. The predicted urgency score is derived from the DistilBERT classifier's output; the model implicitly captures sentiment and urgency-related lexical cues (e.g., 'critical', 'accident', 'trouble') learned during fine-tuning. As shown in Figure 2, the model successfully identified high-urgency terms such as "critical", "accident" and "trouble" and assigned them higher urgency scores. The model achieved a maximum training accuracy of 93.5 percent after five training epochs. Training accuracy increased gradually across epochs, indicating that the model learned meaningful patterns from the generated descriptions without signs of overfitting.

Figure 2 shows the training and validation accuracy curves for the DistilBERT-based urgency scoring model.

Figure 2. Training and validation accuracy curve for the DistilBERT urgency scoring model

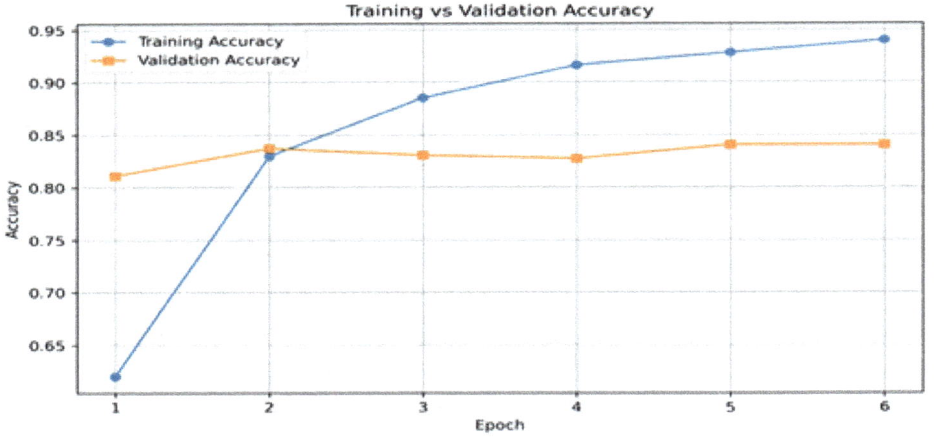

As shown in Figure 2, the validation accuracy curve remains steady at a value of approx. 84% after each epoch. It indicates that the model is able to understand and effectively generalise patterns. As summarised in Table 2, the model achieved an overall classification accuracy of 86% on the test set.

Table 2. Classification report of urgency scoring DistilBERT model

Urgency Class	Precision	Recall	F1-score	Support(N)
Not urgent	0.89	0.85	0.87	59
urgent	0.85	0.83	0.84	148
critical	0.82	0.88	0.85	100

All the classes showed similar results which indicates that the model's ability to avoid false positives is near perfectly balanced with its ability to avoid false negatives for every category.

4.3 Dynamic Urgency Updation based on Follow-up Citizen Comments

One of the key features of the system is its ability to dynamically update the urgency score of an issue based on visually estimated impact from images (0–1), dynamic urgency (U_dyn) refers to time-criticality inferred from the initial report text and subsequent comment text (0–1), engagement (E) refers to community validation signals (e.g., upvotes and comment volume) and priority (P) is the combined ranking score used for operational triage. Feedback is captured through user comments (text updates) and upvotes (validation/impact signal). Comments update urgency, while upvotes contribute to engagement (E) used in the overall priority score. When a user submits a comment on an issue, the text is processed by the urgency scoring model, which generates an updated urgency score. The dynamic urgency score (U_dyn) is calculated as the mean of the initial urgency score (U_0) and the urgency scores derived from subsequent comment texts: U_dyn = mean(U_0, U_comment1, …, U_commentk). Using this approach, if an issue is initially classified as urgent, can be reclassified as critical if citizens' responses indicate increased concern.

5. DISCUSSION

5.1 Operational Efficiency

The main objective of this work was to check the usability of a multimodal AI-based system in handling citizen's complaints. It aimed to observer the utility of such AI-based systems in making process faster for traditional manual process which are slow. The results indicate that the model performs effectively in the initial screening of reported issues. The system achieved an average precision score of approximately 0.86 across the tested categories, demonstrating reliable classification performance under controlled conditions. However, the main aim of the work was not classification accuracy but the significant reduction in processing time.

Under the traditional manual process, the time between a citizen submitting a complaint and authorities reviewing the complaint was several days. After implementing the AI-based system this time can be reduced to few minutes. This considerable improvement indicates that a major challenge in urban service delivery is not in solving issues rather in the administrative processes required to review, categorise and route large volumes of complaints.

With the help of AI-based systems, the time taken in initial stages of complaint handling is reduced. It also reduces the workload on administrative staff. These findings support the shift towards smart urban governance, where technology is used to improve societal outcomes, as discussed by Meijer and Rodríguez Bolívar (2016).

Use of such AI-based systems will make problem reporting faster but there is a possibility of some errors due to limitations of such systems. To overcome such issues, human intervention is also required. For example, any complaint related to damaged roads due to water may be due to water leakage. In this case, the actual issue is related to water infrastructure but the system classifies it as road infrastructure problem wrongly. Additional information using human intervention is needed in such cases to solve actual cause of the problem..

5.2 Data Imbalance and Reporting Bias

As observed from Table 1, the model achieved high F1-score 0.97 and 0.95 for safety hazards and potholes, respectively. However, for issues like garbage dumps and illegal parking, the F1-score reduced to 0.33 and 0.22. This poor performance correlates directly with the lack of data, as these classes had less data (66 for garbage dumps and 7 for illegal parking), which is a reflection of underlying patterns in citizen reporting behaviour. According to Goodchild (2007) citizens act as sensors for those events that directly disrupt their daily routines. A pothole causes physical discomfort while driving and garbage accumulation produces immediate sensory irritation and are likely to be reported. This bias has important implications for urban management. Because the AI model was trained on thousands of images of common issues such as potholes, it learned to classify them with high accuracy. In contrast, the scarcity of data on illegal parking and garbage dumps limited its ability to recognise these categories effectively. This situation creates a risk of what Offenhuber (2014) describes as a crisis of infrastructure legibility.

5.3 Semantic Ambiguity in Text Input

While the image processing faced imbalance issues, the text analysis showed better performance in controlled settings using DistilBERT. The model, fine-tuned on 3,000 generated urban complaint descriptions, demonstrated consistent reliability across categories, with F1-score of 0.85 for the critical category. This indicates the model effectively learned to map high-urgency keywords like "accident" and "trouble" to higher urgency scores. However, this dependency on specific keyword intensity poses a challenge for real-world application. Although the model achieved high precision, 0.89 for 'not urgent' issues, it was trained on synthetic, human-like descriptions rather than noisy, real-time data. In a real-world scenario, users often provide short, vague notes that lack the specific keywords the model was trained to detect. Additionally, while the model generalizes well on standard English (as observed from 0.88 Recall value for critical issues), it may not perform well with the mixed languages and local dialects which is common in diverse urban environment (Balahur & Turchi, 2014).

To address this issue a more structured input design is required that should guide the users at the time of reporting.

5.4 Visual Noise and Real-World Conditions

Using computer vision techniques to extract information from photographs submitted by citizens highlighted the gap between photographs taken in controlled laboratory conditions and photographs taken by citizens in real-world conditions. The model performed well when images were clear and captured in daylight, but its accuracy is reduced when photographs contain noise. For example, photographs taken during early morning or late afternoon, may have shadows which may create sharp, dark shadows that visually resemble road damage to the model. System may also get confused in correctly distinguishing between construction debris and ordinary garbage in photographs. Maeda et al. (2018), in their research showed that environmental noise, particularly shadows and variations in lighting, is a primary reason of inaccurate results in AI-based road damage detection models based on photographs. Real-world photographs generally have blur, glare, partial occlusion and uneven illumination. The model's difficulty in handling these conditions suggests that training exclusively on high-quality, well-lit images can be counterproductive. Models trained on idealised data tend to learn simple visual patterns that do not reliably transfer to the complexity of street-level environments.

5.5 Temporal Dynamics and Alert Fatigue

The temporal analysis showed that urban issues do not follow a linear or stable pattern over time. For example, the number of road related complaints is very high during the monsoon period. If the system relies on static rules, widespread flooding would cause the system's urgency scores to peak, classifying nearly all complaints as critical. While flooding constitutes a serious concern, the uniform assignment of the highest urgency level undermined the system's ability to support prioritisation. When all reports are flagged as urgent, the distinction between routine and life-threatening incidents collapses, rendering the priority mechanism ineffective. This exposes a key limitation of static urgency classification rules. Although Kitchin (2014) highlights the value of real-time dashboards in urban governance, our findings suggest that such dashboards offer limited utility when baseline parameters remain fixed during abnormal conditions.

These indicate the need for adaptive urgency calibration. During large-scale events, the system should dynamically adjust its thresholds, reserving critical alerts for exceptional and life-threatening situations, such as structural failures or major accidents, while treating widespread but expected conditions such as flooded streets during heavy rainfall, as lower-priority signals for that period. The system's failure to adapt resulted in alert fatigue among human operators, who gradually disregarded AI-generated recommendations and reverted to traditional manual decision-making processes.

5.6 Ethical and Legal Considerations

Although AI-enabled civic reporting systems are efficient, they raise several ethical and legal concerns that need to be addressed. One major issue is data privacy. Citizen-submitted complaints may contain sensitive information, including geolocation data and personal identifiers. Without clear data protection policies, such systems may unintentionally expose individuals to privacy risks (Taylor, 2021).

There is also a risk of use of data for monitoring citizen behavior, especially in contexts lacking robust accountability mechanisms. Consent, transparency and purpose limitation must be built into system design from the outset to address these concerns. Biases in training data can reinforce existing inequalities, particularly when systems lack mechanisms for corrective oversight (Eubanks, 2018).

5.7 Comparison with Existing Implementations

Open311 (https://www.open311.org/), a standard for civic issue tracking used in cities like New York, Chicago and Boston, enables citizens to report issues through web portals or mobile apps. These reports are sent to municipal departments for resolution and often made publicly visible to promote accountability.

Use of Open311 increases transparency, quick responses and public trust. However, Open311 platforms often lack dynamic urgency scoring or AI-based triage features. Reports are treated sequentially and systemic biases may arise from uneven reporting activity across neighborhoods (Offenhuber, 2014; Goldsmith & Crawford, 2014). The proposed AI-based framework aims to address these limitations by integrating automated urgency assessment and image analysis, offering a more scalable and equitable solution.

5.8 Institutional Readiness and Long-Term Sustainability

Adopting AI-enabled civic platforms also presents institutional and operational challenges. Municipal governments often lack the technical expertise to maintain advanced machine learning systems. Therefore training of staff training is required to ensure that administrators are able to interpret AI-based systems' outputs and monitor for unintended consequences (Young et al., 2019).

Integrating AI tools into existing workflows requires change in management flow. Public agencies must align new technologies with governance structures and ensure they do not conflict with existing accountability mechanisms. Furthermore, the maintenance of these systems, including retraining models, updating datasets and securing digital infrastructure, incurs ongoing costs that must be factored into planning (Janssen & van den Hoven, 2015).

A sustainable deployment strategy should include multi-stakeholder collaboration, regular performance audits and policy frameworks that address both efficiency and equity concerns.

6. CONCLUSION

The work in this chapter has shown the use of artificial intelligence techniques, specifically natural language processing and computer vision, combined with citizen participation, can enhance the reporting and resolution mechanisms for urban problems. As the population is increasing in cities at a fast speed, traditional approaches to address civic grievances such as manual issue sorting, limited transparency and delayed feedback, are becoming increasingly unsustainable (Chourabi et al., 2012). By combining sentiment analysis based urgency scoring and Convolutional Neural Networks (CNNs) for image classification, the proposed system presents a scalable framework for AI-enabled participatory governance. The urgency module can dynamically update the urgency component (U_dyn) of an issue using the text of user comments and the system computes an overall priority score (P) by combining visual severity (S), dynamic urgency (U_dyn) and engagement (E). This approach enables static reporting systems to convert public feedback into improvement of the system dynamically. Using sentiment analysis, extraction of emotional and attitudinal information from textual reports is possible. This information provides valuable information related to perceived urgency and dissatisfaction. These capabilities support informed decision-making and more responsive prioritization in public service delivery (Medhat et al., 2014).Furthermore, the integration of image classification models addresses the issue of data diversity present in crowdsourced reporting. As shown by Brabham (2009), the effectiveness of crowdsourced civic data is often influenced by noise and misclassification. The proposed system solves this issue by automatically categorizing reported issues, such as potholes, waste accumulation and damaged infrastructure, thereby reducing the administrative burden associated with manual categorization.

Proposed system enables citizens to report issues and also to comment on and upvote existing reports. This provides citizens an opportunity to collectively validate the severity and importance of local problems. This participatory model aligns with the United Nations Sustainable Development Goal 11, which emphasizes inclusive, safe and sustainable urban development, by establishing a transparent and interactive feedback loop between citizens and municipal authorities (Visvizi and Lytras, 2018). Using AI-enhanced digital participation tools in smart city implementations has resulted in improved response rates and giving value to citizen voice in urban governance (Bastos et al., 2022).

Despite its contributions, the proposed system has several limitations. At present, the sentiment analysis component processes only English-language input, which may exclude non-native speakers in linguistically diverse urban contexts. As noted by Pang and Lee (2008), sentiment analysis is highly sensitive to linguistics and contextual information such as sarcasm, which may result in inaccurate urgency assessments. Additionally, the dependence on user-generated images introduces challenges related to image quality, lighting conditions, privacy concerns and citizen anonymity. Other important constraint is requirement of internet connectivity, which may marginalalize low-income or digitally underserved areas where infrastructure issues are often most severe but access to digital reporting platforms is limited (Graham, 2002).

In future, the system can be enhanced by using Augmented Reality (AR) techniques. AR techniques will allow citizens to see subsurface infrastructure overlaid on physical defects (Schall et al., 2009).

In conclusion, this chapter has shown the use of AI-techniques in making a participatory governance. It successfully showed that how governance can be moved from a slow, paper based system to an intelligent, responsive and participatory system where every citizen's voice contributes to the sustainable maintenance of their city.

REFERENCES

Ansell, C., & Gash, A. (2008). Collaborative governance in theory and practice. *Journal of Public Administration: Research and Theory*, *18*(4), 543–571. DOI: 10.1093/jopart/mum032

Balahur, A., & Turchi, M. (2014). Comparative experiments using supervised learning and machine translation for multilingual sentiment analysis. *Computer Speech & Language*, *28*(1), 56–75. DOI: 10.1016/j.csl.2013.03.004

Bastos, D., Fernández-Caballero, A., Pereira, A., & Rocha, N. P. (2022). Smart city applications to promote citizen participation in city management and governance: A systematic review. *Informatics (MDPI)*, *9*(4), 89. DOI: 10.3390/informatics9040089

Batty, M., Axhausen, K. W., Giannotti, F., Pozdnoukhov, A., Bazzani, A., Wachowicz, M., Ouzounis, G., & Portugali, Y. (2012). Smart cities of the future. *The European Physical Journal. Special Topics*, *214*(1), 481–518. DOI: 10.1140/epjst/e2012-01703-3

Bertot, J. C., Jaeger, P. T., & Grimes, J. M. (2010). Using ICTs to create a culture of transparency: E-government and social media as openness and anti-corruption tools for societies. *Government Information Quarterly*, *27*(3), 264–271. DOI: 10.1016/j.giq.2010.03.001

Bosco G, Riccardi V, Sciarrone A, D'Amore R, Visvizi A. (2024). *AI-driven innovation in smart city governance: achieving human-centric and sustainable outcomes*. Transforming Government: People, Process and Policy. DOI: 10.1108/TG-04-2024-0096

Bovaird, A. G., & Löffler, E. (2015). *Public Management and Governance*. DOI: 10.4324/9781315693279

Brabham, D. C. (2008). Crowdsourcing as a model for problem solving. *Convergence (London)*, *14*(1), 75–90. DOI: 10.1177/1354856507084420

Brabham, D. C. (2009). Crowdsourcing the public participation process for planning projects. *Planning Theory*, *8*(3), 242–262. DOI: 10.1177/1473095209104824

Busuioc, M. (2021). Accountability, control and power in data-driven public administration. *Public Administration Review*, *81*(5), 857–859. DOI: 10.1111/puar.13381 PMID: 34690372

Chatfield, A. T., & Reddick, C. G. (2018). A longitudinal cross-sector analysis of open data adoption by U.S. cities. *Government Information Quarterly*, *35*(4), 535–546. DOI: 10.1016/j.giq.2017.02.004

Chourabi, H., Nam, T., Walker, S., Gil-Garcia, J. R., Mellouli, S., Nahon, K., Pardo, T. A., & Scholl, H. J. (2012). Understanding smart cities: An integrative framework. In *Proceedings of the 45th Hawaii International Conference on System Sciences* (pp. 2289–2297). IEEE. DOI: 10.1109/HICSS.2012.615

Eubanks, V. (2018). *Automating inequality: How high-tech tools profile, police and punish the poor*. St. Martin's Press.

Fung, A. (2006). Varieties of participation in complex governance. *Public Administration Review*, *66*(s1), 66–75. DOI: 10.1111/j.1540-6210.2006.00667.x

Gari, N. (2025). *Car parking violation detection* [Data set]. Roboflow Universe. https://universe.roboflow.com/najlaa-gari-gywmx/car-parking-violation-detection/dataset/1

Gil-Garcia, J. R., Pardo, T. A., & Nam, T. (2016). What makes a city smart? Identifying core components and proposing an integrative framework. *Information Polity*, *21*(1), 61–87. DOI: 10.3233/IP-150354

Goldsmith, S., & Crawford, S. (2014). *The responsive city: Engaging communities through data-smart governance*. Jossey-Bass.

Goodchild, M. F. (2007). Citizens as sensors: The world of volunteered geography. *GeoJournal*, *69*(4), 211–221. DOI: 10.1007/s10708-007-9111-y

Graham, S. (2002). Bridging urban digital divides? *Urban Studies (Edinburgh, Scotland)*, *39*(1), 33–56. DOI: 10.1080/00420980220099050

Harrison, C., Eckman, B., Hamilton, R., Hartswick, P., Kalagnanam, J., Paraszczak, J., & Williams, P. (2010). Foundations for smarter cities. *IBM Journal of Research and Development*, *54*(4), 1–16. DOI: 10.1147/JRD.2010.2048257

Heyik, M. A., Erdoğan, M., & Romero-Martínez, J. M. (2025). AI-powered meta analysis of geospatial participatory platforms for ecosocial transition in urban design and planning. *Urban Governance*, *5*(4), 411–425. DOI: 10.1016/j.ugj.2025.09.006

Himan, A. (2025). *Urban Issues Dataset* [Data set]. Kaggle. https://www.kaggle.com/datasets/akinduhiman/urban-issues-dataset

Hollands, R. G. (2008). Will the real smart city please stand up? *City (London, England)*, *12*(3), 303–320. DOI: 10.1080/13604810802479126

Imran, M., Castillo, C., Lucas, J., Meier, P., & Vieweg, S. (2020). AI for disaster response. *Proceedings of the International AAAI Conference on Web and Social Media, 14*(1), 357–366. DOI: 10.1145/2567948.2577034

Janssen, M., & Helbig, N. (2018). Innovating and changing the policy cycle. *Government Information Quarterly*, *35*(4), S99–S105. DOI: 10.1016/j.giq.2015.11.009

Janssen, M., & Kuk, G. (2016). The challenges and limits of big data algorithms in technocratic governance. *Government Information Quarterly*, *33*(3), 371–377. DOI: 10.1016/j.giq.2016.08.011

Janssen, M., & van den Hoven, J. (2015). Big and open linked data (BOLD) in government: A challenge to transparency and privacy? *Government Information Quarterly*, *32*(4), 363–368. DOI: 10.1016/j.giq.2015.11.007

Jurafsky, D., & Martin, J. H. (2023). *Speech and language processing* (3rd ed.). Pearson., https://web.stanford.edu/~jurafsky/slp3/

Kim, Y. (2014). *Convolutional neural networks for sentence classification. Proceedings of the 2014 Conference on Empirical Methods in Natural Language Processing (EMNLP)*, 1746–1751. DOI: 10.3115/v1/D14-1181

King, S. F., & Brown, P. (2007). *Fix my street or else: Using the Internet to voice local public service concerns.* In *Proceedings of the 1st International Conference on Theory and Practice of Electronic Governance (ICEGOV 2007)* (pp. 72–80). Association for Computing Machinery. DOI: 10.1145/1328057.1328076

Kitchin, R. (2014). *The data revolution: Big data, open data, data infrastructures and their consequences.* SAGE Publications.

Krizhevsky, A., Sutskever, I., & Hinton, G. E. (2012). ImageNet classification with deep convolutional neural networks. *Advances in Neural Information Processing Systems*, *25*, 1097–1105. DOI: 10.1145/3065386

Linders, D. (2012). From e-government to we-government. *Government Information Quarterly*, *29*(4), 446–454. DOI: 10.1016/j.giq.2012.06.003

Liu, B. (2012). Sentiment analysis and opinion mining. *Synthesis Lectures on Human Language Technologies*, *5*(1), 1–167. DOI: 10.1007/978-3-031-02145-9

Maeda, J., Sekimoto, Y., Seto, T., & Kashiyama, H. (2018). Road damage detection using deep neural networks. *IEEE International Conference on Systems, Man and Cybernetics*, 1–6. DOI: 10.48550/arXiv.1801.09454

Maske, Y., Jakate, S., Thakare, C., & Lokhande, S. (2025). *Urban civic issues image dataset: Potholes and garbage (QR4Change)* (Version 2) [Data set]. Mendeley Data. DOI: 10.17632/zndzygc3p3.2

Medhat, W., Hassan, A., & Korashy, H. (2014). Sentiment analysis algorithms and applications. *Ain Shams Engineering Journal, 5*(4), 1093–1113. DOI: 10.1016/j.asej.2014.04.011

Meijer, A., & Rodríguez Bolívar, M. P. R. (2016). Governing the smart city: A review of the literature on smart urban governance. *International Review of Administrative Sciences, 82*(2), 392–408. DOI: 10.1177/0020852314564308

Ministry of Housing and Urban affairs. (2017). Swacchta – MoHUA: Citizen Grievance redressal platform under Swachh Bharat Mission (Urban). Govt. of India https://swachhbaharatmission.gov.in

Motet Hansen, M., & Dahiya, B. (2025). Traffy Fondue: A smart city citizen engagement platform. *Frontiers in Sustainable Cities, 7*, 1491621. DOI: 10.3389/frsc.2025.1491621

Nabatchi, T., & Amsler, L. B. (2014). Direct public engagement in local government. *American Review of Public Administration, 44*(4, suppl), 63S–88S. DOI: 10.1177/0275074013519702

Nam, T., & Pardo, T. A. (2011). *Conceptualizing smart city with dimensions of technology, people and institutions*. In *Proceedings of the 12th Annual International Conference on Digital Government Research: Digital Government Innovation in Challenging Times*. (pp. 282–291). ACM. DOI: 10.1145/2037556.2037602

Offenhuber, D. (2014). Infrastructure legibility: A comparative analysis of open311-based citizen feedback systems. *Cambridge Journal of Regions, Economy and Society, 8*(1), 93–112. DOI: 10.1093/cjres/rsu001

Pang, B., & Lee, L. (2008). Opinion mining and sentiment analysis. *Foundations and Trends in Information Retrieval, 2*(1–2), 1–135. DOI: 10.1561/1500000011

Peixoto, T., & Fox, J. (2016). When does ICT-enabled citizen voice lead to responsiveness? *World Development, 79*, 159–172.

Porumbescu, G. (2015). Does e-government enhance trust? *Public Administration Review, 75*(4), 675–686.

Sanh, V., Debut, L., Chaumond, J., & Wolf, T. (2019). *DistilBERT, a distilled version of BERT: smaller, faster, cheaper and lighter*. arXiv. /arXiv.1910.01108DOI: 10.48550

Schall, G., Mendez, E., Kruijff, E., Veas, E., Junghanns, S., Reitinger, B., & Schmalstieg, D. (2009). Handheld Augmented Reality for underground infrastructure visualization. *Personal and Ubiquitous Computing*, *13*(4), 281–291. DOI: 10.1007/s00779-008-0204-5

Shayamunda, R., & Bhanye, J. (2024). Digital democracy in action: Impact of civic tech innovation on public service delivery. In G. Onyango & G. Karuri-Sebina (Eds.), *Digitalisation and public policy in Africa* (Studies in national governance and emerging technologies). Palgrave Macmillan. DOI: 10.1007/978-3-031-75079-3_8

Shin, B., Floch, J., Rask, M., Bæck, P., Edgar, C., Berditchevskaia, A., Mesure, P., & Branlat, M. (2024). A systematic analysis of digital tools for citizen participation. *Government Information Quarterly*, *101954*(3), 101954. DOI: 10.1016/j.giq.2024.101954

Tan, K. L., Lee, C. P., & Lim, K. M. (2023). A survey of sentiment analysis: Approaches, datasets and future research. *Applied Sciences (Basel, Switzerland)*, *13*(7), 4550. DOI: 10.3390/app13074550

Taylor, L. (2021). Public data governance: When openness and privacy collide. *Big Data & Society*, *8*(2), 1–13. DOI: 10.1177/20539517211042490

United Nations. (2025). *World urbanization prospects. The 2025 revision*. United Nations Department of Economic and Social Affairs.

Veale, M., & Brass, I. (2019). Administration by algorithm? In Karen Yeung & Martin Lodge (Eds.), *Algorithmic Regulation*. Oxford University Press. https://doi.org/10.1093/oso/9780198838494.003.0006.

Vieweg, S., Hughes, A. L., Starbird, K., & Palen, L. (2010). *Microblogging during two natural hazards events: What Twitter may contribute to situational awareness. Proceedings of the SIGCHI Conference on Human Factors in Computing Systems*, 1079-1088. DOI: 10.1145/1753326.1753486

Visvizi, A., & Lytras, M. D. (2018). Rescaling and refocusing smart cities research: From mega cities to smart villages. *Journal of Science and Technology Policy Management*, *9*(2), 134–145. DOI: 10.1108/JSTPM-02-2018-0020

Wirtz, B. W., Weyerer, J. C., & Geyer, C. (2019). Artificial intelligence and the public sector. *International Journal of Public Administration*, *42*(7), 596–615. DOI: 10.1080/01900692.2018.1498103

Young, M. M., Bullock, J. B., & Lecy, J. D. (2019). Artificial discretion: A framework for understanding the impact of artificial intelligence on public administration. *Perspectives on Public Management and Governance*, *2*(4), 301–313. DOI: 10.1093/ppmgov/gvz014

Zheng, Y., Capra, L., Wolfson, O., & Yang, H. (2014). Urban computing: Concepts, methodologies and applications. *ACM Transactions on Intelligent Systems and Technology*, *5*(3), 38. DOI: 10.1145/2629592

Chapter 3

AI-Supported Augmented Reality in Smart Cities:

Administration Between Innovation and Institutional Adaptation

Enrico Moch
https://orcid.org/0009-0005-4722-0961
GrandEdu Research School, Germany

Jan Vrba
https://orcid.org/0000-0002-8404-5091
Akademia Jagiellońska w Toruniu, Poland

Tobias Oberdieck
https://orcid.org/0009-0002-2017-4991
GrandEdu GmbH, Germany

Lars Arnold Ritter
https://orcid.org/0009-0008-8988-0556
University of Library Studies and Information Technologies, Bulgaria

ABSTRACT

Smart cities have become a central frame of reference for contemporary urban governance. Public administrations are increasingly using artificial intelligence to analyse complex data environments and support administrative decision making processes. At the same time, augmented reality is opening up new forms of visualisation by embedding analytical results directly in spatial and administrative contexts. Both technologies are changing how information is generated, interpreted and used in

DOI: 10.4018/979-8-3373-7804-6.ch003

public decision-making processes. This chapter analyses AI-supported augmented reality applications in smart cities from an administrative science and governance-oriented perspective. The focus is not on technical performance characteristics, but on institutional adaptation processes within public organisations. Based on a comparative qualitative case study analysis, three internationally established smart cities are analysed: Singapore, Barcelona and Amsterdam. These cases represent different governance models and administrative logics that characterise the use of AI-based and immersive systems.

1.1 INTRODUCTION AND PROBLEM CONTEXT

Smart cities have established themselves as a defining frame of reference for modern urban development (Meijer et al., 2016). Public administrations are faced with the task of reconciling growing urban complexity, data-intensive control requirements and rising expectations of transparency and performance (Kitchin, 2014). Digital technologies are no longer merely supporting this development, but are increasingly shaping it (Dunleavy et al., 2006). In this context, artificial intelligence and augmented reality are becoming increasingly important. AI-based systems enable data-based analyses, forecasts and decision support, thereby expanding the analytical scope of action of public administrations. Augmented reality complements this development by changing administrative forms of perception and interaction and integrating digital information into real environments in a context-specific manner. The combination of both technologies fundamentally shifts the processes of information generation, interpretation and integration in administrative decision-making structures. This results in new institutional possibilities for systematically analysing complex issues and at the same time communicating them in a comprehensible manner. Planning processes can be visualised spatially, scenarios simulated and decision-making bases clearly presented (van Winden et al., 2016).

At the same time, new institutional challenges are emerging. Existing administrative structures are historically geared towards rule-based systems, clarity of responsibilities and the allocation of accountability. Adaptive and visually powerful systems do not fit seamlessly into this logic. Tensions arise where algorithmically generated recommendations interact with formal decision-making procedures or where visual representations influence the perception of administrative considerations. Questions of responsibility, traceability and democratic control are becoming more prominent (Ansell & Gash, 2008). Technological innovation does not unfold its effects in isolation, but in interaction with institutional frameworks, organisational routines and governance structures (Lodge & Wegrich, 2014). This chapter examines AI-supported augmented reality applications in smart cities from an administrative science perspective. The focus is on the institutional embedding of these technologies and the adaptation processes of public organisations. While the efficiency and innovation potential of AI has been extensively researched, governance aspects are often considered in isolation. An integrative analysis of these dimensions has been largely lacking to date (Moch et al., 2025). The focus is not on technical performance evaluation, but on the structural effects on decision-making processes, role understandings and governance arrangements. For empirical depth, three internationally established smart cities are analysed comparatively: Singapore, Barcelona and Amsterdam. These cases represent different institutional logics, control models and forms of administrative adaptation. They make it possible to systematically identify similarities and differences in the use of AI-supported augmented reality (Prakash & Karvonen, 2026).

1.2 THEORETICAL BACKGROUND AND STATE OF RESEARCH

Research on smart cities is characterised by a wide variety of perspectives. Earlier work looked at digital urban development primarily from a technical point of view. The focus was on networked infrastructures, data-based control and efficiency gains through automation. Cities were often understood as controllable systems whose performance could be enhanced through improved information flows (Kitchin, 2014). This perspective has provided important impetus, but remains insufficient when digital technologies intervene deeply in administrative decision-making processes. More recent approaches shift the focus to governance and administration. Smart cities are increasingly understood as socially embedded systems in which technical systems, institutional rules and organisational practices are closely interlinked. Administration no longer appears merely as a user of digital solutions, but as a shaping actor that must integrate innovations into existing structures of responsibility, legal obligations and normative expectations. This perspective brings the institutional prerequisites of digital transformation more into focus (Meijer et al., 2016).

Digital governance research is picking up on this development and analysing how digital systems are changing government action. Data-based applications influence not only work processes, but also decision-making logic, forms of accountability and the relationship between administration, politics and the public. AI-based systems in particular generate new forms of knowledge by recognising patterns, deriving forecasts and formulating recommendations for action. For decision-makers, this creates a tension between data-based support and their own professional judgement (Janssen & Kuk, 2016). Institutional administrative research offers a suitable framework for analysing these tensions. Administration is understood here as a historically grown order characterised by formal rules, informal norms and established routines.

Stability, reliability and legal binding are considered constitutive features. Technological innovation thus encounters structures that are not primarily geared towards flexibility, but rather towards predictability. Changes therefore rarely occur abruptly, but rather in gradual adaptation processes (Lodge & Wegrich, 2014). Approaches to institutional change emphasise that public organisations adopt innovation selectively. New technologies are adapted, limited or embedded in existing routines. These processes are not an expression of backwardness, but serve to secure responsibility and legitimacy. This perspective is particularly important in the case of technologies with a high degree of intervention, as it explains why administrations do not adopt digital systems unfiltered (Ansell & Gash, 2008). Augmented reality plays a special role in this debate. Unlike purely data-based applications, it directly changes the perception of administrative issues. Digital information is spatially located and made visually tangible. In conjunction with AI systems, representations are created that not only communicate analysis results but also provide an interpretative framework. Decision support thus takes on a visual dimension that influences cognitive processes. Previous research on augmented reality in the public sector has focused primarily on areas of application such as urban planning, infrastructure management and citizen communication. User acceptance, display quality and technical performance are frequently examined. Institutional effects on administrative organisations, role understanding and decision-making processes, on the other hand, are only considered to a limited extent (van Winden et al., 2016). A similar gap can be found in the literature on AI in administration. Numerous studies address efficiency potentials and risks of algorithmic bias, while questions of institutional embedding receive comparatively little attention (Wirtz et al., 2018).

This chapter addresses this background. It combines smart city research, digital governance approaches and institutional administrative research to analyse AI-supported augmented reality as part of a comprehensive administrative adaptation process. Administration is not understood as a passive recipient of technological innovation, but as an active space for design in which stability and change are in a constant state of tension (Prakash & Karvonen, 2026).

1.3 CONCEPTUAL FRAMEWORK

The conceptual framework of this chapter is based on the assumption that public administration acts as an institutionally bound actor. Administrative decisions are made within stable regulatory frameworks, organisational routines and normative expectations. Digital technologies intervene in this structure without completely dissolving it. Their effect unfolds in interaction with existing structures, not outside them (Lodge & Wegrich, 2014). From a governance perspective, administration can be understood as a place of competing control logics. Political objectives, legal obligations, technical expertise and organisational responsibilities all influence decision-making processes simultaneously. Digital systems change this constellation by introducing new forms of knowledge production and decision support (Dunleavy et al., 2006). AI-based analyses generate forecasts and patterns, while augmented reality makes these results spatially and visually accessible. This changes how administrative issues are perceived, evaluated and prioritised (Janssen & Kuk, 2016). For the analysis of institutional adaptation, three analytical dimensions are distinguished that are closely interrelated and together form the framework of the study. The first dimension concerns administrative decision-making processes. AI-supported augmented reality applications influence which information is considered relevant and how uncertainty is handled. Visual representations can reduce complexity and provide orientation. At the same time, they direct attention and frame interpretation. Institutionally, the question arises as to how such effects are integrated into formal decision-making processes and how data-based recommendations and human considerations relate to each other (Janssen & Kuk, 2016). The second dimension relates to organisational roles and competencies. The use of adaptive and immersive systems changes the requirements for expertise and responsibility. Administrative staff must interpret algorithmic results, classify visual representations and reflect on their limitations. At the same time, the normative responsibility for decisions remains anchored in the administration.

Organisational learning processes thus become a central prerequisite for institutional adaptation (Wirtz et al., 2018). The third dimension concerns governance structures and legitimacy. Public administration depends on transparency, traceability and democratic control. AI-supported analyses and immersive visualisations pose new challenges to these principles. The traceability of algorithmic recommendations, documentation of decision-making processes and clear allocation of responsibilities are becoming increasingly important. Governance arrangements must be adapted to the AI-based in order to secure trust and ensure institutional stability (Meijer et al., 2016). These three dimensions form the analytical framework for the comparative analysis of the case studies. They allow AI-supported augmented reality to be viewed not as an isolated technology, but as a catalyst for institutional negotiation. The focus is on interactions between technology, organisation and governance. For empirical application, the framework is applied to three different institutional contexts. Singapore represents a highly coordinated, state-controlled approach. Barcelona represents a governance-oriented model with an emphasis on public values. Amsterdam serves as an example of experimental and learning-oriented administration. The three cases make it possible to systematically compare institutional adaptation processes and identify differences in decision-making logic and governance structures (Prakash & Karvonen, 2026).

1.4 RESEARCH QUESTION AND OBJECTIVE

Based on the theoretical and conceptual framework, the research focuses on the institutional effects of AI-supported augmented reality applications in public administrations of smart cities (Meijer et al., 2016). The focus is not on the technical performance of individual systems, but rather on their influence on administrative decision-making processes, organisational roles and governance structures (Lodge & Wegrich, 2014). The guiding research question is how AI-supported augmented reality applications change decision-making processes, competence requirements and governance arrangements in public administrations in the context of smart cities (Wirtz et al., 2018). In addition, the study examines the institutional conditions under which these technologies contribute to administrative performance and where limits to adaptation become apparent (Lodge & Wegrich, 2014). The aim of the chapter is to systematically analyse and comparatively classify institutional adaptation processes. The study aims to show how administrations navigate between innovation pressure and institutional stability and what strategies they develop to embed new technologies responsibly (Prakash & Karvonen, 2026).

This contributes to the further development of smart city and governance research, which understands digital transformation not as linear progress but as an institutional negotiation process (Meijer et al., 2016). At the same time, the chapter pursues a practice-oriented objective. Public administrations should be provided with analytically sound guidelines for introducing AI-AR applications in a reflective manner, securing them institutionally and managing them in the long term (Wirtz et al., 2018). The analysis makes it clear that technological innovation has only limited impact without corresponding organisational and governance-related adjustments (Lodge & Wegrich, 2014).

1.5 METHODOLOGICAL APPROACH AND CASE STUDY LOGIC

A qualitative-analytical approach is chosen to answer the research question. This approach is particularly suitable for investigating institutional structures, organisational practices and governance arrangements, as it is context-sensitive and theory-driven. Quantitative impact analyses are not the main focus, as the interest lies in structural and procedural effects (Lodge & Wegrich, 2014). The chapter is based on a comparative case study analysis of three internationally established smart cities: Singapore, Barcelona and Amsterdam. These cities were deliberately chosen because they represent different institutional logics, control models and governance traditions. At the same time, they have documented applications of data-based and visual decision-making systems in the public sector (van Winden et al., 2016). The case studies were selected according to clear criteria. The institutional context of the administration, the design of governance structures and the maturity of the digital systems used were taken into account. The aim is to highlight differences and similarities in institutional adaptation without considering individual cases in isolation (Meijer et al., 2016). The analysis follows the dimensions developed in the conceptual framework. Administrative decision-making processes, organisational roles and governance structures are systematically examined and correlated. In this way, institutional tensions, adaptation strategies and governance effects can be identified and compared (Lodge & Wegrich, 2014). The empirical basis is formed by publicly available strategy documents, administrative reports, project descriptions and relevant scientific studies. These sources enable a well-founded analysis of institutional arrangements and their change through the use of AI-supported augmented reality (Meijer et al., 2016).

1.6 CASE STUDY ANALYSIS

1.6.1 Singapore

Singapore is considered a case study with a high degree of government control, clear responsibilities and strong strategic coordination (Bork-Hüffer, 2017). Digital urban development there is not just a technical modernisation project, but part of a long-term government programme that closely links administration, infrastructure, security and urban planning (Bork-Hüffer, 2017). This context is particularly revealing for the analysis of AI-supported augmented reality because institutional adaptation does not primarily result from spontaneous individual initiatives, but rather from systematic embedding in existing control structures (Prakash & Karvonen, 2026). The starting point is characterised by three features. First, the administration has a high capacity for standardisation and coordination across departmental boundaries (Lodge & Wegrich, 2014). Second, the use of data-based systems is widely established in the public sector and is understood as an integral part of administrative performance (Meijer et al., 2016). Thirdly, political expectations are strongly focused on effectiveness, reliability and predictable implementation (Bork-Hüffer, 2017). These characteristics favour the use of AI and visual systems, but at the same time increase the requirements for institutional control and accountability (Meijer et al., 2016).

In Singapore, the use of AI-supported visual systems can be observed particularly well in integrated urban planning and urban infrastructure management (Ruhlandt, 2018). Administrative decisions in areas such as transport, construction, land use, crisis management and security are often based on the linking of heterogeneous data sources (Meijer et al., 2016). AI systems are used here to consolidate large amounts of data, recognise patterns and generate forecasts (Janssen & Kuk, 2016). Augmented reality is added as an interface that makes these results spatially visible and thus supports operational and strategic use (Ruhlandt, 2018). This coupling is relevant for administration because it connects two levels. On the one hand, there are computer-assisted assessments that structure possible courses of action (Janssen & Kuk, 2016). On the other hand, there are visual representations that present complex issues in a way that can be used immediately in meetings, situation discussions or planning rounds (Ruhlandt, 2018). The technology thus acts not only as a tool, but also as a form of knowledge organisation (Wirtz et al., 2018).

With regard to decision-making processes, Singapore exhibits a pattern that can be described as controlled integration (Meijer et al., 2016). AI-based results are used to support decision-making, but not to replace it (Janssen & Kuk, 2016). The administration retains formal responsibility, while at the same time the actual significance of algorithmic proposals is growing (Lodge & Wegrich, 2014). Visual representations reinforce this effect because they draw attention to specific aspects and translate uncertainty into vivid scenarios (Janssen & Kuk, 2016). How these effects are embedded in existing procedures is institutionally relevant. In a highly coordinated administrative environment, clear expectations arise regarding the traceability of proposed actions, documentable decision-making processes and stable review mechanisms (Meijer et al., 2016). This allows the administration to expand the use of technical systems without undermining the basic principle of accountability (Lodge & Wegrich, 2014). At the same time, there is a growing risk that visual plausibility will override technical considerations (Janssen & Kuk, 2016). In an environment that is strongly focused on effectiveness, there is a danger that the visibility of a scenario will be perceived as sufficiently convincing, even if uncertainties or model limitations are not adequately discussed (Janssen & Kuk, 2016). The institutional response often lies in the design of multi-stage decision-making processes. Technical assessments are understood as input variables that are supplemented by technical review, legal classification and internal organisational coordination (Lodge & Wegrich, 2014). This creates a balance that ensures both performance and accountability (Meijer et al., 2016).

Singapore illustrates that AI-AR applications are shifting the competency profiles in administrations (Wirtz et al., 2018). In addition to technical and legal competencies, the ability to interpret algorithmic evaluations and critically read visual representations is becoming increasingly important (Janssen & Kuk, 2016). This applies not only to technical specialists, but also to decision-makers who have to translate the results into politically responsible steps. This development creates two institutional requirements. The first requirement concerns qualification and organisational learning. Administrations must build up skills that enable them to recognise model assumptions, limitations of the data available and sources of error (Wirtz et al., 2018). A second requirement concerns the distribution of roles.

When technical systems consolidate proposals, it must remain clear who is responsible for selection, consideration and decision-making. Without a clear allocation of roles, a grey area arises in which responsibility is effectively dispersed (Lodge & Wegrich, 2014). Singapore generally tends towards formal clarity of responsibilities, which reduces the risk of diffusion of responsibility (Lodge & Wegrich, 2014). At the same time, the practical challenge remains that the line between recommendation and decision can become blurred in everyday life when systems are built into operational routines (Janssen & Kuk, 2016). Internal cooperation is also changing. Data, models and visual representations promote coordination between units, but can also create new dependencies. An administrative unit that provides a visual overview of the situation gains influence over the prioritisation of other units. Institutionally, this reveals a new type of internal power relationship that operates not through hierarchy but through information advantage (Janssen & Kuk, 2016).

In the area of governance and legitimacy, the case of Singapore shows a tension between strong control capabilities and high expectations of oversight (Bork-Hüffer, 2017). On the one hand, coordinated administration allows for the rapid introduction and standardisation of digital systems. On the other hand, there is a growing need for rules on transparency, documentation and control because AI systems and visual representations are not automatically self-explanatory (Meijer et al., 2016). Legitimacy arises here less through broad public negotiation and more through performance promises, stability and institutional reliability (Bork-Hüffer, 2017). This makes control mechanisms within the administration particularly important. Governance structures are designed to stabilise the use of technology through rules, audits and chains of responsibility (Lodge & Wegrich, 2014). Questions of traceability are particularly relevant here. If an AI-based assessment suggests an action, it must be clear which database, model assumptions and uncertainties underlie it (Janssen & Kuk, 2016). If augmented reality presents this assessment visually, it must also be ensured that the representation is not misunderstood as objective truth (Wirtz et al., 2018). The institutional challenge is to treat the visual level as part of a responsible decision-making process. This includes documentation standards, a clear separation between analysis and decision-making, and the ability to visualise alternative scenarios rather than just providing a plausible picture (Meijer et al., 2016).

An administration with a high level of coordination can establish such standards. At the same time, the success of the systems increases the risk of routine formation. The more effectively a system functions in everyday life, the less willingness there is to regularly review model assumptions (Janssen & Kuk, 2016). Institutionally, this is a risk because long-term stability is based not only on function but also on controlled accountability (Lodge & Wegrich, 2014).

Singapore is a suitable case for comparison because institutional adaptation there takes place under conditions of high control capacity (Bork-Hüffer, 2017). The introduction of AI-supported visual systems is planned, controlled and closely linked to administrative responsibilities (Meijer et al., 2016). Decision-making processes are supported but not formally replaced (Janssen & Kuk, 2016). Roles and competencies are expanded without delegating responsibility to technology (Lodge & Wegrich, 2014). Governance structures emphasise internal control and documentable procedures (Meijer et al., 2016). A comparison with Barcelona and Amsterdam is likely to show that Singapore has a stronger tendency towards standardisation and performance orientation. The question of how public values, external transparency and democratic control are shaped will be different in the two European cases. It is precisely this difference that makes the case selection analytically productive.

1.6.2 Barcelona

Barcelona is considered a reference case for smart city development with a strong normative and governance-oriented focus (Calzada, 2019). In contrast to highly centralised control models, the primary focus here is not on administrative efficiency, but on the institutional embedding of digital technologies in democratic processes, public values and transparent administrative structures (Calzada, 2019). This context is particularly relevant for the analysis of AI-supported augmented reality applications, as technological innovation is explicitly linked to questions of legitimacy and accountability (Meijer et al., 2016). Barcelona's starting point is characterised by three structural features. First, digital urban development is closely linked to political models of openness, transparency and public welfare orientation (Calzada, 2019). Second, the city has a distinctive governance structure in which administration, politics, civil society and technological actors are intertwined (Ansell & Gash, 2008).

Thirdly, there is a high sensitivity to power asymmetries that can arise from data-based systems (Zuboff, 2019). This constellation fundamentally shapes the way AI and visual technologies are handled.

In Barcelona, AI-supported visual systems are primarily used in urban planning, traffic control and participation processes. Augmented reality is not only used for internal decision-making support, but also for external communication of complex planning and control issues (Capra, 2018). AI-based analyses provide forecasts and scenarios that are made accessible to different stakeholder groups by means of visual representations (Calzada, 2019). The system logic differs significantly from purely administrative use. Technologies are understood as a means of supporting deliberative processes (Ansell & Gash, 2008). Visual representations are intended to facilitate understanding, not to replace decision-making guidelines. Institutionally, this sets a different focus. The question is less about how quickly and efficiently decisions can be made, but rather how decisions can remain comprehensible, justifiable and publicly communicable (Meijer et al., 2016).

In the area of administrative decision-making processes, Barcelona shows a pattern of reflexive use (Meijer et al., 2016). AI-based assessments are understood as one element among many that is embedded in political and administrative deliberation processes (Ansell & Gash, 2008). Augmented reality acts as a medium for visualising different scenarios and presenting their consequences in a comparable way (Capra, 2018). The visual level thus serves not primarily to reduce uncertainty, but to reveal options for action (Calzada, 2019). It is institutionally relevant that visual plausibility is deliberately relativised (Meijer et al., 2016). Administrative decisions are not made solely on the basis of a convincing image, but are supplemented by argumentative and legal review (Lodge & Wegrich, 2014). This practice slows down the decision-making process, but increases institutional robustness. Decisions retain their deliberative character, even when technical systems are involved (Ansell & Gash, 2008). At the same time, an area of tension arises. The more visual representations are integrated into political discussions, the greater their influence on perception and priority setting (Janssen & Kuk, 2016).

Even in a governance-oriented environment, visual evidence can shift the weight of argument. Institutionally, this requires clear rules on how visual scenarios are incorporated into decision-making processes and how alternative representations remain visible (Meijer et al., 2016).

Barcelona illustrates that AI-AR applications are creating new role profiles in administration (Wirtz et al., 2018). In addition to traditional technical and legal competencies, skills in communicating, translating and critically evaluating technical results are becoming increasingly important (Janssen & Kuk, 2016). Administration acts more as a moderator between technical analyses, political decisions and public perception (Ansell & Gash, 2008). This development increases the requirements for qualifications. Employees must not only understand systems, but also communicate their results in a way that is appropriate for the target audience, while at the same time pointing out their limitations (Wirtz et al., 2018). The ability to openly address uncertainty is becoming an institutional competence (Meijer et al., 2016). Unlike in highly hierarchical systems, there is less pressure to make quick decisions, but more responsibility for transparent presentation (Calzada, 2019). Role responsibility remains clearly anchored in the administration (Lodge & Wegrich, 2014). AI systems provide input, not decisions (Janssen & Kuk, 2016). Nevertheless, the internal distribution of power is shifting. Units that develop data models and visual scenarios are gaining influence over discourse and agenda setting (Calzada, 2019). Institutionally, attempts are being made to offset this effect through open data strategies, interdisciplinary teams and participatory formats (Meijer et al., 2016).

In the area of governance and legitimacy, Barcelona is showing an explicit politicisation of digital technologies (Calzada, 2019). The use of AI and augmented reality is not treated as a purely technical issue, but as a matter of public responsibility (Ansell & Gash, 2008). Legitimacy arises here less through performance promises than through transparency, participation and institutional control (Meijer et al., 2016). Governance structures are designed to ensure traceability (Meijer et al., 2016). This includes open documentation, public discussion of assumptions and the possibility of visualising alternative scenarios (Calzada, 2019). Visual representations are not understood as objective depictions, but as interpretative tools that require critical assessment (Capra, 2018).

This approach strengthens democratic control but increases the complexity of administrative control (Lodge & Wegrich, 2014). Decision-making processes become slower and more prone to conflict. Institutionally, this tension is accepted as a necessary price to pay for legitimacy and public accountability (Ansell & Gash, 2008). For AI-AR applications, this means that their use is more limited and regulated than in more performance-oriented models (Calzada, 2019).

Barcelona is a suitable case for comparison because institutional adaptation here takes place under conditions of strong normative orientation (Calzada, 2019). AI-supported augmented reality applications are not primarily used as efficiency tools, but as a means of supporting transparent and participatory governance (Meijer et al., 2016). Decision-making processes remain deliberative, roles are designed to be mediating, and governance structures emphasise public values (Ansell & Gash, 2008). Compared to Singapore, there is less standardisation but greater sensitivity to the power effects of visual and data-based systems. Compared to Amsterdam, Barcelona is more politically framed and less experimental. These differences form the basis for the final comparative analysis.

1.6.3 Amsterdam

Amsterdam stands for an approach to urban digitalisation that is characterised by a willingness to experiment, institutional learning and cooperative governance (Capra, 2018). Digital innovation is not understood here as a linearly plannable process, but as an iterative search process that connects administration, business, science and civil society (Prakash & Karvonen, 2026). This context is particularly revealing for the analysis of AI-supported augmented reality applications, as institutional adaptation is deliberately designed to be open and tested step by step (Ruhlandt, 2018). The starting point is characterised by three features. First, the city pursues a strongly network-based governance model in which formal responsibilities are combined with project-related cooperation (Capra, 2018). Second, there is a strong culture of testing and learning in which pilot projects are explicitly understood as provisional arrangements (van Winden et al., 2016). Thirdly, there is a high level of sensitivity to issues of data protection, transparency and public responsibility (Meijer et al., 2016). This combination has a particular impact on the use of AI and visual technologies.

In Amsterdam, AI-AR applications are mainly found in urban planning, mobility management and spatial analysis of urban developments (Capra, 2018). Augmented reality is used to spatially represent planning variants, traffic flows or environmental impacts and to discuss them with various stakeholders (Capra, 2018). AI-based analyses provide forecasts, simulations and scenarios that serve as a starting point for negotiation (Janssen & Kuk, 2016). The system logic differs significantly from more standardised models. Technologies are not introduced as stable decision-making instruments, but as experimental tools whose benefits, limitations and side effects are continuously reflected upon (van Winden et al., 2016). Institutionally, this creates a framework in which technological innovation is linked to questions of responsibility and legitimacy from the outset (Meijer et al., 2016).

In the area of administrative decision-making processes, Amsterdam shows a pattern of cautious integration (Meijer et al., 2016). AI-supported analyses and visual representations are used to explore decision-making options, not to determine them (Janssen & Kuk, 2016). Augmented reality is used for the joint exploration of scenarios and the visualisation of possible consequences (Capra, 2018). Decisions remain the result of a negotiation process between the administration, politicians and other stakeholders (Prakash & Karvonen, 2026). Institutionally, this leads to a decoupling of analysis and decision-making. Technical systems generate knowledge that is deliberately treated as provisional and context-dependent (Ruhlandt, 2018). This approach reduces the risk of visual plausibility serving as a substitute for professional consideration (Janssen & Kuk, 2016) At the same time, decision-making processes are prolonged as additional reflection and coordination steps are planned (Lodge & Wegrich, 2014). An area of tension arises where experimental procedures meet formal administrative logic. Projects that appear successful in pilot formats must be transferred to existing decision-making processes (van Winden et al., 2016). This shows that the openness of the experimental framework can conflict with legal and organisational requirements (Lodge & Wegrich, 2014). Institutional adaptation here consists less in standardisation than in translating learning outcomes into permanently sustainable procedures (Ruhlandt, 2018).

Amsterdam illustrates that AI-AR applications are creating new roles in administration (Wirtz et al., 2018). Employees act not only as specialists or decision-makers, but increasingly as mediators between technology, politics and the public (Prakash & Karvonen, 2026). The ability to communicate uncertainty and classify results is becoming increasingly important (Janssen & Kuk, 2016). Competence requirements are shifting towards interdisciplinary collaboration (Wirtz et al., 2018).

Administrative staff must understand technical analyses without being developers themselves (Janssen & Kuk, 2016). At the same time, the ability to openly address normative issues and tolerate conflicts is in demand (Meijer et al., 2016). Organisational learning processes are explicitly promoted, for example through project-based teams and temporary experimental spaces (van Winden et al., 2016). Role responsibilities remain deliberately clear. Decisions are not delegated to systems (Lodge & Wegrich, 2014). Nevertheless, a new form of internal dependency arises, as units with access to data and visualisations can shape discourse (Capra, 2018). Institutionally, attempts are made to limit this effect through transparency, open data and broad participation (Meijer et al., 2016).

In the area of governance and legitimacy, Amsterdam demonstrates a highly reflexive approach (Ruhlandt, 2018). The use of AI-supported visual systems is continuously questioned and linked back to public values (Meijer et al., 2016). Legitimacy here arises less from efficiency or performance promises than from openness, willingness to learn and institutional control (Prakash & Karvonen, 2026). Governance structures are designed to keep technological innovation reversible (Ruhlandt, 2018). Pilot projects can be terminated, adapted or realigned (van Winden et al., 2016). Visual representations are understood as discursive tools, not as objective representations (Capra, 2018). This attitude strengthens democratic control but creates uncertainty about long-term controllability (Lodge & Wegrich, 2014). Institutionally, this uncertainty is accepted and understood as part of responsible digitalisation (Prakash & Karvonen, 2026). The price for this is greater coordination effort and lower predictability (Lodge & Wegrich, 2014). For AI-AR applications, this means that their use remains more fragmented and scales less quickly than in more hierarchical systems (Ruhlandt, 2018).

Amsterdam is a suitable case for comparison because institutional adaptation here takes place under conditions of deliberate openness (Ruhlandt, 2018). AI-supported augmented reality applications are used as learning tools, not as stable control tools (van Winden et al., 2016). Decision-making processes remain exploratory, roles are mediating, and governance structures emphasise reversibility and public responsibility (Meijer et al., 2016). Compared to Singapore, there is less control but a higher degree of reflexivity. Compared to Barcelona, there is a stronger focus on experimentation with less political framing. These differences form the basis for a precise comparative analysis of institutional adaptation strategies.

1.7 COMPARATIVE SYNTHESIS OF THE CASE STUDIES

The three case studies show that AI-supported augmented reality functions less as an isolated technology and more as an institutional impulse that reveals existing administrative logics and triggers adaptation processes (Meijer et al., 2016). Differences arise not primarily from technical maturity, but from governance structures, political framing and organisational learning capacity (Ruhlandt, 2018). Singapore, Barcelona and Amsterdam represent three different modes of institutional embedding. These modes can be described as controlled integration, normatively framed governance and experimental learning. Singapore stands for a highly coordinated administrative system in which technological systems are introduced and standardised in a planned manner (Bork-Hüffer, 2017). AI-supported analyses are used as performance-enhancing decision support, while augmented reality serves as an operational interface that enables consolidation and rapid orientation (Janssen & Kuk, 2016). Institutional adaptation here takes place primarily through formalised procedures, clarity of responsibilities and internal control mechanisms (Lodge & Wegrich, 2014). Barcelona demonstrates an approach in which technological innovation is deliberately linked to public values, transparency and democratic embedding (Calzada, 2019). AI-AR systems are used not only for internal control, but also for communication about options for action (Meijer et al., 2016). Institutional adaptation is supported by deliberative processes, public communication and normative governance structures (Ansell & Gash, 2008). Visual representations are treated as interpretative tools whose impact is reflected upon and limited (Capra, 2018). Amsterdam represents a learning-oriented and project-based form of digitalisation (Ruhlandt, 2018).

Technologies are tested in pilot constellations, adapted and, in some cases, discarded (van Winden et al., 2016). AI-supported analyses and augmented reality are used to explore scenarios (Capra, 2018). Institutional adaptation takes place through organisational learning, cooperation networks and the translation of experimental findings into permanent procedures (van Winden et al., 2016). Reversibility and reflexivity are part of the legitimation process here (Meijer et al., 2016). These differences create a clear logic for comparison. Singapore maximises controllability through standardisation, Barcelona maximises legitimacy through public values, and Amsterdam maximises learning ability through experimental formats. AI-supported augmented reality acts as an amplifier of these institutional characteristics in all three cases.

1.7.1 Institutional areas of tension and governance effects

The first area of tension concerns responsibility and decision-making authority. AI-based recommendations and visual scenarios shift the actual distribution of weight in the decision-making process (Janssen & Kuk, 2016). Formal responsibility remains with the administration (Meijer et al., 2016), but the question of the actual justification for decisions becomes more complex (Lodge & Wegrich, 2014). Singapore addresses this through clear responsibilities and documented review steps. Barcelona integrates technical recommendations more strongly into argumentative and public justification logic. Amsterdam decouples analysis and decision-making and treats recommendations as preliminary contributions. In all cases, a governance effect arises. Responsibility must be re-operationalised so that the use of technical support does not lead to informal delegation (Meijer et al., 2016). A second area of tension concerns traceability and transparency. AI-based models generate results whose internal logic is not readily apparent (Janssen & Kuk, 2016). Augmented reality increases comprehensibility, but at the same time can create the impression of objectivity (Li et al., 2025). Singapore focuses on internal traceability and chains of control. Barcelona prioritises external transparency and the public visibility of assumptions. Amsterdam emphasises openness in the process and focuses on reversibility as a control principle. The governance effect is that transparency needs to be redefined. It is not enough to show results. What is required is the institutional capacity to make assumptions, uncertainties and alternatives recognisable (Meijer et al., 2016). A third area of tension concerns changing roles and skill requirements. AI-AR systems are creating new job profiles (Wirtz et al., 2018).

Employees must interpret technical results, critically read visual representations and communicate their limitations (Janssen & Kuk, 2016). In Singapore, this is more pronounced than professionalisation within standardised processes. In Barcelona, mediation between technology, politics and the public is becoming a core competence. In Amsterdam, interdisciplinary collaboration and project-based learning dominate. The governance effect lies in the shift in competence definitions. Administration requires not only specialist knowledge, but also evaluation skills, translation skills and institutional reflexivity (Meijer et al., 2016). A fourth area of tension concerns visual evidence and political control. Augmented reality changes perception (Li et al., 2025). Scenarios can structure debates, direct attention and set priorities (Janssen & Kuk, 2016). Visual plausibility can override argumentative deliberation, even if no formal automation takes place (Janssen & Kuk, 2016). Singapore reduces this risk through procedural embedding and internal control. Barcelona attempts to limit it through public discussion, alternative representations and normative framing. Amsterdam counters it with experimental formats that explicitly address uncertainty. The governance effect is that visual systems can act as a new form of administrative power (Meijer et al., 2016). Institutional mechanisms must therefore make not only models but also visualisations controllable.

1.7.2 Interim conclusion of the empirical analysis

Overall, the case studies show that AI-supported augmented reality does not replace administration, but reframes decision-making and control processes (Meijer et al., 2016). Institutional adaptation is the decisive factor for success. The use of such technologies is viable where the assignment of responsibility, traceability and competence building are institutionally secured (Lodge & Wegrich, 2014). Limits to adaptation become apparent where visual plausibility has an uncontrolled effect, where responsibilities become blurred or where transparency can no longer be credibly established (Janssen & Kuk, 2016).

1.8 DISCUSSION

The comparative analysis of Singapore, Barcelona and Amsterdam shows that AI-supported augmented reality in smart cities cannot be understood as a technical addition. Rather, the technology changes the conditions under which administration generates knowledge, deals with uncertainty and justifies decisions (Meijer et al., 2016).

This makes it clear that digital transformation in the public sector is not primarily a question of technical performance, but rather a question of institutional adaptation (Ruhlandt, 2018). This perspective puts into perspective widespread narratives that describe smart cities as a progressive logic of technical optimisation and shifts the focus to governance, responsibility and organisational learning ability (Kitchin, 2014). A first point of discussion concerns the epistemic dimension of administrative action. AI systems generate pattern suggestions, forecasts and evaluations from data (Janssen & Kuk, 2016). Augmented reality translates these results into spatial and visual formats that can appear as evidence (Wirtz et al., 2018). This provides administrations with not only more information, but also a different form of knowledge. This form of knowledge is condensed, model-bound and often only interpretable to a limited extent (Janssen & Kuk, 2016). Institutionally, this creates a new tension between professional judgement and model-based plausibility (Lodge & Wegrich, 2014). The case studies show that administrations must address this tension rather than resolve it. Singapore stabilises it through standardised procedures and internal controls. Barcelona addresses it through public values, transparency and discursive embedding. Amsterdam keeps it open through experimental formats and gradually translates learning outcomes into permanent procedures. In all cases, it is clear that administrations must ensure the epistemic quality of systems not only technically, but also institutionally (Meijer et al., 2016). A second point of discussion concerns responsibility and accountability. AI-AR systems generate decision support, but at the same time they change the nature of justification (Janssen & Kuk, 2016). Where arguments used to be derived from files, expertise and normative considerations, model-based evidence is now added. This evidence is often difficult to explain fully, but is particularly convincing when presented visually (Wirtz et al., 2018).

Institutionally, there is a risk of informal delegation (Lodge & Wegrich, 2014). The case studies show different institutional responses. Singapore focuses on clear responsibilities and review steps. Barcelona strengthens the obligation to provide justification and normatively framed public communication. Amsterdam decouples analysis and decision-making more strongly and emphasises reversibility. These differences indicate that responsibility must be understood not only as a legal principle but also as an organisational practice (Meijer et al., 2016). A third point of discussion concerns the governance of transparency and traceability. Augmented reality can increase the comprehensibility of results, but at the same time create a new form of opacity (Wirtz et al., 2018). Visibility is not the same as traceability (Janssen & Kuk, 2016). A convincing image can obscure complex model assumptions.

Transparency must therefore be considered in two ways. Firstly, as transparency of data and model logic. Secondly, as transparency of visual framing (Meijer et al., 2016). The case studies illustrate that these two levels require different institutional solutions. Singapore emphasises internal transparency to ensure operational control. Barcelona emphasises external transparency and treats visualisations as discursive tools that should be publicly negotiable (Calzada, 2019). Amsterdam emphasises process openness and learning ability (Ruhlandt, 2018). This leads to a theoretical implication. Digital governance must treat visual evidence as an independent governance object (Meijer et al., 2016). A fourth point of discussion concerns organisational roles and competence profiles. AI-AR applications are changing not only processes but also the division of labour in administrations (Wirtz et al., 2018). New interface roles are emerging between technology and decision-making. These roles vary in the different cases. Singapore is professionalising them within standardised structures. Barcelona is developing them as a mediating competence in politically sensitive contexts. Amsterdam is anchoring them in project-based teams and networks. What they have in common is that classic administrative skills are not being devalued, but must be supplemented (Lodge & Wegrich, 2014). A fifth point of discussion concerns the logic of institutional adaptation. The three cases show no technological inevitability. They show institutional choices (Ruhlandt, 2018). Singapore prioritises controllability and standardisation, Barcelona prioritises public values and democratic embedding, and Amsterdam prioritises learning and reversibility. This leads to a key insight. AI-supported augmented reality reinforces existing institutional logics rather than replacing them (Meijer et al., 2016). These points lead to an overarching conclusion. The success of AI-AR-based administration depends less on technical innovation than on institutional governance (Ruhlandt, 2018). Administrations must introduce systems in such a way that responsibility, traceability and control are ensured. If this is successful, AI-AR systems can strengthen administrative performance by structuring complexity and improving communication (Wirtz et al., 2018). If this is not successful, new forms of institutional fragility arise, such as diffusion of responsibility, visual persuasion without justification, or the creeping loss of democratic control (Meijer et al., 2016).

1.9 CONTRIBUTION TO RESEARCH AND PRACTICE

The chapter contributes to research on three levels. On the first level, it expands smart city research to include an administrative science perspective that treats technology not as a driver but as an institutional challenge. The work shows that smart cities are not primarily technological projects but governance configurations. This shifts the discussion from infrastructure and efficiency to institutions and responsibility (Meijer et al., 2016; Ruhlandt, 2018). On a second level, the chapter contributes to digital governance research by systematically incorporating the visual dimension of digital systems. Much of the work on AI in the public sector focuses on models, data and algorithmic bias (Janssen & Kuk, 2016; Wirtz et al., 2018). The combination with augmented reality makes it clear that the level of representation itself is relevant to governance. Visual evidence can structure decision-making processes and influence political priorities (Meijer et al., 2016). Therefore, digital governance must regulate not only model logic but also visualisation logic. This extension is a clear theoretical added value. On a third level, the chapter combines institutional theory with empirical case study analysis. The three cases show different modes of institutional adaptation. Controlled integration, normatively framed governance and experimental learning form an analytical grid that can be used beyond individual cities. This creates a framework that is also applicable to other urban contexts and makes institutional variability explainable (Ruhlandt, 2018; Prakash & Karvonen, 2026). Several guiding principles emerge for practical application. Firstly, administrations should not treat AI-AR systems as a substitute for judgement, but as structured support that is always supplemented by technical and legal review (Lodge & Wegrich, 2014). Secondly, responsibility allocation and documentation standards should be defined from the outset. This includes clarifying who is responsible for data quality, who reviews model assumptions, who approves visualisations and how decisions are justified (Meijer et al., 2016). Thirdly, administrations should understand competence building as a core component of implementation. Without competence, either uncritical adoption or institutional blockage will result (Wirtz et al., 2018). Fourthly, visualisations should be made governance-capable. This means keeping alternative scenarios visible, communicating uncertainty and reflecting on representation-related framing effects (Janssen & Kuk, 2016). Fifthly, the introduction should be gradual, but not arbitrary. Pilot logic must be translatable into permanent procedures, otherwise innovation will remain fragmented (van Winden et al., 2016).

These guidelines show that technological innovation only increases administrative performance if institutional adaptation is considered and actively managed. Administration needs not only systems, but also rules, competencies and control mechanisms (Meijer et al., 2016).

1.10 LIMITATIONS

The study has several limitations that are important for interpreting the results. The case study analysis is qualitative and context-specific. It does not allow for statistical generalisation, but provides theory-driven insights into institutional processes (Ruhlandt, 2018). The selection of three internationally prominent cities increases comparability and documentability, but may create a bias, as these cities have high resources and strong innovation capacity. Results may differ in municipalities with fewer resources (Meijer et al., 2016). Another point concerns the data basis. The analysis is based on publicly available documents and scientific studies. Informal practices, organisational cultural dynamics and internal conflicts therefore remain partially hidden. Especially in sensitive areas such as security or crisis management, publicly available information may be strategically filtered (Lodge & Wegrich, 2014). Future research should reduce this limitation through interviews, participant observation or in-depth process analyses (Ansell & Gash, 2008). Finally, the term AI-supported augmented reality is broad. Systems vary greatly in terms of their field of application, data basis and degree of maturity. This chapter focuses on institutional effects and deliberately abstracts from technical details. This abstraction makes sense from an analytical point of view, but can only depict differences between specific system types to a limited extent. Future work could differentiate more clearly between which system architectures produce which institutional effects (Wirtz et al., 2018).

1.11 CONCLUSION AND OUTLOOK

This chapter has shown that AI-supported augmented reality does not replace administration in smart cities, but changes the conditions of administrative action (Meijer et al., 2016). AI systems generate new forms of model-based knowledge (Janssen & Kuk, 2016). Augmented reality makes this knowledge spatially visible and influences perception and priority setting (Wirtz et al., 2018). This combination acts as an institutional impulse that challenges the allocation of responsibility, traceability, understanding of roles and governance structures (Lodge & Wegrich, 2014).

The comparative analysis of Singapore, Barcelona and Amsterdam makes it clear that institutional adaptation takes place in different modes. Singapore stands for highly controlled integration and standardisation (Bork-Hüffer, 2017), Barcelona for normatively framed governance and democratic embedding (Calzada, 2019; Ansell & Gash, 2008), and Amsterdam for experimental learning and reversibility (Ruhlandt, 2018; van Winden et al., 2016). In all cases, the sustainability of technology use depends on whether responsibility, control and competence building are institutionally secured (Meijer et al., 2016). There are two key implications for the further development of smart city governance. First, administrations must understand the governance of visual evidence as a separate task. It is not enough to regulate AI models. Visualisations must also be designed in such a way that uncertainty remains visible and alternative interpretations are possible (Janssen & Kuk, 2016; Wirtz et al., 2018). Second, institutional adaptation should be understood as a strategic process. Digital systems only have an impact if they are integrated into decision-making processes, responsibility structures and control mechanisms (Lodge & Wegrich, 2014). The outlook reveals several research perspectives. Of particular interest is the long-term impact of visual decision support on political negotiation processes (Ansell & Gash, 2008). Another relevant question is how administrations deal with routine formation when systems are used over many years (Ruhlandt, 2018). In addition, research on smaller municipalities and resource-poor contexts is needed to understand institutional adaptation under less favourable conditions (Meijer et al., 2016). Finally, the connection between technical design, visual framing and normative responsibility is a field that needs to be further developed both empirically and theoretically (Wirtz et al., 2018). Overall, the work makes it clear that the quality of smart cities cannot be measured solely in terms of technological innovation. The decisive factor is whether the administration is able to embed digital systems in an institutionally responsible manner and ensure democratically legitimised control even under conditions of data-based and visual decision support (Meijer et al., 2016).

REFERENCES

Ansell, C., & Gash, A. (2008). Collaborative governance in theory and practice. *Journal of Public Administration: Research and Theory*, *18*(4), 543–571. DOI: 10.1093/jopart/mum032

Bork-Hüffer, T. (2017). Beyond Smart City. Singapore's "Smart Nation" strategy and the competition for model status. *Geographische Rundschau*, *69*(7–8), 36–40.

Calzada, I. (2019). Deciphering smart city citizenship: The techno-politics of data and urban co-operative platforms. *Revista Internacional de Estudios Vascos*, *63*(1–2), 42–81.

Capra, C. F. (2018). The Smart City and Its Citizens: Governance and Citizen Participation in Amsterdam Smart City. In I. Management Association (Ed.), E-Planning and Collaboration: Concepts, Methodologies, Tools, and Applications (pp. 321-341). IGI Global Scientific Publishing. https://doi.org/DOI: 10.4018/978-1-5225-5646-6.ch015

Dunleavy, P., Margetts, H., Bastow, S., & Tinkler, J. (2006). New public management is dead. Long live digital era governance. *Journal of Public Administration: Research and Theory*, *16*(3), 467–494. DOI: 10.1093/jopart/mui057

Janssen, M., & Kuk, G. (2016). The challenges and limits of big data algorithms in technocratic governance. *Government Information Quarterly*, *33*(3), 371–377. DOI: 10.1016/j.giq.2016.08.011

Kitchin, R. (2014). The Real-Time City? Big Data and Smart Urbanism. *GeoJournal*, *79*(1), 1–14. DOI: 10.1007/s10708-013-9516-8

Li, R., Yuen, K. F., Wang, Y., & Lu, Y. (2025). System dynamics–based framework for modelling and assessing smart city resilience. A case study of Chengdu, China. *Sustainable Cities and Society*, *107*, 107056. DOI: 10.1016/j.scs.2025.107056

Lodge, M., & Wegrich, K. (2014). *The problem-solving capacity of the modern state. Governance challenges and administrative capacities*. Oxford University Press.

Meijer, A., Gil-Garcia, J. R., & Bolívar, M. P. R. (2016). Smart city research. Contextual conditions, governance models, and public value assessment. *Social Science Computer Review*, *34*(6), 647–656. DOI: 10.1177/0894439315618890

Moch, E., Oberdieck, T., Barenkamp, M., & Ritter, L. A. (2025). *KI-Anwendungen im Unternehmen – Effizienz steigern, Innovation fördern, Governance sichern*. Wirtschaftsinformatik & Management., DOI: 10.1365/s35764-025-00578-x

Prakash, D., & Karvonen, A. (2026). Institutional logics of the smart city and the emergence of new configurations of local governance. *Cities (London, England)*, *171*, 106727. DOI: 10.1016/j.cities.2025.106727

Ruhlandt, R. W. S. (2018). The governance of smart cities. A systematic literature review. *Cities (London, England)*, *81*, 1–23. DOI: 10.1016/j.cities.2018.02.014

van Winden, W., Oskam, I., van den Buuse, D., Schrama, W., & van Dijck, E.-J. (2016). *Organising smart city projects: Lessons from Amsterdam*. Amsterdam University of Applied Sciences.

Wirtz, B. W., Weyerer, J. C., & Geyer, C. (2018). Artificial intelligence and the public sector. Applications and challenges. *International Journal of Public Administration*, *42*(7), 596–615. DOI: 10.1080/01900692.2018.1498103

Zuboff, S. (2019). *The age of surveillance capitalism. The fight for a human future at the new frontier of power*. PublicAffairs.

Chapter 4
AI Regulations and Policies for Data Privacy Protection in Indonesia

Bintang Mahardika Pramanda Aji
https://orcid.org/0009-0008-7858-4903
Universitas Muhammadiyah Malang, Indonesia

Mohammad Jafar Loilatu
https://orcid.org/0000-0001-6921-6879
Universitas Muhammadiyah Malang, Indonesia

Sheha Putri Septaninda
Universitas Muhammadiyah Malang, Indonesia

Saiman saiman
Universitas Muhammadiyah Malang, Indonesia

Farhan Muhammad Idris
Universitas Muhammadiyah Malang, Indonesia

Ali Roziqin
https://orcid.org/0000-0001-8336-3103
Universitas Muhammadiyah Malang, Indonesia

Meylyana Brigidta Zulfanabil
Universitas Muhammadiyah Malang, Indonesia

Tri Sulistyaningsih
https://orcid.org/0000-0003-1620-166X
Universitas Muhammadiyah Malang, Indonesia

ABSTRACT

This study examines the relationship between AI policy and data privacy in Indonesia, focusing on social media, public services, and electronic government systems. Using a Regulatory Impact Assessment (RIA) approach with normative legal and public policy analysis, the study draws on national surveys, policy documents, and academic literature. Privacy Calculus Theory and Social Exchange Theory are applied to explain personal data sharing behavior in digital environments. The findings indicate

DOI: 10.4018/979-8-3373-7804-6.ch004

that high internet and social media use, particularly among individuals aged 15–34, is not supported by adequate digital security literacy, encouraging oversharing and increasing risks of online fraud, identity theft, and account hacking. Furthermore, the implementation of the Personal Data Protection Law remains limited in regulating AI-based data processing, especially regarding algorithm transparency, accountability of automated decision-making, and oversight mechanisms.

INTRODUCTION

The rapid development of artificial intelligence (AI) has transformed the digital world, but it has also highlighted gaps in laws and regulations protecting user data privacy. Risks such as data exploitation by internet businesses are becoming increasingly concerning as AI becomes more integrated into communications, business, and education (Kirana & Silalahi, 2025). According to the 2025 Indonesian Internet Penetration Survey conducted by APJII, the national internet connectivity rate has reached 80.66%, or approximately 229 million people out of the total Indonesian population. Of this number, 38.01% actively use social media platforms such as TikTok, Facebook, and Instagram, and the majority (83.39%) access them via smartphones, with an average usage of 4-6 hours per day (Arif, 2025).

The heavy reliance on AI has created a data explosion. Every online activity leaves a digital footprint, from information searches and online purchases to interactions on social media. (Li & Zheng, 2024)These footprints are processed by algorithmic systems to personalize content, ads, or recommendations based on user behavior. (Laksito et al., 2025)The increasing number of internet users also increases vulnerability to the risk of personal data leaks. The 2025 APJII survey showed that more than 16% of respondents admitted to having experienced personal data theft and account hacking, (APJII, 2025)while 24.89% of respondents admitted to having faced security incidents, such as losing access to digital accounts (Sonni et al., 2025).

Sri Wulandari (2025) Highlighting the need for specific legislation that leverages AI to prevent data breaches and enhance legal protection, (Disemadi, 2021) Indonesia's personal data protection regulations, including the 2022 Personal Data Protection Law (PPN Law), remain inadequate to address the challenges of using AI in data management. While this law serves as an important legal foundation, its implementation is considered weak, due to the lack of specific provisions regarding algorithm transparency and accountability mechanisms for personal data processing. Wulandari emphasized the need for more adaptive regulatory updates, emulating the principles of the GDPR and the European Union's AI Law, namely transparency, accountability, and explainability, to ensure that AI systems used in data processing do not result in privacy violations. (Milossi et al., 2021).

The 2023 PT Bank Syariah Indonesia (BSI) customer data leak case highlights the weaknesses of the 2022 Data Protection and Data Security Law. Due to inadequate oversight and the absence of an audit mechanism for digital data processing systems, data leaks continued to occur even after the 2022 Data Protection and Data Security Law was enacted. (Revalina Annisa Antoine, 2025). This case demonstrates that automated systems and algorithms, which underpin data management processes, cannot be transparently accounted for under applicable laws and regulations. A closer look at (Ardika, 2025) also cited the same problem with the lack of transparency and accountability inThe 2022 Data Protection and Data Security Law: Data of millions of e-commerce users leaked to online forums due to weak security system oversight (Rosadi et al., 2022; Shrestha et al., 2024a).

To ensure the effective and accountable implementation of AI technology in the Indonesian government's digital transformation, a robust governance framework is needed. Research on e-Government progress in Indonesia shows that while discussions and developments in e-Government come from various fields, a comprehensive understanding of current research and development trends is still lacking (Roziqin, 2025). Accelerated changes in digital bureaucracy during the COVID-19 pandemic have created new opportunities and challenges for the secure and reliable digitalization of the Indonesian government, particularly regarding data privacy protection.

Experience in implementing digital policies in various regions shows that infrastructure, technological literacy, and cross-sector coordination remain major obstacles to implementing digital systems that protect user privacy. Therefore, protecting data privacy through AI policies is closely linked to governance system reform and increasing the capacity of government institutions to manage information technology. The (Roziqin, Fajrina, et al., 2022)The Primary objective of this study is to assess legal weaknesses and vulnerabilities related to algorithm transparency, the legal obligations of electronic system administrators, and oversight procedures for AI-based data processing. This aims to increase the flexibility and compliance of Indonesian data protection laws with international norms.

This study examines the relationship between artificial intelligence (AI) policy and data privacy protection by referring to the application of theories such as Social Exchange Theory (SET) and the Privacy Calculus Model (PCM), which seek to balance aspects of technological innovation, security, and individual rights. By comparing various international frameworks such as the GDPR, CCPA, and the European Union's Artificial Intelligence Act, this study analyzes the extent to which the principles of transparency, accountability, and privacy by design are applied in the context of national policies. The results of this study contribute to strengthening the direction of comprehensive and adaptive regulation, where the use of AI is strictly regulated as part of the legal system for personal data protection. (Abdullah, 2024; Judijanto et al., 2024).

LITERATURE REVIEW

AI and Data Protection

AI and data protection demonstrate that the development of AI technology brings new risks to privacy and data governance, necessitating a more stringent regulatory approach. (Ricciardi Celsi & Zomaya, 2025)One key issue in the relationship between AI and data protection is the use of generative models that can generate or reproduce personal data never directly provided by individuals. (Almada, 2024)This is due to the training process on large, often poorly controlled data sets. This risk raises concerns about the potential for sensitive data leakage and the re-emergence of out-of-context personal information. (Obioha Val et al., 2025)Furthermore, the misuse of deepfake technology and data reconstruction has also been cited as a relevant threat to information security and individual privacy protection. (Wachter et al., 2017).

In the context of data protection, the GDPR remains the primary legal instrument governing how personal data should be processed, including when used in the development or operation of AI systems. (Feretzakis et al., 2025)Data processing by AI must have a valid legal basis as defined in Article 6 of the GDPR, such as consent, legitimate interests, or legal obligations. Furthermore, Lim, (2024)The processing of sensitive data is subject to Article 9 of the GDPR, which sets out stricter requirements, including the requirement for clear justification and additional safeguards (Kingsto, 2017). Therefore, the development and use of AI must implement measures such as data minimization, transparency, and purpose limitation to remain compliant with GDPR principles. Article 22 of the GDPR protects individuals from decisions made entirely by automated systems without meaningful human evaluation. (Lazcoz & de Hert, 2023)AI systems are considered high-risk if they impact individuals' fundamental rights, security, or public services. This category includes AI in recruitment, public services, credit scoring, and biometric systems. Requirements for high-risk AI include process documentation, accuracy, robustness, human oversight, and a data protection impact assessment. (Sarra, 2025).

The integration of Privacy Calculus Theory and Social Exchange Theory in this research literature review is conducted analytically to explain the behavior of Indonesian digital users, not merely as a conceptual foundation. Privacy Calculus Theory is used to explain how individuals weigh the benefits and risks of sharing personal data in the digital environment. In the Indonesian context, the high use of social media and AI-based services encourages users to prioritize immediate benefits, such as ease of communication, content personalization, and social benefits, while long-term risks related to data security and algorithmic processing tend to be overlooked. Social Exchange Theory complements this analysis by showing that digital interactions are perceived as profitable social exchanges, thus encouraging oversharing practices as part of an effort to gain social recognition and economic value. The integration of these two theories is relevant to explaining why oversharing practices remain high in Indonesia despite low digital security awareness, and why formal regulation alone is insufficient without interventions that take into account the dimensions of user behavior.

Managing AI and Data Regulation

AI Governance and Data Regulation is an interdisciplinary field that integrates the governance of artificial intelligence technologies with the regulatory framework for data protection in the era of digital transformation. This concept encompasses a set of principles, policies, procedures, and oversight mechanisms designed to ensure that the development, implementation, and use of AI systems are conducted responsibly, ethically, and in accordance with applicable data protection standards. In the debate surrounding AI regulation, its fundamental foundation, data, is often overlooked. For AI to be successful and transparent, explainable, and auditable when necessary, we need to ensure the underlying data is of good quality (Mittelstadt, 2019).

Managing AI is not just about the technical aspects of algorithm development; it also encompasses legal, ethical, social, and economic dimensions that ensure AI systems operate within regulatory boundaries that protect fundamental individual rights, particularly the privacy and security of personal data. (Wachter et al., 2020) As data grows unprecedentedly and privacy standards become increasingly stringent, traditional data management approaches are no longer effective. An AI-based data governance approach offers opportunities to optimize critical processes, work with regulations in real time, and enhance data privacy measures. (Cihon et al., 2020).

This concept is becoming increasingly important given that AI relies on vast amounts of data for its training and operation, which poses risks to privacy, bias, discrimination, and misuse of personal information. (Biega et al., 2020)Therefore, data regulatory frameworks such as the GDPR in Europe, the PIPL in China, and various privacy laws across jurisdictions are becoming crucial instruments in governing how data is collected, processed, stored, and used in AI systems, with the goal of creating an AI ecosystem that is safe, trustworthy, and oriented toward protecting the public interest. The regulatory landscape for AI and data privacy in 2025 is experiencing significant convergence, with emerging and existing laws around the world presenting a set of overlapping obligations for business organizations. (Rocher et al., 2019).

Research on artificial intelligence (AI)-based personal data protection in Indonesia is still dominated by normative and sectoral approaches and has not integrated elements of regulation, technology utilization, and implementation governance.

Abidin & Tina (2024) stated that although the Personal Data Protection Law (PDP Law) and the ITE Law have provided a general legal framework, they have not yet regulated specific AI issues such as automated profiling, algorithm-based decision-making, and adequate oversight mechanisms. Arief (2025) also stated that AI can serve as a tool to improve personal data protection and reduce human error. However, this research focused only on specific regulatory requirements and failed to comprehensively examine institutional readiness, resource capacity, and governance risks associated with its implementation. In contrast, Rosadi et al. (2022) focused on privacy protection in the use of AI in the financial sector, using privacy rights theory and a legal approach. However, they did not link this to a framework for stakeholder collaboration or an empirical evaluation of existing policies.

Studies have tended to focus on normative or sectoral legal approaches, emphasizing the existence and urgency of regulations, without systematic evaluation of policy effectiveness, institutional readiness, user behavior, and cross-sectoral AI governance mechanisms. Furthermore, the empirical dimension reflecting the gap between the legal framework (law on the books) and personal data protection practices (law in action) has not been adequately examined. Therefore, there is a significant need for research that combines analysis of data protection regulations, the use of artificial intelligence, and collaborative governance based on regulatory impact evaluation (RIA), supported by national empirical evidence. The purpose of this research is to gain a better understanding of how personal data protection policies in Indonesia function in the AI era.

RESEARCH METHODS

This research uses the Regulatory Impact Assessment (RIA) research method, which is a highly relevant and comprehensive approach in analyzing public policy formulation. (Amelia Azis et al., 2023)RIA functions as a process, tool, and logic of thinking, including problem identification, goal setting, development of policy alternatives, cost-benefit analysis, and implementation strategies. This method is able to assess whether regulations are necessary, effective, and provide benefits that outweigh their costs. RIA also increases transparency and public participation, reduces implementation costs, and bridges political and academic approaches. In normative legal research, RIA allows for analysis of aspects of legal drafting as well as the economic, social, and political impacts of a policy, with the principles of neutrality, minimally effective regulation, participation, transparency, and cost-benefit effectiveness.

This approach is used to understand digital data governance policies, including algorithm transparency and the legal responsibilities of electronic system administrators. This study analyzes academic literature, policy documents, surveys, and research reports related to privacy and AI regulation, particularly in Indonesia. This study focuses on social media data and digital policies to assess the alignment of national policies with global data protection principles The analytical technique used is content analysis with a public policy theory approach, which examines the formulation, implementation, and evaluation of data protection policies. Using this framework, this study highlights strengthening transparency, accountability, and public participation in the oversight of AI use, thereby protecting data privacy while supporting technological innovation.

This research explicitly positions its contribution to filling a methodological gap by using the Regulatory Impact Assessment approach in evaluating AI policy in Indonesia. To date, studies on AI regulation and personal data protection have tended to use a normative-juridical approach that focuses on analyzing legal articles and principles, without comprehensively assessing the policy's impact. The RIA approach allows for a more comprehensive analysis by assessing regulatory needs, the effectiveness of existing policies, and the social, economic, and institutional impacts of AI implementation in personal data processing. Through the RIA, this research is able to assess the extent to which existing regulations are able to respond to algorithmic risks, the readiness of supervisory institutions to carry out their oversight functions, and potential implementation gaps between the public and private sectors. Thus, the RIA serves as an evaluative framework that bridges the gap between legal norms and AI policy practices in Indonesia.

DISCUSSION RESULTS

1. Number of Digital Attacks in Indonesia

According to Katadata's Databoks, digital attacks in Indonesia are increasingly prevalent, targeting various groups, particularly citizens, students, and private sector employees, indicating weak personal data protection and the national cybersecurity system. The following data shows digital attacks in Indonesia...(Katadata Insight Center, 2021)

Figure 1. Digital attacks in Indonesia

Based on Figure 1, Digital Attacks in Indonesia, it can be seen that digital attacks in Indonesia have become a widespread phenomenon and have affected various levels of society, both individuals and institutions. (Katadata Insight Center, 2021) The graph shows the variation in the number of digital attacks experienced by various groups and professional organizations. The group with the highest number of attacks is the general public, with a total of 65 cases, followed by students or university students with 64 cases. (Katadata Insight Center, 2021)These two groups top the list as the main targets of digital attacks. (Rinaldo & Puspitasari, 2024)The high numbers in this category indicate that the general public, especially individual users and young people who are active in the digital world, are easy targets for cyber attackers. (Ilaina & Nugraha, 2025). This can occur due to the still low level of digital literacy, weak personal data protection systems, and the tendency of people to share personal information on social media without adequate protection (Katadata Insight Center, 2021).

Furthermore, private sector employees were also the target of a significant number of digital attacks, with a total of 54 cases. (Katadata Insight Center, 2021)This fact indicates that the private sector faces a significant potential risk of data breaches, given the large number of business activities now conducted online, including financial transactions, internal communications, and customer data storage. (Nadhifa et al., 2025; Setiawan & Najicha, 2022). Meanwhile, organizational staff or activists recorded 26 cases of digital attacks. (Katadata Insight Center, 2021) This group is often targeted because of their important role in public policy or advocacy for social causes. (Ilaina & Nugraha, 2025)Attacks on this group can include hacking of social media accounts, the spread of false information, or cyberattacks aimed at silencing public voices. Creative workers, with 19 cases, were also among the affected groups. (Katadata Insight Center, 2021)Professions in this field generally have high exposure to digital platforms, such as designers, content creators, and digital artists. (Abdillah et al., 2024).

Their involvement in online public spaces makes them more vulnerable to identity theft, misappropriation of works, or copyright infringement through digital attacks. (Abdillah et al., 2024) Furthermore, civil society organizations recorded 14 cases of attacks, indicating that non-governmental organizations or civil society groups involved in social and advocacy fields are not immune to cyber threats. (Ilaina & Nugraha, 2025)Meanwhile, journalists or media workers and public institutions each recorded 10 cases of attacks. (Rinaldo & Puspitasari, 2024)Attacks on journalists and media outlets are often related to reporting sensitive news or efforts to uncover public issues, and therefore can be considered a form of attack on press freedom. (Posetti et al., 2020).

The targeting of public institutions highlights weaknesses in the government's cybersecurity system that need to be strengthened, particularly in protecting public data. (Roziqin, Kismartini, et al., 2022)Academics also experienced eight cases of digital attacks, demonstrating that the world of education and research is not immune to the threat of hacking, for example, of research data or institutional information. (Shrestha et al., 2024b)Several other groups that also experienced digital attacks, albeit in smaller numbers, were businesspeople or entrepreneurs and celebrities with six cases each; government employees and private companies with five cases each; and lawyers, media outlets, and student organizations with two to three cases (Katadata Insight Center, 2021). While these numbers are relatively small, this demonstrates that digital attacks are widespread and can affect anyone regardless of social status, profession, or public role (Nadhifa et al., 2025).

Overall, the data from the graph shows that Indonesia faces serious challenges in digital security. (Nadhifa et al., 2025)Attacks targeting citizens, students, professionals, and public institutions highlight weaknesses in personal data protection systems across various sectors. (Rinaldo & Puspitasari, 2024). This situation emphasizes the importance of raising public awareness about digital security, educating people about personal data protection, and strengthening law enforcement against cybercrimes. (Katadata Insight Center, 2021). The government, along with the private sector, needs to strengthen cybersecurity regulations and infrastructure to ensure that all digital activities in Indonesia are safe, transparent, and secure. (Kirana & Silalahi, 2025b).

2. Number of electronic media users in Indonesia

According to the 2025 Indonesian Internet Profile Survey conducted by APJII, the estimated number of people connected to the internet in 2025 will reach

229,428,417, or 80.66% of Indonesia's 284,438,900 population. Using a multistage random sampling (margin of error $\pm 1.1\%$), the survey was conducted from April 10 to July 16, 2025, with a sample of 8,700 respondents spread proportionally across 38 provinces. This indicates a continuous increase in national penetration from 2022 to 2025 (APJII, 2025).

Figure 2. Number of electronic media users

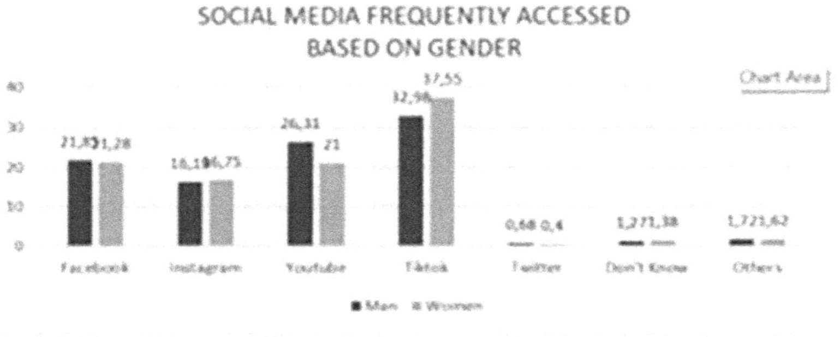

Based on the graph titled Frequently Accessed Social Media by Gender, TikTok shows the most frequently accessed platform by both genders, with a higher percentage for women (37.55%) compared to men (32.98%), while YouTube is accessed more by men (26.31% compared to 21.00% for women), Facebook is almost equal between men and women (21.85% compared to 21.28%), and Instagram is slightly more popular among women (16.75% compared to 15.19%). The relatively small contribution figures for other platforms, such as Twitter, the "don't know" category, and "other," indicate that social media usage is focused on a few main applications. (APJII, 2025).

However, the increased use of electronic media also comes with the potential for data security threats. (Nadhifa et al., 2025). Some users have experienced online fraud, personal data theft, and virus attacks, while others admitted to being unaware or indifferent to digital security practices, according to the results of the APJII survey. (APJII, 2025). Although many users have followed basic rules such as using strong passwords and being wary of applications that request personal data, around 20% of respondents admitted to never protecting their data. (Katadata Insight Center, 2021). These results indicate that increasing digital literacy, especially in terms of cybersecurity, is crucial to ensuring the safe, productive, and sustainable use of electronic media. (Kurnianingrum, 2020).

In addition to the increasing number of internet users, APJII noted that smartphones are the most widely used device for electronic media, with a usage rate of

94.40% (APJII, 2025). This shows that smartphones are the dominant device in Indonesian people's digital activities. (Roziqin, Kismartini, et al., 2022)Laptops or personal computers are far below at 39.06%, followed by smart TVs at 18.16%, and tablets are only used by 10.24% of respondents. (APJII, 2025)These results indicate that easily accessible handheld devices dominate almost all electronic media activities, including information consumption, entertainment, and communication. (Effendi, 2019).

For digital activities, internet users most frequently use the internet to communicate via text messages (87.93%), use social media (86.40%), and search for information (79.01%) (APJII, 2025). Activities such as online shopping, video streaming, and digital work also continue to increase. Conversely, the increase in electronic media use is also in line with the rise in national internet penetration. Internet penetration (Katadata Insight Center, 2021)continues to increase from 77.02% in 2022 to 78.19% in 2023, and reaches 80.66% in 2025, indicating the growth of infrastructure and people's dependence on digital services (APJII, 2025).

The 15-19 and 20-24 age groups are the most frequent internet users, with penetration rates of 99.90% and 99.64%, respectively, indicating the dominance of the younger generation in electronic media consumption. (APJII, 2025)Although the areas with the highest penetration are still in urban areas, rural areas show significant growth as the development of digital networks becomes more widespread. This data supports the assumption that electronic media is becoming increasingly popular and increasingly embedded in various levels of Indonesian society. (Rajagukguk et al., 2023).

3. Privacy Data Protection Regulation

The background to the data privacy policy arises from the increasing risk of personal data misuse with the development of digital technology. Online services such as social media, e-commerce, digital banking, and health apps collect vast amounts of data, raising concerns about identity theft, unauthorized tracking, and data commercialization. (Priyadi et al., 2025). Global cases such as the Cambridge Analytica scandal demonstrate how easily data can be manipulated without strong regulation. (Myrna Fitria, n.d.), prompting various countries to formulate stricter data protection measures.

In Indonesia, the increasing number of public and private data breaches has highlighted weaknesses in cybersecurity infrastructure and data governance. (Setiawan et al., 2022). This has led to public demands for legal certainty, leading to the enactment of the Personal Data Protection Law (HPPA) as a legal basis for data controllers to ensure security, processing consent, and transparency. (Ahmad Tarikh, 2025)Beyond responding to incidents, this policy is also crucial for maintaining public trust in the digital economy, ensuring the safe and sustainable growth of online services and fintech.(Pujianto et al., 2018) (Jefry et al., 2025).

Table 1. Privacy data protection regulations

Regulation	Function	Lack
1. Electronic transactions	Electronic transaction regulations are legal rules governing digital transaction activities, such as e-commerce, online banking, fintech, digital government services, and electronic data exchange. These regulations serve to ensure security, legal certainty, and good governance in the digital space.	The inability to keep up with rapid technological developments, frequent overlapping regulations, and ineffective law enforcement, along with suboptimal consumer protection, limited oversight of digital actors, and low digital literacy leave the public vulnerable to cybercrime.
2. SPBE	The SPBE regulation ensures that digital government administration is directed, standardized, and secure. This regulation governs the integration of systems and data between institutions, ensures information security, and increases the efficiency and accountability of electronic-based public services.	The lack of detailed technical regulations creates room for differing interpretations between agencies, which can hinder system synchronization. Furthermore, the regulations do not fully address adaptive evaluation and update mechanisms, resulting in some rules quickly becoming outdated. The SPBE regulations also remain weak in addressing cross-sector collaboration, including private sector involvement and national data integration, resulting in incomplete and incomplete implementation.
3. Personal Data Protection	The Personal Data Protection Act aims to safeguard individuals' privacy rights by ensuring that personal data is managed securely and is not misused. This regulation provides legal certainty, establishes the responsibilities of data controllers, and increases public trust in digital services.	The causes lie in weak law enforcement, unclear technical security standards, and limited oversight of data controllers. Furthermore, regulations often fail to keep pace with the rapid development of digital technology, creating loopholes that can be exploited for data misuse. Low public privacy literacy also hampers the effectiveness of regulations.
Personal Data Protection Act	a. Protecting citizens' rights to privacy and personal data. Providing a national legal framework that comprehensively regulates data protection. b. Regulate the obligations of data controllers/processors to be transparent, secure, and accountable. c. Providing law enforcement mechanisms through administrative, criminal, and compensatory sanctions.	a. To date, there are no specific regulations governing AI-based data processing, such as profiling and automated decision-making. b. Data supervisory authorities have not yet fully understood its implementation. c. Compliance readiness between large and small business sectors still has the potential to be unequal. d. Cross-border data transfer regulations are not as stringent as international standards (e.g., GDPR). e. Legal protection has not been balanced with digital literacy among the public and strong law enforcement.

The Electronic Transaction Regulation (SPBE), the Personal Data Protection Law (PDPA), and the Personal Data Protection Law (PDPA) form an interconnected legal framework to ensure security, legal certainty, and digital governance in Indonesia. (Akbar et al., 2025)The PDPA regulates digital activities such as e-commerce, online banking, fintech, and government services, to create consumer protection and legal certainty. (Widijowati, 2023)The PDPA ensures standardized, secure, and integrated digital governance across institutions, while increasing the efficiency and accountability of electronic-based public services. (Almadani et al., 2024)Meanwhile, the PDPA Law provides a clear legal basis for personal data protection, regulating the obligations of data controllers and processors, law enforcement mechanisms, and principles of transparency and accountability.

In the context of AI, this regulation is particularly relevant because this technology relies on processing large amounts of data, including sensitive data and individual behavior. (Akbar et al., 2025)The use of AI in public services, finance, and digital government requires compliance with the Personal Data Protection (PDP) Law, algorithm audits, and risk-based regulatory mechanisms for high-risk AI systems. The integration of electronic transaction regulations, SPBE, and the PDP Law emphasizes the need for data security. (Domi Dwi Kurniasandi, 2022) Effective oversight, algorithm transparency, and accountability of data controllers, so that technological innovation can go hand in hand with the protection of individual rights and legal certainty for society (Junaidi & Rozlinda Mohamed Fadzil, 2024).

A comparative analysis shows that the Indonesian context presents fundamentally different regulatory challenges than mature jurisdictions such as the European Union or the United States. Indonesia has a very high internet penetration rate of 80.66 percent and strong social media usage, particularly among the productive age group. However, this is not accompanied by adequate digital security literacy, as reflected in the fact that 53.6 percent of the population still falls into the low data protection category. In this situation, AI-based data processing takes place in a vulnerable digital ecosystem, where users tend to overshare without adequate understanding of algorithmic risks. Unlike the European Union, which is supported by a comprehensive regulatory framework, algorithm audit mechanisms, and strong oversight bodies, Indonesia is still in the regulatory development stage through the 2022 Personal Data Protection Law, which does not yet specifically address algorithm transparency, profiling, and automated decision-making. These different contexts indicate that successful regulatory approaches in developed countries cannot be directly applied in Indonesia without adjustments to national social conditions, digital literacy levels, and institutional capacity.

Discussions on artificial intelligence and personal data protection are still dominated by normative and conceptual approaches, particularly those referring to global regulatory frameworks such as the GDPR and AI governance principles.

However, this literature has not clearly identified the unanswered issues in the context of implementing AI-based data processing regulations in developing countries. In Indonesia, the research gap is evident in the limited analysis of how existing regulations translate into algorithm-based data management practices, including limited oversight mechanisms for AI systems, unclear accountability for automated decisions, and the absence of a systematic evaluation of the effectiveness of the 2022 Personal Data Protection Law in regulating dynamic technology. Therefore, this research addresses the need to examine the gap between regulatory design and the reality of AI implementation in personal data processing in Indonesia, a topic that has not been widely addressed by previous research.

4. LEVEL OF PERSONAL DATA PROTECTION FOR INDONESIANS IN 2021

Public awareness of personal data protection remains a challenge in Indonesia. This is evident from the results of a national survey conducted by the Ministry of Communication and Informatics in collaboration with the Katadata Insight Center in October 2021. (Cindy Mutia Annur, 2022). The survey showed that the majority of people have not implemented adequate personal data protection measures in their daily digital activities. Fifty-three percent of respondents reported a low level of personal data protection, while only 46.4 percent indicated a high level of protection. These findings confirm that more than half of internet users in Indonesia still do not prioritize the security of their identity in the digital space (Katadata Insight Center, 2021).

Figure 3. Level of privacy data protection

Data from a survey conducted by the Ministry of Communication and Informatics and the Katadata Insight Center shows that the low level of personal data protection among Indonesians is not simply a matter of technical ignorance, but reflects a weak digital security culture at the user level. (Rohan et al., 2023)With 53.6% of respondents falling into the low data protection category, it is clear that the majority of the public lacks the habit of or awareness of the risks of data breaches online. (Tran, 2024)This situation stands in stark contrast to the increasing use of digital services, which actually demand higher levels of personal data protection. (Alsharida et al., 2023).

The high number of users who are careless in managing personal information can be explained by digital behavior patterns recorded in the survey, such as posting phone numbers, birth dates, family details, and current locations on social media. (Gangire et al., 2020)Furthermore, the habit of uploading sensitive documents such as photos of ID cards or travel tickets indicates that people do not yet fully understand the potential for data misuse for digital crimes, including identity theft, online fraud, and social engineering. (Nguyen et al., 2024)This means that people do not yet position personal data as an important asset to be protected, but rather as part of the activity of sharing on social media. (Schreiber, 2020).

Another argument that can be drawn from these findings is that digital literacy has not kept pace with internet penetration. The survey covered 10,000 respondents from various regions, aged 13-70, thus indicating that low data protection is not limited to a particular age group or region. (Mersinas & Bada, 2023). In other words, the problem is structural: internet access is increasing rapidly, but people's digital security awareness and behavior have not kept pace with this development. This indicates a critical gap between technology use and users' ability to protect their digital identities. (Papp & Lovaas, 2021)Thus, the data clearly demonstrates that efforts to protect personal data in Indonesia are not sufficient through the development of regulations and policies alone, but also require educational and literacy interventions to empower people to behave safely in the digital space. (Van Binh et al., 2023). Without changes in user behavior, the risk of data breaches and identity theft will remain high despite the existing legal framework. (Hartzog, 2021).

We found that the nature of social media use is influenced by the level of digital literacy. This finding is in line with the views of Dinev and Hart (2006) in Privacy Calculus Theory, which states that individual decisions regarding social media use and personal data sharing are influenced by the user's cognitive ability to assess privacy benefits and risks. (Dinev & Hart, 2006; Trepte, 2021)Individuals with low digital literacy levels tend to emphasize immediate benefits such as ease of communication and personalized AI-based services, rather than long-term risks such as data leaks and misuse of personal information. (Festic et al., 2021)This condition is reflected in the Indonesian context, where high levels of social media use and excessive data sharing occur alongside low levels of personal data protection and a weak understanding of algorithmic and AI-based data processing mechanisms. (Keykha & Rezaie Kahkhajale, 2024).

5. PEOPLE WHO SHARE PERSONAL DATA ON SOCIAL MEDIA

Figure 4. People sharing personal data on social media

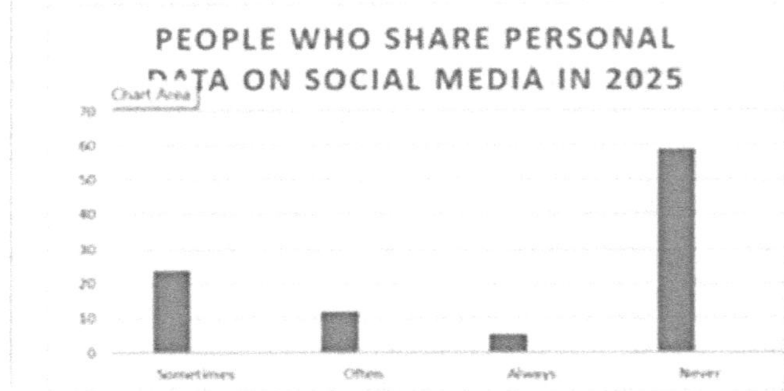

A survey conducted by the Ministry of Communication and Informatics (Kominfo) revealed that approximately 41% of respondents frequently share personal data on social media. (Kementerian Komunikasi Dan Digital, 2025.)Specifically, 23.7% do so occasionally, 12% do so quite frequently, and 5.2% always share personal information. (Katadata Insight Center, 2021). Meanwhile, the majority of respondents, namely 59%, stated that they never share their personal data online. The report emphasized the importance of education regarding digital security practices and increasing public awareness regarding potential risks to personal data and cybersecurity. (Kementerian Komunikasi Dan Digital, 2025). On the other hand, the most common data protection action taken by respondents was adjusting privacy settings on social media accounts, with a proportion reaching 62.3%. The survey covered 18,564 individuals aged 15–64 years and 11,901 business units, spread across 514 districts/cities throughout Indonesia. (Katadata Insight Center, 2021; Kementerian Komunikasi Dan Digital, 2025).

These results indicate that the majority of internet users in Indonesia are still reluctant to share personal data. Sharing on social media isn't accompanied by an awareness of the risks involved, as demonstrated by the number of respondents who continue to share personal data. (Katadata Insight Center, 2021)This 41% figure indicates that some people don't view personal data as an asset that must be carefully guarded. Cybercriminals can exploit simple data such as birth dates, phone numbers, addresses, and current locations uploaded through stories or posts.(Abdillah et al., 2024; APJII, 2025)

Furthermore, the majority of users who share personal data are from the productive age group who are active on social media, particularly those aged 15 to 34. This group lacks understanding of digital security threats, despite their digital technology expertise (Edy Susilo et al., 2025). This situation highlights the gap between technological literacy and the ability to protect digital identities. As criminals exploit information voluntarily shared by users, cases of online fraud, phishing, identity theft, and account hacking continue to increase in Indonesia. (Alpiah et al., 2024; Katadata Insight Center, 2021).

Furthermore, according to Dinev and Hart (2006), using the Privacy Calculus Theory framework, personal data sharing behavior among productive age groups is influenced by a perception of benefits that is more dominant than risks. Younger generations who are active on social media tend to view digital platforms as social and economic spaces that provide direct benefits, such as social recognition, ease of communication, and access to artificial intelligence-based digital services. With limited digital security literacy, privacy risks are perceived as abstract and distant, thus not a primary consideration in decision-making. As a result, *excessive data sharing practices* are increasingly common and open up opportunities for cybercriminals to commit online fraud, phishing, identity theft, and account hacking by exploiting publicly available digital footprints.

The high number of digital crime cases that use personal data as a gateway is also related to this phenomenon of excessive data sharing. Most social engineering attacks are successful because the perpetrators obtain most of the data from users' own uploads. (Abdillah et al., 2024). Location data, family information, daily routines, and important documents such as identity cards or travel tickets are often shared without considering the risk of misuse. This situation supports the argument that personal data protection is heavily influenced by digital media user habits and applicable laws. (APJII, 2025; Edy Susilo et al., 2025).

Although more than 50% of respondents have changed their account privacy settings, this is ineffective if data sharing is not controlled. For digital protection, security features and collective awareness are needed to prevent increasingly complex cyber threats. Consequently, this data (Alpiah et al., 2024; Katadata Insight Center, 2021)Suggests that society must make greater efforts to learn more about digital security. Unless digital culture shifts to a more cautious approach, cybercrime will continue to plague society. From the availability tool, law, and technology data protection, things will Keep going happen. (APJII, 2025).

Therefore, there is a need big For research that combines analysis of regulations, data protection, use of artificial intelligence, and governance collaborative-based evaluation impact regulation (RIA) with support of empirical national data. The purpose of the study is For get greater understanding of how the policy on personal data protection in Indonesia functions in the AI era. Compared with other conditions This present challenge has different regulations because Indonesia is in a phase of transition in which the adoption of digital technology and AI is on the rise rapidly, while enforcement law, legislation, and public Not yet developed evenly. Deep gap study. This is done with an analysis contextual which shows that Indonesia is unique in the matter implementation global standards and as ecosystem regulations that have unique social, institutional, and technological factors. This helps us understand development policy, data protection, and AI governance at the enterprise level nationally in a way more relevant and practical.

Increasing AI adoption in digital services show trend of increasingly complex processing of personal data, massive and complex. The main issues discussed in the chapter are increasing risk, violation of privacy, consequence use algorithm in making automatic decisions, data utilization for profiling, and limitations of the supervision mechanism. Problems were analyzed as a consequence of the imbalance between accelerated innovation in technology and readiness regulations to provide adequate protection to the right data subject. Behavior sharing of personal data by users is explained as part of the dynamics of social in the digital ecosystem, influenced by the perception benefit technology. However, the discussion focused on how design AI policy and governance shape risk structure to personal data protection. With this approach, this issue is addressed by placing the individual in context, while the analysis is mainly directed at regulations, mechanisms, supervision, and accountability of AI-based data processing.

Framework law on personal data protection in Indonesia still faces challenges in arranging AI-based data processing explicitly, especially related to transparency algorithm, automatic decision-making, and accountability organizer system electronics. Condition This implications for limitations protection of the right of data subjects and potential occurrence of misuse of personal data. Discussion in the chapter. This is to describe the challenge as part from problem policies that require attention. Serious in development regulations to the front. Use of empirical data combined with international literature international give base for analysis to discuss data protection in the AI era. Approach comparative with framework regulations, international enrich perspective policies, and enable identification practice best relevant with Indonesian context. This is strengthen contribution to academic and policy from the discussion presented.

CONCLUSION

The study's findings indicate that the high level of social media and AI-based digital technology use in Indonesia, particularly among the productive age group 15-34, has not been matched by adequate levels of digital security literacy and personal data protection. Although this age group possesses relatively good technical skills in operating various digital platforms and optimally utilizing technological features, they tend to lack an understanding of the long-term consequences of sharing personal data in the digital space. This situation encourages the practice of *oversharing*, where personal information is shared voluntarily without carefully considering security risks. As a result, the digital space is becoming increasingly vulnerable to various forms of cybercrime, such as online fraud, phishing, identity theft, and account hacking, which continues to show an increasing trend in Indonesia. These findings highlight the significant gap between technological proficiency and critical awareness in protecting users' digital identity and privacy.

From a theoretical perspective, the findings of this study can be explained through the Privacy Calculus Theory framework, which views user behavior as the result of a rational process of weighing the benefits and risks of using digital technology. In the context of social media and artificial intelligence-based services, users tend to value immediate benefits such as ease of access to information, intensity of social interaction, personalization of services, and digital economic opportunities as more dominant factors than abstract and less directly perceived privacy risks. This imbalance in privacy calculations is further exacerbated by low digital security literacy, limited public understanding of algorithm-based data management mechanisms, and suboptimal implementation and enforcement of personal data protection regulations. Therefore, this study emphasizes that efforts to protect users in the digital era cannot rely solely on regulatory approaches, but also require a comprehensive strategy through increasing digital literacy, transparency of AI governance, and strengthening the accountability of electronic system providers so that the use of digital technology can take place safely, ethically, and sustainably.

REFERENCES

Abdillah, A., Widianingsih, I., Buchari, R. A., & Nurasa, H. (2024). Big data security & individual (psychological) resilience: A review of social media risks and lessons learned from Indonesia. *Array (New York, N.Y.)*, *21*, 100336. DOI: 10.1016/j.array.2024.100336

Abdullah, A. M. (2024). Protection of Privacy Rights Against Personal Data Collection by Generative AI Based on Conversations with Users. *Padjadjaran Law Review*, *12*(2), 145–156. DOI: 10.56895/plr.v12i2.1796

Abidin, F., & Tina, A. (2024).. . *Indonesia's Legal Policy on Protecting Personal Data from Artificial Intelligence Abuse.*, *07002*, 1–11.

Ahmad Tarikh, R. A. B. (2025). *COMPARATIVE ANALYSIS OF DATA PROTECTION LAW BETWEEN INDONESIA AND THE EUROPEAN UNION: A CASE REVIEW OF CAMBRIDGE ANALYTICA*. www.kominfo.go.id/content/detail/34906/pemeriksaan-dugaan-kebocoran-data-bpjs-kesehatan/0/berita_

Akbar, N., Kurnia Sitorus, H., Arifin, MY, & Nasution, P. (2025). Legal Protection of Consumer Personal Data in Digital Transactions. *Indonesian Law Journal, 2* (1).

Almada, M. (2024). *Law & Compliance in AI Security & Data Protection*.

Almadani, M., Cahyani, A. A. D., & Khadafi, M. (2024). The Effect of Electronic-Based Government System (SPBE) Implementation on Performance Accountability in the Regional Secretariat of South Sulawesi Province. [Management of Apparatus Resources]. *MSDA Journal*, *12*(1), 96–132.

Alpiah, S., Asbari, M., Saputri, I. A., & Adilya, N. R. (2024). Oversharing: The Urgency of Privacy in the Digital Age. [JISMA]. *Journal of Information Systems and Management*, *3*(1), 42–47. DOI: 10.4444/JISMA.V3I1.877

Alsharida, R. A., Al-rimy, B. A. S., Al-Emran, M., & Zainal, A. (2023). A systematic review of multiple perspectives on human behavior in cybersecurity. *Technology in Society*, *73*, 102258. DOI: 10.1016/j.techsoc.2023.102258

Amelia Azis, R., Olivia, F., & Arianto, H. (2023). REGULATORY IMPACT ASSESSMENT (RIA) IN POLICY FORMULATION. In *Regulatory Impact Assessment (RIA) In Policy Formulation Lex Jurnalica* (Vol. 20, Issue 1).

APJII. (2025). *INTERNET PENETRATION SURVEY AND INTERNET USAGE BEHAVIOR 2025*.

Ardika, I. W. C. (2025). Legal Review of Personal Data Protection in the Digital Era: A Case Study of E-Commerce User Data Leaks. *Indonesian Journal of Law and Justice*, *2*(3), 11. DOI: 10.47134/ijlj.v2i3.3601

Arief, S. (2025). *Article 7 Regulatory Arrangements and Utilization of Artificial Intelligence (AI) in Realizing Personal Data Protection in Indo... 19% Overall Similarity*. 1–13.

Arif, M. (2025). *APJII General Arfizar Zulkarnaen, B.* INTERNET PENETRATION SURVEY AND INTERNET USAGE BEHAVIOR IN.

Biega, A. J., Potash, P., Daumé, H., Diaz, F., & Finck, M. (2020). Operationalizing the principles of the law of data minimization for personalization. *Proceedings of the 43rd ACM SIGIR International Conference on Research and Development in Information Retrieval*, 399–408.

Cihon, P., Maas, M. M., & Kemp, L. (2020). Should artificial intelligence governance be centralized? Design lessons from history. *Proceedings of the AAAI/ACM Conference on AI, Ethics, and Society*, 228–234. DOI: 10.1145/3375627.3375857

Cindy Mutia Annur. (2022). *The Level of Personal Data Protection of Indonesian Citizens is Still Low. The Level of Personal Data Protection of Indonesian Citizens (2021).*

Dinev, T., & Hart, P. (2006). An extended privacy calculus model for e-commerce transactions. *Information Systems Research*, *17*(1), 61–80. DOI: 10.1287/isre.1060.0080

Disemadi, H. S. (2021). The Importance of Special Regulations and the Utilization of Artificial Intelligence in Realizing Personal Data Protection in Indonesia. *Jurnal Wawasan Yuridika*, *5*(2), 177. DOI: 10.25072/jwy.v5i2.460

Domi Dwi Kurniasandi, S. N. A. N. I. C. (2022). *REGULATIONS CONCERNING PERSONAL DATA PROTECTION IN THE USE OF E-COMMERCE SERVICES.* https://www.cnnindonesia.com/teknologi/20231231054937-192-1043657/daftar-dugaan-

Edy Susilo, M., Prayudi, P., & Yanu Florestiyanto, M. (2025). Oversharing Behavior of Gen Z on Social Media. *SHS Web of Conferences, 212*. DOI: 10.1051/shsconf/202521204022

Effendi, A. Y. (2019). Mobile Phone Addiction: Smartphone Use Among the Digital Generation of People with Disabilities in Indonesia. *2nd International Conference on Strategic and Global Studies (ICSGS 2018)*, 90–98.

Feretzakis, G., Vagena, E., Kalodanis, K., Peristera, P., Kalles, D., & Anastasiou, A. (2025). GDPR and Large Language Models: Technical and Legal Barriers. *Future Internet*, *17*(4), 151. Advance online publication. DOI: 10.3390/fi17040151

Festic, N., Büchi, M., & Latzer, M. (2021). Still there: Digital inequality and its evolution in the information society. *SCM Studies in Communication and Media*, *10*(3), 326–361. DOI: 10.5771/2192-4007-2021-3-326

Gangire, Y., Da Veiga, A., & Herselman, M. (2020). Information security behavior: Development of a measurement instrument based on self-determination theory. *International Symposium on Human Aspects of Information Security and Assurance*, 144–157. DOI: 10.1007/978-3-030-57404-8_12

Hartzog, W. (2021). What is privacy? That's the wrong question. *U.Chi. L. Rev.*, *88*, 1677.

Ilaina, A. S. A., & Nugraha, I. F. (2025). Indonesia's Cybersecurity Capability Gap in Mitigating Cyberattacks on Digital Public Services 2020-2025. *Triwikrama: Journal of Social Sciences*, *8*(6), 141–150.

Jefry, B., Gultom, E., & Yuanitasari, D. (2025). MISUSE OF CONSUMER PERSONAL DATA BY COMPANIES: A LEGAL STUDY FROM THE PERSPECTIVE OF CONSUMER PROTECTION LAW AND PERSONAL DATA PROTECTION LAW. *Indonesian Education Journal*, *6*(5), 1.

Judijanto, L., Saiful Basri, T., Madah Khulaili Harsya, R., Yuli Vandika, A., & Shandy Utama, A. (2024).. . *Legal Study of the Impact of Artificial Intelligence on Data Privacy Protection in Indonesian Cyber Law.*, *3*(02), 68–76. DOI: 10.58812/shh.v3.i02

Junaidi, & Rozlinda Mohamed Fadzil. (2024). The Importance of Legal Protection of Personal Data in E-Commerce Transactions Involving Artificial Intelligence. *Walisongo Law Journal (Walrev), 6* (2), 96–108. DOI: 10.21580/walrev.2024.6.2.25548

Katadata Insight Center. (2021). *Status of Digital Literacy in Indonesia 2021. Ministry of Communication and Digital*. (undated). Accessed December 16, 2025, from https://www.komdigi.go.id/berita/siaran-pers/detail/imdi-2025-naik-ke-4453-indonesia-makin-cakap-digital

Keykha, B., & Rezaie Kahkhajale, Z. (2024). Monitoring Postgraduate Students' Digital Literacy Based on Elements of the UNESCO Digital Literacy Competency Framework. *Academic Library and Information Research*, *58*(2), 47–60.

Kingsto, J. (2017). *Using Artificial Intelligence to Support Compliance with the General Data Protection Regulation*.

Kirana, K. B., & Silalahi, W. (2025). Challenges of Artificial Intelligence (AI) Regulation from the Perspective of Personal Data Protection Law in Indonesia. *Cerdika: Indonesian Scientific Journal*, *5*(6), 1807–1817. DOI: 10.59141/cerdika.v5i6.2711

Kurnianingrum, T. P. (2020). The importance of protecting consumer personal data in the digital economy era. *Studies*, *25*(3), 197–216.

Laksito, J., Pratiwi, B., & Ariani, W. (2025). Harmonization of Data Privacy Frameworks in Artificial Intelligence: Comparative Insights from Asia and Europe. *Perkara: Journal of Law and Political Science*, *2*(4), 579–588. DOI: 10.51903/perkara.v2i4.2229

Law, I. (2024). *European Union Artificial Intelligence Law. April.*

Lazcoz, G., & de Hert, P. (2023). Humans in GDPR and AIA governance of automated and algorithmic systems. A crucial prerequisite for preventing dereliction of responsibility. *Computer Law & Security Review*, *50*. Advance online publication. DOI: 10.1016/j.clsr.2023.105833

Li, W., & Zheng, X. (2024). Social Media Use and Attitudes Toward AI: The Mediating Roles of Perceived Fairness and AI Threat. *Human Behavior and Emerging Technologies*, *2024*, 1–11. Advance online publication. DOI: 10.1155/2024/3448083

Lim, J. (2024). *The Urgency of Personal Data Protection Related to Data Processing in the Form of Artificial Intelligence in Indonesia.*

Mersinas, K., & Bada, M. (2023). A behavior change approach to cybersecurity and the need for ethics. *International Conference on Cybersecurity, Situational Awareness and Social Media*, 107–129.

Milossi, M., Alexandropoulou-Egyptiadou, E., & Psannis, K. E. (2021). AI Ethics: Algorithmic Determinism or Self-Determination? A GDPR Approach. *IEEE Access : Practical Innovations, Open Solutions*, *9*, 58455–58466. DOI: 10.1109/ACCESS.2021.3072782

Mittelstadt, B. (2019). Principles alone cannot guarantee ethical AI. *Nature Machine Intelligence*, *1*(11), 501–507. DOI: 10.1038/s42256-019-0114-4

Myrna Fitria, D. I. P. A. H. S. (n.d.). LEGAL PROTECTION AND RESPONSIBILITY FOR PERSONAL DATA INFORMATION LEAKS IN ELECTRONIC SYSTEM ORGANIZERS BASED ON A TRADE SECRET PERSPECTIVE. *Indonesian Scientific Journal, January* 2025 (1), 1–8. http://cerdika.publikasiindonesia.id/index.php/cerdika/index

Nadhifa, C. L., Irama, O. N., Lubis, A. S., & Harahap, J. P. R. (2025). CYBER RISK MANAGEMENT IN THE DIGITAL ERA: ANALYSIS OF MITIGATION STRATEGIES AND PREVENTIVE INNOVATIONS AGAINST CYBER CRIME IN INDONESIA. [MICJO]. *Indonesian Multidisciplinary Center Journal, 2*(3), 2610–2619. DOI: 10.62567/micjo.v2i3.868

Nguyen, T. T., Tran, T. N. H., Do, T. H. M., Dinh, T. K. L., Nguyen, T. U. N., & Dang, T. M. K. (2024). Digital literacy, online safety behavior, and e-payment intention. *Journal of Open Innovation, 10*(2), 100292. DOI: 10.1016/j.joitmc.2024.100292

Obioha Val, O., Gbadebo, MO, Olaniyi, OO, Chinye, NC, & Balogun, AY (2025). Innovative regulation of open-source intelligence and AI deepfakes in managing public trust. *Michael Olayinka and Olaniyi, Oluwaseun Oladeji and Chinye, Noah Chukwufumnanya and Balogun, Adebayo Yusuf, Innovative Regulation of Open-Source Intelligence and AI Deepfakes in Managing Public Trust (January 30, 2025).*

Papp, G., & Lovaas, P. (2021). Assessing Cybersecurity Awareness of Small Institutions Using the Human Aspects of Information Security Questionnaire (HAIS-Q). *Intelligent Computing: Proceedings of the 2021 Computing Conference,* Volume 3, 933–948.

Posetti, J., Aboulez, N., Bontcheva, K., Harrison, J., & Waisbord, S. (2020). *Online violence against women journalists. 'Online Violence against Women Journalists', edn.* UNESCO.

Priyadi, A., Trisno, A., Banjarnahor, H., & Sugianto, F. (2025). Building Digital Trust through Enforcement of Personal Data Protection Laws. In *Literacy Syntax* (Vol. 10, Issue 5).

Pujianto, A., Mulyati, A., & Novaria, R. (2018). UTILIZATION OF BIG DATA AND PROTECTION OF CONSUMER PRIVACY IN THE DIGITAL ECONOMY ERA. *Bijak Scientific Magazine, 15*(2), 127–137. DOI: 10.31334/bijak.v15i2.201

Rajagukguk, W., Heatubun, A., & Pane, M. (2023). Demographic and socioeconomic determinants of internet use in Indonesia. *ARPHA* Preprints, *4*, e109500.

Revalina Annisa Antoine, NSFHHP (2025). *Misuse of Personal Data in Digital Transaction Technology in the Digital Banking Industry (Case Study of PT. Bank Syariah Indonesia).*

Ricciardi Celsi, L., & Zomaya, A. Y. (2025). Perspectives on Managing AI Ethics in the Digital Age. *Information (Basel), 16*(4), 318. DOI: 10.3390/info16040318

Rinaldo, & Puspitasari, D. (2024). Digital Risks in Developing Countries: Escalation of Cyber Threats in Indonesia (2020–2023). *Data: Journal of Information Systems and Management, 2* (3), 152–163. DOI: 10.61978/data.v2i3.697

Rocher, L., Hendrickx, J. M., & De Montjoye, Y.-A. (2019). Estimating re-identification success in incomplete datasets using generative models. *Nature Communications, 10*(1), 3069. DOI: 10.1038/s41467-019-10933-3 PMID: 31337762

Rohan, R., Pal, D., Hautamäki, J., Funilkul, S., Chutimaskul, W., & Thapliyal, H. (2023). A systematic literature review of cybersecurity scales assessing information security awareness. *Heliyon, 9*(3), e14234. DOI: 10.1016/j.heliyon.2023.e14234 PMID: 36938452

Rosadi, S. D., Yuniarti, S., & Fauzi, R. (2022)... *PROTECTION OF DATA PRIVACY IN THE ERA OF ARTIFICIAL INTELLIGENCE IN THE FINANCIAL SECTOR.*, *1*(2), 353–366.

Roziqin, A., Kismartini, Fajrina, AN, Salahudin, & Sulistyaningsih, T. (2022). The Development of e-Government in Indonesia: A Bibliometric Analysis. *COLLNET Journal of Scientometrics and Information Management, 16* (1), 49–74.

Roziqin, A. (2025). *Analysis of Indonesian government policy on. 24* (1), 92–107. DOI: 10.1108/PAP-08-2020-0039

Roziqin, A., Fajrina, A. N., Sulistyaningsih, T., & Roziqin, A. (2022). *Development of e-Government in Indonesia: A bibliometric analysis.* DOI: 10.1080/09737766.2021.2007036

Sarra, C. (2025). Artificial Intelligence in Decision-Making: A Consistency Test between the "EU AI Law" and the "General Data Protection Regulation.". *Athens Law Journal, 11*(1), 45–62. DOI: 10.30958/ajl.11-1-3

Schreiber, A. (2020). Privacy Blueprint: The Battle to Control the Design of New Technologies. By Woodrow Hartzog. [Cambridge, MA: Harvard University Press, 2018. x+ 366 pp. Hardcover £28.95. ISBN 978-06-74976-00-9. *The Cambridge Law Journal, 79*(2), 377–380. DOI: 10.1017/S0008197320000355

Setiawan, HB, Fatma, &, & Najicha, U. (2022). PROTECTION OF PERSONAL DATA OF INDONESIAN CITIZENS RELATED TO DATA LEAKS. *Citizenship Journal, 6* (1).

Setiawan, H. B., & Najicha, F. U. (2022). Protection of Indonesian citizens' personal data regarding data leaks. *Journal of Citizenship, 6*(1), 976–982.

Shrestha, A.K., Barthwal, A., Campbell, M., Shouli, A., Syed, S., Joshi, S., & Vassileva, J. (2024a). *Navigating AI to Uncover Adolescents' Privacy Concerns: An In-Depth Exploration and Systematic Review.*

Shrestha, A. K., Barthwal, A., Campbell, M., Shouli, A., Syed, S., Joshi, S., & Vassileva, J. (2024b). Navigating AI to address adolescent privacy concerns: An in-depth exploration and systematic review. *ArXiv Preprint ArXiv:2412.16369.*

Sonni, A. F., Mau, M., Akbar, M., & Putri, V. C. C. (2025). AI and Digital Literacy: Impact on Information Resilience in Indonesian Society. *Journalism and Media, 6*(3), 100. DOI: 10.3390/journalmedia6030100

Sri Wulandari, Y. (2025). ARTIFICIAL INTELLIGENCE AND DATA PROTECTION: A FAIR REGULATION ANALYSIS FOR THE INDONESIAN LEGAL SYSTEM. In *THE JURIS: Vol. IX* (Edition 1). http://ejournal.stih-awanglong.ac.id/index.php/juris

Tran, H. (2024). *Understanding user information behavior: An analysis of data protection measures on digital platforms.*

Trepte, S. (2021). A model of social media privacy: Privacy and communication in the context of social media affordances. *Communication Theory, 31*(4), 549–570. DOI: 10.1093/ct/qtz035

Van Binh, T., Minh, D. T., Linh, L. T. H., & Van Nhan, T. (2023). Location-based service information disclosure on social networking sites: The influence of privacy calculus, subjective norms, trust, and cultural differences. *Information Services & Use, 43*(1), 39–62. DOI: 10.3233/ISU-230180

Wachter, S., Mittelstadt, B., & Floridi, L. (2017). Why is a proper explanation of automated decision-making missing from the General Data Protection Regulation? *International Data Privacy Law, 7*(2), 76–99. DOI: 10.1093/idpl/ipx005

Wachter, S., Mittelstadt, B., & Russell, C. (2020). *WHY JUSTICE CAN'T BE AUTOMATED: BRIDGING THE GAP BETWEEN EU NON-DISCRIMINATION LAW AND AI.* 1–72.

Widijowati, D. (2023). *Improving Consumer Protection in Electronic Commerce Transactions* (Vol. 3, Issue 4).

Chapter 5
Legal Challenges of AI and AR in Governance

Ayesha Farooqi
https://orcid.org/0009-0000-4556-4211
Poornima University, Jaipur, India

ABSTRACT

Use of artificial intelligence and augmented reality in the governance system is reforming the process of immigration to support the administration, decision-making and participation by the population. Even though these technologies are expected to bring greater efficiency, transparency and innovativeness in public services, they equally present a considerable ethical and legal dilemma. The chapter analyzes ethical standards and the law that regulates AI and AR use in governance, and specifically issues of accountability, data privacy, algorithmic bias, surveillance and democratic values. It examines regulatory loopholes, cross-jurisdictional issues and endangers to civil liberties, boasting of the necessity of transparency, fairness and humanism in governance models. The chapter gives a full background to responsible deployment of AI and AR in the governance of the people by critically analyzing the existing practices and the emerging policy approaches.

1. INTRODUCTION

1.1 Evolution of Artificial Intelligence and Augmented Reality in Public Administration

Globalization of modern digital technologies in the state has increased during this decade by factors of increasing the demand of efficiency, transparency and responsiveness in governance. Artificial intelligence, in its turn, has become one

DOI: 10.4018/979-8-3373-7804-6.ch005

of the key instruments of this change, allowing governments to automate their administrative functions, analyze repentallion amounts of information, and assist in decision-making in all areas of the policy. Examples include predictive apps that can be used to allot resources, artificial intelligence to decide who qualifies to receive a service in society, and AI-driven fraud tools, which demonstrate that algorithmic systems are now being intensively integrated into the machinery of governance. Such trends represent a wider transition into a data-driven kind of public administration, frequently called algorithmic or intelligent governance (Bathaee, 2018).

Being more recent in governance uses, augmented reality has as well started redefining the process of interaction of the public authorities with the physical and social space. AR technologies impose the digital information on the real-world environment so that the public officials and citizens can see data, infrastructure plans, or emergencies in the field. AR, used in urban planning, allows the stakeholders to visualize a planned development prior to the construction process, whereas in the field of public safety and emergency response, it helps in situational awareness and training. With comparison to AI, which in the main operates in the background processing the information and supporting the decision-making process, AR operates in the direct sphere of human perception and interaction with the public spaces and it develops new patterns of governance engagement.

The intersection of AI and AR leads to a qualitatively new phase of the functioning of the administration. The combination of these technologies brings together algorithmic decision-making and immersive visualization and dims the line between analysis, action, and perception. Although such convergence presents a highly valuable set of instruments to governance innovation, it increases ethical and legal issues as it introduces technological mediation on a deeper level into the social decision making process. To put it in perspective, the ethical and legal dilemmas that come with the implementation of AI and AR in governance cannot be fully understood without some knowledge on how these technologies have developed over the years (Bostrom & Yudkowsky, 2014).

1.2 Electronic Governance and New technology

Digital governance means applying digital technologies, which can improve the formulation, implementation, and assessment of the policy in the sphere of the government. It includes e-government services, policy making that is based on data,projects of smart cities and platform based citizen engagement. AI and AR are higher levels in this expanded digital governance system not just past digitization to automation, prediction, and immersive or interactive. Their incorporation represents the desire of governments to enhance the delivery of services, make them cheaper and react better to the multi-dimensional challenges facing the society (Brauneis & Goodman, 2018).

Huge amounts of diverse information that are beyond human analytical abilities can be processed with the help of AI-driven systems by the public institutions. These systems are able to assist in activities like risk scoring in the criminal justice, preventive maintenance of infrastructure and optimization of transportation systems. AR, however, increases governance through having easy-to-use interfaces that simplify the access to complicated data by both the decision-makers and the citizens. Indicatively, AR-based dashboards may be used to visualize environmental records or other forms of congestion in urban space directly, allowing informed debate and plan development.

The implementation of new technologies in governance however does not just signify the technical upgrading of governance but also a change in the exercise of authority, discretion, and accountability. The field of digital governance is becoming more based on automated or semi-automated systems that shape or affect the results of the populace. The change brings some fundamental concerns regarding transparency, legitimacy, and the place of human judgments in governance. With the introduction of AI and AR into the institutions workflow, ethical and legal concerns will have to keep up with the technological capacities of the latter in order to make the governance procedure democratic, just, and responsible (Butcher & Beridze, 2019).

1.3 The drivers of AI and AR Adoption in Governance

The increased use of AI and AR in governance is motivated by a number of factors. The complexity of modern policy challenges is one of the main motivators, such as climate change, urbanization, crises of health of the population, and security threats. These problems cause the immense amounts of information and demand quick and evidence-based answers that cannot be facilitated by traditional administrative procedures. AI provides pattern recognition, forecasting, and optimization tools, whereas AR can be used to improve situational knowledge and coordination in the complicated environment (Carabantes, 2020).

The second force is the demand by the people to have a more efficient and transparent governmental services. The citizens are becoming more and more determined to see digital interfaces that reflect the convenience and responsiveness of the services in the privacy sector. The applications of chatbots, use of AI in creating portals to provide automated services, and the use of AR in public consultations are meant to facilitate these expectations by eliminating bureaucratic resistance and enhancing accessibility. Governments see such technologies as a way to restore the lost trust of the people and increase their engagement, especially in situations where the administrative inefficiency has compromised the legitimacy.

Adoption is also affected by economic and political pressure. The governments are challenged by the limitations of finances and employability of the staff, which prompts the interest in the automation as a saving mechanism. Meanwhile, geopolitical rivalry and innovative technologies provide states with motivation to embrace innovative digital technologies in order to remain globally competitive. These drivers, though not less powerful, tend to focus more on efficiency and innovation instead of on ethical reflection, a tendency that puts more pressure on the risk of the fact that the law and normative considerations will be outpaced by the use of technologies (Cath, 2018).

1.4 AI and AR Ethical and Legal Implications in Governance

The ethical and legal importance of AI and AR in governance is connected with their abilities to control the ways of how the population decides, impacts the rights of individuals and changes their power relations between the state and citizens. AI systems can have an influence on access of the citizens to public services, law enforcement results, or welfare benefits, and AR applications can have an impact on how citizens feel and experience public spaces. These technologies thus work on the interplay of technical design and normative values thus rendering the ethical governance to be one of the chief concerns as opposed to a peripheral issue (Chen et al., 2020).

Regulatory-wise, both AI and AR are a threat to the current regulatory frameworks which were built to consider human-centric decision-making and narrow-scope information systems. The questions emerge on the subject of liability of automated decisions, due process of algorithmic governance, and the adherence to data protection laws. AR also makes it harder to analyze the law since it provides the mechanism of continuous data recording, real-time enhancement of the public space, bringing up the question of consent, surveillance, and the freedom of expression to the common areas.

Figure 1. Multi-layer governance framework illustrating legal and ethical challenges of AI and AR in public administration

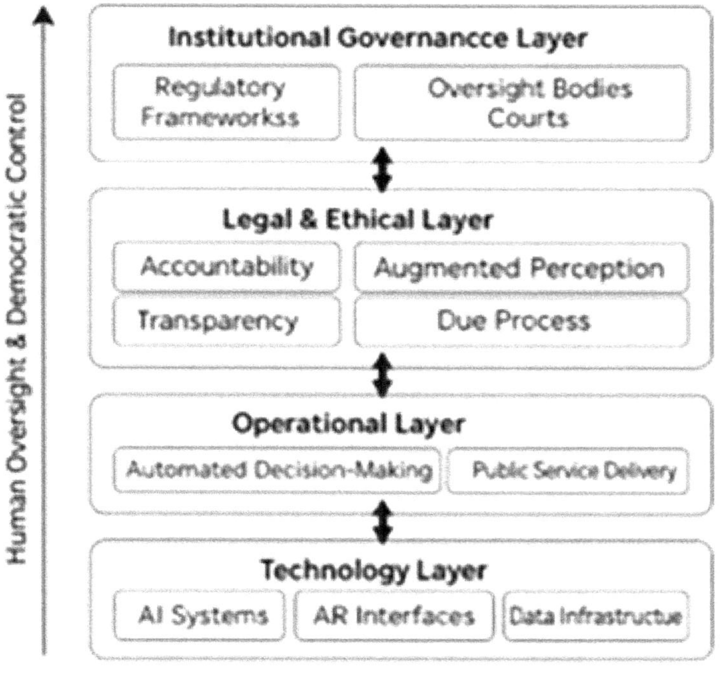

With regards to ethics, the use of AI and AR in governance brings up issues of fairness and accountability, as well as democratic control. The risks that exist are that algorithmic bias, lack of transparency in deciding, and unequal distribution of access to digital technologies might strengthen social inequalities. Furthermore, the convincing and engaging character of AR can affect the behavior of people in slightly different ways, endangering the autonomy and informed consent. To deal with these legal and ethical issues, the combination of technology mastership and the law, the application of ethical theory, and the principles of democratic governance are essential (Cihon et al., 2020).

2. FOUNDATIONS OF ETHICAL GOVERNANCE IN AI AND AR SYSTEMS

2.1 Ethical Theories and Principles in Technology Governance

Moral theories used many years ago found their way to lend some ethical guidance to the AI and augmented reality systems applied to the operation of the public administration. Such normative ethical theories like deontological ethics, consequentialism and virtue ethics are also used to give some backgrounds through which moral implications of new technologies can be assessed. The deontological approaches are associated with attention to individual rights and duties as well as legal protection, which is especially relevant in those situations when AI systems influence access to civic services or police choices. Consequentialist views are more concerned with the results and the common good, which favors the deployment of AI and AR in case they have proven to enhance effectiveness, security, or the general well-being of the population. Virtue ethics, on the contrary, emphasises moral character and responsibility of the public institutions that apply the technologies.

Ethical standards should be converted to guidance rules in the governance setting that design and deployment of systems. Fairness, proportionality, accountability, respect of human dignity are some of the widely accepted principles of ethical public administration. These principles when the AI systems automate or aid the decision-making require keen consideration with regards to the manner in which data are gathered, the way models are trained, and the result they produce. In the same manner, AR applications which change the perception of the people should be developed to ensure that it is not manipulative, misrepresentative or isolating to some groups. Technical governance would therefore necessitate the incorporation of normative values being part of the technological procedures rather than the incorporation of ethics as the limitation factor (Cunneen et al., 2019).

AI/AR technologies are dynamic that makes it difficult to conduct a moral analysis as the behavior of the system can change over time, due to learning and/or adaptation. This casts doubt on continued moral accountability and continued ethical scrutiny. Institutions of the public thus need to embrace flexible ethical theories which are able to adjust to the change in technology but consistent with the principles of democracy. Ethical governance in this regard is not a-one time evaluation task but a continuous evaluation, reflection and correction process.

2.2 Competitiveness, Market Accessibility, and Non-use of Buying Power

One of the essential aspects of ethical governance is transparency, especially when the AI systems shape the decisions made by people that impact their rights and social life. Transparency in a governance context relates to the availability of information regarding the objectives of the system, sources of data and the logic behind making decisions to stakeholders. Nonetheless, various AI models, particularly, the ones that use intricate machine learning methods are opaque systems whose derivations cannot be easily interpreted. This transparency is a big challenge to accountability by the masses and damages faith in automated governance (Dafoe, 2018).

Explainability can find a solution to this problem because it allows the stakeholders to clarify how and why AI systems achieve specific results. Explainable AI plays a critical role in the functioning of a state or local government when it comes to the due process, appeals, and informed regulation and court supervision. Citizens who have been victims to algorithmic decision making process must be in a position to be provided with meaningful explanations as officials in the government need to know the limitation in the system and uncertainty involved. Another issue on explainability concerns AR systems because the superimposition of all digital information over physical places may tend to influence the perceptions more subtly without necessarily revealing underlying sources of data and assumptions.

Accountability goes hand in hand with transparency and explainability since it clarifies the responsibility of system outcomes. Accountability can be shared in AI and AR-based governance with system designers, data provider, government officials and institutions. Moral governance involves proper delegation of responsibility in order to enhance that evils may be resolved and rectified. Transparency and explainability are not enough to safeguard the interests of the populace in the absence of accountability measures. These principles have resulted in an interdependent system that aids in the ethical supervision and the democratic legitimacy (Felzmann et al., 2019).

2.3 Value-Sensitive and Human-Centred Design

Human-centered design also focuses more on primacy of human values, needs and agency in technological systems development. This can be done in the context of governance applications so that the use of AI and AR technologies would be in the interests of the population and do not remove human judgment or autonomy. The value-sensitive design also takes this view further by systematically applying ethical values to technical specifications and design decisions. Such approaches are especially applicable to the situation within the context of the performance in the public sector, when technologies should be able to suit different populations and promote democratic principles.

The design of the governance should be human centered by engaging stakeholders or human beings that make sense such as the participation of the public servants, citizens and civil society organizations. Design processes involving participation enable harm, bias and accessibility issues to be recognized during the initial stages of the system development. In the case of AI systems, it might entail assessing the impact of the data collection practice on marginalized populations or how AI-programmed decisions comply with the legal regulations. In the case of AR applications, human-centered design has a solution regarding the problem of inclusivity, usability, and psychological impact of immersive technologies in the public spot (Firlej & Taeihagh, 2021).

Value-sensitive design is also conscious of the fact that values can be mutually conflicting or gradually change. To illustrate the point, efficiency results of automation can be incompatible with fairness or procedural justice. These trade-offs and mechanisms demand open discussion of these design choices and how to have a second or third tier of revisiting these decisions as the social expectations evolve. Public institutions can be more accountable to the principles of ethics and democracy by focusing on human-oriented and value-specific solutions, which will allow integrating AI and AR systems into the framework of moral guidelines.

2.4 Ethics Structure and Governance Model in the Institution

The technical design of AI and AR alone is insufficient in the ethical governance; the situation should be complemented with the institutional structures, which will facilitate oversight, accountability, and address compliance. More ethics committees, advisory boards and governance structures have been instituted within public institutions that are focused on determining emerging technologies. These organizations give cross-functional competence and assistance in applying abstract moral ideas into functioning policies and principles (Gasser & Almeida, 2017).

The institutional structures are vital in organising the process of ethical governance between departments and level of government. They promote uniform data governance, risk evaluation and participation of stake holders. Within the framework of AI and AR, institutional ethics models need to touch upon such issues as the procurement standards, the responsibility of vendors, and the lifecycle of the deployed systems. Lack of such structures will make ethical considerations to be integrated or sidelined in the bureaucratic processes.

Lastly, the learning and adaptation should be supported by effective structures of governance. With the development of AI and AR technologies, some ethical issues can arise, which was not expected in the early stages of implementation. The institutions should thus be able to create feedback processes, monitoring processes, and revision processes to be responsive to the new risks and societal concerns. The introduction of ethics into governance as an institution is what guarantees that the continuous application of AI and AR in the administration is ethical and not a post-hoc consideration (Goodman & Flaxman, 2017).

3. LEGAL FRAMEWORKS AND REGULATORY LANDSCAPES

3.1 Existing Laws Applicable to AI and AR in Governance

Artificial intelligence and augmented reality implementation in government work lacks a legal vacuum; it overlaps with a large set of the existing legal frameworks that were neither designed to support human decision-making or standard information technology. The administrative law, constitutional law, data protection regulations, and specific statutes of various sectors all influence the possibilities of using AI and AR by the authorities. Such concepts as: legality, proportionality, due process, and non-discrimination do not disappear as more automated or augmented processes are employed in the process of decision making. These are the laws that hold that all decisions which are made by the government. either human or algorithm based should be open to review, to explanations and reconsideration.

The legalists that relate specifically to AI- and AR-enabled governance include data protection and privacy laws. The use of AI systems can be based on big data with personal or sensitive information, whereas AR applications can imply continuous data capture in open or semi-open areas. Laws including data protection laws provide stipulations of legal transformations of data use, reasons, data reduction, and person rights. It should be the duty of public institutions to make sure that the AI and AR implementations meet such requirements, even in cases when the data undergoes their usage in the predictive analytics or real-time visualization (Helbing, 2019).

Moreover, the acquisition and use of AI and AR technologies are affected by the legal procurement sector and the systems of accountability in the field of the state. Governments have to find a way of negotiating contracts with the private vendors and at the same time ensuring that transparency and competition policies are met. These legal concerns signify that the current legislation offers biased regulation of AI and AR, yet it was not intended to address adaptive, learning systems and immersive technologies. Consequently the legal interpretation tends to push the old traditional notions to fit the emerging technological realities.

3.2 Regulatory Loopholes and Challenges in jurisdiction

Yet, no matter how applicable the existing laws are, there are still critical regulatory gaps in the AI and AR in the field of public administration. Most of the legal frameworks presuppose distinct decision-makers and tools, which lose its clarity when there is a generation of a recommendation or automated results by AI systems. Concerns are raised whether the outputs of the algorithms are administrative decisions and the allocation of responsibility should in the case of errors. The uncertainties result in ambiguities that cause confusion among the public institution as well as those who are affected (Huq, 2019).

Jurisdictional issues also lead to complex regulation especially in the cases where AI systems are created, hosted, or trained internationally. The existence of cloud-based infrastructures and multinational providers of technology implies that data processing and the algorithmic decision-making might not be within the territory where the outcomes of governing may be experienced. It gets more complicated in this case to determine applicable law, authority of enforcing laws, and remedies. AR apps used in open areas can also imply cross-border information flows and company patent issues that demand pressure on established jurisdiction.

These regulatory gaps are enhanced by the fast rate of technical transformation. Regulatory bodies and legislatures regularly find it hard to keep up with the speed of innovation thus resulting in reactive and not proactive regulation. Without any clear rule, the public authorities can be guided by the discretional interpretation or soft-law tools, i.e. guidelines and codes of conduct. It is true that these tools are flexible, but they might not be enforceable and consistent, which highlights the necessity of more consistent regulatory measures (Janssen et al., 2020).

3.3 International Governance and Cross-border Standards

Since AI and AR technologies are global, globalization is an important factor in setting the standards of governance. To ensure that AI is morally and legally used within the state of affairs, international bodies and regional agencies have started crafting frameworks and principles to help regulate the application of AI. These projects can foster the human rights protection, transparency, and accountability and ease the operations of the interoperability measures amongst the different jurisdictions. As much as AR-specific governance is underdeveloped, there are principles that resemble that of immersive technologies that influence the world of publicity and contact with people (Jobin et al., 2019).

The international standards play a number of significant roles. They are the points of reference in the national regulation, decrease fragmentation and contribute to cross-border cooperation in the fields of digital public services and smart city projects. In the case of public institutions, compliance with the international standard might improve the legitimacy and trustworthiness of the institutions, especially when implementing technologies with extensive social impacts. But the problem is that it is not always easy to translate high-level principles into binding laws within the countries because the legal systems of the countries differ in structure and ability.

Sovereignty and democratic accountability also appear to be the issues of cross-border governance. In a situation where international standards are used in determining domestic policy decisions, there could be conflicts between international norms and the local values. There is thus a need to harmonize a balance between respect to national legal traditions. To ensure successful international governance of AI and AR, it is important that they include an inclusive discussion among the states, the civil rights organizations, and the developers of technologies, so that the standards adopted are based on varying opinions and safeguard primary human rights.

3.4 Enforcement, Compliance and Legal Remedies

Laws regulating AI and AR in governance can only be functional when there is a solid enforcement mechanism and compliance. EDM procedures should be put in place by the public institutions to make sure that the deployed systems are used in ways that are in compliance with the legal aspects of their lifecycle. This involves impact studies, recording the decision making procedures and frequent audits in order to detect possible infractions. Conformity checking mechanisms are also essential to AI systems, which change over time because adherence to them does not mean continued legality.

The legal solutions are of importance in safeguarding people against AI- and AR-enabled governance. Mechanisms should also be made available to be able to challenge decisions made, seek explanations, and receive redress in case of harm by the citizens. There is a problem with courts and their external controls because those cases that involve complex algorithms or immersive technologies are more difficult to resolve. Certain specialized knowledge to evaluate evidence and the liability might be needed, which has shown that there is a requirement to build capacity in legal institutions to judge and regulate (Goyal, 2025).

Figure 2. Pathways illustrating legal risks and regulatory responses associated with AI and AR in governance

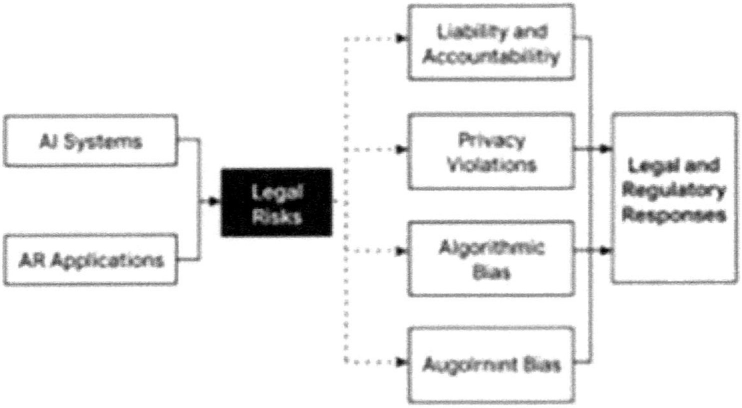

The implementation is also based on the transparency and cooperation with the technology providers and the state authorities. The presence of access to relevant system information running on a contractual basis in order to allow access to audit and investigation. Lack of access undermines accountability and the law enforced is problematic. There is a need to enforce, comply and remedy therefore further in ensuring that the application of AI and AR in governance is in compliance with the rule of law and democracy.

4. DATA PRIVACY, SURVEILLANCE, AND CIVIL LIBERTIES

4.1 Data Collection, Consent, and Ownership in AI-Driven Governance

The use of AI in the creation of governance systems requires mass data in most cases where they may include personal, behavioral data as well as contextual information regarding the citizens of the nation or state. Such data are used by governments to deliver services in a more efficient way, anticipate risks as well as allocate the resources of people in a better manner. Specifically, the size and the heterogenous nature of data collection provoke serious ethical issues related to consent and property. In contrast to a traditional administration data collection process, AI systems often operate on continuous stream of data, rely on secondary data usage, and infer attributes, which makes it hard to understand how their data is being utilized and it is not easy that the individual may agree to any such use in qualitative or useful manner (Kleinberg et al., 2018).

Power imbalances between the government and the population make consent in a public governance context always complex. People can be unable to choose not to donate data when the use of the necessary services requires the involvement in digital systems. AI also makes consent more difficult by allowing the use of data after the initial use, like repurposing administrative data to do predictive analytics. Such practices interfere with the basic principles of privacy and beg the question as to whether any consent to such situations can be regarded as informed and voluntary.

AI-based governance also has ambiguous data ownership. Although governments are raising claims claiming that they are stewards of the common information, the subject individuals are demanding the rights to control their personal information. Laws have a difficult time balancing these two competing interests, especially where data are manipulated by the third-party vendor or stored in a cloud infrastructure. By resolving the issue of data ownership and consent, it is necessary to reconsider the privacy governance models so that citizens have the meaningful control over their data and that the legitimate uses of data by the public should be facilitated (Kroll et al., 2016).

4.2 Surveillance and Public Trust by AI

One of the most disputed ways of implementing AI in governance is the use of AI in such actions as law enforcement, border control, or safety of people. Surveillance systems powered by AI-based strategies by use of facial recognition, behavioral analysis, and predictive policing technologies allow the uninterrupted observation and automatic evaluation of potential risks never seen in history. Although advocates believe that these systems increase the level of security and efficiency, opponents are crying foul that it will infringe on the rights of civil liberties as well as eroding trust that the people put in it (Leenes & Lucivero, 2014).

AI-powered surveillance moves the regulating paradigm towards anticipatory management of individuals, in which a person can become the subject of control on the basis of probabilities, but not on the foundations of concrete actions. With this change, some ethics and legal issues such as presumption of innocence, freedom of movement, and freedom of expression also come with serious concerns. These issues are further boosted by the fact that the AI surveillance systems are opaque and people are usually unaware of the process by which they are surveyed or the manner in which decisions are made.

Surveillance is a heavily influential factor in the views of governance in the public. Over surveillance or one that is inadequately controlled may lead to an atmosphere of mistrust and self-censorship, thus undermining the democracy process. It take trust, which means being transparent on any surveillance, and ensuring that they are kept within rigid legal framework and commensurate to the known interest of the people. In the absence of these policies, intelligent surveillance will undermine the validity of the social institutions (Leenes et al., 2017).

4.3 AR Applications, and Privacy Risk in the Public Space

The concept of augmented reality presents new privacy issues due to the blurring of digital space and the physical streets. In governance the AR applications can be applied to navigation, information to people, city planning or even crowd control. Systems of this sort are usually based on immediate data recording in the form of cameras, sensors, and location tracking which has questioned the aspect of constant surveillance in common places. In comparison to the traditional surveillance tools, AR is happening on the perception level, influencing the ways in which individuals experience the overpublic space.

The weaknesses of AR in terms of privacy are increased by the impossibility of separating between non-malicious information overlays and the hidden data gathering. Citizens do not know that they might designate their movements, gestures, or interactions and track them as recording or analysis to back AR functionalities. Such invisibility weakens informed consent and puts in question the current privacy standards which require a distinct difference between observation and interaction (Goyal, Dandotiya, Kumari, Kaloria et al, 2025).

The legal safeguards of privacy in a social area are usually less as compared to a personal setting, and such aspects pose a gap in the regulations of AR technologies. With the increasing number of AR in governance, legal frameworks should resolve the issue of privacy rights in the augmented setting. It is important that the civil liberties in the era of the immersive governance technologies are kept in order to do not transform the public spaces into the realm of the liberties.

4.4 Tradeoffs between Security, Innovation and Civil Liberties

Governments are under constant pressure on how to both use AI and AR to gain security and innovations and resolve concerns of civil liberties. The data-intensive technologies may justify safeguarding the population in a hazardous state by means of crime prevention or disaster management in some circumstances. Nevertheless, in the absence of articulated boundaries and regulation, such rationalizations will creep into the area of generalized surveillance and control. Proportionality, neediness and accountability during the deployment of AI and AR systems are ethical manufactures.

The resolution of such competing priorities requires solid law enforcement, at least through independent checks and balances and participation by the populace. Intrusive technologies should be reviewed and subject to democratic questioning on a regular basis using impact assessments and transparency reports and the use of sunset clauses. The civil liberties organizations and citizens have to have the means of questioning and affecting the policies of AI and AR governance (Mittelstadt et al., 2016).

Finally, it is recommended that in order to make AI- and AR-enabled governance legitimate, a social contract based on the rights protection and trust is preserved. Democratic freedoms need to be strengthened and not weakened through innovation. The realization of this balance is among the most urgent problems of the modern system of governance.

5. BIAS, FAIRNESS, AND DISCRIMINATION IN AI-ENABLED GOVERNANCE

5.1 Algorithmic Bias in Public Decision-Making Systems

Algorithms bias happens when AI systems make disproportionately different outputs to various social categories. Such biases may be deadly in governance settings because they affect access to social services, policing activities, or welfare benefits. Disparity can be the cause of bias in the training information, false assumptions of the model, or previous disparities ingrained in administrative data. By reproducing or magnifying such patterns, AI systems will threaten to instill discrimination on the pretext of being objective.

The AI systems that are used in the public sector usually process the data that mirror previous policy choices and social systems. When these data have discrimination in them, AI models that are geared on these data might propagate unfairness. As an illustration, systems of predictive policing can be biased towards minority communities because they are trained on historic crime patterns, which conserves the patterns of surveillance and discipline. The issue of algorithmic bias, therefore, contradicts the principle of equality before the law (Pagallo et al., 2019).

To overcome bias, the first approach is to note that AI systems cannot be a neutral means but they are socio-technical structures affected by human decisions. Ethical governance requires the active identification of bias, reduction and constant control to avoid discriminatory results in the decision-making process of the masses.

5.2 Equity, Inclusion, and Social Justice Issues

In addition to technical bias, governance powered by AI is associated with other concerns that extend to equity and social justice. Automated systems can be biased against those with limited access to digital technology, language, or other irregular life factors causing them to fall outside of the model. AR-based public services can also dis include disabled people or people who do not know about immersive technologies. These are some of the exclusionary implications that negate the promise of digital governance as a weapon of inclusive delivery of services to the population.

The issue of equity is especially urgent in the context of an implementation where human discretion is substituted with AI systems but lacks proper protective measures. Human officials are able to be empathetic and contextum based, but the AI systems can be strict in following rules on incomplete information. This inflexibility may discriminate especially those who are vulnerable and prefer discretion and one-on-one evaluation. Certain practices that can ensure equity are maintenance of human control and developing systems that are able to adapt to diversity and complexity (Rahwan, 2018).

Participatory inclusion is the other aspect of social justice in AI governance. Representing the affected communities in designing and assessing AI and AR systems should be a future truth. Unless this is done, then the governance technologies will instead of contributing to the reduction of power imbalance, they will contribute to its strengthening.

5.3 Mitigation Strategy and Algorithms Auditing

To reduce bias and discrimination in the AI-enabled governance, technical, organizational, and legal models should be used. Algorithms auditing has been seen as one of the most important ones in determining fairness, transparency and compliance. Audit also entails a systematic scrutiny of information, model action, and consequences to determine discriminatory patterns and unexpected outcomes. Audits should be carried out on a regular basis and they should be done in a non-partisan way in a manner that ensures accountability in the governance of the people (Goyal, Dandotiya, Qurashi et al, 2025).

Such techniques as data balancing, fairness-conscious modeling, and explainable AI approaches, showing how decisions are achieved, are the examples of such technical mitigation. Institutional commitments to equity and include are however not possible without technical fixes. The government structures need to put in place governance systems that require the measurement of disparities and rectifying it in case inequality has been identified.

Legal procedures are also important in discrimination. The anti-discrimination laws should be understood and applied in a manner that considers the application of algorithms in making decisions. Inclusion of people in their right to explanation, appeal and redress improves safeguards against the unfair AI systems. Holding auditing, governance, and legal enforcement jointly would create an all-encompassing strategy of ensuring fairness in AI-driven governance.

5.4 Long-Term Implication on Democratic Equality

Not only the individual decisions but also the texture of democratic equality, the long-term consequences of bias in AI-enabled governance are further than that. Otherwise, the risk of treating people unequally as part of the algorithmic discrimination can become normal and undermining the confidence towards any institutional setting. Citizens can feel that they are being governed unfairly or arbitrarily and this undermines the democratic legitimacy and social cohesion (Stahl & Coeckelbergh, 2016).

On the other hand, ethical development and regulation of AI and AR give a chance to promote equity by detecting inequity and enhancing policy focus. AI can be used to help establish evidence-based interventions that can minimize inequality, when it is correlated with social justice goals. To achieve this possibility, there must be conscious legal and ethical frameworks which focus on fairness as a fundamental graduate of governance (Taeihagh & Lim, 2019).

Finally, maintaining bias-free and inclusive AI governance is the key aspect to maintain the idea of democracy in a more digital state. Technological innovation in the field of public administration should keep equity on its core.

6. RESPONSIBILITY AND LIABILITY IN ARTIFICIAL INTELLIGENCE AND AR IMPLEMENTATION

6.1 Automated and Augmented Decision Accountability

The application of artificial intelligence and augmented reality to the governmental sphere completely transforms the classical concepts of accountability in the process of making decisions that are made publicly. Under traditional forms of administration, the responsibility is well assigned to human authorities with discretion and judgment. In situations where the decisions are automated or largely left to the AI system, though, the responsibility is shared among many players, such as system designers, data suppliers, vendors as well as the government. Such a spread of responsibility builds ambiguity on whom to take responsibility in case something goes wrong, hurt, or rights are violated (Ulnicane et al., 2021).

Such AI-enabled decision-making devices can be seen, more often, as decision-support systems instead of true agents but their suggestions can have a great influence in reality. Officials of the state can also act on the results of algorithms in preference to effective human direction because they seem objective or more efficient. Under these circumstances, differentiating between the blame on the human decision-maker who trusted the system and the institution that gave go-ahead to its use is hard. The issue of augmented reality adds an additional difficulty to the question of responsibility since it shapes and influences human perception and actions in the present moment and may exclude the understanding of the decisions made due to the mediation of technology deliberately or inadvertently.

Since ethical and legal governance requires, it is important to have a framework of responsibility established. Even when technologies are of primary importance, the roles and responsibility of all the stakeholders of AI and AR systems should be established by public institutions, and human responsibility should be maintained. Governance would lose its accountability in the absence of accurate accountability of responsibility, and there would be lack of the rule of law and trust.

6.2 Legal Liability and Redress Mechanisms

The important aspect of accountability is legal liability that entails due redress in case of harm by AI-/AR- enabled governance. The conventional liability regimes lie in determinable human behavior or negligence, an EA that is questioned by complicated algorithms. In the case that an AI system renders an incorrect or discriminative corrective, there are multiple ways to identify the legal accountability of legal liability and establish whether leafloss was caused by inaccurate data, the development of the model, system implementation, or the failure to delegate very carefully. This complication is normally beyond the ability of the legal doctrines in place.

The matters of liability are rather delicate in the context of governance since the coercive power is exercised by the government over the citizens. Victims of automated decision making should be provided with remedies that are effective and these should include challenging decisions, getting explanations, and even compensation where feasible. Courts and administrative tribunals get challenges in provisions of such cases, since they will need to evaluate technical evidence and non-human behavior. This case highlights the importance of the creation of legal frameworks that would directly take into account algorithmic decision-making in public administration (Wirtz et al., 2019).

AR-related liability creates other complexities that arise particularly when it is in the open spaces. When AR systems give wrong information or lead to accidents, there are questions regarding the liability to damage that could be brought by perceptual augmentation. The issue of responsibility between the government, technology provider or the user must be determined through a keen legal study. Ensuring that rather than legal protection and justice taking a hit to the head, strengthening liability regimes to consider AI and AR technologies is necessary to make sure that governance innovation is not affected.

6.3 Mixed Human Governance and Hybrid Governance Models

The concept of human supervision has been acknowledged as one of the foundations of responsible AI governance. Instead of substituting human judgment, AI and AR systems must exist in a system of hybrid governance, which integrates aspects of technological abilities with human judgment. These kinds of models make sure that the automated outputs can be reviewed, contextually interpreted, and ethically evaluated by some trained public officials. Human control is also another means of protection against system mistakes, favoritism and unexpected outcomes (Goyal, 2025).

Good surveillance demanded something more than formal human intervention; it demanded practical ability to override or reach into or challenge algorithmic advice. Arguably, public officials need to be educated to know their limitations within the systems, and to make their own judgment other than accepting AI outputs as an authority. In AR treated governance, management of the same involves making sure that immersive interfaces do not fraudulently affect decision making or behavior without the conscious awareness.

Accountability is also facilitated through hybrid models of governance by ensuring that there are clear lines of responsibility. Whenever human beings are the ultimate decision makers, accountability can be laid down more easily and prove helpful in offering explanations to the people involved Nevertheless, it is a method that needs institutional dedication to supervision and resources adequate to prevent the bias associated with automation. The development of governance systems that would promote efficiency and accountability is one of the primary issues involved in the implementation of AI and AR (Sætra, 2020).

6.4 Warning Bells and Supplier Controllability

Responsibility in AI- and AR-facilitated governance is also largely based on the quality of opportunities to write down and track the decision-making procedures. Documentation carries a record of system design decisions, source of data, updates of model and context of deployment. Such records play a crucial role in the audit of the system behavior, incidents investigation and compliance to the legal and ethical codes. Accountability mechanisms become terribly undermined unless there is sufficient documentation (Goyal, Dandotiya, Kumari, Sheikh et al, 2025).

Auditability is the ability to review AI and AR systems methodically in terms of compliance, performance, and equitably. Audits can be performed by an internal oversight organization, external experts, or the independent regulators of the governing system. Frequent audits can find out the risks, prejudices, and deviants of intended usage. In the case of AR systems, the auditability is also about the evaluation of the digital overlays at the context of user perception and behavior in the open spaces.

Traceability helps to make sure that certain final results can be traced back to the inputs to a specific system or the decision made. This skill is paramount in solving conflicts, taking accountability as well as system design. Traceability increases with more complex respondent systems, which are more adaptive, however, it is mandatory when it comes to accountability. Responsible AI and AR governance then comes with the cost of purchasing documentation, auditability and traceability infrastructure (Goyal, Kumari, Kushwah et al, 2025).

CONCLUSION

The adoption of artificial intelligence and augmented reality in governance is a radical change in the functioning of the institutions of the population and their decision-making and interaction with citizens. As this chapter has demonstrated, AI and AR can be used to a great potential in terms of improving efficiency, transparency, and innovation in the sphere of the government. Meanwhile, their implementation provokes some complicated ethical and legal issues that challenge the very core of the democratic governing system such as the problem of privacy, monitoring, bias, responsibility, and the rights protection. These are internal issues rather than peripheries in defining where the emerging technologies are going to empower or defeat citizen trust and legitimacy.

It is also clear in the chapter that the current rules and ethical standards are effective backgrounds but not adequate in themselves to take care of the active and systemic risks introduced by AI and AR. These technologies are adaptive, opaque and immersive and traditional model of regulation, liability, and control is complicated by their nature. To solve such complexities, there is a need to change the reactive governance to proactive, value-oriented design and regulation. The ethical aspect should be integrated across the lifecycle of both the AI and AR systems, in the collection of data and the design process of the system, deployment and the monitoring of the systems. It is also essential that the substantial human control is maintained, and the strengthening of the checks and balances that facilitate the access to explanation, redress, and the democratic control.

To address this, in the future, AI and AR require responsible governance, which can be relied upon through long-term interdisciplinary cooperation between policy-makers, legal experts, technologists, and civil societies. Democratic institutions need to transform around the changing technology, but should not turn their backs on their own commitments to the equality and transparency and the rule of law. Governments can use the power of AI and AR to address their needs and protect civil liberties and democratic principles by creating strong ethical frameworks, revising the standards of law, and ensuring that right people take part in this technological governance. The future of governance in the age of valuable and immersive technologies will finally be determined not by the possibility of technology, but by the ethical and legal decisions on how these vehicles will be applied in the common interest.

REFERENCES

Bathaee, Y. (2018). The artificial intelligence black box and the failure of intent and causation. *Harvard Journal of Law & Technology, 31*(2), 889.

Bostrom, N., & Yudkowsky, E. (2014). The ethics of artificial intelligence. In The Cambridge Handbook of Artificial Intelligence (pp. 316–334). DOI: 10.1017/CBO9781139046855.020

Brauneis, R., & Goodman, E. P. (2018). Algorithmic transparency for the smart city. *Yale Journal of Law & Technology, 20*, 103.

Butcher, J., & Beridze, I. (2019). What is the state of artificial intelligence governance globally? *RUSI Journal, 164*(5–6), 88–96. DOI: 10.1080/03071847.2019.1694260

Carabantes, M. (2020). Black-box artificial intelligence: An epistemological and critical analysis. *AI & Society, 35*(2), 309–317. DOI: 10.1007/s00146-019-00888-w

. Cath, C. (2018). Governing artificial intelligence: Ethical, legal and technical opportunities and challenges.

Chen, S. Y., Kuo, H. Y., & Lee, C. (2020). Preparing society for automated vehicles. *Sustainability (Basel), 12*(19), 7844. DOI: 10.3390/su12197844

Cihon, P., Maas, M. M., & Kemp, L. (2020). Fragmentation and the future. *Global Policy, 11*(5), 545–556. DOI: 10.1111/1758-5899.12890

Cunneen, M., Mullins, M., & Murphy, F. (2019). Autonomous vehicles and embedded artificial intelligence. *Applied Artificial Intelligence, 33*(8), 706–731. DOI: 10.1080/08839514.2019.1600301

Dafoe, A. (2018). *AI governance: A research agenda*. University of Oxford.

Felzmann, H., Villaronga, E. F., Lutz, C., & Tamò-Larrieux, A. (2019). Transparency you can trust. *Big Data & Society, 6*(1), 2053951719860542. DOI: 10.1177/2053951719860542

Firlej, M., & Taeihagh, A. (2021). Regulating human control over autonomous systems. *Regulation & Governance, 15*(4), 1071–1091. DOI: 10.1111/rego.12344

Gasser, U., & Almeida, V. A. (2017). A layered model for AI governance. *IEEE Internet Computing, 21*(6), 58–62. DOI: 10.1109/MIC.2017.4180835

Goodman, B., & Flaxman, S. (2017). European Union regulations on algorithmic decision-making. *AI Magazine, 38*(3), 50–57. DOI: 10.1609/aimag.v38i3.2741

Goyal, N. K. (2025). Security and privacy in IoT, fog, and blockchain networks. In Energy-Efficient Deep Learning Approaches in IoT, Fog, and Green Blockchain Revolution (pp. 371–398). IGI Global Scientific Publishing. DOI: 10.4018/979-8-3373-0300-0.ch015

Goyal, N. K. (2025). Weaponizing misinformation and cyberattacks on supply chains. In *Mass Media and Impact of Fake News on Supply Chains* (pp. 177–210). IGI Global Scientific Publishing., DOI: 10.4018/979-8-3373-2175-2.ch007

Goyal, N. K., Dandotiya, M., Kumari, M., Kaloria, S., & Anushya, A. (2025). AI-powered haptic devices for patient rehabilitation. In *Integrating AI With Haptic Systems for Smarter Healthcare Solutions* (pp. 143–170). IGI Global Scientific Publishing., DOI: 10.4018/979-8-3373-2307-7.ch007

Goyal, N. K., Dandotiya, M., Kumari, M., Sheikh, M. F., & Sharma, S. (2025). Emerging job roles leveraging artificial intelligence. In *Empowering Sustainable Performance and Competitive Advantage in Tourism* (pp. 89–126). IGI Global Scientific Publishing., DOI: 10.4018/979-8-3373-4546-8.ch004

Goyal, N. K., Dandotiya, M., Qurashi, J. A., Kumari, M., & Sharma, S. (2025). AI-driven predictive analytics for disease management. In *Utilizing AI of Medical Things for Healthcare Security and Sustainability* (pp. 231–276). IGI Global Scientific Publishing., DOI: 10.4018/979-8-3373-0690-2.ch008

Goyal, N. K., Kumari, M., Kushwah, V., Dandotiya, M., & Vijay, A. (2025). Evaluating blockchain security: Trade-offs in consensus mechanisms. *IET Conference Proceedings*, 2024(38),80–88. https://doi.org/DOI: 10.1049/icp.2025.0775

Helbing, D. (2019). Societal, economic, ethical and legal challenges of the digital revolution. In Towards Digital Enlightenment (pp. 47–72).

Huq, A. Z. (2019). Racial equity in algorithmic criminal justice. *Duke Law Journal*, *68*(6), 1043–1134.

Janssen, M., Brous, P., Estevez, E., Barbosa, L. S., & Janowski, T. (2020). Data governance for trustworthy AI. *Government Information Quarterly*, *37*(3), 101493. DOI: 10.1016/j.giq.2020.101493

Jobin, A., Ienca, M., & Vayena, E. (2019). The global landscape of ethics guidelines. *Nature Machine Intelligence*, *1*(9), 389–399. DOI: 10.1038/s42256-019-0088-2

Kleinberg, J., Ludwig, J., Mullainathan, S., & Sunstein, C. R. (2018). Discrimination in the age of algorithms. *The Journal of Legal Analysis*, *10*, 113–174. DOI: 10.1093/jla/laz001

Kroll, J. A., Barocas, S., Felten, E. W., Reidenberg, J. R., Robinson, D. G., & Yu, H. (2016). Accountable algorithms. *University of Pennsylvania Law Review*, *165*, 633.

Leenes, R., & Lucivero, F. (2014). Laws on robots, laws by robots. *Law, Innovation and Technology*, *6*(2), 193–220. DOI: 10.5235/17579961.6.2.193

Leenes, R., Palmerini, E., Koops, B. J., Bertolini, A., Salvini, P., & Lucivero, F. (2017). Regulatory challenges of robotics. *Law, Innovation and Technology*, *9*(1), 1–44. DOI: 10.1080/17579961.2017.1304921

Mittelstadt, B. D., Allo, P., Taddeo, M., Wachter, S., & Floridi, L. (2016). The ethics of algorithms. *Big Data & Society*, *3*(2), 2053951716679679. DOI: 10.1177/2053951716679679

Pagallo, U., Casanovas, P., & Madelin, R. (2019). The middle-out approach. *The Theory and Practice of Legislation*, *7*(1), 1–25. DOI: 10.1080/20508840.2019.1664543

Rahwan, I. (2018). Society-in-the-loop. *Ethics and Information Technology*, *20*(1), 5–14. DOI: 10.1007/s10676-017-9430-8

Sætra, H. S. (2020). Political harms of algorithmic governance. *Technology in Society*, *62*, 101283. PMID: 32536737

Stahl, B. C., & Coeckelbergh, M. (2016). Ethics of healthcare robotics. *Robotics and Autonomous Systems*, *86*, 152–161. DOI: 10.1016/j.robot.2016.08.018

Taeihagh, A., & Lim, H. S. M. (2019). Governing autonomous vehicles. *Transport Reviews*, *39*(1), 103–128. DOI: 10.1080/01441647.2018.1494640

Ulnicane, I., Knight, W., Leach, T., Stahl, B. C., & Wanjiku, W. G. (2021). Framing governance for contested technologies. *Policy and Society*.

Wirtz, B. W., Weyerer, J. C., & Geyer, C. (2019). Artificial intelligence and the public sector. *International Journal of Public Administration*, *42*(7), 596–615. DOI: 10.1080/01900692.2018.1498103

Chapter 6
Fusion Technologies in Governance:
From Algorithmic Intelligence to Augmented Reality

Kamini Pareek
https://orcid.org/0009-0003-3994-7285
Poornima University, Jaipur, India

Neetu Sharma
Poornima Institute of Engineering and Technology, Jaipur, India

Navin Kumar Goyal
https://orcid.org/0009-0006-0901-294X
Poornima Institute of Engineering and Technology, Jaipur, India

Sanjay Kumar Sinha
https://orcid.org/0000-0003-0351-2549
Poornima Institute of Engineering and Technology, Jaipur, India

Sunil Kushwaha
Poornima University, Jaipur, India

Nikhil Kumar Goyal
https://orcid.org/0009-0007-4532-8033
Poornima University, Jaipur, India

ABSTRACT

The combination of AI algorithms and extensive augmented reality technologies, is revolutionizing the service delivery in the occupational sector in the form of intelligent, immersive, and citizen-driven digital ecosystems. The government is able to process vast quantities of data automatically, predict the needs of the society and automate its operations through AI, and use AR to engage more people through superimposing real-time, context-driven information onto the environment of the user involved. Collectively, the technologies will aid in responsive and accountable governance in the sector of healthcare, urban governance, transport, education, and emergency services. Their intersection enhances transparency, efficiency, and

DOI: 10.4018/979-8-3373-7804-6.ch006

accessibility and it also allows to engage citizens and government systems more intuitively. These opportunities, however, have their share of challenges associated with privacy, capacity of the infrastructure, digital equity, and regulation.

1: INTRODUCTION

1.1 Understanding AI Algorithms

Artificial intelligence algorithms underlie the modern public services as they provide governments with the ability to study data, automatize routine operations and make more correct decisions. Machine learning, deep learning, and rule-based models, which extract the patterns out of big datasets, are the main components of these systems. These algorithms are used to inform and manage inefficiencies and enable future predictions in terms of demand and needs, as well as services can be implemented to individual or community-level demands when applied to public health, transportation, taxation, or portals providing citizen services. This capacity to process huge quantities of data has moved governance out of the reactive mode to the proactive mode of planning (Gigerenzer, 2023).

Figure 1. Types of AI algorithms

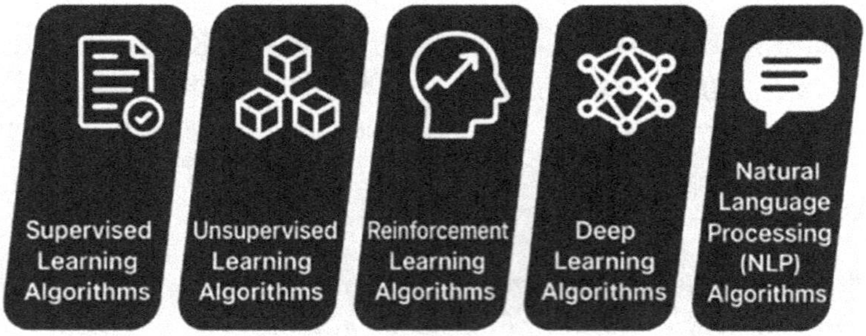

The AI algorithms are being modified to address more complex challenges like anomaly detection, fraud, smart routing, and social welfare optimization as more and more public services are becoming interconnected. The systems can be effectively utilized over time because of the new information, and so it should be used particularly by governments that intend to deal with the changing aspects of problems such as congestion in a city, environmental risks and safety of the community. Nonetheless, the use of AI in the government is associated with transparency, fairness, and accountability as well and the policymakers need to work around the design and effect of the algorithmic decision making.

1.2 History of Augmented Reality Technologies

AR has evolved to be an experimental technology in the niche yet an effective means of communication in the public administration. AR was initially widely used in entertainment and commercial sectors, but now it is adopted by the governments to improve interactions with the citizens. AR gives digital information a physical context and therefore enables users to have real-time contextual information whether navigating around a public building, getting civic information, or getting familiar with the urban planning proposal. It is a visual, imersive communication process that eases the mental burden and gives the citizens direct, practical information (Nordström, 2022).

The increasing accessibility of smart phones and wearables and apps based on AR has offered speed to adoption in many sectors of the general population. AR tools are now used by municipal offices, emergency workers, and service centers to see underground infrastructure, provide remote assistance, and provide field workers training without having use of specific equipment. As AR can be more user-friendly and integrated, governments can see the opportunities of AR to decrease service wait times, enhance the accuracy of field work, and increase the trust of the citizens to the government through the open and interactive communication (Floridi et al., 2020).

1.3 AI and AR Meeting in the Contemporary Governance

The combination of AI algorithms and augmented reality technologies is a significant technological breakthrough in the process of modernizing the work of public services. AI offers an analytical intelligence, whereas AR offers a user-friendly interface, where the insights are conveyed in a visual way. A combination of these technologies allows real-time guidance, automatic decision support, and individual service experience. To illustrate, an AI model has the potential to process traffic data in the city and instantly present routing options via an AR-based interface and allow the officials (or citizens) to engage with solutions in real time. Such convergence comes in handy to improve operational efficiency and facilitate a service that is more inclusive to the people.

The integration also enhances the humanity of the approach in the public systems by simplifying complex data which are not comprehendible by non-technicians. AR overlays allow citizens to engage in AI-informed insights to the creation of a more transparent governance space. AI-supported visual support can be availed to field officers, healthcare workers, and emergency teams and enhance their accuracy and responsiveness. With the transition to citizen-oriented and data-based government approaches, the combination of AI and AR technologies puts the public administration under the conditions of more dynamic, personalized, and intelligent network services (Gigerenzer, 2022).

2. AI ALGORITHMS IN PUBLIC SERVICE DELIVERY

2.1 Machine Learning Models for Government Decision-Making

Machine learning models have taken the centre of the modern world of governance as it has given the ability of the public institutions to detect trends, distribute resources and react effectively to the arising challenges. These models are based on historical and real time information that are used to predict outcomes of disease outbreaks, economic changes, congestion, and welfare needs. Governments will also be able to make decisions quicker and smarter by automating the analytical process that did not involve much manual work. The probability of human error is also minimal in machine learning, which means that administrative outcomes are of more consistency (De Sousa et al., 2019).

Figure 2. Model selection for machine learning in government decision-making

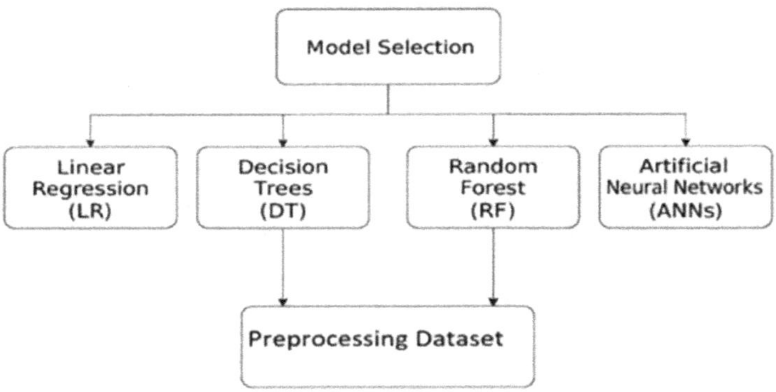

With the rise in the sophistication of the collective demands, machine learning systems are being developed to assist in the execution of more advanced forms of decision-making. Classification, clustering, and predictive models are now used by governments to identify fraud, determine eligibility in the social schemes, and allocate public goods in the most efficient manner possible. The tools are also useful in simulating the future by the policy makers and hence planning and risk management is improved. Simultaneously, machine learning implementation should also be tightly regulated to ensure the transparency and prevent the revision of the prejudices inherent in historical data. Hence, the introduction of the ML systems should entail powerful moral principles and its consistent observation to guarantee the fairness and responsibility.

2.2 Predictive Training in Public Safety as well as Resource Allocation

Predictive analytics is extremely important in improving the safety of people by detecting trends indicate that can be used to indicate chances of danger or crisis. By relying on predictive models, law enforcement agencies are able to predict hotspots of crime, enhance their patrolling approaches, and distribute their officers in the most efficient manner. Equally, emergency services are using such tools to predict any natural disasters, fire outbreak or health crisis so that response teams may be ready in advance to handling an incident before it gets out of hand. This rebuttal-to-proactive safety management also enhances the strength of the community and less resistance in the face of a crisis.

When it comes to resource allocation, predictive analytics can be used to assist governments in planning allocation of medical resources, transport, educational resources, and energy. The models help to make informed investments of the population by studying the demographic changes and seasonal variations and trends in the behavior of the population to prevent wastage of social cash. Predictive systems are also capable of making dynamic changes, enabling authorities to reallocate resources when there is a peak demand. There is a need to hit the right balance between efficiency and expectation of fairness by the government as more integrate these tools and we see that predictive decisions incorporated into social equity and not favoring the disadvantaged groups (Decker et al., 2025).

2.3 Policy implementation and Automated Decision Systems

Automated decision making simplifies the administrative tasks through the provision of a standardization and timely assessment of governmental applications, registering and request of services. These systems read established rules and access logic to establish eligibility or compliance thus reducing the time delays that are characteristic of the more traditional bureaucratic processes. Automated systems achieved by minimizing administrative overheads allow the government workers to concentrate on more complicated tasks involving human element which involve judgment and understanding. The outcome is a governance structure which is more responsive to large scale demand (Wirtz et al., 2019).

As much as the automated systems have a lot of benefits, challenges of transparency and accountability also come in. When citizens cannot determine the way they reach decisions, it may also be important when the algorithm decides which services pass or fail. Hence, the governments have to communicate the rationality of these systems transparently, and give them mechanisms of appeal or revision. Automated decision-making may help to increase the trust of the population in the studies when it is done in a responsible way, as it provides predictable results, and the chances of corruption are minimized. With the ever-changing technology, the successful adoption of the automated systems will be paramount in achieving fair and effective implementation of the policies (Sun & Medaglia, 2019).

3. AUGMENTED REALITY FOR ENHANCED PUBLIC ENGAGEMENT

3.1 AR Interfaces for Public Information Delivery

The technology known as Augmented Reality is changing the face of how governments communicate through the overlaying of digital content in the physical space in a manner that can be intuitively learned by the citizens. Conventional ways of communicating through public service interfaces work well like posters, websites, and notice boards but fail to reach various target audiences and present complicated information in an easily understandable manner. AR interfaces are, however, able to enable individuals to see instructions, routes or processes in an interactive 3D format which is displayed directly in their immediate environment. This immersive communication form minimizes the level of confusion, enhances understanding and closes the divide between online and offline channels of public service delivery.

The governments are promptly implementing AR as a platform to dispatch real-time alerts, public safety protocols and infrastructure data. Those citizens scan QR codes placed on the places where people can view 3D explanations of the government schemes, procedures, or emergency actions. Such information delivery can come in especially handy in areas that are multilingual, as the information displayed can be easily understood by visual means and language barriers can be broken. With the development of AR being more available via smartphones and wearable technology, its ability to enhance citizen awareness and a sense of trust will only continue to increase, becoming one of the fundamental instruments of next-generation public information systems (Züger & Asghari, 2023).

3.2 Public Immersion Public Awareness and Civic Education

The immersive AR experiences provide governments with a chance to develop civic education and social awareness activating rather passive information. Instead of surfing long documents or watching physical trainings, the citizens are engaged in AR simulations, showing them the aftermath of the undertaking (climatic choices, traffic offense, or disaster-response actions and so on). Such virtual contexts enable the people to learn more about the complicated civic concerns by making them experience and learn more about the problems and more extensively they get to understand them (Van Noordt & Tangi, 2023).

AR-based modules have specific use in education and community outreach programs, when citizens can see the insides of water systems, the processes in medical institutions, the system of voting and the conservation of nature. Watching these systems in their own space, people will have a better understanding of the value of the public services and how they contribute to the life of the community. In addition, AR will support individualized learning experiences, with users being able to read about things on their own time. Consequently, the AR based civic education can not only inform, but also empower the citizens through curiosity, engagement and responsibility (Equey et al., 2024).

3.3 AR usage to provide Citizen Inclusion and Accessibility

The technologies supported by Augmented Reality can allow making public services more accessible by offering adjustable digital extensions to a diverse audience including people with disabilities. AR can transform complicated text into easier visual instructions, give gesture-based instructions, or give audio explanations of governmental procedures. AR can be adapted to spoken language so as to enable citizens impaired with hearing to follow the instructions through visual cues whereas haptic-feedback enhanced AR could be helpful to citizens with visual defects. These accommodative functions make public services to be fair and accessible by all the social groups.

In addition to accessibility, AR is important in promoting social inclusion through overcoming the digital divide. The less technologically exposed citizens are able to engage in AR experiences that are easy to use and not as daunting as a conventional interface. The use of AR kiosks in places where people congregate, government buildings, and in local communities aids in breaking the barrier by providing a physical interaction which is not dependent on advanced digital literacy. The more AR systems will be made a part of the governance, the greater their opportunities to expand participation and increase a shared civic identity can become. By designing AR inclusively, it is guaranteed that the digital transformation in the public sector accords both personal gains and common assets to every citizen, irrespective of age, literacy and other backgrounds (Al-Ansi et al., 2024).

4. DECISION-MAKING, PLANNING, AND OPERATIONAL EFFICIENCY WITH AI-AR SYSTEMS

4.1 AI-Driven Insights for Real-Time Public Sector Decision-Making

Artificial Intelligence is a disruptive factor in aiding real-time decision-making to rely on massive amounts of operational information and detect valuable patterns that a human administrator may miss. As these AI insights are combined with Augmented Reality, they can be acted upon in real-time since administrators view data overlay in the real world when performing an inspection, public safety review, or looking at infrastructure. As an illustration, a governmental bridge or drainage system inspector can be provided with AI-generated risk indicators superimposed on AR glasses, with the person being able to decide on the basis of precise, geo-specific intelligence. The effect of this integration is a reduction in the delays, the minimization in guess work and the informed decisions made due to dynamic and evidence based analysis (Wang et al., 2024).

Also, AI-powered AR applications assist administrators to model a variety of different situations in order to learn how their decisions will affect them. This predictive ability is useful in the planning of public interventions, like that of traffic diversion, maintenance of waste, flood management or allocation of resources. The decision-makers do not use documents or fixed dashboards but are communicating with 3D projections, which are changing in accordance with the real-world conditions. These visual simulations enhance interdepartmental collaboration because various stakeholders can be able to view and discuss the same contextual data and eventually enhance coordination and policy accuracy (Chen & Chen, 2024).

4.2 AR-Based Urban Planning, Infrastructure Surveillance, and Urban Utilities

AR interfaces are a great help in urban planning because the planners are able to see a proposed structure or a zoning change and environmental impacts on the real landscape. With a combination of AI-based analytics in all these AR models, planners can now have access to various details about the population growth, mobility trends, the land-use forecasts, and ecological limitations. Such a two-layered system is more focused and transparent in terms of planning in order to allow cities to experiment with various development plans without disrupting pre-existing infrastructure. Using realistic 3D overlays, the stakeholders are able to test the long-term effect of new roads, bridges, housing development, or the green spaces with a better understanding of the spatial and social implications (Buçinca et al., 2021).

It is also efficient in infrastructure monitoring once AI-AR tools would be implemented as maintenance and inspection tasks. The AR devices allow the technicians to see the conditions inside the structure, sensor readings and warning signs of failures on a physical object. This will reduce the risk of human error and will enable the agencies to use a preventive maintenance model instead of responding to an emergency. In the case of the general utility like electricity, water flow, and garbage management, AI-AR systems can provide nonstop monitoring of the functioning and supply-demand dynamics. The capabilities allow cities to be more efficient, minimize the number of services outage, and enhance the satisfaction of citizens by responding to the needs promptly and effectively (Rodrigues, 2020).

4.3 AI-AR aid to fight crisis responses and emergency management

In the case of emergency situations, the AI and AR provide very responsive operational environment, facilitating quick assessment and communication as well as mobilization. Artificial intelligence algorithms have the potential to handle real-time sensor, drone, camera, and citizen report data to identify anomalies and forecast areas of concern and recommend the most appropriate response strategies. AR builds upon such experiences by overlaying the dangers, including areas of evacuation and structural frailty, onto the field of vision of the emergency responders. Such spatial awareness contributes a lot to safety and accuracy in those cases when fast decisions can save lives (McKinney et al., 2020).

AR based navigation helps the emergency teams by showing safe routes, locating the wounded ones, and the plan of the building during an emergency rescue in a new environment. AI also enhances coordination, analyzing and advising deployment priorities and predicting the way a crisis will develop. When the interacting parties have a synchronized AR interface, communication is more effective and efficient as there is less miscommunication that happens when people are under stress. In the long term, this type of technologies will aid in the creation of more intelligent and resilient systems of public safety that can address the impact of natural catastrophes, infrastructure issues, and epidemic cases on a large scale (Angwin et al., 2016).

5. ENHANCING TRANSPARENCY, ACCOUNTABILITY, AND CITIZEN ENGAGEMENT

5.1 AI-AR Tools for Public Service Transparency and Performance Visibility

The combination of AI and Augmented Reality opens a whole new concept of transparency in the work of governmental services as complex governmental processes are transformed into transparent and immersive environment with visual contexts. The traditional public administration is typically ineffective when it comes to the obscure reporting, disjointed information and minimal anticipation of how the public funds are used. These barriers can be slowly broken down with the help of data processing through AI and visualization with AR. It allows citizens to observe the performance of the services available in real time, project progress and budget use by merely engaging with AR applications which project the pertinent data on the physical environment. As a rules example, a citizen noticing an under-construction public building by pointing an AR device at it may overlay AI-analysed timelines, resource utilisation, structural plans, and actual completion on the site. This will not only create confusion but will also avoid misinformation, and create clarity regarding government work without having to be a technical literate person.

Monitoring transparency in the context of public referencing, policy deliberation, etc. is also achieved by combining AI intelligence with AR visualization. Citizens and administrators do not have to examine bulky paperwork or technical frameworks, as AR projections of data demonstrate the effects of the economy, hypothetical risk instances, and contrasting policy consequences. Artificial intelligence processes past data, forecasts with regard to the future, and identifies possible bottlenecks, whereas AR will present this results through intuitive formats, like spatial overlays or 3D visualization. This enhances the decision making ability of the government and its citizens alike as everybody is able to know what will happen in case the policy is adopted or not. This leads to transparency being an experience and not an empty promise and a situation in which the public trust builds up organically (Engel et al., 2025).

Moreover, proactive transparency is also initiated by AI-AR tools, which provide constant updates, as opposed to an occasional one. The citizens do not wait any longer to find out the progress of a project by traveling once an annual report or an official announcement is made. Instead, through AR dashboards, they are able to have updated AI-generated insights every day, or even every hour. This information democratization makes sure that the governments become accountable on a real time and they cannot conceal their inefficiency or delays. The increased transparency also promotes internal accountability in the government departments, which promote their coordination and minimize the chances of administrative fraud or performance gaps. Using this model, transparency is an obligation between the state and the community.

5.2 Improving Government Accountability Through AI-Based Monitoring and AR Visualizations

The power of AI algorithms in enhancing the accountability of the people cannot be overstated because AI is responsible in the end time by constantly checking on service delivery, anomaly detection, and even creating red flags that indicate areas of inefficiency. Combined with AR visualizations, such analytic insights will help curb state authorities in accomplishing greater accuracy, timeliness, and ease in carrying out the process. As an example, AR glasses an auditor visits a construction site can be linked to an AI system that analyzes the intended infrastructure with the one that exists before the eyes of the system user. Irregularities, including wrong sizes, lack of stuff, or more than allowable delays are evidently pointed out. This diminishes the subjectivity of reporting and gives little room to corruption, manipulation and misrepresentation of project status. Through this, accountability is no longer a paper process, but a real-time evaluation process with evidence backing (van Bekkum & Borgesius, 2021).

The AI-AR devices also enable formal and reliable inspection trails. All the observations of the officials working in the field may be recorded in AR-recorded images, authenticated and tagged by AI systems, and stored in secure online repositories. The records are objective data that will be used to audit the future or checks on citizens, or legal checks. Such documentations also destroy confusion of what the inspectors saw or how projects changed along the way. It also makes sure the responsible parties are liable to the mistakes or failures as there is a clear chain of evidence. The result of such systems is procedural fairness that prevents any false accusation and at the same time safeguards the public resources.

Also, AI-AR responsibility systems include enhancing responsiveness in administration. The system will raise alerts about emerging problems, including a decline in the quality of provided services, increased number of complaints received by the citizen, or when the system starts showing indications of a failing infrastructure, the relevant departments can be alerted promptly to take corrective action. AR visualization allows field teams to clearly comprehend the location of the problem and correct the situation. Government agencies reduce the impact of service disruptions, and the services performance standards through accelerating detection and intervention. By gradually implementing AI-AR monitoring, the ethical culture of the public institutions will become strong, and the accountability will be operated as a result of the new norm instead of a response to the necessity (Gomez & Ilarri, 2024).

5.3 Participatory Governance and citizen interaction which is AR enabled

Combined AI and AR technologies transform the citizen interaction with the process of government and make it more singular, more open, and involving. Rather than restricting the engagement to official methods like holding public hearings or profile surveys, AR allows individuals to enjoy the benefits of being physically engaged with future urban plans and policy proposals as well as service designs. As an example, a redevelopment plan of an urban area can be demonstrated as a full-scale simulation of AR that will superimpose future infrastructures onto the current setting: parks, roads, transportation systems. AI evaluates the responses of citizens, trends on sentiment, and forecast the usage and AR enables one to see what might happen. Once the involvement ceases to be a mere reading and turns into experience, opinion of the masses gets much more informed and colorful.

The inclusivity dimension is especially important since the AR tools contribute to breaking the barriers in literature, language as well as technological knowledge. Artificial intelligence translation, voice recognition, and shorter visual stories can help the marginalized populations participate in the governance process meaningfully. A citizen with language barriers or unable to fight with documents will be able to engage in experiences with AR which is based on symbols, sound instructions and the needless interactions. The implementation of AI-AR systems can be located both in community centers and in general kiosks and mobile devices so that the interaction process is not based on individual access to costly equipment. This renders participatory governance fair and inclusive bringing the voices of people who were not historically included in political procedures (Rukanova et al., 2021).

Besides, AI-AR technologies augment the feedback between citizens and authorities. AR dashboards can be used to help government agencies visualize the sentiment of people, through the compilation of aggregated responses of a particular location or theme. Decision-makers have an understanding of the communities that agree or disagree with certain policies, and the reason. Citizens in their turn will observe how their feedback contributes to real policy changes and it will reinforce the sense of agency and trust. This will form a governance model that is not episodic but constant and citizens feel like participants in the design of the public service and not passive recipients. By providing this ongoing interaction, AI-AR technologies can help build the world of the future which is highly democratic, transparent, and built on mutual responsibility.

6. ENHANCING CITIZEN ENGAGEMENT AND EXPERIENCE THROUGH AI–AR INTEGRATION

6.1 Personalized and Context-Aware Public Interactions

The deployment of AI and AR technologies in the sphere of public initiatives is radically changing the relationship of citizens with the government, making them more personal and more intuitive and contextual. The use of traditional interfaces in the services of a government tends to use the predetermined forms, verification, lengthy procedures that cause irritation and ineffectiveness among users. On the contrary, AI-based personalization enables systems to dynamically vary following the past, passion, and the present demands of a citizen. These interactions are more real when they are augmented with AR, allowing citizens to interact with public information and infrastructure in the natural and immediate sense. The citizenry no longer needs to search through convoluted bureaucratic sites and can instead be provided with customized directions which are superimposed on their physical locations to ease the burden of confusion and simplify the public services.

Using AI, it is possible to observe the behavior of users, the patterns of queries, and the history of using the offered services to pre-empt what kind of support the customer needs. As the example on one citizen applying a public-service AR app at a transport center, AI algorithms access his/her past transportation data, his/her location, and other time-changing factors to provide correct route recommendations or point-to-point information. The contextual awareness generated with this integration will be useful in the elimination of redundant stages so that the citizens are not overwhelmed with irrelevant information. Further, this form of personalization results to a scenario where interactions in the public will be humanized because the system seems to know what the situation requires as opposed to providing a generic response (Rosado et al., 2024).

The AR immersion also adds to the clarity of complicated situations that were formerly to be supported by a physical presence. AR-based superimpositions can be used by citizens who attend governmental hospitals, governmental administrative buildings, or any other welfare offices to find the necessary counters, required documents, or service ranks. AI subsequently modifies the AR guidance (on a real-time basis) to match the evolving conditions, including the crowd density, the number of available staff, or an emergency situation. Such adaptability makes the user experience more supportive and smooth at a state of the moment. Finally, the contextual awareness and customization support the enhancement of citizen empowerment, minimize barriers to accessibility, and assist in changing the perception of public-service ecosystem into a more involving and routinely responsive space.

6.2 AR-based Navigation and the Dissemination of Public Information

The concept of augmented reality has provided fresh opportunities to publicize information more visually, intuitively, and easily. Non-modern methods of communication, including signage, pamphlets, or websites, can be effective only with certain groups of the population, as literate citizens and, more so, people who lack literacy or have problems with bureaucratic language. AR can assist in alleviating this disconnection by bringing actual data to life in the form of an interactive visual aspect directly in the lens of a citizen. AR-guided navigation can be a useful tool in assisting the user to maneuver around the public spaces, learn procedures, and find the necessary services with ease when paired with AI algorithms to recall relevant information in real-time.

The routes to trains and buses offered by the public transport system can be very illustrative of such change since AR appears can give real-time information about the route and delays, and track changes by merely scanning a device at the station map or at the train track. The AI models work with real data about operational activities in real-time and display it in AR format so that the citizens can make adequate decisions without interpreting the complicated schedules or announcements. Similar developments are going on in government hospitals as AR-guided navigation is used to relieve stress on patients and visitors in the country by giving them a visual course of action to get to diagnostic centers, consultation rooms, and even emergency departments. The interface turns into a digital companion that will make citizens feel freer to interact with spaces in the city (Hamid & Huda, 2025).

The AI and AR platforms are beneficial to the situation awareness of the citizens and government in the context of the context of public safety and emergency services. In the case of crisis like in case of a natural disaster or in the case of massive events on the ground, AR can overlay evacuation paths, risk area or safety messages onto the physical landscape, enabling individuals to find their way through unfamiliar and or even hectic environments. The AI systems are making sure that these overlays are correct through continuous analysis of sensor data, satellite images and communication feeds. Offloading cognitive citizens by converting received information and making it agency-oriented visual indicators, AR helps them make quicker and more thoughtful decisions under conditions of both crisis and routine. The outcome is a more effective user-centered public information ecosystem that can be changed real-time according to the changing environment.

6.3 Improving Accessibility and Reducing Digital Exclusion

Among the most influential benefits of the integration of AI and AR, one may note the lack of distance between citizens who invariably encounter pressure in their interactions with public measures. The disabled people who may be visually impaired, have mobility problems, have learning or memory impairments, or who have language problems may experience problems in moving around the government offices or in following the instructions in the procedures. The use of AI algorithms with natural language processing, image recognition and translation abilities, which can be implemented in real-time will be helpful to decode the information that is difficult to understand and reform it to present it in a manner that fits individual requirements. Even these modifications are more effective when offered in AR because a multi-sensory support can be provided to users with regard to their particular accessibility needs.

AR applications that enable the blind citizens to listen to descriptions of the visual icons like building signs, labels in documents, or follow arrows is beneficial to blind citizens can see visual free information and therefore deduce its meaning. With improved independence, AI systems can study the environment based on cameras on their devices, detect objects, and provide a narrative on their relevance. In the case of hearing-impaired individuals, AR may present captivated messages, sign language indicators or emphasize significant visual objects in the general location. Such adaptations will ensure that public-service spaces are more accommodating and less rely on human mediators, thus ensuring that the experience is more just to everyone using it.

Another important concern of the issue of digital exclusion in the delivery of public services and particularly those with insufficient technological knowledge or digital illiteracy. User-friendly interfaces can also be customized to the level of comfort that the individual requires; this is where AI can simplify the instructions, support voice guidance or step-by-step AR overlays which can be used to break down complex instructions. This will minimize intimidation but will make the citizens develop confidence when utilizing digital services. Moreover, training modules created with AR programs can assist one to learn the way to find the government services by demonstrating how to do it virtually, without confusion and becoming more independent. Together, focusing on accessibility and digital inclusion, both AI and AR assist in reducing structural disparities and making sure that the technological change will reach the whole citizenry rather than solely digitally savvy communities (Almahmoud et al., 2025).

7. CHALLENGES, RISKS, AND GOVERNANCE CONSIDERATIONS

7.1 Ethical and Privacy Concerns

The inclusion of AI algorithms and augmented reality in the domain of the public service makes the number of ethical and privacy concerns enormous, and it has to be considered thoroughly. The scope of tolerable data utilization turns out to be more challenging to determine with the increase in the scope of AI systems gathering, analyzing, and concluding upon the information provided by citizens to provide a personalized service to them. The applications of AR, especially those that use real-time functionality and are available in open areas, serve as an additional point of complexity since they do not only capture personal data of the user but also the location and data about other people. This blurring can lead to scenarios in which people can be filmed or examined without their knowledge or permission, which conflicts with the old concept of privacy. The governments, accordingly, should strike a balance between the utility of these technologies and the ethical considerations to safeguard the citizens as well as keep the institutions of the country open and accountable.

The other significant issue is the biases that can be instilled in the AI algorithms. AI models used by public services can be based on the large datasets which can reproduce history of inequities or distorted demographic trends unwillingly. In cases where these biases are recreated in policing systems, welfare distribution systems, or even in public health systems, the results of such systems may be disproportionately unfavorable to vulnerable groups. Placed over AI-based decision-making, AR interfaces can also serve to reinforce biased interpretations of context, resulting in an action that is misinformed by the workers of a public organization or an automated system. When the biased prompts are sent to a frontline worker or automated kiosk, even slight visual overlays can influence the decisions, which embraces inequities even more (Ainslie et al., 2023).

The third ethical issue is associated with the issue of informed consent because the nature of AI and AR technologies complicates the citizens to clearly understand the use of what information is shown, how it is analyzed, and why. Old consent systems are no longer effective as technologies constantly trace real-time space and personality data. It is possible that many users are not aware that AI algorithms combined with AR devices can create inferences that are much more than their immediate data may reveal, including predictions of behavioral tendencies, moods or socioeconomic indicators. Creating effective consent regimes will become an inherent need of governance, and not a fixation but a mere administrative formality, and the governments will be required to adopt new communication strategies that will make citizens have a personal meaningful meaning of the consequences of their engagement in the work of the AI-enabled types of systems.

7.2 Data Protection and Security Problems

The issue connected with AI and augmented reality in the context of the public services refers to the security vulnerability of both the data volume the facilities are working with and the aspect of being real-time (AR interactions). Powerful data sets are essential to the functionality of AI systems, and storage and migration of such data are the best attack points by cyberattacks. These risks are intensified by the use of AR applications since the latter utilize continuous environmental scanning and usually sends the visual and spatial contents to networks to process them. Provided that attackers receive access to these data streams, they might be able to recreate sensitive surroundings, monitor movement directions by users, or modify visual overlays on which public officials work. This gives new possibilities of using surveillance without precedent, identity theft, and specific targeted cybercrime, and strong cybersecurity frameworks are indispensable (Al-Mhiqani et al., 2024).

The other level of security concern is the manipulation of algorithms. In such applications of AI in the government, like resource allocation or emergency management, adversarial attacks can only compromise AI models by supplying subtly modified input data in order to obtain incorrect outputs. Such disruptions are even more hazardous when combined with AR interfaces since the operators at the frontline are dependent on visual indicators or digital markers that could be authentic and yet were probably violated. Such manipulations may confuse the emergency responders, interfere with the management of public transport, or prevent medical aid provided with the help of AR-guided instruments. The fact that such attacks are sabotageable with the resulting consequences depicts how critical constant tracking, backup measures and possibility to restore to manual functions are necessary.

Another hurdle is related to data sovereignty and cross-sovereign data transfers particularly when national-owned AI systems are created by foreign contractors or are hosted by cloud systems situated across borders. AR systems and devices usually rely on global positioning systems, remote switches, and third-party APIs, which can make sensitive data in the public sector vulnerable to jurisdictions with varied privacy regulations. In such a way, governments should develop consistent data governance plans that can solve the problem of ownership, control, and local storage so that the implementation of AI and AR technologies was not a threat to national security or the freedom of citizens. In the absence of these protective measures, advantages of technological advancement will soon be diminished by the drawbacks that could lead to lack of credibility among the community (Alaeifar et al., 2024).

7.3 Regulatory, Policy and Governance Requirements

With the development of the public-service system towards the use of AI algorithms and AR interfaces, the regulatory and governance systems will require adjustments. The current policies of digital governance were printed in conventional information systems and they were usually not specific enough to handle the dynamic, predictive, and immersive essence of the AI-AR technologies. Governments need to shift towards adaptive forms of regulation that would keep up with changes in technology and at the same time retain consistent monitoring mechanisms. This entails setting standards of transparency of algorithms, raising the independent auditing of the AI models deployed in the services of the state and recreating them to be fair and justified, and displaying them to the stakeholders in a comprehensible way (Kazimierczak et al., 2024).

The interdisciplinary look should be included in the process of the policy development as well since it entails the integration of technologists, legal professionals, ethicists, social scientists and leaders of communities. It should not just be regulation regarding technical specifications only, it should extend to other social effects, specifically in respect to equity and access. Publix services should be inclusive and rules should ensure availability of access features of AR interfaces and make sure that AI based systems do not increase digital gaps. The governments should ensure that every citizen, irrespective of their level of digital illiteracy, can be able to engage fully in AI-enabled government services in an unbiased and un-exclusionary way.

Another consideration in governance is the establishment of accountability frameworks that would deal with errors, misuse, and unintended consequences. With more tasks being performed through AI and AR systems that were previously handled by human personnel, the question of whether the party is liable during an instance of system malfunction or adverse consequences is a complicated question to answer. The government authorities should specify the authorized bodies to regulate automated judgments and means by which the population can remind or object AI-powered results. Dissatisfaction redress systems, publicity websites, citizen scrutiny boards can become attentive elements of the administrative infrastructure of AI-AR incorporation. In the absence of these, the validity of digital transformation activity in the public sector can be doubted, which can negatively affect its acceptance and belief (Groumpos, 2010).

CONCLUSION

It is a paradigm that the utilization of AI and augmented reality in permissible services alter the way governments, design, and render system-related provision to the citizens. With the growing complexity of challenges in the public sector, these technologies can help administrations shift the model of these processes to be reactive, paper-based, but then move upwards to proactive. intelligent and immersive services. With sophisticated analytics, real-time data processing and intuitive AR displays, governments can now read citizen demands more precisely, ease processes and minimize the strain that has typified the experiences of using social services. This is not just a technological change, but a structural change, which signals in another wave of modernization where accessibility, inclusiveness and transparency are the key pillars of governance.

On the operational level, AI and AR in combination open opportunities to restructure workflows, to automatize baseline operations, and to provide high-context guidance to citizens in a variety of settings like a hospital, transportation, and even an administrative office. They have a statistical addition that improves efficiency, lessens human error, and makes the delivery of information more understandable and interesting. Notably, these technologies serve the functions of supporting the public officials as offering decision-support, predictive insights, and enhanced visualizations tools that enhance planning, resource allocation, and emergency response. When used responsibly, AI--AR ecosystems can increase the productivity of workforce and build a higher level of trust among the population towards the government systems by creating a more uniform, reliable, and human-centered service delivery.

Nevertheless, the impact of AI-AR integration is not completely achievable without governments taking action concerning the ethical, regulatory and social side of its usage. The aspects of privacy, data security, and algorithmic fairness, as well as equal access, should be seen as primary instead of secondary concerns. In addition, the issue of digital inclusion and access should be kept at the center of attention so that the advancement in the field of technology will not introduce new inequalities. The future of AI-based public services is in favor of a balanced solution to the issues that is an approach of combining innovation to accountability, empathy to efficiency, modernization to justice. Since government is going to persist in considering immersive and intelligent technologies, it must go ahead and embrace this new direction in a responsible and thoughtful way to create a system of providing services to people that is not only smarter, but also fairer, open and transparent, and in regard to the needs of all citizens.

REFERENCES

Ainslie, S., Thompson, D., Maynard, S., & Ahmad, A. (2023). Cyber-threat intelligence for security decision-making: A review and research agenda for practice. *Computers & Security*, *132*, 103352. DOI: 10.1016/j.cose.2023.103352

Al-Ansi, A. M., Garad, A., Jaboob, M., & Al-Ansi, A. (2024). Elevating e-government: Unleashing the power of AI and IoT for enhanced public services. *Heliyon*, *10*(23), e40591. DOI: 10.1016/j.heliyon.2024.e40591 PMID: 39654738

Al-Mhiqani, M. N., Alsboui, T., Al-Shehari, T., Abdulkareem, K., Ahmad, R., & Mohammed, M. A. (2024). Insider threat detection in cyber-physical systems: A systematic literature review. *Computers & Electrical Engineering*, *119*, 109489. DOI: 10.1016/j.compeleceng.2024.109489

Alaeifar, P., Pal, S., Jadidi, Z., Hussain, M., & Foo, E. (2024). Current approaches and future directions for Cyber Threat Intelligence sharing: A survey. *Journal of Information Security and Applications*, *83*, 103786. DOI: 10.1016/j.jisa.2024.103786

Almahmoud, Z., Yoo, P. D., Damiani, E., Choo, K. K. R., & Yeun, C. Y. (2025). Forecasting Cyber Threats: Future mitigation technologies. *Technological Forecasting and Social Change*, *210*, 123836. DOI: 10.1016/j.techfore.2024.123836

Angwin, J., Larson, J., Mattu, S., & Kirchner, L. (2016). Machine Bias: Software used to predict future criminals and its racial biases. In *Ethics of Data and Analytics*. Auerbach Publications.

Buçinca, Z., Malaya, M. B., & Gajos, K. Z. (2021). To trust or to think: cognitive forcing functions can reduce overreliance on AI in AI-assisted decision-making. Proceedings of the ACM on Human-computer Interaction, 5(CSCW1), 1-21.

Chen, Y., & Chen, Z. (2024). Can e-government online services offer enhanced governance support? *Journal of Innovation & Knowledge*, *9*(3), 100526. DOI: 10.1016/j.jik.2024.100526

De Sousa, W. G., de Melo, E. R. P., Bermejo, P. H. D. S., Farias, R. A. S., & Gomes, A. O. (2019). How and where is artificial intelligence in the public sector going? A literature review and research agenda. *Government Information Quarterly*, *36*(4), 101392. DOI: 10.1016/j.giq.2019.07.004

Decker, M., Wegner, L., & Leicht-Scholten, C. (2025). Procedural fairness in algorithmic decision-making: The role of public engagement. *Ethics and Information Technology*, *27*(1), 1. DOI: 10.1007/s10676-024-09811-4

Engel, C., Linhardt, L., & Schubert, M. (2025). Code is law: How COMPAS affects the way the judiciary handles the risk of recidivism. *Artificial Intelligence and Law*, *33*(2), 383–404. DOI: 10.1007/s10506-024-09389-8

Equey, C., Priftis, A., Trabichet, J. P., & Hutzli, V. (2024). Designing a digital citizen-centered service. *Technological Forecasting and Social Change*, *202*, 123280. DOI: 10.1016/j.techfore.2024.123280

Floridi, L., Cowls, J., King, T. C., & Taddeo, M. (2020). How to Design AI for Social Good: Seven Essential Factors. *Science and Engineering Ethics*, *26*(3), 1771–1796. DOI: 10.1007/s11948-020-00213-5 PMID: 32246245

Gigerenzer, G. (2022). *How to Stay Smart in a Smart World: Why Human Intelligence Still Beats Algorithms*. MIT Press.

Gigerenzer, G. (2023). Psychological AI: Designing Algorithms Informed by Human Psychology. *Perspectives on Psychological Science*. Advance online publication. DOI: 10.1177/17456916231180597 PMID: 37522323

Gomez, I., & Ilarri, S. (2024). Enriched traffic datasets for smart cities (Madrid): Integrating sensors, infrastructure, and weather data. *Data in Brief*, *57*, 110878. DOI: 10.1016/j.dib.2024.110878 PMID: 39309711

Groumpos, P. P. (2010). Fuzzy Cognitive Maps: Basic Theories and Their Application to Complex Systems. In Glykas, M. (Ed.), *Fuzzy Cognitive Maps. Studies in Fuzziness and Soft Computing* (Vol. 247). Springer., DOI: 10.1007/978-3-642-03220-2_1

Hamid, S., & Huda, M. N. (2025). Mapping the landscape of government data breaches (2006–2023). *Social Sciences & Humanities Open*, *11*, 101234. DOI: 10.1016/j.ssaho.2024.101234

Kazimierczak, M., Habib, N., Chan, J. H., & Thanapattheerakul, T. (2024). Impact of AI on the Cyber Kill Chain: A Systematic Review. *Heliyon*, *10*(24), e40699. DOI: 10.1016/j.heliyon.2024.e40699 PMID: 39720055

McKinney, S. M., Sieniek, M., Godbole, V., Godwin, J., Antropova, N., Ashrafian, H., Back, T., Chesus, M., Corrado, G. S., Darzi, A., Etemadi, M., Garcia-Vicente, F., Gilbert, F. J., Halling-Brown, M., Hassabis, D., Jansen, S., Karthikesalingam, A., Kelly, C. J., King, D., & Shetty, S. (2020). International evaluation of an AI system for breast cancer screening. *Nature*, *577*(7788), 89–94. DOI: 10.1038/s41586-019-1799-6 PMID: 31894144

Nordström, M. (2022). AI under great uncertainty: Implications and decision strategies for public policy. *AI & Society*, *37*(4), 1703–1714. DOI: 10.1007/s00146-021-01263-4 PMID: 34511737

Rodrigues, R. (2020). Legal and human rights issues of AI: Gaps, challenges and vulnerabilities. *Journal of Responsible Technology*, *4*, 100005. DOI: 10.1016/j.jrt.2020.100005

Rosado, D. G., Sánchez, L. E., Varela-Vaca, Á. J., Santos-Olmo, A., Gómez-López, M. T., Gasca, R. M., & Fernández-Medina, E. (2024). Security risk assessment and management for business process models. *Journal of Information Security and Applications*, *84*, 103829. DOI: 10.1016/j.jisa.2024.103829

Rukanova, B., Tan, Y.-H., Slegt, M., Molenhuis, M., van Rijnsoever, B., Migeotte, J., Labare, M. L. M., Plecko, K., Caglayan, B., Shorten, G., van der Meij, O., & Post, S. (2021). Identifying the value of data analytics for government supervision: Insights from customs domain. *Government Information Quarterly*, *38*(1), 101496. DOI: 10.1016/j.giq.2020.101496

Sun, T. Q., & Medaglia, R. (2019). Mapping the challenges of Artificial Intelligence in the public sector: Evidence from public healthcare. *Government Information Quarterly*, *36*(2), 368–383. DOI: 10.1016/j.giq.2018.09.008

van Bekkum, M., & Borgesius, F. Z. (2021). Digital welfare fraud detection and the Dutch SyRI judgment. *European Journal of Social Security*, *23*(4), 323–340. DOI: 10.1177/13882627211031257

Van Noordt, C., & Tangi, L. (2023). The dynamics of AI capability and its influence on public value creation in public administration. *Government Information Quarterly*, *40*(4), 101860. DOI: 10.1016/j.giq.2023.101860

Wang, Y., Huang, X., Zhang, T., Jiang, B., & Wang, X. (2024). Impact of fiscal decentralization and local government competition on the supply of basic public services. *Heliyon*, *10*(4), e26511. DOI: 10.1016/j.heliyon.2024.e26511 PMID: 38420436

Wirtz, B. W., Weyerer, J. C., & Geyer, C. (2019). Artificial Intelligence and the Public Sector—Applications and Challenges. *International Journal of Public Administration*, *42*(7), 596–615. DOI: 10.1080/01900692.2018.1498103

Züger, T., & Asghari, H. (2023). AI for the public. How public interest theory shifts the discourse on AI. *AI & Society*, *38*(2), 815–828. DOI: 10.1007/s00146-022-01480-5

Chapter 7
AI Algorithms and Augmented Reality Integration With Public Services

Angga Muhammad Galih
https://orcid.org/0009-0009-2998-9514
Universitas Esa Unggul, Indonesia

Muhammad Adi Zacky Zahran
https://orcid.org/0009-0000-8736-5376
Universitas Esa Unggul, Indonesia

Binastya Anggara Sekti
https://orcid.org/0000-0001-5489-4888
Universitas Esa Ungggul, Indonesia

Gusti Muhammad Sardana
https://orcid.org/0009-0001-4281-2432
Universitas Esa Unggul, Indonesia

Bartholomeus Dimanche Carl Beth
https://orcid.org/0009-0006-1088-9212
Universitas Esa Ungggul, Indonesia

Ryan Putra Laksana
Universitas Esa Unggul, Indonesia

ABSTRACT

This chapter examines the integration of Artificial Intelligence (AI) and Augmented Reality (AR) in public service delivery, highlighting their combined potential to improve efficiency, decision-making, and citizen engagement. AI provides analytical intelligence for automation, prediction, and data processing, while AR enhances visualization and real-time interaction within physical environments. The chapter explores applications across healthcare, administration, urban planning, and emergency response, as well as challenges related to ethics, infrastructure, and governance. It concludes that AI–AR synergy offers a transformative pathway toward smarter, more responsive, and citizen-centered public services.

DOI: 10.4018/979-8-3373-7804-6.ch007

1. INTRODUCTION

The rapid advancement of digital technologies over the last twenty years has transformed nearly every aspect of public-sector operations, and government services are no exception. Two of the most significant innovations driving this shift are Artificial Intelligence (AI) and Augmented Reality (AR). Their growing integration is beginning to alter the way governments conceptualize, implement, and assess public service delivery. AI brings powerful tools for processing vast amounts of data, generating predictions, and automating decisions, while AR adds immersive, context-sensitive visual layers that help users engage with complex information more intuitively. Together, these technologies create opportunities not only to streamline daily operations but also to rethink public-sector structures more broadly, paving the way for services that are more transparent, inclusive, efficient, and centered on citizen needs.

Historically, the delivery of public services has faced a series of persistent and widely recognized obstacles, including cumbersome bureaucratic processes, resource constraints, fragmented institutional structures, and unequal access across various regions and demographic groups. Newman, Mintrom, and O'Neill (2022) note that bureaucratic systems have frequently been viewed as "inflexible, wasteful in their pursuit of budget maximization, and overly dependent on rigid rules and procedures," all of which undermine their ability to act efficiently and respond effectively to public needs (Newman et al., 2022).

Traditional public service systems often oblige citizens to go through lengthy and complex procedures, visit several government offices, and complete paper-based forms that can easily lead to delays or mistakes. At the same time, public institutions must frequently operate with tight budgets, limiting their ability to modernize or sustain large workforces capable of meeting rising service demands. Within these constraints, emerging technologies such as AI and AR offer valuable opportunities to rethink how public services are structured and delivered. They can help reduce administrative burdens, simplify decision-making processes, enable real-time access to information, and support the creation of more interactive and user-centered service experiences.

Although digital government initiatives have advanced in recent years, a number of contemporary challenges continue to hinder effective service provision. One major issue is the increasing complexity of society's needs. As communities become more diverse and interconnected, citizens expect services that are inclusive, flexible, and accessible at any time. Yet many digital platforms still operate in rigid and static ways, offering limited real-time assistance or customization. Governments also face the challenge of managing overwhelming volumes of data generated across sectors such as healthcare, education, transportation, emergency management, and public administration. Without sophisticated analytical tools, much of this information remains unused.

The rapid expansion of digital communication channels has further raised expectations for transparency, accountability, and speedy responses. People now expect personalized and immediate support similar to what private digital platforms offer. This shift places additional strain on public organizations, particularly those with limited technological capacity or outdated infrastructure. Moreover, persistent digital inequality continues to restrict equitable access to public services. Differences in digital literacy and technology access mean that not all individuals can fully benefit from online government services. These ongoing challenges reinforce the importance of more advanced, adaptive, and immersive tools areas where AI and AR offer significant potential to drive meaningful transformation. As noted by Latupeirissa et al. (2024), even well-designed digitalization efforts often struggle due to unequal access, limited infrastructure, and inconsistent service coverage among different social groups (Latupeirissa et al., 2024).

The incorporation of AI and AR into public service delivery provides a strong foundation for overcoming many existing challenges. AI offers the ability to conduct advanced data analysis, automate routine administrative tasks, improve predictive accuracy, and supply decision-makers with insights grounded in empirical data. When these capabilities are paired with AR, the resulting information can be displayed in immersive and intuitive formats, allowing both government employees and the public to interpret complex data within real-world contexts. For instance, AR tools driven by AI could guide citizens step-by-step through administrative procedures using visual overlays, enabling them to understand forms, find service locations, or monitor application progress in real time. In healthcare settings, AR-supported telemedicine enhanced by AI diagnostic tools can present clinicians with patient information directly within their field of view, improving diagnostic precision and consultation efficiency. In urban planning and transportation management, AI-generated insights can support decision-making, while AR can project proposed infrastructure or policy changes onto actual physical spaces, helping residents and stakeholders visualize potential outcomes before any action is taken. Emergency response operations can also benefit, as AR headsets equipped with AI-enabled situational awareness may assist responders in navigating dangerous areas, identifying individuals in need, and accessing critical information in real time.

These illustrations reveal how combining AI and AR can shift public service delivery away from slow, manual, and reactive processes toward systems that are more intelligent, proactive, and highly interactive. Rakšnys et al. (2024) similarly emphasize that AI significantly enhances the efficiency, analytical capability, and decision-making processes within public sector institutions (Rakšnys, 2025).

The growing relevance of AI–AR integration becomes even clearer when considered alongside global trends toward smart governance and digital public administration. Many countries are now channeling significant investment into smart city programs aimed at improving resource efficiency, environmental monitoring, transportation systems, and public safety. While AI is central to these initiatives, its effectiveness ultimately depends on how easily human decision-makers can interpret the insights it produces. AR fills this gap by merging digital information with the physical world, enabling public officials to view complex data within the context where it is most meaningful. AR also helps connect digital services with physical interactions, making public interfaces more inclusive for individuals who may find conventional systems difficult to navigate.

When combined, AI and AR can also strengthen government transparency by translating dense information into visual forms that are easier for the public to understand. For instance, AR dashboards can show how budgets are distributed or how policy choices influence infrastructure and community well-being. These innovations have the potential to rebuild and strengthen public trust, encouraging greater civic participation and engagement.

Integrating these technologies is equally important for improving internal government operations. Many tasks performed by public institutions demand high accuracy, fast processing, or coordination on a scale that exceeds human capacity. AI can sift through and interpret massive datasets far more efficiently than human analysts, while AR can create immersive training environments that allow personnel to develop critical skills without being exposed to real-world hazards. For example, civil servants can train for natural disaster response using AR simulations enhanced with AI-generated scenarios that resemble actual conditions similar to the EasyVizAR system designed for first responders, which overlays crucial situational data to support rescue activities (Ponto et al., 2025).

Given the wide-ranging potential of these technologies, this chapter sets out to examine the key foundations, challenges, and relevance of integrating AI and AR in public service contexts. It provides a conceptual entry point for understanding how these tools can reshape not only day-to-day administrative operations but also the broader dynamics between governments and the communities they serve. The chapter seeks to offer a comprehensive introduction to the historical, technological, and societal factors that drive interest in AI and AR, while outlining the transformative possibilities they bring to public service delivery models.

It also defines the scope for the chapters that follow, establishing the theoretical importance and practical value of the subject. Throughout, the chapter underscores the importance of interdisciplinary collaboration, ethical oversight, and deliberate strategic planning to ensure that technological progress remains aligned with public priorities and societal expectations. As governments work to upgrade their service systems amid rising demands and increasing complexity, the convergence of AI and AR emerges as a promising direction for developing more transparent, responsive, and citizen-focused public services. Consequently, this chapter lays the groundwork for examining how these technologies can be deployed effectively, what advantages they may offer, and what considerations policymakers must keep in mind as digital transformation continues to evolve.

2. FUNDAMENTAL CONCEPTS

2.1 Definition and Characteristics of Artificial Intelligence

Artificial Intelligence (AI) is one of the most influential technological developments of the twenty-first century, enabling machines to perform tasks that traditionally required human cognitive abilities, such as learning, pattern recognition, language understanding, and decision-making. Conceptually, AI draws on computational methods that support reasoning, perception, and adaptive behavior. The intellectual foundations of AI date back to the mid-twentieth century, particularly Alan Turing's seminal work *Computing Machinery and Intelligence*, which introduced the Turing Test as a criterion for machine intelligence (Turing, 1950). This work continues to shape contemporary AI research and theory (J. J. Chen, 2025).

Modern AI systems differ from traditional software through their ability to learn from data, generalize knowledge to new contexts, and operate autonomously. Current AI development is largely driven by data-centric paradigms such as machine learning, deep learning, and reinforcement learning, rather than fixed rule-based programming (Mishra, 2024). While contemporary AI systems demonstrate scalability, robustness, and transferability, they remain limited to narrow task domains, require extensive data and computational resources, and face challenges related to bias, interpretability, and contextual understanding.

2.2 Relevant AI Algorithms: Machine Learning, NLP, Computer Vision

Artificial Intelligence (AI) operates through advanced computational algorithms that enable machines to analyze data, recognize patterns, and generate meaningful insights. Among its key domains, Machine Learning (ML), Natural Language Processing (NLP), and Computer Vision (CV) play central roles in analyzing qualitative, social, and contextual data. ML forms the foundation of modern AI by allowing systems to learn from data through supervised, unsupervised, and semi-supervised approaches, making it particularly valuable in research contexts where labeled data are limited. Its versatility supports applications across public policy, health, engineering, and social sciences, and enables multidimensional analysis when combined with NLP and CV (Huebner et al., 2021).

NLP focuses on enabling machines to process human language, addressing challenges such as ambiguity and context dependency. Advances in transformer architectures have led to Large Language Models like GPT and BERT, which support tasks such as text classification, summarization, and qualitative data analysis (Khetarpal et al., 2022). CV enables interpretation of visual data through techniques such as feature extraction, object detection, and image segmentation, with Convolutional Neural Networks forming the backbone of contemporary visual analysis.

2.3 Supporting Platforms, and Components of Augmented Reality

While Large Language Models are the primary AI technologies transforming qualitative research, while Augmented Reality (AR) offers emerging possibilities for innovative, though still exploratory, methodological approaches. Cloud-based AI platforms such as Google Cloud AI, AWS, Azure Cognitive Services, and IBM Watson enable accessible implementation of NLP functions for qualitative data preparation and preliminary analysis. In contrast, open-source frameworks like TensorFlow, PyTorch, Hugging Face, and spaCy provide greater customization through fine-tuning and specialized model development, albeit requiring higher technical expertise. AR technologies, including spatial computing and multimodal sensing, support novel data collection methods such as spatially tagged ethnographic observations and participatory annotation. Integrating AI with AR may enable real-time contextual analysis during fieldwork, though its methodological value requires critical evaluation.

3. AI–AR INTEGRATION FRAMEWORK

3.1 Conceptual Framework for AI–AR Integration

The The integration of Artificial Intelligence (AI) and Augmented Reality (AR) can be understood through a conceptual framework that positions AI as the cognitive engine and AR as the immersive visual interface. In this framework, AI performs analytical functions such as data processing, pattern recognition, prediction, and decision support, while AR communicates these insights by overlaying contextual information onto the physical environment. The framework is grounded in three core principles: context-awareness, real-time responsiveness, and user-centered interaction. Context-awareness enables precise spatial alignment of AI-generated content through sensors and spatial mapping technologies, while real-time responsiveness ensures low-latency visualization for timely decision-making. User-centered interaction emphasizes intuitive engagement via gestures, voice, and spatial navigation, enhancing usability and situational awareness (Stefanidi et al., 2022).

A central concept is the synergy between perception and cognition: AR enhances perception through visual cues, whereas AI enhances cognition by interpreting and augmenting their meaning. This synergy supports data-driven yet intuitive decision-making, as demonstrated in healthcare applications where AR visualizes patient data while AI analyzes trends and anomalies (Oun et al., 2024). The framework further highlights integrated sensor, processing, algorithmic, and visualization layers operating in continuous feedback loops to enable responsive and citizen-centered public services.

3.2 Interaction Mechanism Between AI Algorithms and AR Interfaces

The interaction mechanism between AI algorithms and AR interfaces explains how both technologies communicate and reinforce one another to create a seamless and responsive user experience. This mechanism follows a multi-stage workflow that begins with environmental perception and ends with visualization and interaction. Initially, real-world data are captured through sensors, cameras, LiDAR, GPS, microphones, and other input devices, then processed by AI models to perform tasks such as object recognition, speech interpretation, predictive analytics, and natural language understanding.

After AI systems generate insights, these outputs are transformed into spatial information that can be visualized accurately within augmented reality environments. Advanced spatial computing techniques such as simultaneous localization and mapping (SLAM), depth sensing, and scene interpretation ensure precise alignment between digital overlays and physical objects. This accuracy is essential for public-sector applications like infrastructure inspection, where LiDAR-enhanced SLAM and multimodal sensor-fusion techniques enable reliable mapping and trajectory estimation (Zhang et al., 2025).

he interaction mechanism further relies on multimodal communication, presenting AI outputs through visual, auditory, or haptic cues while allowing user interaction via voice, gestures, gaze, or movement. This creates a dynamic feedback loop in which AI continuously adapts to user behavior and environmental changes. Real-time synchronization is critical in time-sensitive public services such as emergency response and infrastructure assessment. Low-latency performance is achieved through optimized computation, edge computing, and high-speed networks like

5G, as demonstrated in emerging real-time AR frameworks for structural evaluation (Awadallah et al., 2024). Adaptive personalization further enhances inclusivity by tailoring AR guidance to users' skills and needs.

Lastly, the interaction mechanism incorporates adaptive personalization. AI learns from user behavior, preferences, and past interactions to tailor AR experiences. For instance, in a public administration setting, a citizen service kiosk equipped with AI–AR can adjust the level of guidance based on a person's digital literacy. Experts may receive concise overlays with advanced options, while novices may access step-by-step AR tutorials. This adaptive mechanism ensures inclusivity and improves user satisfaction, making AI–AR systems more effective across diverse public populations.

3.3 System Architecture for Integrated Solutions

A well-structured system architecture is essential for seamless integration of Artificial Intelligence (AI) and Augmented Reality (AR) in public-sector applications. Typical AI–AR architectures consist of interconnected layers, including sensing and input, data management, AI processing, AR rendering, user interface, and communication networks. The sensing and data management layers collect, organize, and secure large volumes of heterogeneous data from sources such as cameras, IoT devices, and environmental sensors, ensuring scalability, privacy, and regulatory compliance.

The AI processing layer executes machine learning, computer vision, and predictive analytics, operating at the edge or in cloud environments depending on latency and computational requirements. Outputs are transformed by the AR rendering layer into spatially aligned visual elements, relying on accurate mapping and real-time scene understanding, as demonstrated in recent evaluations of mixed-reality platforms (Do et al., 2024). The user interface layer enables intuitive interaction while minimizing cognitive load, with empirical studies highlighting the benefits of ergonomically optimized AR interfaces for prolonged professional use (Wu et al., 2023). Finally, high-speed communication networks underpin real-time synchronization, ensuring reliable performance in time-critical public service operations.

3.4 Data Security, Interoperability, and Privacy Considerations

The integration of Artificial Intelligence (AI) and Augmented Reality (AR) in public service environments raises critical challenges related to data security, privacy protection, and system interoperability. Because AI–AR systems often process sensitive information such as personal identifiers, health data, geolocation records, and behavioral patterns, robust security mechanisms are essential to maintain public trust and ensure legal compliance. Effective protection requires end-to-end encryption, secure authentication, key management, and continuous monitoring to mitigate cyber threats targeting government systems.

Privacy protection is equally crucial and demands compliance with national and international data governance regulations, particularly concerning biometric data, facial recognition, and location tracking. Transparent communication, informed consent, and privacy-enhancing technologies such as anonymization, differential privacy, and federated learning can significantly reduce privacy risks.

Interoperability further determines the effectiveness of AI–AR adoption, as public institutions often rely on heterogeneous digital infrastructures. Standardized data formats, shared APIs, and common communication protocols are necessary to enable cross-agency collaboration. Ethical governance frameworks must also address algorithmic bias, accountability, and equitable access, especially in sensitive sectors such as healthcare and law enforcement.

4. APPLICATIONS IN PUBLIC SERVICES

The integration of Large Language Models and artificial intelligence technologies into public service delivery represents a significant paradigm shift in how governments and public institutions interact with citizens, manage resources, and fulfill their administrative responsibilities. Public services, traditionally characterized by bureaucratic processes, paper-based documentation, and human-intensive workflows, are undergoing digital transformation through AI adoption. This chapter examines how LLMs and related AI technologies are being deployed across critical public service domains, exploring both the benefits realized and challenges encountered. Understanding these applications provides valuable context for researchers studying public administration, policy implementation, and the broader societal implications of AI integration into governmental functions (Latupeirissa et al., 2024; Newman et al., 2022)

4.1 Public Government Healthcare (AR + Telemedicine + AI)

The healthcare sector represents one of the most consequential domains for AI application in public services, where technological innovation directly impacts citizen wellbeing, healthcare accessibility, and clinical outcomes. The convergence of Augmented Reality, telemedicine platforms, and AI-powered analytics is fundamentally reshaping public healthcare delivery, particularly in contexts where geographic distance, resource limitations, or public health emergencies create barriers to traditional in-person medical care (Wosny & Hastings, 2024).

AI-Enhanced Telemedicine has emerged as a critical component of modern public healthcare systems, accelerating dramatically during the COVID-19 pandemic when social distancing requirements necessitated remote medical consultations. LLM-powered systems now support telemedicine in multiple ways. Intelligent triage systems analyze patient-reported symptoms through conversational interfaces, asking clarifying questions and providing preliminary assessments that help direct patients to appropriate care levels emergency services, urgent care, primary care appointments, or self-care guidance. These AI triage systems process natural language descriptions of symptoms, cross-reference medical databases, and apply clinical decision rules to generate recommendations, significantly reducing the burden on human healthcare providers while improving access for patients in remote or underserved areas (Bennis & Mouwafaq, 2025).

During virtual consultations, AI systems provide real-time clinical decision support to healthcare providers, analyzing patient histories, current symptoms, and relevant medical literature to suggest differential diagnoses, recommend diagnostic tests, or flag potential drug interactions. LLMs trained on vast medical corpora can rapidly synthesize information from electronic health records, research publications, and clinical guidelines, presenting concise, contextually-relevant information that enhances provider decision-making without requiring extensive manual literature review. Post-consultation, AI systems automatically generate clinical documentation from conversation transcripts, extract key medical concepts, populate structured data fields in electronic health records, and draft patient instructions reducing administrative burden and allowing providers to focus on patient interaction rather than documentation (Hitch, 2024).

Augmented Reality in Public Healthcare introduces innovative capabilities particularly valuable for medical education, surgical planning, and remote expert consultation. AR-enabled telemedicine allows specialists at major medical centers to virtually "see" what rural or remote healthcare providers observe, overlaying diagnostic guidance, anatomical references, or procedural instructions onto the provider's field of view during examinations or procedures. For complex surgeries, AR systems project pre-operative imaging (CT scans, MRIs) onto patients' bodies, helping surgeons visualize internal anatomy and plan optimal approaches. In medical training contexts, AR simulations enable healthcare students to practice procedures, learn anatomy through interactive 3D models, and develop clinical skills in safe, controlled environments before treating actual patients.

Predictive Analytics and Population Health Management represent another crucial AI application in public healthcare. Machine learning algorithms analyze aggregated health data from electronic medical records, public health surveillance systems, and social determinants of health to identify disease outbreak risks, predict healthcare demand, and target preventive interventions toward high-risk populations. During the COVID-19 pandemic, AI models processed data on case counts, mobility patterns, vaccination rates, and demographic factors to forecast infection trends, hospital capacity needs, and optimal resource allocation strategies supporting public health decision-making under conditions of extreme uncertainty.

However, deploying AI in public healthcare raises significant ethical considerations and practical challenges. Algorithm bias where AI systems perform less accurately for demographic groups underrepresented in training data can exacerbate existing healthcare disparities. Data privacy concerns arise when sensitive medical information is processed by AI systems, particularly cloud-based commercial platforms. The "black box" nature of complex AI models creates challenges for clinical accountability when algorithms influence diagnostic or treatment decisions. Ensuring equitable access to AI-enhanced healthcare services, maintaining appropriate human oversight of algorithmic recommendations, and establishing clear liability frameworks when AI-supported decisions lead to adverse outcomes remain ongoing policy challenges requiring careful governance.

4.2 Administrative Public Services (AI + Services Diagnostics)

Administrative public services including licensing, permits, social benefits, taxation, and regulatory compliance historically involved time-consuming paperwork, long processing times, and frustrating citizen experiences navigating complex bureaucratic requirements. AI technologies are transforming these services through automation, intelligent document processing, predictive analytics, and conversational interfaces that make government more responsive, efficient, and accessible.

Intelligent Virtual Assistants and Chatbots powered by LLMs now serve as front-line interfaces for citizen interactions with government services. These conversational AI systems handle routine inquiries about service eligibility, required documentation, application procedures, and case status, operating 24/7 without the constraints of traditional office hours. Citizens can ask questions in natural language rather than navigating complex website hierarchies or waiting in phone queues. Advanced systems maintain conversation context, ask clarifying questions, and guide users through multi-step processes, significantly improving user experience particularly for citizens with limited digital literacy or language barriers. Multilingual LLMs enable government services to communicate effectively with diverse linguistic communities without requiring human translators for routine interactions (Newman et al., 2022).

Automated Document Processing represents a major AI application streamlining administrative workflows. Government agencies process enormous volumes of documents tax returns, benefit applications, business licenses, building permits, immigration forms traditionally requiring extensive manual review by civil servants. AI systems now automatically extract information from submitted documents, verify completeness, cross-reference claims against databases, identify inconsistencies requiring human review, and route applications through appropriate approval workflows. NLP algorithms interpret unstructured text in supporting documents, extracting relevant information and flagging potential issues. OCR combined with LLMs processes handwritten forms, scanned documents, and images, converting them into structured data for downstream processing (Hitch, 2024).

Predictive Service Diagnostics uses machine learning to anticipate citizen needs, identify service delivery problems, and optimize resource allocation. By analyzing historical patterns of service requests, demographic data, seasonal trends, and external factors, predictive models forecast future demand for specific services. For example, tax authorities use ML models to predict which returns likely contain errors or require additional documentation. Social service agencies predict which benefit recipients face elevated risks of homelessness or other crises, enabling targeted preventive interventions (Latupeirissa et al., 2024).

Fraud Detection and Compliance Monitoring represent critical AI applications protecting public resources. Machine learning algorithms analyze patterns in benefit claims, tax filings, procurement contracts, and regulatory submissions to identify anomalies indicating potential fraud, waste, or abuse. Unlike rule-based systems, ML models detect subtle correlations and unusual combinations of factors suggesting previously unidentified fraud schemes. These systems process vast transaction volumes impossible for human auditors to review comprehensively, focusing investigative resources on highest-risk cases while allowing legitimate claims to proceed efficiently (Bennis & Mouwafaq, 2025).

Challenges in Administrative AI Deployment include ensuring algorithmic fairness and avoiding discriminatory impacts. If training data reflects historical biases for example, disproportionate enforcement scrutiny toward certain demographic groups AI systems may perpetuate or amplify these disparities. Lack of transparency in automated decision-making raises due process concerns: citizens affected by algorithmic decisions deserve explanations and opportunities for appeal. Technical challenges include integrating AI systems with legacy government IT infrastructure, maintaining data quality across fragmented databases, and ensuring cybersecurity for sensitive citizen information. Organizational challenges involve retraining civil servants for new roles emphasizing judgment, exceptions handling, and human oversight rather than routine processing.

4.3 Public Emergency Transportation and Disaster Response (Smart AI)

Emergency response and disaster management constitute high-stakes environments in which artificial intelligence supports rapid decision-making, situational awareness, and coordinated action to reduce casualties and losses. In intelligent transportation systems, AI-enabled computer vision and predictive models detect incidents, manage congestion, and optimize emergency vehicle routing, including dynamic traffic signal control to create priority corridors during crises (Weber et al., 2023). Emergency service dispatch increasingly relies on machine learning and natural language processing to prioritize calls, extract critical information in real time, and recommend appropriate resource deployment based on historical patterns and incident characteristics (Kim et al., 2020).

AI also enhances disaster prediction and early warning systems by integrating meteorological, geospatial, and social media data to improve forecasting accuracy and identify emerging threats before formal reports are issued (Motra et al., 2021). Post-disaster damage assessment benefits from computer vision applied to satellite and aerial imagery, enabling rapid mapping of affected areas. Despite these advantages, effective AI deployment requires robust infrastructure, human oversight, and ethical safeguards to ensure accountability, reliability, and equitable emergency response outcomes (Motra et al., 2021).

4.4 Disaster Management Mobility

Disaster mobility management encompasses the complex challenge of moving people, equipment, and supplies efficiently during emergency situations evacuations, mass casualty transport, relief supply distribution, and displaced population relocation. AI technologies address the dynamic, large-scale optimization problems inherent in disaster mobility, where conditions change rapidly, information is incomplete, and decisions carry profound humanitarian consequences.

Evacuation Planning and Management represents perhaps the most critical disaster mobility challenge. AI systems analyze multiple factors population distribution, road network capacity, expected disaster timing and impacts, available transportation resources, shelter capacity to generate optimized evacuation plans. Agent-based models simulate how populations will respond to evacuation orders under different scenarios, accounting for behavioral factors like compliance rates, departure timing, destination choices, and route selection. These simulations identify potential bottlenecks, estimate clearance times, and suggest interventions (contraflow lane reversal, staged evacuations, targeted public messaging) to improve outcomes.

Real-time evacuation monitoring uses mobile device location data, traffic sensors, and social media analysis to track actual population movement during evacuations, comparing observed patterns against predictions. When bottlenecks emerge or compliance proves lower than expected, AI systems rapidly recalculate optimal strategies and recommend adjustments. Natural language generation creates updated public guidance reflecting current conditions: "Highway 10 is experiencing severe congestion; if you haven't left yet, consider alternative route via Highway 23" or "Shelter capacity at Location A is full; proceed to Location B instead."

Relief Supply Chain Optimization employs machine learning to predict needs for food, water, medical supplies, temporary shelter materials, and other critical resources across affected areas. AI systems synthesize damage assessments, population estimates, infrastructure status, and historical disaster patterns to forecast demand. Optimization algorithms then determine optimal supply pre-positioning before disasters, distribution center locations, transportation routing through damaged infrastructure networks, and allocation across multiple affected communities balancing urgency, equity, and logistical efficiency. These systems continuously update as new information becomes available and situations evolve.

Medical Evacuation and Patient Transportation during mass casualty incidents requires rapid triage and optimal patient-destination matching. AI decision support systems analyze patient conditions, available transportation assets (ambulances, helicopters, medical transport aircraft), receiving hospital capacities and capabilities, and transport times under current conditions. The system generates recommended patient assignments maximizing survival probability while considering capacity constraints, specialized care requirements, and transportation resource availability. Unlike pre-planned protocols, AI systems adapt dynamically as situations evolve hospitals reach capacity, additional patients are discovered, or transportation routes become impassable.

Displaced Population Management involves coordinating movements of potentially millions of people displaced by large-scale disasters. AI platforms integrate data on displaced populations (locations, numbers, demographics, special needs), available shelter facilities, transportation resources, and ongoing relief operations. Optimization algorithms match displaced persons to appropriate shelters considering factors like family reunification, cultural/linguistic compatibility, medical needs, and transportation accessibility. These systems help prevent secondary humanitarian crises where displaced populations overwhelm receiving communities or individuals cannot locate family members across multiple shelter locations.

Infrastructure Restoration Prioritization determines which roads, bridges, airports, and ports should be repaired first to maximize emergency response effectiveness and recovery progress. AI systems model the network effects of different restoration sequences how repairing particular road segments enables access to larger populations, facilitates specific relief operations, or supports economic recovery. These optimization problems involve complex interdependencies where infrastructure repairs enable other repairs, creating cascading benefits but also requiring careful sequencing.

Ethical challenges in disaster mobility AI include ensuring equitable treatment across all affected populations regardless of socioeconomic status, race, disability, or other protected characteristics. Algorithmic optimization based purely on efficiency metrics might systematically disadvantage vulnerable groups who are harder to reach or have less visibility in data systems. Balancing utilitarian optimization (maximizing overall welfare) against principles of fairness and human dignity requires careful algorithm design incorporating equity constraints and human oversight of automated recommendations.

4.5 Public Education and Civil Service Training

The application of AI technologies in public education and civil service training represents investment in human capital development preparing citizens with knowledge and skills for productive participation in society and economy while ensuring government employees possess competencies for effective public service delivery. LLMs and related AI systems are transforming educational content delivery, personalized learning, assessment, and professional development across public sector contexts.

Personalized Learning Systems powered by AI adapt educational content, pacing, and instructional approaches to individual learner characteristics, needs, and progress. Machine learning algorithms analyze student performance patterns, identifying knowledge gaps, predicting which concepts students will find challenging, and recommending targeted interventions. LLM-based tutoring systems provide individualized explanations, generate practice problems at appropriate difficulty levels, answer student questions in natural language, and offer encouragement and motivational feedback. For public education systems serving diverse student populations with varying backgrounds, learning styles, and support needs, AI personalization helps ensure all students receive instruction suited to their individual circumstances rather than one-size-fits-all approaches that serve some students well while leaving others behind.

Automated Assessment and Feedback extends beyond multiple-choice testing to evaluate complex written work, project-based assignments, and demonstrated competencies. NLP algorithms assess student essays, providing feedback on argumentation quality, evidence usage, writing mechanics, and conceptual understanding. While human teachers remain essential for high-stakes evaluation and nuanced judgment, AI systems provide rapid formative feedback on practice assignments, enabling students to iterate and improve before final submission. For civil service training contexts, AI systems evaluate scenario-based responses, case study analyses, and simulated decision-making exercises, identifying areas where employees demonstrate proficiency versus requiring additional development.

Intelligent Content Creation and Curriculum Development employs LLMs to generate educational materials, adapt content for different reading levels, translate materials for multilingual populations, and create diverse examples illustrating concepts across varied cultural contexts. AI systems analyze curriculum standards, learning objectives, and student performance data to identify content gaps, suggest instructional sequences, and recommend resources addressing specific learning challenges. For rapidly evolving fields like cybersecurity, data analytics, or emerging policy areas, AI-assisted curriculum development helps educational programs remain current with accelerating knowledge change.

Administrative Efficiency in Educational Institutions benefits from AI automation of routine tasks scheduling classes, managing enrollments, processing student records, responding to common inquiries, and generating reports freeing educators and administrators for higher-value activities directly supporting student learning and development. Predictive analytics identify students at risk of academic difficulty, disengagement, or dropout, enabling proactive interventions. Resource optimization models improve facility utilization, course offerings, and staffing allocation based on enrollment patterns and student needs.

Professional Development for Civil Servants increasingly incorporates AI-enhanced learning platforms providing on-demand training, microlearning modules, and continuous skill development aligned with evolving public service requirements. LLM-powered systems serve as knowledge repositories where employees access policy guidance, procedural documentation, and best practices through conversational interfaces rather than searching complex document libraries. Simulation-based training uses AI to create realistic scenarios where civil servants practice handling difficult citizen interactions, emergency responses, or complex regulatory decisions in safe environments where mistakes become learning opportunities rather than real-world consequences.

Equity and Access Considerations remain paramount in educational AI deployment. Systems must work effectively for students with disabilities, English language learners, students from low-income families potentially lacking internet access or devices, and rural students where technology infrastructure may be limited. Algorithmic bias that systematically underestimates capabilities of particular demographic groups or reinforces educational inequities represents a serious concern requiring ongoing monitoring and mitigation. Privacy protections for student data, transparency about AI use in educational settings, and maintaining appropriate human relationships between teachers and students despite increasing AI mediation require careful policy frameworks and implementation practices that prioritize student welfare above technological efficiency or cost reduction.

5. CASE STUDIES

5.1 Cities and Countries Successfully Implementing AI–AR Solutions

The global adoption of AI–AR technologies in public service delivery has accelerated significantly, with numerous countries and major cities demonstrating meaningful progress across domains such as administration, healthcare, transportation, public safety, and urban development. These early adopters serve as important reference points for understanding how AI–AR integration can reshape government operations and improve citizen services at scale.

Several leading smart cities provide noteworthy examples. Singapore, through its Smart Nation initiative, has combined AI-driven analytics with AR visualization to enhance functions such as building inspection, urban mobility planning, and real-time crowd management. Likewise, Seoul has embedded AI–AR capabilities into its digital governance model, utilizing AR-enhanced dashboards for environmental and traffic monitoring, immersive tools for cultural engagement, and emergency response systems that overlay evacuation and hazard information supported by predictive AI models. Dubai has also made significant investments in AI–AR technologies, deploying AR-based training for public-sector personnel, AR-supported infrastructure visualization, and AI-driven maintenance forecasting across its transportation and utilities sectors.

Across Europe and Asia, similar advancements can be observed. Helsinki integrates AI-powered environmental modeling with AR overlays to support sustainable planning and encourage citizen participation in climate-related decision-making. Meanwhile, Tokyo employs AI–AR systems for disaster preparedness, allowing residents and officials to visualize evacuation routes, hazard maps, and real-time transit guidance. These varied initiatives demonstrate that although implementation strategies differ according to local priorities, the impact of AI–AR technologies is consistently substantial, offering improved efficiency, safety, and accessibility in public service ecosystems.

5.2 AI–AR Use in Smart Government Projects

Smart government projects represent some of the most forward-thinking applications of AI–AR integration, blending immersive analytics with automated intelligence to create service ecosystems that are more responsive and citizen-centric. Across various domains, AI and AR have been strategically deployed to enhance decision-making, improve operational efficiency, and elevate the overall user experience .

In the domain of urban planning, AI–AR systems allow planners and policy-makers to simulate infrastructure projects directly within the physical environment. By overlaying 3D building models, zoning boundaries, and environmental impact predictions onto real-world landscapes, AR interfaces help visualize AI-generated forecasts concerning traffic congestion, population density, energy consumption, and environmental risks. This immersive approach supports participatory planning, enabling citizens to view proposed developments more clearly and participate in more informed consultations. Research in smart urban analytics confirms that AR-based visualization integrated with AI-driven prediction models enhances accuracy, public understanding, and stakeholder decision-making (Suleymanoglu et al., 2024).

Within public transportation, smart government projects have introduced AI-powered predictive analytics integrated with AR navigation tools. AI models analyze real-time data from sensors, vehicles, and commuter patterns, predicting congestion or delays. AR displays then guide passengers through stations, show optimal routes, or project real-time arrival information. Some governments have also used AR for driver assistance, where AI analyzes surroundings to provide hazard warnings, speed recommendations, and lane guidance.

In healthcare, governments have adopted AI–AR systems for remote diagnostics, medical training, and public health management. AR devices enhanced with AI-vision algorithms allow surgeons or paramedics to access patient data, anatomy overlays, or real-time diagnostic insights during emergency procedures. Training simulations with AI-driven scenarios enable medical personnel to practice complex procedures within immersive, risk-free environments. Public health agencies also use AI-powered analytics visualized through AR dashboards to track disease spread, allocate resources, or model intervention outcomes (Oun et al., 2024).

Public safety and emergency response are among the areas where AI–AR integration has shown remarkable impact. AI-powered risk detection systems analyze surveillance data, environmental sensors, or social media feeds to detect anomalies such as fires, accidents, or crowd surges. AR headsets worn by emergency responders then project hazard maps, object labels, victim locations, or safe evacuation routes directly into their field of view. Real-time integration allows responders to make faster, better-informed decisions even in chaotic or low-visibility conditions (Ponto et al., 2025).

In the field of public administration, AI–AR solutions help streamline citizen services through interactive AR kiosks or mobile applications. These tools allow citizens to complete bureaucratic tasks such as submitting forms, renewing permits, or paying taxes using AR-based guidance. AI algorithms provide natural language support, personalized recommendations, and automated documentation processing. Some governments have used AR to visualize complex legal or administrative information, supported by AI models that interpret policies or identify relevant regulations.

Finally, smart government initiatives have expanded into education and workforce development, where AR-enhanced training modules supported by AI performance analytics help civil servants acquire new skills. Whether for maintenance crews learning to repair infrastructure through AR overlays, or customer service agents training in AI-driven simulations, governments are using these tools to modernize workforce capabilities. These smart government projects demonstrate that AI–AR integration is not merely a technological enhancement but a fundamental shift in how governments design, deliver, and evaluate public services.

5.3 Analysis of Success Factors and Implementation Challenges

The effective implementation of AI–AR technologies in public services requires an integrated alignment of strategic vision, institutional readiness, and public trust. International experiences demonstrate that strong political leadership and clearly articulated long-term digital transformation strategies are critical enablers, supported by sustained investment and inter-agency coordination. Robust digital infrastructure including high-speed connectivity, interoperable data ecosystems, and scalable cloud or edge computing ensures reliable and real-time AI–AR performance. Equally important is organizational capacity, as public sector personnel must be equipped with appropriate skills, adaptive workflows, and digital literacy to integrate these technologies into daily operations.

At the same time, governments face persistent challenges such as high implementation costs, technical limitations, fragmented institutional structures, and significant privacy and security risks. Addressing these issues requires coordinated governance frameworks, ethical data management, and sustainable funding models that balance innovation with accountability and societal acceptance.

5.4 Lessons Learned

Global experiences with AI–AR deployment reveal a set of key insights that can help governments shape more effective digital transformation strategies. Successful implementations often begin with targeted pilot projects that test feasibility and user experience before wider rollout, emphasizing the need for iterative development anchored in user-centered design. These initiatives also show that technological integration must be accompanied by cultural and organizational change, supported through leadership commitment, workforce training, and inter-agency coordination.

Strong data governance frameworks are essential to ensure data quality, transparency, and legal compliance, while strategic partnerships with industry, academia, and civil society can accelerate innovation and distribute costs. Moreover, governments must design systems with scalability and future adaptability in mind, relying on modular architectures and open standards to accommodate rapid technological evolution. Together, these lessons highlight that AI–AR adoption is a long-term, strategic process requiring continuous refinement, responsible governance, and sustained investment to enhance public service effectiveness and promote more inclusive, resilient, and citizen-focused government systems.

6. CHALLENGES AND FUTURE OPPORTUNITIES

The integration of Large Language Models (LLMs), artificial intelligence, and augmented reality into qualitative research and public services presents a landscape filled with both obstacles and transformative promise. As adoption accelerates, understanding the technical, ethical, and institutional challenges as well as the emerging opportunities becomes critical for practitioners, policymakers, researchers, and citizens. This chapter summarizes the key constraints shaping current implementation and the future directions likely to influence research and public sector transformation.

6.1 Technical Challenges: AI Accuracy, Real-Time Processing, AR Hardware

Technical constraints continue to pose significant obstacles to dependable AI implementation, particularly in contexts that require high accuracy and nuanced interpretation. Performance often varies widely depending on the task, domain, and quality of input data. In qualitative research, for instance, errors in transcription and automated content analysis remain common, especially when dealing with accents, specialized terminology, overlapping dialogue, or subtle contextual cues. Even sophisticated large language models may produce hallucinated responses outputs that sound convincing but are factually incorrect highlighting the risks of relying on automated analyses without rigorous human validation. Real-time processing further complicates deployment, as complex reasoning or multimodal tasks can introduce latency that is incompatible with fast-paced public-sector environments such as emergency response or transport management. These issues are exacerbated in low-connectivity settings, where cloud-based processing becomes unreliable, and edge-based solutions remain limited by device capabilities and reduced model accuracy.

Hardware limitations in augmented reality also affect overall system reliability. Current AR headsets continue to face constraints including short battery duration, narrow fields of view, and ergonomic discomfort during prolonged use. Their sensing systems are highly sensitive to environmental fluctuations such as poor lighting, reflective surfaces, and rapidly changing surroundings conditions common in public service and field research settings. These shortcomings can undermine situational awareness and lead to interruptions or inaccuracies in spatial data collection. In addition, reliable data governance presents an ongoing challenge, as AI systems depend on large, high-quality datasets that are often scarce, fragmented, or locked within outdated institutional infrastructures. The computational resources required to train, update, and maintain advanced AI models remain substantial, further limiting accessibility for researchers and public institutions operating under restricted budgets.

6.2 Ethical, Legal, and Regulatory Issues

The integration of AI into research and public service environments raises a range of ethical and legal challenges that demand careful governance. Algorithmic bias remains a major concern, particularly when training data embeds historical inequities that may disadvantage marginalized groups in public decision-making or distort minority perspectives in qualitative analysis. Privacy risks intensify as AI systems process sensitive health, financial, biometric, and location data, often in ways that conflict with transparency and data-minimization requirements found in regulations such as the GDPR. Questions of accountability further complicate deployment, as responsibility for AI-driven decisions becomes diffused across developers, data providers, and implementing institutions, underscoring the need for robust oversight and clear documentation. Transparency and explainability also pose difficulties, since the most advanced AI models remain highly opaque despite the availability of interpretability tools that offer only partial insight an issue that is especially problematic for high-stakes applications. Moreover, informed consent becomes harder to guarantee when AI systems infer information beyond what participants knowingly disclose, necessitating more adaptive and granular consent mechanisms. These challenges are compounded by uneven regulatory landscapes across jurisdictions, highlighting the need for governance frameworks that protect rights while remaining flexible enough to accommodate rapid technological evolution.

6.3 Opportunities: Digital Twins, Spatial AI, Autonomous Public Services

Despite the challenges surrounding its deployment, the integration of AI and AR presents substantial opportunities to reshape public services and research practices. Digital twin technologies enable policymakers and scholars to experiment with potential interventions in virtual replicas of physical or social environments, allowing cities to model transportation reforms or disaster-response strategies and researchers to explore organizational or community dynamics. Advances in spatial AI which combine computer vision, natural language processing, and geospatial analytics further enhance the ability to analyze how activities and inequalities manifest across locations, supporting more equitable resource allocation and more informed emergency planning. Emerging autonomous and semi-autonomous service models also allow AI to manage routine administrative tasks, freeing human personnel for cases requiring discretion or empathy, while multimodal AI broadens analytical depth and improves accessibility for diverse user groups. Additionally, predictive systems help identify early risks in areas such as public health, welfare, and housing, enabling proactive interventions and more personalized services. Finally, AI-driven platforms can strengthen democratic participation by synthesizing public feedback and supporting multilingual communication at scale, offering new avenues for inclusive civic engagement.

Figure 1. AI–AR public service opportunity

6.4 Future Trends and Innovations

Future developments will emphasize explainable AI, enabling transparent reasoning; federated learning, supporting privacy-preserving collaboration; and human-AI teaming, optimizing complementary strengths. Continual learning systems will adapt to evolving environments, while ethical AI by design frameworks embed societal values into development processes. Ultimately, the future of AI-enhanced research and public services depends not only on technological advances but on wise governance, inclusive design, and sustained commitment to public good.

Figure 2. AI-AR integration challenge map

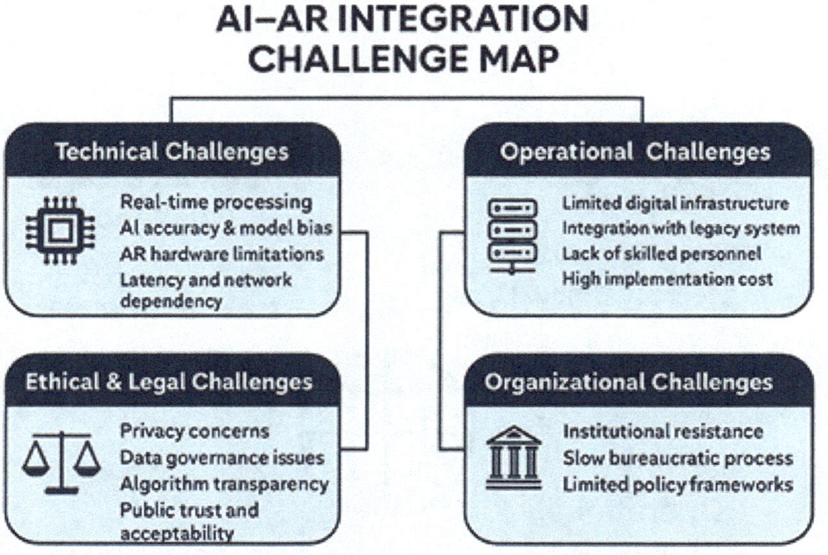

7. RECOMMENDATIONS FOR PRACTITIONERS AND POLICYMAKERS

7.1 Suggested Implementation Framework

Establishing an effective implementation framework for AI–AR integration in public services requires a strategic approach that balances technological innovation with organizational readiness. Practitioners should begin by conducting a comprehensive needs assessment to identify public service areas where AI–AR can generate the highest value such as public safety, transportation, healthcare, education, licensing systems, or citizen engagement platforms. This assessment must be supported by data-driven evaluations to ensure that AI and AR technologies solve actual service bottlenecks rather than becoming isolated digital experiments. A phased implementation model is recommended, beginning with pilot projects that test narrowly scoped use cases. These pilots allow assessment of technical feasibility, citizen acceptance, cost implications, and regulatory considerations before broader deployment.

A key component of the implementation framework is the establishment of robust governance structures. These include steering committees composed of public officials, IT professionals, legal experts, and citizen representatives who provide oversight and ensure that AI–AR projects align with institutional mandates. Standards for transparency, performance evaluation, and ethical guidelines should be embedded in governance frameworks from the outset. Public agencies must also adopt agile project management methodologies that support iterative prototyping, user testing, and continuous improvement. Unlike traditional public sector projects that follow rigid linear processes, AI–AR systems evolve rapidly and require dynamic adaptation.

The communication and networking layer connects all system components and enables data exchange across devices and platforms. The architecture may incorporate 5G, Wi-Fi 6, mesh networks, or satellite communication depending on the operational environment. High-speed connectivity is crucial for simultaneous AI processing and AR rendering, particularly in public safety or infrastructure management scenarios. Another essential dimension is technological interoperability. AI algorithms and AR platforms often run on systems developed by different vendors, using distinct data formats and standards; practitioners should therefore adopt open architectures and standardized APIs that enable seamless data exchange to avoid vendor lock-in and support long-term scalability. Collaboration across agencies is also crucial for instance, an AI-powered AR navigation solution for emergency responders will perform far more effectively if it can integrate real-time feeds from traffic management, weather stations, and geospatial databases (Baheer et al., 2020; Hernández et al., 2020)

Finally, practitioners should implement strong monitoring and evaluation mechanisms. Key performance indicators (KPIs) should measure user satisfaction, service delivery speed, error reduction, fiscal efficiency, and equity impacts. These indicators inform continuous optimization and justify further investment in AI–AR infrastructure. Policymakers should use evaluation data to refine regulations and support responsible scaling of successful initiatives.

7.2 Human Resource and Capacity Building Strategies

Developing human resource capacity is a critical requirement for the effective adoption of AI–AR technologies in public services. Public employees must be equipped not only to operate these systems but also to understand their foundational concepts in order to make informed decisions. Training should be structured across competency levels from basic digital literacy to advanced technical skills and strategic management capabilities. Frontline personnel such as inspectors, educators, and healthcare workers may require practical instruction on AR interface navigation and interpreting AI outputs, while technical teams need deeper knowledge of algorithms, data governance, cybersecurity, and system maintenance. For managers and policymakers, capacity building must emphasize budgeting, organizational change, and ethical oversight. Cross-disciplinary collaboration is equally important, as AI–AR systems sit at the intersection of technology, behavioral science, and public administration. Partnerships with universities and research institutions can further strengthen these efforts through specialized programs, professional certifications, and applied research initiatives.

Beyond technical training, capacity building also requires cultivating an institutional culture that supports innovation and adaptability. Public sector organizations often exhibit risk-averse tendencies, which can hinder experimentation with new technologies. Incentive mechanisms such as recognition programs, career advancement opportunities, and performance-based rewards can encourage employees to engage with AI–AR initiatives. Establishing internal innovation labs or digital transformation units offers a structured environment for developing and testing prototypes outside traditional bureaucratic constraints. Addressing talent shortages may also require governments to adopt flexible hiring models, collaborate with external experts, or recruit specialized professionals through fellowships and short-term contracts. To ensure long-term sustainability and reduce dependence on external vendors, procurement agreements should include explicit knowledge-transfer provisions that enable public institutions to maintain and evolve AI–AR systems independently.

7.3 Policy Development and Technological Roadmap

Developing effective policies for AI–AR integration requires a forward-looking approach that considers legal, ethical, technical, and socio-economic implications. Policymakers must begin by establishing clear regulatory frameworks governing data collection, usage, and retention. Because AI–AR systems often rely on real-time data from sensors, cameras, and user interactions, there is heightened risk of violating privacy rights. Policies should therefore mandate data minimization, transparency of data flows, opt-in consent mechanisms, and strict limitations on biometric and location tracking. Cybersecurity policies must also address vulnerabilities in AR devices and cloud-based AI systems, ensuring that robust encryption, authentication, and vulnerability assessment practices are in place.

Beyond data governance, policymakers should define standards for algorithmic fairness, explainability, and accountability. AI systems must be regularly audited to detect bias or discriminatory outcomes, especially in sensitive areas like public safety, welfare eligibility, or healthcare triage. Requirements for human oversight should also be codified, ensuring that automated decisions do not become opaque or unchallengeable. In the context of AR interfaces, policies should also govern the accuracy and safety of visual overlays, particularly for applications such as navigation support, emergency response, or medical diagnostics (Mehrabi et al., 2021).

A technological roadmap is essential to guide long-term investments. Governments should outline timelines for infrastructure upgrades, cloud adoption, sensor deployment, and cross-agency data integration. The roadmap should also anticipate emerging trends such as 5G/6G connectivity, spatial computing, edge AI, and wearable AR devices. By aligning public investments with technological evolution, policymakers can avoid obsolescence and ensure that systems remain adaptive. Additionally, roadmaps should incorporate sustainability considerations, ensuring that AI–AR deployments are energy-efficient and environmentally responsible (M. Chen et al., 2023).

Finally, policy frameworks should support innovation ecosystems by simplifying procurement processes for emerging technologies, offering grants for pilot projects, and fostering public–private innovation accelerators. These measures enable governments to test new ideas quickly while maintaining regulatory safeguards.

7.4 Collaboration Between Academia, Industry, and Government

Cross-sector collaboration is essential for the effective implementation of AI–AR systems, as no single institution holds the full range of expertise, infrastructure, and resources required for such complex initiatives. Academic institutions contribute through research, curriculum development, and objective evaluation of pilot programs, ensuring that technological innovations remain evidence-based and aligned with societal values. Industry partners add technical depth, scalable solutions, and rapid innovation capacity, though their involvement must be guided by transparent procurement processes and safeguards that protect public interests. Government agencies serve as coordinators and regulators by defining societal needs, setting equitable access standards, and creating supportive policy and funding environments. To operationalize these collaborative roles, structured mechanisms such as multi-stakeholder advisory groups, innovation sandboxes, co-laboratories, data-sharing frameworks, and long-term research partnerships are crucial. These arrangements not only accelerate development and real-world testing but also strengthen transparency and public trust by incorporating diverse expertise throughout the design and evaluation stages.

8. CONCLUSION

The integration of Artificial Intelligence (AI) and Augmented Reality (AR) within public service systems marks a major evolution in how governments conceptualize and execute service delivery. Rather than functioning as isolated technological upgrades, AI and AR together represent a structural modernization of governance, operational workflows, and public engagement processes. AI contributes analytical intelligence processing large datasets, identifying trends, making predictions, and automating complex administrative tasks while AR translates these insights into real-world contexts through immersive, spatially aligned interfaces. Their convergence supports public systems that operate with greater speed, accuracy, transparency, and citizen responsiveness.

Across government domains, the combined application of AI and AR unlocks substantial benefits. In healthcare, the technologies enhance remote consultation, support real-time diagnostics, and strengthen medical training through simulated environments. Administrative functions are improved through automated procedures, intelligent assistants, and streamlined citizen touchpoints. Emergency services gain operational efficiency via AI-driven threat detection and AR-guided field operations that enhance situational awareness. Urban planning and transportation also benefit significantly: AI-driven projections paired with AR visualization allow policymakers and communities to observe potential impacts of development projects directly within the physical landscape, supporting more inclusive and data-informed decision-making. However, realizing these advantages requires clear governance structures, ethical safeguards, and regulatory frameworks that address algorithmic fairness, privacy, interoperability, and long-term system sustainability.

Equally important is the readiness of the public workforce and the trust of the citizens they serve. Public servants must adapt to new modes of operation introduced by AI–AR tools, which demands ongoing training, digital literacy development, and strong organizational change management. Citizen confidence must also be cultivated through transparent practices, responsible data management, and mechanisms that ensure accountability and fairness. Looking ahead, continued advancements in spatial computing, edge AI, digital twins, and multimodal interaction are expected to expand the capabilities of AI–AR systems even further. Governments that invest strategically in infrastructure, human capital, and ethical governance will be better prepared to harness these technologies to enhance efficiency, resilience, inclusivity, and overall service quality. Together, AI and AR hold the potential to transform public institutions into interconnected, intelligent ecosystems capable of delivering more responsive and equitable public services.

REFERENCES

Awadallah, O., Grolinger, K., & Sadhu, A. (2024). Remote collaborative framework for real-time structural condition assessment using Augmented Reality. *Advanced Engineering Informatics*, *62*, 102652. https://doi.org/https://doi.org/10.1016/j.aei.2024.102652. DOI: 10.1016/j.aei.2024.102652

Baheer, B. A., Lamas, D., & Sousa, S. (2020). A Systematic Literature Review on Existing Digital Government Architectures: State-of-the-Art, Challenges, and Prospects. In *Administrative Sciences* (Vol. 10, Issue 2, p. 25). DOI: 10.3390/admsci10020025

Bennis, I., & Mouwafaq, S. (2025). Advancing AI-driven thematic analysis in qualitative research: a comparative study of nine generative models on Cutaneous Leishmaniasis data. BMC Medical Informatics and Decision Making, 25doi: PubMedDOI: 10.1186/s12911-025-02961-5

Chen, J. J. (2025). From Turing's conception of machine intelligence to the evolution of AI in early childhood education: Conceptual, empirical, and practical insights. *AI. Brain and Child*, *1*(1), 1. DOI: 10.1007/s44436-025-00002-6

Chen, M., Cao, Y., & Liang, Y. (2023). Determinants of open government data usage: Integrating trust theory and social cognitive theory. *Government Information Quarterly*, *40*(4), 101857. https://doi.org/https://doi.org/10.1016/j.giq.2023.101857. DOI: 10.1016/j.giq.2023.101857

Do, T. L., Sanhae, K., Hwang, L., & Lee, S. (2024). Real-Time Spatial Mapping in Architectural Visualization: A Comparison among Mixed Reality Devices. In *Sensors* (Vol. 24, Issue 14, p. 4727). DOI: 10.3390/s24144727

Hernández, J. L., García, R., Schonowski, J., Atlan, D., Chanson, G., & Ruohomäki, T. (2020). Interoperable Open Specifications Framework for the Implementation of Standardized Urban Platforms. In *Sensors* (Vol. 20, Issue 8, p. 2402). DOI: 10.3390/s20082402

Hitch, D. (2024). Artificial Intelligence Augmented Qualitative Analysis: The Way of the Future? [PubMed]. *Qualitative Health Research*, *34*. Advance online publication. DOI: 10.1177/10497323231217392

Huebner, M., Meltzer, D. E., Ma, W., & Arrow, H. (2021). Correction: The Masters athlete in Olympic weightlifting: Training, lifestyle, health challenges, and gender differences. *PLoS One*, *16*(2), e0247110. DOI: 10.1371/journal.pone.0247110 PMID: 33566849

Khetarpal, K., Riemer, M., & Rish, I. (2022). Towards Continual Reinforcement Learning. *Revista Perspectivas (Cochambamba)*, *75*, 1401–1476.

Kim, M., Suh, I., & Chung, Y. D. (2020). MARS: A multi-level array representation for simulation data. *Future Generation Computer Systems*, *111*, 419–434. https://doi.org/https://doi.org/10.1016/j.future.2019.11.010. DOI: 10.1016/j.future.2019.11.010

Latupeirissa, J. J., Dewi, N. L., Prayana, I. K., Srikandi, M. B., Ramadiansyah, S. A., & Pramana, I. B. (2024). Transforming Public Service Delivery: A Comprehensive Review of Digitization Initiatives. In *Sustainability* (Vol. 16, Issue 7, p. 2818). DOI: 10.3390/su16072818

Mehrabi, N., Morstatter, F., Saxena, N., Lerman, K., & Galstyan, A. (2021). A Survey on Bias and Fairness in Machine Learning. *ACM Computing Surveys*, *54*(6), 1–35. Advance online publication. DOI: 10.1145/3457607

Mishra, A. (2024). A Comprehensive Review of Artificial Intelligence and Machine Learning : Concepts, Trends, and Applications. *International Journal of Scientific Research in Science and Technology*, *11*(5), 126–142. DOI: 10.32628/IJSRST2411587

Motra, G. B., Sah, B. K., & Jha, P. (2021). Structural condition assessment and retrofitting of Shital Niwas building (presidential palace). *Progress in Disaster Science*, *10*, 100174. https://doi.org/https://doi.org/10.1016/j.pdisas.2021.100174. DOI: 10.1016/j.pdisas.2021.100174

Newman, J., Mintrom, M., & Neill, D. O. (2022). *Digital technologies, artificial intelligence, and bureaucratic transformation. 136*(April 2021).

Oun, A., Hagerdorn, N., Scheideger, C., & Cheng, X. (2024). Mobile Devices or Head-Mounted Displays: A Comparative Review and Analysis of Augmented Reality in Healthcare. *IEEE Access : Practical Innovations, Open Solutions*, *12*, 21825–21839. DOI: 10.1109/ACCESS.2024.3361833

Ponto, K., Hartung, L., Zhao, Y., Sprecher, B., Tredinnick, R., & Banerjee, S. (2025). EasyVizAR: Supporting First Responders Through the Use of Collaborative Augmented Reality Tools. In *Applied Sciences* (Vol. 15, Issue 21, p. 11498). DOI: 10.3390/app152111498

Rakšnys, A. V. (2025). *THE USES OF ARTIFICIAL INTELLIGENCE IN THE PUBLIC SECTOR : CHALLENGES AND PROSPECTS. 24*(3).

Stefanidi, Z., Margetis, G., Ntoa, S., & Papagiannakis, G. (2022). Real-Time Adaptation of Context-Aware Intelligent User Interfaces, for Enhanced Situational Awareness. *IEEE Access : Practical Innovations, Open Solutions*, *10*, 23367–23393. DOI: 10.1109/ACCESS.2022.3152743

Suleymanoglu, B., Soycan, M., & Toth, C. (2024). 3D Road Boundary Extraction Based on Machine Learning Strategy Using LiDAR and Image-Derived MMS Point Clouds. In *Sensors* (Vol. 24, Issue 2, p. 503). DOI: 10.3390/s24020503

Weber, M., Engert, M., Schaffer, N., Weking, J., & Krcmar, H. (2023). Organizational Capabilities for AI Implementation Coping with Inscrutability and Data Dependency in AI. *Information Systems Frontiers*, *25*(4), 1549–1569. DOI: 10.1007/s10796-022-10297-y

Wosny, M., & Hastings, J. (2024). Applying Large Language Models to Interpret Qualitative Interviews in Healthcare. [PubMed]. *Studies in Health Technology and Informatics*, *316*. Advance online publication. DOI: 10.3233/SHTI240530

Wu, S., Hou, L., Chen, H., & Zhang, G. (Kevin), Zou, Y., & Tushar, Q. (2023). Cognitive ergonomics-based Augmented Reality application for construction performance. *Automation in Construction, 149*, 104802. https://doi.org/https://doi.org/10.1016/j.autcon.2023.104802

Zhang, D., Tan, W., Zelek, J., Ma, L., & Li, J. (2025). SLAM-TSM: Enhanced Indoor LiDAR SLAM With Total Station Measurements for Accurate Trajectory Estimation. *IEEE Transactions on Intelligent Transportation Systems*, *26*(2), 1743–1753. DOI: 10.1109/TITS.2024.3504487

KEY TERMS AND DEFINITIONS

Algorithmic Fairness: A set of principles ensuring that AI systems operate without bias or discrimination, particularly important in public sector decision-making.

Artificial Intelligence (AI): Technology that enables machines to analyze data, recognize patterns, and make autonomous decisions to support complex public service operations.

Augmented Reality (AR): A visualization technology that overlays digital information such as models, text, or analytics onto the physical world, improving situational awareness.

Digital Twins: Virtual replicas of physical environments or systems used for simulation, planning, and real-time monitoring using integrated AI–AR insights.

Edge Computing: A computing paradigm where AI processing occurs near the data source (e.g., on devices or local servers) to reduce latency in time-critical public services.

Interoperability: The ability of different technological systems to communicate and share data seamlessly, crucial for cross-agency AI–AR applications.

Natural Language Processing (NLP): An AI technique for understanding and generating human language, used in chatbots, virtual assistants, and automated document processing.

Predictive Analytics: AI methods used to forecast future events or service demands, enabling proactive planning in healthcare, transportation, and disaster management.

Real-Time AR Visualization: An AR capability that displays AI analytics instantly within the physical environment, supporting high-speed operations like emergency response.

Spatial Computing: The set of technologies that allow digital systems to understand and interact with physical environments, essential for accurate AR anchoring.

Chapter 8

Designing Human-Centered Public Services Through AI-Driven Augmented Reality Systems

Dharmendra Kumar Gupta
https://orcid.org/0009-0003-9219-9757
Poornima University, Jaipur, India

ABSTRACT

AI and AR in the combination form a radical change in how governments imagine the conceptualization and provision of public services, which allows customers to experience immersive, context-dependent, and personalized experiences. The human-centered design of the public services also incorporates technology in a design that has a responsible grasp in the needs, accessibility challenges and environmental limitations of the citizens so as to have meaningful participation. The AI-assisted AR applications will contribute to the improvement of transparency, reduction of the time spent working through the bureaucratics, real-time multilingual communication, or visual overlay of the features allowing civilians to learn more about their city, react to crises, access healthcare, and interact with the government. This chapter will look at the design architectures, application paradigms, and guidelines on governance needed to safely, equitably.

DOI: 10.4018/979-8-3373-7804-6.ch008

1. INTRODUCTION

1.1 Evolution of Public Service Design from Traditional Systems to Digital Ecosystems

Traditionally the design of a public service was based on the centralized and process based approach where administrative efficiency was given more importance than the experience of the user. The citizens were supposed to adapt to strict workflows, physical documents, and standard procedures irrespective of their personal needs and socio-economic constraints. As the population had become more diverse, and demand on the population was expected to grow, and more people turned to digital devices, this model could not cope anymore and only led to exclusion, delays, and mistrust in the public institutions. The migration to digital service portals was the first significant transformation but most of the earlier digital systems were merely physical bureaucracy replicated online without a way of reconsidering accessibility or the impact on a person (Mikropoulos & Natsis, 2011).

The age of the Internet obliged to come up with a model according to which the administrative processes should become adjusted to the citizens, rather than the opposite. Human-centered service design was one such response that focused on empathy based research, usability, transparency, and constant feedback loop to make services match with human experience. It is more interested in maximizing results, to the citizens, rather than maximizing work to institutions, especially to vulnerable populations, e.g., older citizens, disabled citizens, non-native speakers of the language, or citizen with a lack of technological knowledge. It is the shift of the paradigm of providing services to the possibility of using, understanding, and meaning services.

With the growing use of immersive technologies, the development of the public service design has moved beyond websites and mobile apps to the next-generation interactive systems. The use of Artificial Intelligence to power Augmented Reality makes it possible to provide real-time personalization, contextual support, sensory integration, and penal interaction with the infrastructures of the population. AI-AR systems can make citizens work within highly complex systems; instead, they guide citizens in real time within the surroundings and according to their needs, simply redefining what it means to be a citizen of the digital society (Slater & Wilbur, 1997).

1.2 Principles of Smart Public Systems Human-Centered Design

The human-oriented public service design is based on the emotional, cognitive and practical needs of citizens and not the convenience of operation of the government institutions. The design approach demands designers and policymakers to practice user ethnography, participatory research and prototyping as well as iterative evaluation throughout the system lifecycle. This strategy will make services inclusive throughout the process and lessens the cognitive burden on the citizen through procedural ambiguity and interface complexity. To truly be human-centered, digital public systems must be made to work in real-life conditions and not in an ideal laboratory environment.

The philosophy of the design also dictates the adaptation to the variety of the human capabilities. The citizens differ in terms of digital literacy, cognitive capabilities, cultures, and communication preferences. The systems should hence be able to facilitate other forms of interaction, including multimodal input, spoken instructions, gesture-sensitive computation, multilingual instructions and AR overlay as necessitated by accessibility. Rather than designing one user journey, the human-centered design realizes that the route of pathway of public services should be flexible, responsive, and adaptable because, there is no two citizens (citizens) who will have the same circumstances and expectations of government services (Merchant et al., 2014).

Human-centered design systems put even more emphasis on emotional experience. The feeling of being empowered, clear and trusted during the interaction with the government as well affects the level at which citizens view and trust the public institutions in their perception. One of the chances that AI-AR systems can offer to instill confidence into the system is the real-time instructions, visual confirmation of the task completion, and less reliance on third-party intermediaries. By being in control and guaranteed fairness and transparency the citizens will have more power and strengthen the institutions (Wen et al., 2023).

1.3 Human-Technology Relationships in Transformation of the Public Service

Digital transformation is never a substitution of analog procedures with automated processes; also it is a paradigm shift of the connection between man and the institutions of the populace. The case of AI and AR in service delivery to the population also poses important questions regarding agency, control, and trust. The use of automation can be the best way to streamline the process, but the state should not undermine autonomy by causing citizens to feel monitored, controlled, or assessing them through algorithms. The transformation should be done with the help of technology which should not be seen as a control but as a supplement to the level of the human decision making and simplification of the civic engagement.

Creation of a productive human-technology relationship in the services of the population requires a purpose. Citizens have to know the purpose of collection of data by a system, the means of producing decisions, and the way they can challenge or mitigate mistakes. Personalization is a useful concept only when it includes transparency and informed consent with the help of AI. Similarly, AR interfaces should be developed in such a way that they provide guidance and not control, to provide assistance but not to affect decision-making and psychological addictiveness. Maturing human-technology relationship is anchored on collaboration and in such a relationship, technology enhances human capacity, as opposed to substituting it (Goyal et al., 2025).

One critical feature of the said change is viewing citizens as a partner not an object of the technological government operation. The ecosystem of human centred AI-AR facilitates real time feedback and exchange of data such that the general platforms can develop with the needs of their communities. When citizens provide more than usage data, but experience information, the government will have a constant situational awareness to produce a better service delivery. This process of developing dynamically through cooperation by means of the cycle enables development of public systems that maintain the dignity of humans, their agency, and ownership of technology as civilians.

2. ROLE OF ARTIFICIAL INTELLIGENCE IN PUBLIC SERVICE EXPERIENCE PERSONALIZATION

2.1 AI as a Catalyst for Adaptive and Responsive Public Service Delivery

Artificial Intelligence has brought a paradigm shift on the response of the public services to citizen needs since the systems can become dynamic as opposed to using previously set workflow. The old style of providing public services presupposes a set of procedures that are applicable to all the users, in most cases, disregarding individual factors like age, language, disability, or urgency of a particular request. AI in turn overturns this trend and emulates a perpetual learning process based on user activity, past data, and situational variables to create personalized support pathways. Rather than providing generic information, AI-based systems filter the content and interaction models, which match the individual needs of any citizen, enhancing its efficiency and user-friendliness.

The flexibility of AI is particularly transformational in the contexts, where procedural complexity has been traditionally introducing a profound obstacle to the involvement of the population. As a case example, the procedure of receiving medical care benefits or licenses renewal might differ based on age or eligibility criteria. The algorithm of the AI is intelligent enough to read these variables and adapt the interface and support messages according to the user profiles. This customization does not just make work easier, but happens to be more effective in the reduction of the procedures anxiety and mental burden, providing citizens with a feeling of clarity and empowerment during the entire digital experience with governmental websites (Dunleavy & Dede, 2014).

Moreover, AI helps to apply individual timing and communication plans, as it predicts the time of intervention or reminder that a citizen needs. Instead of making people record the deadlines by hand or wade through bureaucracy, AI systems will alert the user when documents need to be done next, give instructions on what actions to take, and identify and point out incompleteness before it turns into an impediment. Such a change in reactive personal navigation to active directed relationship is a radical advance in the provision of public services, enhancing inclusiveness and procedures.

2.2 Data-based Dynamic Results to Equity and Access

The principle of AI-based personalization is based on the possibilities of processing various information sources during which it is not only the identity of the user that is registered, but also social facts and behavior patterns. It is not aimed at placing citizens in the strict divisions but seeking to find out the barriers to the services that can be encountered by certain citizens and make adjustments to the system on a dynamic basis. As an example, the first stages of hesitation when filling out forms may manifest digital literacy difficulties, and the system will be transferred to simplified layouts, audio support, or walkthroughs. With the constant learning, AI becomes not passive interface, but active facilitator of the public access (Ibáñez & Delgado-Kloos, 2018).

To achieve a human-centered approach to data-driven personalization, it is important to find the balance between smart automation and consideration of the user autonomy. The citizens should be convinced that personalization is not obtrusive or discriminatory on the one hand. This is by ensuring the use of clear consent models that effectively communicate the type of data collected, its purpose and the manner in which the data benefits service delivery. Selfless and ethical personalization of the programs will make the services of the state more democratic instead of strengthening social positions. Typically, those who in the past had difficulties with government processes get a customised interaction channels that are based on their realities as opposed to presumptions regarding profile-based generalised citizens.

The factor of having access to AI regardless of disabilities is also being supported as it recognizes contextual and emotional experiences. An example is that non-native speakers can also find multilingual conversational agents necessary, whereas large visuals and reduced depth of navigation can be needed by the elderly users. Live guidance modules can be triggered by AI tools that identify that the user is frustrated or confused in real time. It is the capacity to determine impediments in order to prevent them before they create interference to the engagement so that personalization will add to fairness, dignity, and fluent civic participation (Cao et al., 2023).

2.3 Predictive AI to smooth experiences of receiving public services

Predictive intelligence bridges the gap between historical trends analytics and real-time analytic capabilities to offer an insight into what citizens require even before they have encountered difficulties. Traditional systems only respond when an error has traveled or some request has been placed but predictive AI can tell the anticipated obstacles beforehand and make changes to the workflow. By way of illustration, it can identify any discrepancies in documentation requirement and rectify them even prior to any submission being made by the users thus reducing the number of repeated visit; failure rates of the service provided and the level of dissatisfaction by the users. Such a change in corrective to preventive interaction maximizes the outcomes of services without increasing the administration load (Danry et al., 2020).

Another way through which predictive models improve user experience is by having a priority based on urgency and social relevancy. As an example, patients receiving emergency benefits or medical aid can be automatically transferred to accelerated virtual service provision, and the needy demographic will get appropriate treatment. Through community-level analytics, predictive AI can assist agencies to deploy resources where demand is likely to explode, in the case of a natural disaster or a tourism season wave. This forms an ecosystem of services which is not only responsive but also anticipatory and provides stability and nimbleness even in cases of uncertainty.

When predictive AI develops further, going beyond automation, and transforms into a relationship, its actual worth is realized. Predictive systems enhance their cognition of the preferences and social contexts of the individual through constant feedback loops, forming enduring relationships between citizens and technology. These digital relationships of a long-term character are the basis of trust in the public platform since the citizens are feeling heard, respected and understood. The relationships are enhanced through predictive intelligence, which provides continuity in a seamless manner in the course of public services and the administrative interactions that are based on the human context, instead of the bureaucracy (De La Torre et al., 2024).

3 AUGMENTED REALITY AS AN INTERFACE FOR ACCESSIBLE AND INCLUSIVE CIVIC ENGAGEMENT

3.1 Redefining Public Interaction through Immersive AR Interfaces

Augmented Reality is a pioneering shift in civic engagement that changes the public space and government service to a place of interactivity and information-laden setting. As compared to the traditional digital platforms where the user is expected to process the information presented on a screen and by text, AR projects the contextual information onto the real world. This eliminates the chances of confusion caused by bureaucratic or navigation complications to citizens as the instructions are presented at the right place and at the right time. AR systems based on AI help to simplify the navigation of public buildings, transport centers, municipal service centers and medical facilities, deeming institutional logic Visible signs and visual instructions. The interface is no longer a wall and this is actually one of its functions; it is an amplifier that fuses the actual world with the digital counterpart on the fly.

Figure 1. AI-driven human-centered public service interaction

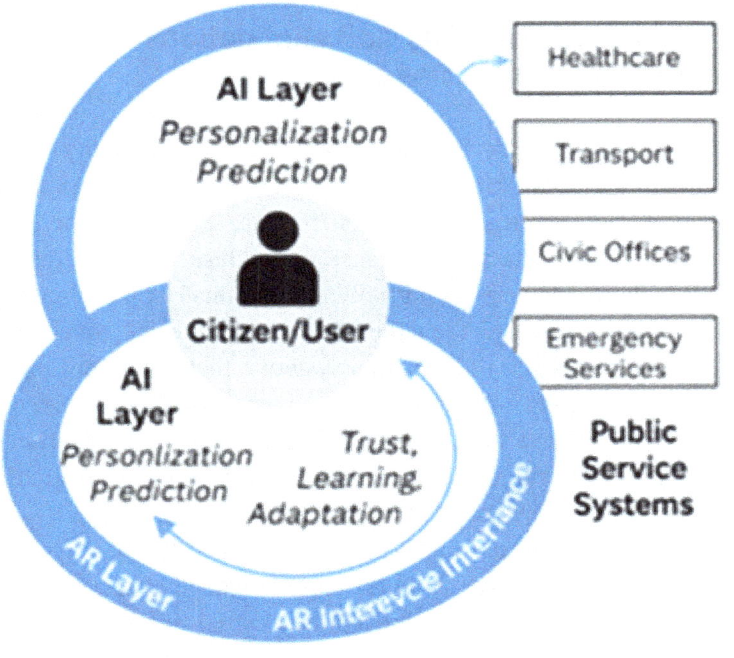

The AR interaction that is immersive will help close the universal divide between the citizens and the authorities as people will not rely on their literacy level, prior knowledge or acquaintance with government processes. Once a person comes to a public office, the AR prompts could bring up the service counters, clarify the requirements and discuss the sequence of actions step-by-step. This eliminates confusion and strengthens aspect of control in user in areas that evoke panic or anger amongst users. AR enhances a greater level of interaction and fair access to services that were once challenging to navigate without external help by restructuring interaction between the citizens and the government around being transparent and confident.

Invisibility of technology is also crucial towards comfort and acceptance. AR systems are user-friendly and do not require the user to master new tools and terminologies as they automatically work in the background with wearables or their mobile phones. The citizens engage in the environment in a natural way whereas the system changes in response to their gaze and gesture and dynamic locality. A gradual change happens on the way that entails the minimization of screen interactions in favor of space by physical spaces which react to the needs of citizens intelligently. This spatial relationship is an essential step towards the realization of human, conversational and intuitive public service ecosystems rather than procedural and inflexible (Lee et al., 2024).

3.2 Multimedia Accessibility and elimination of communication obstacles

AU should provide strong platforms to ensure the inclusivity of the public in the utilization of services through the provision of various sensorial, cognitive and communication orientations. A lot of the citizens are actually hampered not out of an inability to do things but due to the touchstones with services that demand uniform forms of interaction. AR systems partially address this because they promote multimodal interaction systems wherein the user can utilize voice, touch, movements of the eyes, and interpretations of the visual system rather than inputting a lot of text. Pictorial instructions and animations displayed through AR are easier to understand by people who do not have sufficient reading proficiency compared to written materials. This gives strength to the individuals who have been systematically under served by text based publics of use (Bukhari et al., 2025).

AR also facilitates a fair participation of the sensory disabled. As an illustration, in the case of deaf citizens, AR can offer sign language avatars to translate orally announced messages or instructions on a policy in real-time. In the case of visually impaired citizens, voice-based AR navigation would help them navigate through crowded areas in the most accurate manner, since the conventional signage would not assist them much. AR makes access normal so that, rather than creating special systems to meet the needs of specific disability groups, all citizens can access the benefits in the manner that is most natural to them. This universality avoids the effects of stigmatization and enforces the principle that accessibility is an area of collective social responsibility and not a professional service.

AR is also an effective way to address language barriers that historically cut off migrants, tourists, and linguistic minorities to the basic services. Real time translation between text and audio can be placed on physical documents, directional signs and notices to anyone. AI can make the translation dynamic to dialect, context, and cultural nuance which would lead to better understanding as well as honor. Information is delivered to every citizen in the way that respects their communication style of choice and lingual identity. Such an increased sense of belonging and involvement in civic life is a result of this increased inclusivity (Bangor et al., 2008).

3.3 Resolving the Trust, transparency, and institutional legibility with AR

The mistrust in opaque decision-making and unclear institutional processes are issues that are a major problem in engaging the public service in the UK, as well as in addressing the complexities of the existing procedures. AR technologies have the power to build trust because it makes government actions visible, comprehendible, and traceable. In case of a citizen filling forms or service requests, the AR interfaces can show the current status of the application, the steps that are to be undertaken, and the authorities. The demystification of the administrative mechanisms in the system which had been remote and closed previously is being achieved. When processes can be followed by the eye and audit trails are cleared of fog, the sense of fairness and responsibility is gained automatically.

AR helps to be transparent not only in communication but in decision-making. There are numerous instructions in the public sector which use either technical or policy lingo, which cannot be deciphered by an ordinary citizen. AR overlays enable citizens to point or click on the terms that they do not comprehend, and get a simplified guidance, context of the policies, and examples, instantly. Rather than defaulting to the middlemen like agents, or privately hired consultants, the citizens learn how to interpret their rights, duties, and services offered to them on their own. This freedom of action strengthens democratic participation in that it establishes an informational level ground in different socio-economic groups (Bunt et al., 2012).

The presence of AR also demystifies the institutional setting, making it less emotional. Most individuals would not wish to visit government offices due to the fear of making mistakes, being judged or as a result of inefficiency. AR modifies these interactions and makes them objective, neutral, and soothingly clear. The citizen does not have to just guess or wait to be interpreted on the vagueness of the rules; rather, help is given in a consistent and non-discriminative way. In the event that technology is an open intermediary, there is increased institutional legibility and the reduction of emotional distance. The citizens start to realize that rather than facing threatening authorities they can also be partners when it comes to well-being promotion and it is the main task of human-centered governance.

4 PERSONALIZATION, LEARNING, AND BEHAVIOURAL ADAPTATION IN AI-DRIVEN AR PUBLIC SERVICE SYSTEMS

4.1 AI-Powered Behavioural Personalization for Public Service Navigation

The AI-enabled AR systems make it possible to build the degree of personalization that is essentially transforming the way citizens get through the offering of the public services. The traditional mode of providing services to the people presumes that the entire population is requiring the same kind of words, help and knowledge. Conversely, AI-powered AR is dynamic to the behaviour of each individual and their learning rate, as well as the pattern of interaction. This implies that two citizens who came to the same municipal office can be given entirely different guidance on the basis of their previous knowledge, comfort levels and service history sizeable. This real-time adaptability does not only remove the frustrations and anxieties that are commonly related to the strict and formatted service seeming conditions but also fosters the user experience to grow naturally as opposed to a machine (Arrieta et al., 2020).

Success is personalization where AI pays attention to symptoms of behaviour such as stuttering, eye-style, and the same question. When the system senses confusion on a certain step say, documentation of license renewal, it will provide clarifications, background and other possible explanations. It will be able to make the choice of providing more graphic representations, simplified definitions of legal applications, or walkthroughs with voice based instructions based upon what it thinks the user is comfortable with. When the environment is full of paperwork, long queues, and the uncertainty of the bureaucracy, personalization is used to feel welcomed instead of being lost. Proactive teaching reduces the occurrence of errors and has the capacity to perform demanding tasks at a faster rate with the absence of human reliance.

In addition to the individualization of moment by moment, the continuity of the interactions in the public is provided by AI-driven AR. The system studies the past interactions and is capable of predicting future service demands. An illustration is, a resident who has visited the facility to have his/her property registered could subsequently use anticipatory reminders, procedural assistance and AR overlays in future instances when they need to obtain some tax records or renew property-related certificates. By personalizing, continuity is turning the delivery of the public services into predictive rather than reactive assistance making the engagement within the relationship between the citizens and the governments not a one-time event but rather a continual process of support as a result of continuity (Ali et al., 2023).

4.2 Adaptive Learning Mechanisms and Contextual Intelligence in Service Delivery

The AI capabilities in AR do not only aid its citizen user, but they constantly develop through the adaptive learning process to optimize assistive methods. All these interactions will improve on the situational models of the system regarding the citizen behaviors in procedural environments. When systems identify areas of repetitive friction (ex: bad handling of terms, missing paperwork, frequent missteps with navigation) it makes its content delivery strategies more user-focused, and better-suited to the environment. This learning is not completely statistical; it is contextual, that is, the AI does not only understand what was wrong, but why so in this particular user / task environment (Dhanorkar et al., 2021).

The contextual intelligence is especially effective in the multilingual and multicultural public spaces. Rather than have users select a fixed language preference, AI finds linguistic matches, substituting without issues across language, dialect, and simplification depending on reaction of users. When the user takes a prolonged moment to read through the text that has been translated or when he/she tilts his head under the signage, the system will interpret this action as an indication to switch to the visual icons or verbal descriptions. By doing so, contextual intelligence does not dictate a particular best mode of communication; instead, it finds out the best mode of communication at any given situation. This decreases the cognitive load and makes the services of the government more user-friendly to the different populations (Silic et al., 2025).

The adaptive learning also enhances reliability in the delivery of government services as Information disseminated has minimal variation. Human workers can give directions at different times, workload, mood, and style of communication, but AR powered by AIs can provide the same quality of explanations all the time. Nonetheless, individualization is not erased by the consistency, it simply provides a basis of equality and justice as individuality deals with the special comfort and a sense of empowerment. The combination of the two traits, unbiased and personalized guidance, is what eventually determines the usefulness of the contextual artificial intelligence in the sphere of the public service system (Maathuis & Datcu, 2025).

4.3 AR-Feedback Loop Behavioural Nudging and Civic Empowerment

The AR systems with AI capabilities can create an impact on the civic behaviour with positive nudging effects, thus ensuring compliance, responsibility, and active engagement without being imposed. AR can also use contextual prompts and these prompts highlight advantages instead of threats as regulation would be enforced using penalties. On the one hand, the system can remind citizens about possible punishment, i.e. fines related to failure to renew waste management permits; on the other hand, the system can emphasize the benefits, i.e. reduced charges when they renew it earlier or the statistics of the impact on the environment. Soft coercion that is intrinsic in AR encourages motivation as opposed to evading or being resentful, which enables governments to gain policy compliance by enabling empowerment.

AR can become an even more effective form of behavioural nudging when interactive feedback loops are developed to reward task performance and encourage civic discipline. The AR interface can give notice in a visual form, social impact data, or offer an action follow-up when a citizen performs a procedural step, such as uploading a required document, filling in a form, or participating in a public consultation, and then enhance their participation. This is what turns civic participation into a process worth encountering which is psychologically satisfying. The citizens not only obey but also feel that their action is part of a bigger civic cause, be it environmental sustainability, or communal health or community development (Mattioli & Paternò, 2023).

Notably, behavioural nudging should have ethical alignment so not to be psychologically manipulative. Instead of and cap on the impulsiveness accessing the subconsciousness of citizens, nudges are expected to enhance their ability to make informed choices. AR-based motivational designs should be based on a high degree of user autonomy so that citizens could feel themselves as decision-makers, not as the objects of persuasive algorithms. An openness concerning nudging purpose, the alternative to change personalization preferences, and the maintenance of citizen agency are significant ethical standards. Under such circumstances, AR can be used as not only an instrument of enhancing the rate of task accomplishment but also a way of developing informed, driven, and active civic engagement in the whole society (Mattioli & Paternò, 2023).

5 TRUST CONSIDERATIONS IN AI-DRIVEN AR PUBLIC SERVICE SYSTEMS

5.1 Boundaries in AI-Mediated Public Service Interactions

The introduction of AR systems based on AI raises with the introduction of AI-based AR systems in the services of the population serious ethical issues of independence, agreement, and openness. AR overlays contrast with the real world and affect the decision-making process in real time, whereas, in the traditional digital platforms, the user actively pursues the information. This user-friendliness comes at a cost of being easily integrated, yet this can also be associated with some apprehensions about the nature of invisible persuasion, particularly when algorithms lead their users to focus on the governmental priorities and do not make their purpose clear. To align with the ethical factor, AI-powered AR should be designed in such a way that it prevents assistance to border on manipulation. The citizens must not be coerced into making decisions that favor institutions sacrificing on individual right or free will.

Figure 2. Framework showing how transparency, accountability, and oversight support trustworthy AI-driven AR public services

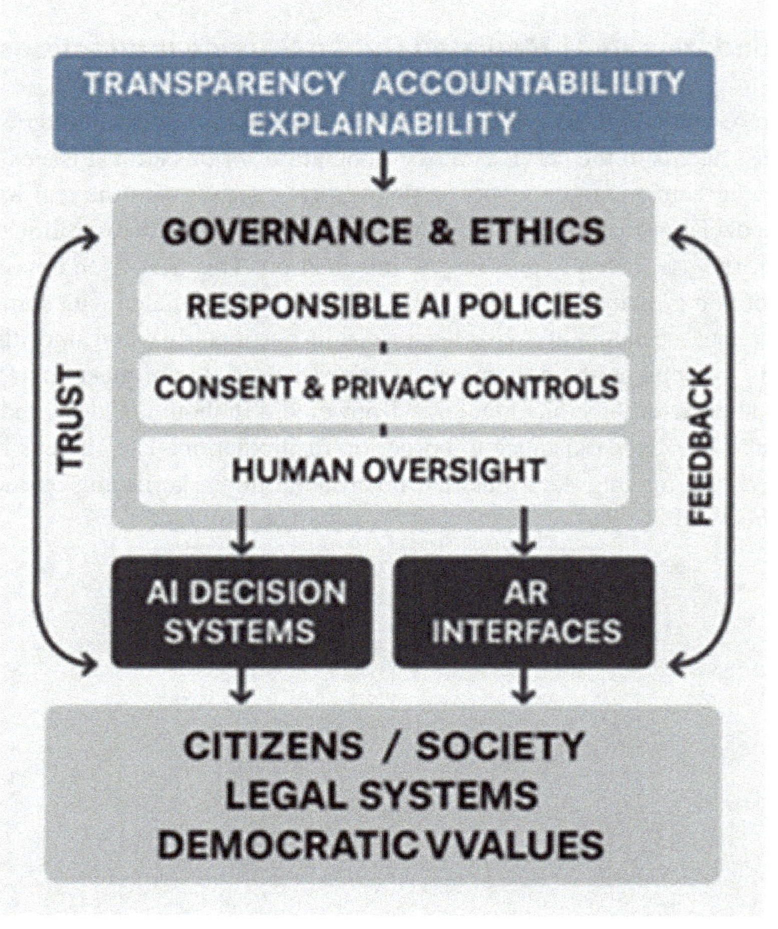

It is necessary to have a clear visibility of AI intervention when and how in ethical practice. When an AR system suggests a certain action or shows steps in a sequence, or points out certain pathways of the procedure, the user would know what is behind it. AR might end up being an instrument of behavioural control in the guise of support, unless it is transparent. As an example, when the AI focuses on the expedited routes of certain social groups without telling people plainly about the factors they take into account, it may lead to an unwanted discrimination. The design thinking on ethics then requires that the personalization algorithms should be rendered understandable and the purpose of suggestions public and not hidden in the interface (Méndez et al., 2023).

Another most important ethical dimension is consent. Personalization involves AI observing the behaviour of citizens, interpreting emotions, monitoring past interactions and modelling the contextual needs. These processes, however, must in no way mean blanket surveillance. Ethical implementation provides citizens with sufficient power to determine what data should be captured by the system, what kind of support needs to be used, and when personalization is supposed to be put on hold. The AI-mediated AR can become the instrument of empowerment as opposed to dependency when autonomy is maintained and clearly respected. This movement not only makes the technological design ethically responsible, but civic culture also bears a considerable responsibility in this, with the necessity of public service innovation being capable of doing this without sacrificing the dignity of an individual (Sahu et al., 2021).

5.2 Legal Accountability and responsibility Arrangements

The legal surface of the delivery of the public services increases due to the use of the AI-based AR systems, and in turn, the responsibility becomes much more complex. When some mistake takes place in one of the traditional public offices, the blame normally falls on an employee or a certain department. However, in the case of misleading guidance by the AI-based AR, loss of user-data, or failure of the procedure, it is hard to define the responsibility. Governments should come up with explicit laws to determine whether the human system developer, software developer, AI model instructor, or the institutional user is in charge of the failures. There will be no chain of accountability, and this can create injustice in case the citizens cannot point any responsible name in case of any mistake (Srinidhi et al., 2024).

The gathering and manipulation of sensitive personal data needed to personalize and provide predictive support have legal implications, as well. Disability records, family records, employment history, financial records, are some of the uniquely sensitive categories under the management of the public services. The range of error is very minuscule when AI-based AR infrastructure employs them to make an inference of behaviour or contextual adjustment. In order to remain legal, AR platforms need to adhere to strict rules of compliance such as data retention policies, restricting the data sharing to limit and encrypted data standards. The people are not supposed to lose privacy just to generate procedural efficiency.

More legal risk is created when AI-based AR is applied to high decisions in administrative contexts like social welfare benefits, taxation, healthcare benefits, or immigration. In case AR overlay information takes citizens through decision-making processes that touch on the rights defined by law, transparency and appeal rules have to be incorporated into the system. When the decision has legal or civil consequences, the citizens should be allowed to steer clear of algorithmic recommendations and seek human consultation of traditional nature. Procedural fairness, due process and protecting rights to democracy must be the legal basis of AI-enabled AR public services rather than seeking maximum administrative efficiency (Ouaissa et al., 2025).

5.3 Developing Social Confidence in AI Sourced AR Public Services

Trust is the key factor that will explain the frequency with which citizens will install and use AI-powered AR in the public sphere. The situations of the public service are often associated with anxiety and responsibility and requirements of the law, and thus, the adoption cannot be relied on only by technological convenience. Citizens should be assured that the system protects their privacy and is acting in their best interest and is not misinterpreting or abusing behaviour. When systems are transparent, predictable and respectful of individual control trust is increased. It dies away in cases where the citizens see manipulation, veiled surveillance, or algorithmic bias. As such, trust is not an aftereffect of the design of technology but a key performance indicator of AI-assisted AR systems.

When the process of AI-mediated support turns out to be reliable in various interactions, it enhances a sense of public trust. Effective results in overcoming complications in delivering services without confusion or two or more visits gradually build up confidence. The AR system also evolves such that the system proves to be a preset guide instead of experiment interface. When human support is there to act as a safety net, trust is also built. People should understand that AI is not going to deprive people of their help but prolong it. The factor of automation and human assistance also means respect to citizen choice and soothes possible opposition in the face of groups that use conventional channels of service delivery (Wang et al., 2024).

Lastly, the public trust is based on the role of communication by governments about the role of AI in the AR systems. The process of algorithmic personalization must not appear to the citizens randomly but, instead, during an explicit process of onboarding, which describes the scope and intention of personalization in all their manifestations. User agency is enhanced by mechanisms of reviewing and removing historical interaction data, balancing the level of support, or blocking behavioural tracking. Once institutions implement ethical visibility and transparency in law, AI-based AR is not just a technology innovation but a trust-building tool that helps to increase civic participation and build legitimacy in the democratic institutions of providing the public services (Ilo et al., 2024).

6 FUTURE DIRECTIONS AND POLICY FRAMEWORKS FOR SCALABLE AND RESPONSIBLE AI-DRIVEN AR PUBLIC SERVICES

6.1 Pathways for Large-Scale Deployment Across Public Service Domains

The future of AI-enhanced AR in the context of the public services remains to be created on the basis of the deployment models that can be scaled and adjusted to the various administrative backgrounds. The initial applications have been on the simplification of front-desk processes, but the real potential of AR reaches to changes of sophisticated systems of delivering services like healthcare access, court-support systems, taxation, immigration, and disability services. In contrast to the hard-core traditionalated portals where one agency requires a different version, the AR driven by AI may be deployed using modular architectures where services are integrated gradually. This modularity provides the agencies with the ability to adopt the system even when comprehensive infrastructure upgrades are not needed which shortens the financial and operational hurdles to adoption (Liao et al., 2021).

Scaling would be possible once the AR solutions are based on the interoperable datasets and the standardized service ontologies. The cross-agency harmonization of data will enable the citizens to transfer across the services in the future without undergoing repetitive paper work or re-filing the information that was verified before. A citizen who had joined a housing service application could subsequently apply school enrollment or tax benefit without having to reenter the identification processes. Integrity like this ensures not only the efficiency but also the emotional relief since citizens do not feel being the victim of the re-births of the same personal information in cyclical bureaucratic break-even. Those scaffolding structures motivate the focus on the idea that adoption of technology does not merely become the element of automation but the succession of establishing ecosystems capable of conducting respect to continuity of human relations with institutions.

Scalability will have to develop with digital equity strategies, however. The mere increase in AR infrastructure without the consideration of the digital divides may actually strengthen inequalities instead of eradicating them. The future deployment models should also have the provision of accessibility to rural populations, low-income families, aged citizens, and persons with disabilities. AR hubs in community centers, libraries, and civic offices can be used as a universal node of access to the list of individuals who lack personal devices. Only mass implementation will have its full transformational impact when its inclusion is inherent in its design and not dealt with as a secondary addition (Mamodiya et al., 2025)[30].

6.2 International Policy Standardization and Legal Preparedness to Intelligent Public Interfaces

As AI-enabled AR technologies become more entrenched within the administrative systems, governments will require policies that will have the potential to be able to control hybrid environments in which digital, material, and algorithmic interactions blend. Conventional IT governance models are preoccupied with data storage and cybersecurity but pay inadequate attention to the new reality, including real-time behavioural monitoring, proactive nudging, and predictive policymaking. The next generation policies have to establish ethical limits to personalization, where AI supplements and does not overtake citizen agency. Regulation is not only about protecting the data that its users have, but also protecting the psychological autonomy, transparency of choice, and equity in algorithmic thinking (Achiam et al., 2023).

The international collaboration may require the world organizations to initiate the international harmonization of the legal frameworks of the algorithmic responsibility of the public service. The absence of uniform policies across borders will put multinational AR vendors in an unequal situation across countries and privatize regulation and externalize the risks. The international legal systems ought to provide guidelines to explainability and auditability of the systems in case of dispute in the algorithm-mediated decision-making setting. The power to appeal the AI-controlled administrative results should be retained by citizens, and the systems of appealing the outcomes should be at the core of the policy development. The legal potential of the AI-driven AR is found not in the safeguarding of the digital right but the expansion of rights of democracy into digital administrative domains (Dogan et al., 2024).

Institutional innovations will also be necessary to guarantee the governments are abreast with technological advancements in the area of governance. Regulatory sandboxes can also be a critical component of a controlled experimentation tool by enabling agencies to test new services based on AR in real settings and trace ethical and legal risks. Policy preparedness is based on ongoing assessment as opposed to an analogous action in terms of regulation. The unceasing change in AI models steers that the regulatory touch should be changed to flexible regulation, where the policy modification should also keep pace with the technology upgrades. This control of fluid guarantees that the innovation does not override the social safety, trust, or even the constitutional values (Sathio et al., 2025).

6.3 Towards Humans-centred Futures and Co-designed Governance Patterns

The ultimate future of the AI-enhanced AR in the sphere of public services is not inevitable but rather the result of technological advances combined with the introduction of co-design approaches that will engage citizens in decisions. When the populace is considered as a stakeholder and not a passive receiver, the service design will become focused on dignity, equity, and social values. The co-design models open access to the testing of AR prototype by different groups of citizens, including elderly, persons with disabilities, migrants, students, and supporters of low literacy levels to set interaction preference grounded not on assumptions, but on lived experience. It is a participatory approach that means that the systems of the public services are tailored to the human diversity as opposed to work out in the best interest of the institutions (Huang & Hu, 2025).

Man-made futures also necessitate trust in the human population to move to the unreserved approval to the active signification. When citizens feel that AI-mediated AR is an empowerment tool, more of them will accept the concept with less resistance to change. Confidence is developed when a system proves empathy, accountability and reliability as time goes by. The prospective public service setting where AI-dependent AR will be a visible, predictable, and emotionally supporting aspect will result in an increased number of individuals being civically engaged and less fearful of the administrative procedures. Once technology is a facilitator of relationships, the process of communication with government does not look like a procedural burden anymore but rather like a lead through and confident experience, even reassuring (Lytvynova & Semerikov, 2021).

However, in the end, the future of AI-powered AR within the sphere of the work of the state apparatus will depend on society's readiness to perceive the development of technology as a way to efficiency or as a possibility to redefine the connection between individuals and state institutions. When applied in a responsible manner, AR systems could transform the concept of providing public services as an act of shared human experiences in the form of algorithmic intelligence and not a strict bureaucratic exchange. Having the potential to transform how public services could be not just smart and automated but also humane, bedside and highly personal through governance structures that adhere to user autonomy, cultural diversity, transparency, and emotional well-being, AI-mediated AR could create a future in which public services become not only smart and automated, but also humane, trustworthy, and extremely personal (Azuma, 1997).

CONCLUSION

The inclusion of AI-based augmented reality in the provision of the public services will be a pivot point in how the governments perceive and pragmatically promote engagement with citizens. Since times immemorial the challenge of seeking complexity in procedures and ensuring accessibility has bedeviled public institutions and has often resulted in systems that inundate users instead of empowering them. By employing AI in AR, this landscape changes as the citizens have been turned to a guided, intuitive, and personalized experience, where those in the public administration have been able to offer assistance when they need it instead of when they succeed in requesting assistance. Citizens are not required to go alone in the government environments but are instead dealing with the digital overlays that give them certainty, clarity, and in so doing, bureaucratic activities are made manageable and transparent.

The usefulness of AI-driven AR, however, is not limited to usability. These systems redefine what a public service means to be a human experience by adapting live based on their behavioural patterns, situational requirements, and emotional backgrounds and responses. Personalization, predictive support, and behavioural nudging will show that technology can no longer serve as a impersonal mediating tool between parties, but rather as an interpersonal guide, in which differences among individuals are treated respectfully and attentively. But the power of these systems is a risk, as well, of the highest degree. These tools that make civic interaction easier to accomplish can be easily exploited to threaten a choice, subvert privacy, or hypothesize inequality unless ethical and legal considerations are prioritized. This is why to this end, transparency, autonomy, and fairness should not be compromised at all as the technology matures.

In perspective, the realisation of AI-based AR systems is scalable with respect to policy frameworks, which are advanced along with technological innovations. The deployment should be inclusive and supported by governance models that will be accountable, protect the digital and psychological rights of citizens, and trust them irrespective of their culture and demographic backgrounds. This technological shift will not be deemed successful by reference to the automation, speed, and reduction of the cost but by the fact whether the public services would be more human, equitable and empowering. In a responsible setting the AI-driven augmented reality can redefine the interaction between governments and citizens making them stronger democratic values by establishing a system of public services that makes people feel knowledgeable, safe, respected, and heavily supported instead of being flooded with bureaucracy.

REFERENCES

Achiam, J., Adler, S., Agarwal, S., ... (2023). GPT-4 Technical Report. *arXiv preprint arXiv:2303.08774*.

Ali, S., Abuhmed, T., & El-Sappagh, S.. (2023). XAI: Trustworthy artificial intelligence. *Information Fusion*, *99*, 101805. DOI: 10.1016/j.inffus.2023.101805

Arrieta, A. B., Díaz-Rodríguez, N., & Del Ser, J.. (2020). Explainable artificial intelligence (XAI): Concepts and challenges. *Information Fusion*, *58*, 82–115. DOI: 10.1016/j.inffus.2019.12.012

Azuma, R. T. (1997). A survey of augmented reality. *Presence (Cambridge, Mass.)*, *6*(4), 355–385. DOI: 10.1162/pres.1997.6.4.355

Bangor, A., Kortum, P. T., & Miller, J. T. (2008). Empirical evaluation of the system usability scale. *International Journal of Human-Computer Interaction*, *24*(6), 574–594. DOI: 10.1080/10447310802205776

Bunt, A., Lount, M., & Lauzon, C. (2012). Are explanations always important? *ACM International Conference on Intelligent User Interfaces*, 169–178.

Cao, J., Lam, K.-Y., Lee, L.-H., Liu, X., Hui, P., & Su, X. (2023). Mobile augmented reality: User interfaces, frameworks, and intelligence. *ACM Computing Surveys*, *55*(9), 1–36. DOI: 10.1145/3557999

Danry, V., Pataranutaporn, P., Mao, Y., & Maes, P. (2020). Wearable reasoner: Enhancing human rationality with an explainable AI assistant. *Augmented Humans International Conference*, 1–12.

De La Torre, F., Fang, C. M., & Huang, H.. (2024). LLMR: Real-time prompting of interactive worlds using large language models. *CHI Conference on Human Factors in Computing Systems*, 1–22. DOI: 10.1145/3613904.3642579

Dhanorkar, S., Wolf, C. T., & Qian, K.. (2021). Broadening XAI design across the AI lifecycle. *Designing Interactive Systems Conference*, 1591–1602.

Dogan, M. D., Gonzalez, E. J., Ahuja, K., et al. (2024). Augmented object intelligence with XR-objects.

Dunleavy, M., & Dede, C. (2014). Augmented reality teaching and learning. *Handbook of Research on Educational Communications and Technology*, 735–745.

Goyal, N. K. (2025). Security and Privacy in IoT, Fog, and Blockchain Networks. In Sathio, A., Rind, M., Awan, S., & Junejo, A. (Eds.), *Energy-Efficient Deep Learning Approaches in IoT, Fog, and Green Blockchain Revolution* (pp. 371–398). IGI Global Scientific Publishing., DOI: 10.4018/979-8-3373-0300-0.ch015

Goyal, N. K., Dandotiya, M., Kumari, M., Kaloria, S., & Anushya, A. (2025). AI-Powered Haptic Devices for Patient Rehabilitation. In Mamodiya, U., Kalam, A., Bossoufi, B., Awad, M., & Somwanshi, D. (Eds.), *Integrating AI With Haptic Systems for Smarter Healthcare Solutions* (pp. 143–170). IGI Global Scientific Publishing., DOI: 10.4018/979-8-3373-2307-7.ch007

Goyal, N. K., Dandotiya, M., Kumari, M., Sheikh, M. F., & Sharma, S. (2025). Emerging Job Roles in the Tourism Sector Leveraging Artificial Intelligence. In Silic, M., Luthia, M., Ahmad, F., & Chakraborty, P. (Eds.), *Empowering Sustainable Performance and Competitive Advantage in Tourism* (pp. 89–126). IGI Global Scientific Publishing., DOI: 10.4018/979-8-3373-4546-8.ch004

Goyal, N. K., Dandotiya, M., Qurashi, J. A., Kumari, M., & Sharma, S. (2025). AI-Driven Predictive Analytics for Disease Management. In Ouaissa, M., Ouaissa, M., Imad, M., Qurashi, J., & Farooq, M. (Eds.), *Utilizing AI of Medical Things for Healthcare Security and Sustainability* (pp. 231–276). IGI Global Scientific Publishing., DOI: 10.4018/979-8-3373-0690-2.ch008

Goyal, N. K., Kumari, M., Kushwah, V., Dandotiya, M., & Vijay, A. (2025). Evaluating blockchain security: Trade offs in consensus mechanisms. *IET Conference Proceedings*, 2024(38), 80–88. DOI: 10.1049/icp.2025.0775

Huang, J., & Hu, Y. (2025). Systematic review of immersive VR in geography higher education. *Journal of Geography in Higher Education*, •••, 1–18.

Ibáñez, M. B., & Delgado-Kloos, C. (2018). Augmented reality for STEM learning: A systematic review. *Computers & Education*, *123*, 109–123. DOI: 10.1016/j.compedu.2018.05.002

Ilo, C., DiVerdi, S., & Bowman, D. (2024). Goldilocks zoning: Gaze-aware VR notification placement. *ACM Symposium on Spatial User Interaction*, 1–12.

Lee, J., Wang, J., & Brown, E.. (2024). GazepointAR: Context-aware multimodal assistant for pronoun disambiguation in wearable AR. *CHI Conference on Human Factors in Computing Systems*, 1–20.

Liao, Q. V., Pribić, M., Han, J., ... (2021). Question-driven design for explainable AI UX. *arXiv preprint arXiv:2104.03483*.

Lytvynova, S. H., & Semerikov, S. O. (2021). *Proceedings of the 4th International Workshop on Augmented Reality in Education.*

Maathuis, C., & Datcu, D. (2025). Transparency of AI-XR systems: Insights from experts. *IEEE AIxVR Conference*, 301–306.

Mattioli, A., & Paternò, F. (2023). Mobile AR app for controlling smart home automations. *Proceedings of the ACM on Human–Computer Interaction*, 7(MHCI), 1–22.

Mattioli, A., & Paternò, F. (2023). *Towards explainable automations in smart homes using mobile AR*. IS-EUD Workshops.

Méndez, J., Satkowski, M., & Rzayev, R. (2023). Explainability in hybrid user interfaces. *IEEE ISMAR-Adjunct*, 251–256.

Merchant, Z., Goetz, E. T., Cifuentes, L., Keeney-Kennicutt, W., & Davis, T. J. (2014). Effectiveness of virtual reality-based instruction: A meta-analysis. *Computers & Education*, *70*, 29–40. DOI: 10.1016/j.compedu.2013.07.033

Mikropoulos, T. A., & Natsis, A. (2011). Educational virtual environments: A ten-year review of empirical research (1999–2009). *Computers & Education*, *56*(3), 769–780. DOI: 10.1016/j.compedu.2010.10.020

Sahu, C. K., Young, C., & Rai, R. (2021). AI in AR-assisted manufacturing: A review. *International Journal of Production Research*, *59*(16), 4903–4959. DOI: 10.1080/00207543.2020.1859636

Slater, M., & Wilbur, S. (1997). A framework for immersive virtual environments (FIVE): Presence in virtual environments. *Presence (Cambridge, Mass.)*, *6*(6), 603–616. DOI: 10.1162/pres.1997.6.6.603

Srinidhi, S., Lu, E., & Rowe, A. (2024). XAIR: XR platform integrating LLMs with the physical world. *IEEE ISMAR*, 759–767.

Wang, Z., Shi, Y., & Wang, Y.. (2024). G-VOILA: Gaze-facilitated information querying. *Proceedings of the ACM on Interactive, Mobile, Wearable and Ubiquitous Technologies*, *8*(2), 1–33.

Wen, Y., Wu, L., He, S., Ng, N. H.-E., Teo, B. C., Looi, C. K., & Cai, Y. (2023). Integrating augmented reality into inquiry-based learning in science classrooms. *Educational Technology Research and Development*, *71*(4), 1631–1651. DOI: 10.1007/s11423-023-10235-y PMID: 37359487

Chapter 9
Enhancing Citizen Engagement and Transparency via Immersive Technologies

Muhamad Rohisul Iman
https://orcid.org/0009-0001-6636-9279
Universitas Esa Unggul, Indonesia

Binastya Anggara Sekti
https://orcid.org/0000-0001-5489-4888
Universitas Esa Unggul, Indonesia

ABSTRACT

The integration of Artificial Intelligence (AI) and Augmented Reality (AR) is redefining digital governance by shifting e-government toward immersive, context-aware, and predictive public services. AI enables decision intelligence through adaptive policies, behavioral insights, and proactive interventions, while AR enhances citizen interaction with spatial, real-time information. This chapter reviews the foundations, technological enablers, challenges, and applications of AI and AR in smart cities, public safety, healthcare, and participatory platforms. It also highlights ethical and regulatory concerns including fairness, accountability, surveillance risks, and institutional readiness. A conceptual framework outlines the architecture and organizational alignment required for effective deployment, followed by future directions stressing interoperability, ethical safeguards, and adaptive policy design.

DOI: 10.4018/979-8-3373-7804-6.ch009

1. INTRODUCTION

1.1 The Emerging Shift Toward Immersive Governance

The evolution of public administration has undergone several paradigm shifts, beginning with the emergence of e-government in the early 2000s, where digital portals served primarily as informational repositories and transactional gateways. While e-government improved efficiency, its interaction model remained largely one-directional, limiting deeper public involvement and reducing the government–citizen relationship to an exchange of documents and completed forms. The subsequent development of smart government expanded this digital foundation by integrating sensors, mobility systems, and analytical tools that enabled real-time system monitoring and data-driven decision-making. Smart governance marked a critical transition toward more responsive institutions, yet it still relied on predominantly screen-based interfaces that constrained how citizens perceived and interacted with public information. As urban environments grow more complex, these constraints have made it increasingly difficult for governments to communicate policies, spatial plans, and public infrastructure decisions in ways that are accessible and intuitive to diverse populations, reinforcing the broader shift in public administration toward more transparent, equitable, and democratized governance practices (Wei et al., 2024).

This evolutionary shift from e-government to immersive governance reflects a broader transformation within public administration toward governance reform, participatory models, and democratic responsiveness. Rather than treating digitalization as a purely technical enhancement, contemporary public administration increasingly frames technological adoption as an institutional and normative change that reshapes state citizen relationships. Bibliometric analyses of public administration research demonstrate a long-term transition from efficiency-oriented administration toward governance paradigms emphasizing transparency, equity, strategic management, and citizen participation, indicating that digital transformation is deeply embedded in the discipline's theoretical evolution (Wei et al., 2024). Within this trajectory, immersive governance can be understood as a continuation of governance reform, where emerging technologies serve not only as service tools but as mechanisms to enhance democratic engagement and institutional legitimacy.

Immersive governance positioned as the next stage of digital transformation emerges from the convergence of Artificial Intelligence (AI), Augmented Reality (AR), and spatial computing. Unlike earlier forms of digital governance, immersive governance is built upon experiential interaction, in which citizens and officials can engage with public data layered directly onto physical environments through AR visualizations, digital twins, and intelligent overlays. Such a paradigm enables users to explore policy impacts, infrastructure changes, and service predictions in context, rather than abstractly. AI functions as the analytical backbone of this model, generating insights, predictive simulations, and adaptive recommendations that power real-time, personalized AR experiences. Research on digital twins highlights the value of spatially grounded decision environments, demonstrating how immersive visualizations allow stakeholders to reason about complex systems more effectively (Glebova et al., 2023). Likewise, studies on navigational and urban AR interfaces emphasize that immersive overlays increase user awareness and safety, providing empirical justification for their use in public administration contexts (Aleva et al., 2024). Furthermore, public acceptance of technologically mediated interactions an essential ingredient for adopting immersive governance has been shown to depend on factors such as perceived usefulness, trust, and individual readiness toward emerging AI-powered tools (Lakshminarayanan et al., 2023), indicating that governments must consider social and psychological dimensions alongside technological capability.

In this emerging landscape, immersive governance does not merely digitize existing bureaucratic processes it redefines how information is perceived, understood, and acted upon. It shifts attention from passive consumption toward participatory exploration, supporting more democratic and transparent forms of engagement. The integration of AI amplifies this transformation by enabling systems that learn from citizen behavior, forecast administrative needs, and deliver context-sensitive information that would be impossible within traditional e-government structures. As governments worldwide confront increasing expectations for transparency, accountability, and adaptive public services, immersive governance presents itself as a structural advancement rather than a technological upgrade. It offers a model capable of bridging institutional complexity with human-centered design, setting the foundation for the next generation of public-sector innovation.

Figure 1. Shift from E-gov to immersive governance model

1.2 Classical Challenges in Citizen Engagement

Citizen engagement has long been one of the most persistent challenges in public administration. Traditional e-government systems often failed to overcome several structural limitations:

1. *Low transparency*, due to information overload or inaccessible design;
2. *Limited participation*, where citizens act only as passive service recipients instead of active contributors;
3. *Lack of real-time communication*, leading to delays in feedback, policymaking, and issue resolution;
4. *Minimal personalization*, because most systems used generic interfaces and one-size-fits-all service models.

These issues collectively weakened public trust and decreased meaningful participation in decision-making processes. Even with the rise of smart city technologies, many services still rely on dashboards and 2D interfaces that fail to represent complex governance contexts effectively. As highlighted by multiple governance studies, meaningful engagement requires environments where citizens can visualize, understand, and interact with information intuitively something traditional systems cannot deliver.

AI and AR provide solutions precisely at this intersection. AR enables the conversion of abstract data into spatial, visual, and interactive public experiences, which strengthens both comprehension and participation. For example, urban planning concepts or budget transparency initiatives can be presented as AR overlays mapped onto real environments. Meanwhile, AI enhances the quality of engagement by providing sentiment analysis, predictive analytics, behavioral pattern recognition, and automated decision support (Marshall & Naff, 2024). These capabilities help governments not only communicate with citizens but also understand them at scale, enabling more inclusive and adaptive governance models.

1.3 The Role of AI as a Driver of Decision Intelligence

One of the central enablers of immersive governance is AI-driven decision intelligence. Traditional government decision-making is often linear, time-consuming, and heavily dependent on manual processes. AI, however, introduces multi-layer analytical capabilities that can process large datasets, simulate scenarios, identify risks, and recommend optimal courses of action. Research shows that AI-based decision engines significantly enhance policy agility, resource allocation, and crisis preparedness (Marshall & Naff, 2024). In public health management, for instance, AI can track disease spread patterns, predict hospitalization surges, and assist in micro-targeted interventions capabilities that proved essential during the post-pandemic era.

In immersive governance, AI does not function in isolation. Instead, it serves as the computational backbone for AR interfaces. For example, AI-powered models can feed real-time data into AR applications used by citizens to visualize public service operations, or by frontline workers to perform field inspections more efficiently. This synergy forms a feedback loop in which AI provides insights, AR communicates them interactively, and citizen responses are captured again by AI to refine predictions. Through such cycles, decision-making becomes more dynamic, transparent, and participatory.

1.4 Augmented Reality as a Tool for Transparency and Interaction

While AI enhances intelligence, AR enhances visibility. AR's ability to embed information into physical environments allows citizens to navigate public services spatially rather than through abstract menus. In contexts such as transportation systems, public safety, and disaster management, AR can project safety instructions, hazard information, and real-time guidance directly onto a user's field of view. Studies confirm that these AR-based interventions reduce user errors, increase situational awareness, and improve safety outcomes (Aleva et al., 2024).

In governance, these strengths translate into new forms of transparency. Budget data, for instance, can be presented as AR visualizations in public spaces; infrastructure development updates can appear as AR overlays on construction sites; and environmental monitoring data can be displayed as live ecosystem indicators in parks or protected areas. Such transformations do more than present information they enable users to *experience* governance. The shift from static documents to immersive public information may become a turning point in rebuilding trust between government institutions and citizens.

1.5 Global Relevance and Post-Pandemic Acceleration

The global COVID-19 pandemic became a catalyst for rapid digitalization across all sectors, including public governance. Remote work, virtual public services, digital identity systems, AI-assisted health analytics, and telepresence solutions surged across nations. Post-pandemic governance studies emphasize that this period accelerated institutional readiness for advanced technologies previously considered futuristic (Aleva et al., 2024). Governments today face heightened expectations for contactless, efficient, transparent, and data-driven services.

AI-AR integration emerges as a logical continuation of this momentum. Countries such as China, South Korea, Singapore, the United States, and member states of the EU have begun experimenting with mixed reality applications for urban navigation, public education, crisis response, and civic participation. These innovations are supported by ethical guidelines emphasizing AI accountability, transparency, and fairness principles highlighted in contemporary AI ethics literature (Marshall & Naff, 2024). The convergence of global digital maturity, technological readiness, and regulatory frameworks creates fertile ground for immersive governance to expand.

1.6 Toward a New Era of Citizen–Government Interaction

Taken together, the transition from e-government to immersive governance represents not just a technological upgrade but a structural modernization of how governments communicate, collaborate, and co-create value with society. AI empowers institutions with predictive, analytical, and adaptive capabilities. AR empowers citizens with intuitive, contextual, and experiential interactions. When combined, these technologies have the potential to transform public services from procedural systems into intelligent, participatory ecosystems.

The remainder of this chapter builds on these foundations by exploring conceptual models, real-world applications, institutional readiness, ethical considerations, and future directions for integrating AI and AR into immersive governance.

2. CONCEPTUAL BACKGROUND

2.1 Defining AI, AR, VR, and XR in Government Contexts

Artificial Intelligence (AI), Augmented Reality (AR), Virtual Reality (VR), and Extended Reality (XR) form the technological foundation of modern digital governance. AI supports automated reasoning, prediction, and policy decision-making, enabling governments to analyze complex administrative data with greater accuracy (Marino-Romero et al., 2025). AR overlays civic information onto the physical environment, helping citizens access real-time updates for planning, infrastructure, or emergency contexts. VR provides fully immersive simulations for public training and education, while XR integrates AR, VR, and mixed-reality elements into a continuous spectrum of immersive tools. Together, these technologies establish the baseline for immersive governance, where intelligent computation and spatial interaction converge to support transparency and enhance public engagement.

2.2 Key Concepts in Immersive Governance

Immersive governance refers to a governance paradigm in which public administration processes such as policy communication, service delivery, and citizen participation are mediated through experiential and spatially embedded digital environments. Rather than relying solely on abstract, screen-based interaction, immersive governance aligns digital transformation with governance reform and democratization by enabling more transparent, participatory, and context-aware engagement between institutions and citizens (Wei et al., 2024).

Decision intelligence describes the application of AI-driven analytics, predictive modeling, and automated reasoning to support evidence-based and adaptive decision-making. In public-sector contexts, decision intelligence enhances administrative capacity by transforming large-scale data into actionable insights, enabling governments to anticipate risks, evaluate outcomes, and improve strategic management beyond traditional reactive governance (Wang & Li, 2024).

Spatial computing refers to the ability of digital systems to understand, map, and interact with physical environments in real time through sensors, spatial mapping, and immersive interfaces. Within immersive governance, spatial computing underpins AR-based public services by anchoring civic information, safety cues, and infrastructure data directly into real-world contexts, improving situational awareness and user comprehension (Zhang et al., 2025).

Predictive public services denote public services that proactively anticipate citizen needs, risks, or system failures using AI-based forecasting and contextual data analysis. By shifting from reactive service delivery toward anticipatory intervention, predictive public services support efficiency, equity, and safety in public administration, particularly in complex urban and public health environments (Obasi & Benson, 2025).

Taken together, the concepts of immersive governance, decision intelligence, spatial computing, and citizen engagement establish an integrated analytical foundation for this chapter. Within this framework, Artificial Intelligence functions as the cognitive layer that enables prediction, learning, and adaptive decision-making, while Augmented Reality serves as the experiential interface that translates complex policy logic and administrative data into intuitive, spatially contextualized interactions for citizens (Wang & Li, 2024). Rather than positioning AI and AR as standalone technologies, this study conceptualizes them as complementary components within a unified governance ecosystem, where algorithmic intelligence informs policy formulation and evaluation, and immersive visualization enhances transparency, comprehension, and participatory engagement (Wei et al., 2024). This integrated perspective provides the conceptual basis for examining how immersive technologies can support more responsive, inclusive, and citizen-centered models of public administration.

2.3 Emerging Technologies in Public-Sector Immersion

Emerging technologies strengthen immersive governance by expanding how citizens interact with digital public services. Wearable devices such as smart glasses and sensor-equipped headsets offer hands-free access and persistent engagement, as emphasized in (Baashar et al., 2023). Their embedded sensors also supply contextual information that adjusts AR overlays based on user location or movement. Intelligent Edge Computing (IEC) further ensures that AR content remains responsive, reducing latency for real-time visual guidance.

Digital twins, as presented in (Glebova et al., 2023), allow governments to model urban or administrative environments, visualize real-time public data, and support interactive AR or XR-based consultations. When combined with spatial-computing techniques that map physical environments in fine detail, these systems ensure that municipal notices, zoning visualizations, or safety alerts are accurately anchored in space. As a unified ecosystem wearables, sensors, IEC, digital twins, and spatial mapping these technologies enable scalable immersive governance that is context-aware, adaptive, and citizen-centered.

2.4 The Role of AI as the Cognitive Layer for Immersion

While AR and XR supply the visual interface, AI functions as the cognitive layer that shapes meaningful interactions. AI interprets public sentiment, analyzes behavioral trends, and adjusts the delivery of information according to user context. It also supports automated classification, issue prioritization, and adaptive guidance within AR-based service portals. In accountability-focused applications, AI-powered integrity monitoring systems detect inefficiencies, irregularities, or anomalies in public-sector operations (Liu et al., 2025). This integration ensures that immersive governance becomes not only interactive but also analytically grounded and transparent.

2.5 HMD Usability Framework and Its Relevance for Citizen AR Experience

The usability of head-mounted displays (HMDs) is crucial to ensuring that immersive governance remains accessible to diverse citizen groups. As described in (Zhang et al., 2025), the HMD usability framework evaluates ergonomics, interaction simplicity, cognitive load, and visual comfort. These dimensions determine whether citizens can engage effectively with AR-based public services.

Integrating wearable sensors and spatial computing into HMDs further enhances personalization and contextual relevance. Sensor data can adjust AR content based on movement or location, while spatial mapping ensures accurate anchoring of public notices, environmental cues, or service instructions. When usability principles guide the adoption of HMD-based AR systems, immersive governance becomes more inclusive, reduces interaction barriers, and aligns with democratic objectives of transparency and equitable participation.

Table 1. Comparison of AI, AR, VR, XR capabilities for public administration

Technology	Capabilities	Advantages	Limitations	Potential for Citizen Engagement
Artificial Intelligence (AI)	Data analysis, predictive modeling, automated decision-making, anomaly detection	Enables evidence-based policies, real-time insights, and proactive governance	Risk of algorithmic bias, data privacy concerns, high computational requirements	Personalized citizen services, transparent monitoring of public projects, AI-driven participatory feedback
Augmented Reality (AR)	Overlaying digital information onto physical environment, interactive visualizations, real-time updates	Enhances spatial understanding, intuitive communication of urban plans, contextual policy visualization	Device dependency (HMDs), usability issues, limited field of view	Visualizing infrastructure projects, interactive participatory planning, immersive policy briefings
Virtual Reality (VR)	Fully immersive digital environments, scenario simulations, training and education	Safe and controlled environment for civic training, emergency simulations, public education	High hardware cost, motion sickness risk, limited mobility	Civic education simulations, emergency preparedness drills, stakeholder workshops
Extended Reality (XR)	Combination of AR, VR, and mixed reality for continuous immersive experiences	Flexible deployment across different devices and contexts, integrated learning and engagement	Complexity in development, resource-intensive, requires high user literacy	Hybrid citizen engagement programs, interactive policy testing, immersive consultations

3. EVOLUTION TOWARD IMMERSIVE GOVERNANCE

3.1 From E-Government to M-Government and AI-Driven Smart Governance

Public administration has evolved from e-government to mobile-enabled governance (m-government) and now toward AI-driven smart governance. Early e-government digitized processes via online portals for document submission, service requests, and information dissemination. While improving accessibility and efficiency, these systems were largely passive, limiting citizen engagement and real-time responsiveness. M-government used mobile devices to enable anytime, anywhere interactions, enhancing immediacy, yet remained primarily reactive.

AI-driven smart governance integrates predictive analytics, real-time monitoring, and intelligent decision-support systems. By analyzing socio-administrative datasets,

AI helps governments anticipate citizen needs, optimize resources, and streamline workflows. This intelligence layer ensures timely, context-aware responses aligned with policy priorities. Incorporating citizen feedback into AI-driven simulations enhances urban planning and participatory governance, promoting transparency and informed decision-making (Nandkumar & Peternel, 2025).

3.2 Integrating 6G, AI, and Digital Twins

A key enabler of immersive governance is the convergence of 6G networks, AI intelligence, and digital twin technologies (Chataut et al., 2024). 6G networks provide ultra-fast connectivity and minimal latency, essential for real-time AR overlays and interactive urban simulations. AI interprets complex civic data, generates predictive models, and adapts experiences for individual users. Digital twins virtual replicas of physical spaces allow citizens and officials to explore infrastructure projects, urban plans, and service scenarios in context. This integration enables immersive, spatially grounded governance where citizens can visualize and interact with policy impacts, creating a more transparent and participatory public administration model. Cross-sector analogies from healthcare VR/AR training and digital twin-enabled simulations highlight the practicality of such systems in complex environments (Chance, 2025).

3.3 Lessons from Cross-Sector Technology Adoption

Evidence from healthcare and sports demonstrates both the benefits and potential risks of digital immersion. In healthcare, VR and AR platforms enhance clinical education, training simulations, and patient engagement, improving knowledge retention and practical skills (Alqutaibi et al., 2024). Similarly, AI-powered sports technologies support personalized training and inclusive participation, showing how intelligent systems can adapt to diverse user needs (Gagandeep et al., 2025). These examples provide valuable insights for public administration, highlighting the importance of user-centered design, ethical oversight, and effective risk management when implementing immersive AI-AR systems. By learning from cross-sector successes and challenges, governments can better anticipate potential pitfalls while promoting citizen engagement and transparency.

3.4 Implications for Immersive Governance

The shift toward immersive governance reflects the convergence of technology, intelligence, and spatial awareness. Integrating AI, 6G, and digital twins enables proactive, data-informed, and citizen-centered engagement. Citizens can explore policies, participate in urban planning, and monitor public services interactively. Cross-sector analogies provide both guidance and caution, emphasizing usability, inclusivity, and ethical safeguards. Immersive governance thus extends beyond a technological upgrade; it is a paradigm where transparency, participation, and intelligent decision-making redefine government–citizen interactions. These frameworks also enhance operational efficiency, adaptive policy implementation, and continuous improvement. By embedding participatory mechanisms, governments can strengthen citizen trust and ensure that urban planning decisions are informed by real-time feedback, fostering accountable and collaborative governance (Nandkumar & Peternel, 2025).

Figure 2. Immersive governance technology stack

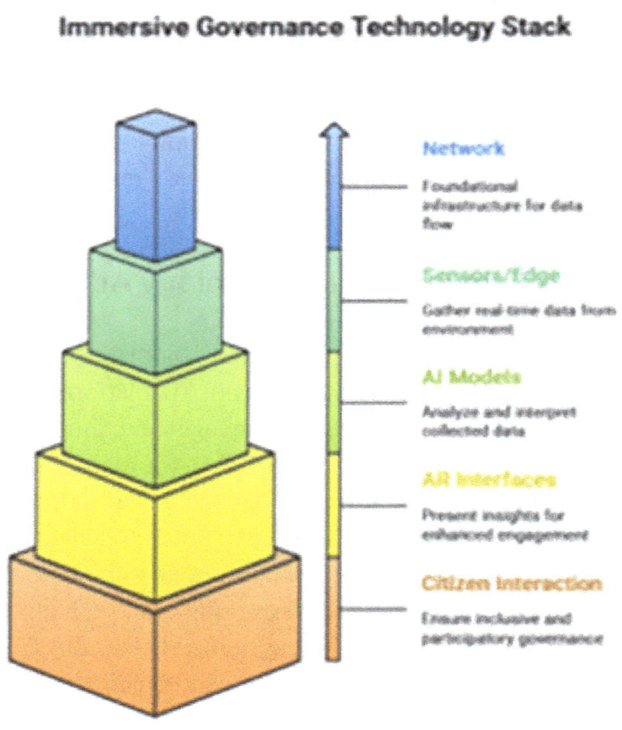

4. AI-POWERED DECISION INTELLIGENCE IN PUBLIC SERVICES

4.1 The Role of AI in Government Decision-Making

Artificial Intelligence (AI) is increasingly shaping modern public administration by enhancing decision-making processes through intelligent data analysis. Traditional governmental decisions often depend on manual evaluation, historical records, and expert judgment, which can be slow and limited in scope. AI, however, enables the processing of large and diverse datasets, offering predictive insights and adaptive recommendations. Predictive modeling helps anticipate citizen needs, optimize resource allocation, and forecast service demands, while automated evaluation systems can assess program effectiveness and identify areas for improvement. Behavioral analysis allows administrators to detect patterns in citizen interactions and respond proactively to emerging trends. This data-driven approach shifts governance from reactive management to proactive, intelligence-informed decision-making, enhancing responsiveness and accountability in public services (Anser et al., 2025).

4.2 AI in Healthcare and Related Sectors: Lessons for Public Administration

AI-driven innovations in healthcare, mental health, and radiology offer transferable models for public administration. In healthcare education, AI-enhanced VR simulations strengthen clinical competence, adaptive learning, and team performance (Chance, 2025). This demonstrates how intelligent systems can provide targeted feedback useful for government training, urban planning simulations, and policy scenario testing.

In mental health, AI analyzes behavioral patterns to deliver personalized interventions, increasing accessibility and autonomy (Anser et al., 2025). Governments can apply similar analytics to understand citizen needs, predict social risks, and tailor services.

Radiology further illustrates AI's anomaly-detection capabilities using CNNs and transformer hybrids (Elhanashi et al., 2025). Public agencies can adopt comparable tools to detect irregularities in budgets, service delivery, infrastructure conditions, or public safety operations.

These sectoral lessons highlight how predictive modeling can enhance emergency preparedness, automated evaluation can streamline departmental performance monitoring, and behavioral analytics can map citizen interaction patterns. Combined, they provide a strong foundation for scalable, data-driven governance.

Figure 3. AI decision intelligence workflow in public services

4.3 Ethical and Operational Challenges

Despite its advantages, AI adoption in public services comes with significant ethical and operational challenges. Bias in datasets and algorithms can lead to unfair outcomes, disadvantaging certain populations or reinforcing structural inequalities (Marshall & Naff, 2024). Privacy concerns are critical, especially when AI systems rely on citizen behavioral data, biometric sensors, or personal health information (Wang & Li, 2024). Data quality, completeness, and standardization are additional constraints, as flawed or inconsistent inputs can produce misleading predictions and undermine trust (Obasi & Benson, 2025).

Governments must therefore implement ethical frameworks, data governance policies, and transparent auditing mechanisms. Training public officials in AI literacy and ensuring continuous human oversight are necessary steps to prevent algorithmic errors or misuse. Moreover, citizen feedback loops should be integrated to validate AI recommendations and ensure that technological adoption aligns with democratic and participatory principles.

4.4 Implications for Citizen Engagement and Transparency

The integration of AI into decision-making directly impacts citizen engagement and transparency. By providing predictive insights, automated evaluations, and behavioral feedback, AI allows citizens to see evidence-based rationales behind policies and services. When combined with AR interfaces or immersive governance tools, citizens can explore data visualizations, monitor public projects, and interact with policy simulations in real time. These immersive, AI-enhanced experiences not only strengthen trust in public institutions but also empower citizens to participate actively in governance. Cross-sector lessons from healthcare and mental health underscore the potential for AI to personalize experiences, enhance accessibility, and facilitate accountability, setting a blueprint for immersive, intelligent governance.

Table 2. Classification of AI decision-intelligence capabilities in governance

Type of AI	Function	Potential	Risk	Public Service Example
Predictive Analytics	Forecast trends, anticipate citizen needs	Improved resource allocation, proactive service delivery	Bias in data, inaccurate predictions	Health service demand forecasting, urban planning
Automated Evaluation Systems	Assess program performance automatically	Efficient monitoring, performance optimization	Over-reliance on AI, lack of human judgment	Social welfare program assessment, budget evaluation
Behavioral Analysis AI	Analyze citizen behavior and feedback patterns	Personalized citizen services, early detection of issues	Privacy concerns, misuse of behavioral data	Public transport usage analysis, emergency response planning
Decision Support AI	Provide recommendations for complex decisions	Enhanced policy-making, evidence-based governance	Data quality issues, ethical concerns	Policy simulations, risk assessment for infrastructure projects
Adaptive Learning Systems	Adjust services based on real-time data	Continuous improvement of public services	Technical complexity, accessibility gaps	Smart city dashboards, citizen engagement platforms

5. AR FOR CITIZEN ENGAGEMENT AND TRANSPARENCY

5.1 AR as a Government Communication Medium

Augmented Reality (AR) is emerging as a powerful communication tool in public administration, enabling governments to present information in more intuitive and accessible ways. By overlaying digital content onto physical environments, AR makes policies, announcements, and service instructions easier to understand than traditional static channels such as printed notices or websites. It provides contextual, immersive experiences for example, visualizing urban planning proposals directly on city streets, showing public health guidance in hospitals, or delivering real-time safety and traffic alerts to pedestrians. These applications make public information more tangible and relevant, helping citizens grasp governmental initiatives more clearly.

AR also enhances participatory governance by allowing users to review zoning changes, infrastructure plans, or community proposals while submitting feedback within the same interface. This creates a more inclusive two-way communication process. Additionally, AR supports civic learning by enabling citizens to understand policies through interaction and observation rather than passive reading, improving comprehension and retention.

5.2 Enhancing Perception of Safety and Trust through AR

One of the critical benefits of AR in public administration is its ability to strengthen perceived safety and trust among citizens. Experimental studies demonstrate that AR interfaces improve situational awareness and reduce perceived risk, especially in public safety and transportation contexts (Aleva et al., 2024). For instance, AR signage guiding pedestrian movement near automated vehicles or construction sites significantly increases awareness, reduces uncertainty, and improves compliance with safety instructions. Similarly, AR visualizations of public infrastructure projects provide transparency regarding resource allocation, project timelines, and environmental impact, which enhances citizen trust in governmental decisions.

To maximize effectiveness, AR systems must consider usability and human factors. Head-Mounted Display (HMD) usability frameworks provide crucial guidance for developing citizen-facing AR applications (Zhang et al., 2025). Factors such as ergonomics, cognitive load, and visual comfort directly influence user engagement and willingness to interact with AR content. Government implementations that neglect these considerations risk low adoption rates and citizen disengagement. Optimized AR interfaces for public use should minimize physical strain, reduce information overload, and support intuitive gestures or gaze-based navigation, ensuring accessibility for users of varying technical literacy.

Figure 4. Building citizen trust with AR

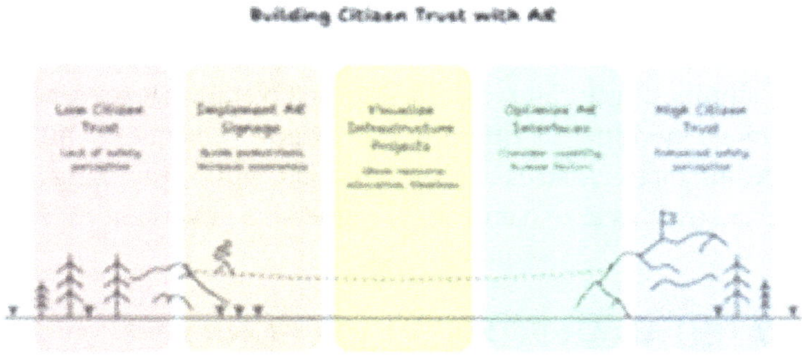

5.3 Case Studies of AR Implementation in Public Services

Several practical examples demonstrate how AR enhances citizen engagement and transparency across different governance domains.

1. **Pedestrian Safety and AR Signage:** AR can be deployed to overlay real-time guidance and safety instructions in high-risk pedestrian zones. This approach not only informs citizens but also reinforces compliance with local regulations, reducing accidents and improving public trust in city management. AR signage can integrate with traffic sensors, updating alerts dynamically based on pedestrian flow and vehicle movement, thereby providing context-sensitive, actionable information (Aleva et al., 2024).
2. **Urban Planning and Policy Communication:** Governments can use AR to visualize proposed spatial changes, such as zoning adjustments, infrastructure development, or environmental management initiatives. Citizens can explore digital models of urban projects directly on-site, offering comments, suggestions, or votes within the AR interface. Such participatory planning fosters inclusivity, strengthens transparency, and improves the alignment of governmental decisions with community preferences.
3. **Emergency Response and Public Awareness:** AR also plays a significant role in crisis management. Immersive visual overlays can guide citizens during natural disasters, health emergencies, or public safety incidents, providing real-time instructions for evacuation routes, shelter locations, or resource distribution. These AR-enhanced communication strategies improve citizen confidence, reduce panic, and enable more efficient coordination between government agencies and the public.

Across these cases, the combination of immersive visualization, HMD usability, and AI-driven analytics ensures that AR solutions provide not only information but also proactive engagement. By incorporating behavioral feedback, predictive modeling, and adaptive content, governments can continuously refine AR implementations to improve accessibility, clarity, and responsiveness. Overall, AR serves as a powerful medium for strengthening the relationship between governments and citizens, making policies visible, interactive, and easier to understand, while promoting transparency, participation, and trust as core elements of immersive governance.

6. INTEGRATED AI–AR FRAMEWORK FOR TRANSPARENT GOVERNANCE

6.1 Conceptual Overview of the AI–AR Governance Framework

The convergence of Artificial Intelligence (AI) and Augmented Reality (AR) presents a transformative approach for creating immersive governance ecosystems. Unlike traditional e-government or smart governance, which largely rely on static digital portals and analytical dashboards, AI–AR frameworks enable real-time, context-sensitive interactions between citizens and public services. In this model, AI functions as the cognitive engine, interpreting complex administrative datasets, predicting citizen needs, and providing actionable insights. AR, in turn, visualizes these insights in the physical environment, creating an intuitive and engaging interface for citizens to interact with government information. Together, AI and AR form an integrated loop where citizen input informs AI analysis, AI produces adaptive recommendations, and AR communicates outcomes in situ, facilitating a dynamic and transparent decision-making ecosystem.

The immersive framework is designed to bridge the gap between raw governmental data and meaningful citizen understanding. While traditional dashboards provide numerical or textual summaries, they often fail to communicate the spatial, temporal, or procedural aspects of policies. Through AI-driven simulations and AR overlays, citizens can perceive policy effects directly on city streets, urban infrastructure, or public facilities. For instance, citizens may view projected environmental impact of a zoning plan through AR visualizations, while AI models dynamically update scenarios based on real-time data and citizen feedback. This integration ensures that governance is not only transparent but also participatory, fostering trust and accountability.

Figure 5. AI–AR governance interaction loop

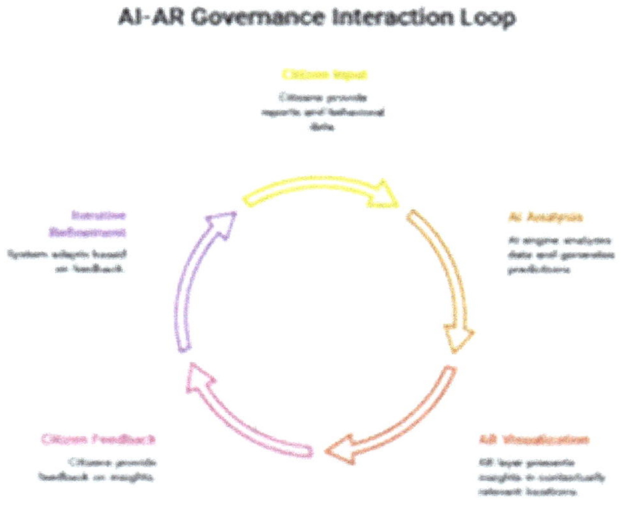

The figure illustrates the data flow from citizen reports and behavioral inputs into the AI engine, where predictive analytics, classification, and scenario modeling generate decision intelligence and policy simulations. These outputs are translated through the AR layer into context-aware visualizations delivered in relevant physical locations, enabling citizens to perceive policy implications directly within their environment. Citizen interactions and feedback captured via AR interfaces are then fed back into the AI models, forming a closed-loop system that continuously refines decision-making, policy evaluation, and public engagement.

6.2 Technical Architecture: AI Engine, AR Display, and Citizen Interaction

The technical backbone of this framework operationalizes AI–AR synergy through three core components: the AI engine, AR display system, and citizen interaction interface. The AI engine performs predictive modeling, automated evaluation, and behavioral analysis. Predictive models anticipate service demand, detect anomalies, and simulate policy scenarios, enabling proactive and evidence-based administrative decisions. Automated evaluation modules assess initiative performance, identify inefficiencies, and provide recommendations to improve service outcomes. Behavioral analysis interprets citizen interaction patterns to optimize service delivery and tailor AR visualizations, ensuring that public communication remains contextually relevant and responsive.

AR displays delivered through head-mounted devices or mobile platforms serve as the bridge between AI outputs and citizens. Unlike standalone AR applications that merely overlay static information, the proposed AI–AR framework operates as an intelligent immersive system. AI modules first analyze multisource administrative and sensor data through prediction, classification, and scenario modeling. The resulting decision intelligence is then translated into context-aware AR visualizations, enabling citizens to perceive policy impacts directly within their physical environment. This bidirectional workflow ensures that citizen interactions captured through AR interfaces continuously refine AI models, forming an adaptive and learning-based governance loop (Glebova et al., 2023). By overlaying digital content onto the physical environment, AR allows users to explore policy simulations, infrastructure information, and public advisories in real time. Interface design emphasizes ergonomics, low cognitive load, and intuitive navigation to maintain accessibility across diverse demographic groups. Citizen feedback collected through interactive AR elements is sent back to the AI engine, forming a continuous learning loop for refining policies based on real engagement.

This architecture is supported by cloud-edge hybrid infrastructures, enabling low-latency processing and adaptive content delivery. Edge computing maintains responsive AR performance in dense urban settings, while cloud systems manage large-scale data aggregation and long-term policy analysis.

6.3 Integration with 6G, IoT, and Intelligent Edge Computing

Next-generation network and computing technologies are critical for the operational viability of AI–AR governance. Integration with 6G networks provides ultra-high bandwidth and extremely low latency, enabling seamless AR content streaming and real-time AI computations across urban landscapes (Chataut et al., 2024). Internet of Things (IoT) devices, such as environmental sensors, traffic monitors, and wearable citizen devices, supply continuous streams of context-rich data to the AI engine. These sensors ensure that AR overlays remain accurate and reflective of real-world conditions, supporting applications such as smart urban planning, pedestrian safety, and emergency response. Intelligent Edge Computing (IEC) complements this architecture by processing data locally, reducing latency, enhancing reliability, and improving privacy for citizens' data (Lakshminarayanan et al., 2023). Together, these technologies allow for scalable, responsive, and highly adaptive governance interventions that respond dynamically to both citizen needs and environmental changes.

6.4 Digital Twin-Enabled Policy Simulation

A key component of the AI–AR framework is the use of digital twins, virtual replicas of physical urban environments, which serve as testbeds for policy experimentation and scenario analysis (Glebova et al., 2023). Digital twins integrate real-time data from IoT networks, demographic statistics, and citizen inputs to simulate the potential impact of public policies before they are implemented in the physical world. Through AR overlays, citizens can visualize these simulations in context, observing how new regulations, infrastructure projects, or environmental policies would affect their immediate surroundings. This capability enhances transparency by making governmental planning processes visible and understandable, and it empowers citizens to provide informed feedback based on tangible, immersive representations of policies.

Digital twin-enabled AR also facilitates iterative experimentation. Policy designers can adjust parameters within the AI engine, observe resulting changes through AR, and collect citizen reactions in real time. This feedback loop accelerates decision-making while minimizing the risk of unintended consequences. Moreover, these immersive simulations foster public trust, as citizens perceive governance decisions as evidence-based, participatory, and adaptive to community input.

6.5 Benefits in Transparency, Engagement, and Public Accountability

The integration of AI and AR within immersive governance offers significant advantages for modern public administration. Transparency is improved as complex administrative datasets are converted into accessible visualizations and real-time simulations, reducing information asymmetry between governments and citizens (Glebova et al., 2023). Engagement is reinforced through interactive interfaces that allow citizens to explore, provide feedback on, and respond to policy data directly within their environment. For example, AR visualizations of urban planning or emergency response scenarios enable citizens to experience policies contextually, fostering understanding and participation (Aleva et al., 2024).

Public accountability is strengthened through AI-driven monitoring and evaluation systems, which provide measurable insights into policy outcomes, while AR ensures that these outcomes are visible, contextualized, and interpretable for citizens. Furthermore, the framework emphasizes ethical and inclusive governance by embedding usability principles, privacy safeguards, and adaptive learning mechanisms, minimizing risks of exclusion, bias, or miscommunication (Zhang et al., 2025). Citizen-centric design ensures that immersive tools remain intuitive, equitable, and accessible, allowing all members of the community to meaningfully engage in governance processes.

Ultimately, the AI–AR integrated framework establishes a new paradigm where governments not only deliver services efficiently but also co-create decisions with an informed, empowered, and participatory citizenry, bridging the gap between administrative complexity and citizen understanding.

7. KEY USE CASES AND SCENARIO MODELING

The practical implementation of AI and AR in public administration provides a diverse set of use cases, demonstrating how immersive governance can enhance citizen engagement, transparency, and participatory decision-making. By integrating predictive analytics, immersive visualization, and interactive interfaces, governments can transform complex datasets into actionable insights while fostering public trust. These scenarios highlight the transformative potential of AI–AR frameworks across multiple sectors.

7.1 Urban Mobility and Digital Twin Planning

Urban mobility is one of the most immediate areas benefiting from immersive governance. AI-powered traffic analysis combined with AR overlays enables real-time visualization of traffic flow, pedestrian movement, and potential hazards. Digital twins create virtual replicas of urban environments, allowing citizens to explore infrastructure projects before implementation. AR signage guides pedestrians safely around construction zones, high-traffic areas, or automated vehicle paths, enhancing situational awareness and compliance with safety instructions (Aleva et al., 2024). Furthermore, by linking citizen feedback to AI simulations, urban planners can dynamically adjust designs or policies, making urban governance more participatory and transparent.

Mini-Case:

In urban mobility governance, traffic congestion, accident risks, and limited public understanding of infrastructure projects remain persistent challenges. AI systems analyze real-time traffic data and historical mobility patterns to predict congestion hotspots and simulate alternative road configurations. These analytical outputs are then visualized through AR overlays deployed at physical locations, allowing citizens to observe projected traffic flows, safety zones, and infrastructure impacts directly within their environment. By experiencing planning outcomes in situ and providing contextual feedback, citizens become active participants in urban decision-making, enhancing transparency and trust in government-led mobility initiatives (Aleva et al., 2024).

7.2 Public Health Visualization and Inclusive Accessibility

Immersive technologies extend to public health and inclusivity. AR dashboards can display localized health data, emergency alerts, and vaccination coverage, giving citizens actionable insights into community health status (Xu et al., 2023). AI models predict resource demand, identify high-risk areas, and optimize emergency response strategies. AR interfaces can be tailored for people with disabilities, offering spatial guidance, adaptive instructions, or assistive navigation in public spaces. Incorporating scenario-based simulations with digital twins allows governments to test interventions and predict outcomes before real-world implementation, enhancing trust and accountability in public health measures.

Mini-Case:

In the public health domain, limited access to localized health information, delayed emergency responses, and insufficient inclusivity for citizens with disabilities pose significant governance challenges. AI-driven models predict healthcare demand, identify high-risk zones, and optimize emergency response strategies based on dynamic population data. Through AR interfaces, health alerts, vaccination coverage, and spatial guidance are delivered in context-aware and accessible formats, including adaptive visual and navigational support for people with disabilities. This immersive approach improves situational awareness, accelerates response times, and strengthens public trust in health governance systems (Xu et al., 2023)

7.3 Smart Civic Education and Participatory Policy Simulation

AI and AR frameworks transform civic education by creating immersive environments where citizens can engage with policy simulations interactively. Participants can explore zoning changes, public service adjustments, or environmental regulations through AR, experiencing consequences of decisions virtually before policies are implemented (Y. Gao, 2025). Gamified modules and scenario-based simulations strengthen civic literacy, enabling citizens to provide informed feedback. When combined with urban mobility and public health scenarios, these educational interventions form a comprehensive system where citizens engage with multiple aspects of governance simultaneously, bridging knowledge gaps, reinforcing inclusivity, and motivating proactive participation. By integrating data from mobility, health, and education domains, AI engines generate adaptive insights visualized through AR, creating an iterative cycle of learning and engagement.

Mini-Case:

Low public understanding of policy changes and regulatory implications often limits meaningful civic participation. AI-enabled policy simulations allow governments to model zoning adjustments, service reallocations, or environmental regulations based on diverse citizen inputs. These simulations are presented through AR-based interactive environments, enabling citizens to explore potential outcomes and trade-offs before policies are implemented. By experiencing policy consequences virtually, citizens develop stronger civic literacy and provide more informed feedback, resulting in governance processes that are more adaptive, responsive, and inclusive (Y. Gao, 2025)

Table 3. Use case mapping to public sector impact

Contribution	Use Case	Impact on Governance
Digital twin modeling & AR overlays	Urban mobility and planning	Improved transparency, participatory urban decision-making
Public health AI visualization	Healthcare awareness & emergency guidance	Enhanced situational understanding and informed citizen choices
Accessibility-focused AR interfaces	Inclusive citizen engagement	Equitable access to government services for all
Smart civic education & AR simulations	Policy literacy and interactive governance	Informed, proactive, and engaged citizenry

These use cases collectively demonstrate the versatility of AI and AR in governance, showing how immersive technologies can bridge the gap between complex administrative processes and citizen understanding. By integrating predictive analytics, interactive visualization, and participatory interfaces, governments are better equipped to deliver transparent, equitable, and effective public services across diverse policy domains.

Beyond individual applications, these scenarios indicate a broader structural shift in public administration. Governance is no longer limited to one-way information dissemination through static digital platforms, but increasingly evolves into a continuous, data-informed, and experiential interaction between governments and citizens. Through AI–AR enabled feedback loops, policy formulation, evaluation, and refinement become iterative and participatory processes, strengthening public trust, accountability, and long-term policy legitimacy.

8. ETHICAL, LEGAL, AND SOCIAL IMPLICATIONS (ELSI)

8.1 Ethical Considerations and Bias in AI-Driven Governance

The integration of Artificial Intelligence (AI) in public administration brings significant ethical challenges. AI algorithms, when applied to public decision-making, can inadvertently introduce bias, undermine fairness, or perpetuate existing inequalities (Wang & Li, 2024). These risks arise from biased training data, opaque decision processes, or algorithmic assumptions that do not reflect the diverse needs of the citizenry. For instance, predictive models for resource allocation or public services may favor certain communities over others, reinforcing social disparities. Ethical governance requires continuous auditing of AI systems, transparent algorithmic processes, and mechanisms for citizens to contest or review automated decisions. Furthermore, automation may reduce human oversight in critical administrative decisions, increasing reliance on machine judgment and raising questions about accountability and moral responsibility in governance.

8.2 Algorithmic Explainability and Transparency

Ensuring transparency in AI-driven governance is essential to maintain public trust. Explainable AI allows citizens and administrators to understand how predictive models and decision-making algorithms generate outcomes. For instance, AI-powered public health visualization and accessibility tools rely on clear reasoning to justify resource allocation or emergency response strategies (Xu et al., 2023). Through AR interfaces, citizens can see how AI models interpret data and influence policy simulations, forming a feedback loop that enhances both transparency and accountability.

8.3 Privacy, Digital Overload, and Automation Dependence

Public deployment of AI and AR interfaces often involves extensive collection of personal or behavioral data, raising privacy concerns. Citizens' location, biometric, or interaction data can be leveraged for predictive modeling, but without proper safeguards, such data may be misused or inadequately protected. AI systems also introduce the risk of "digital overload," where citizens and administrators are inundated with complex, real-time information, potentially leading to decision fatigue or cognitive strain (Obasi & Benson, 2025). Over-reliance on automated systems may further reduce critical human judgment, creating dependencies that diminish adaptive capacity during unforeseen events. Policymakers must therefore balance technological sophistication with transparency, consent, and accessible data governance protocols to protect citizen rights while maintaining effective decision-making.

8.4 AR-Specific Challenges and Inclusivity in Public Spaces

Augmented Reality (AR) introduces unique ethical and safety considerations in public contexts. While AR can enhance citizen engagement and awareness, it can also pose physical safety risks if interfaces distract users in traffic zones, construction areas, or crowded public spaces (Aleva et al., 2024). Ethical deployment requires careful design, clear safety guidelines, and user education to prevent accidents or misuse. Additionally, inclusivity is paramount; AR systems must accommodate citizens with disabilities or varying levels of technological literacy to avoid exclusion (Gagandeep et al., 2025). Ensuring that immersive governance tools are accessible, equitable, and culturally sensitive strengthens legitimacy, enhances trust, and supports the broader goal of participatory public administration.

8.5 Digital Divide and Inclusive Access

Immersive governance frameworks must address inequalities in access to AI and AR technologies. Elderly populations, persons with disabilities, and residents in underserved areas may face challenges engaging with immersive public services. Adaptive AR interfaces and AI-driven accessibility features can mitigate these gaps, offering spatial guidance, personalized instructions, and inclusive citizen engagement (Gagandeep et al., 2025). By integrating these measures, governments can promote equitable participation, ensuring that immersive governance benefits all citizens regardless of technological familiarity or physical ability.

Overall, the Ethical, Legal, and Social Implications (ELSI) of immersive AI–AR governance highlight the necessity of balancing innovation with responsibility. Addressing ethical bias, ensuring explainability, safeguarding privacy, preventing digital overload, and reducing digital divide are critical to sustaining public trust and social equity in immersive public administration.

9. INSTITUTIONAL READINESS AND CAPACITY BUILDING

9.1 Organizational Preparedness for AI–AR Governance

Effective deployment of immersive governance frameworks requires institutions to possess adequate human resources, technological infrastructure, and regulatory alignment. Skilled personnel capable of operating AI engines, managing AR interfaces, and interpreting immersive analytics are essential for sustainable implementation. Institutional readiness also involves establishing clear operational protocols, robust IT infrastructure, and secure data governance mechanisms. Regulatory frameworks must adapt to emerging technologies to ensure ethical, accountable, and legally compliant practices. Without such foundational elements, even technically sophisticated AI–AR systems risk inefficiency, underutilization, or public mistrust.

9.2 Learning from Cross-Sector Experience

Public institutions can leverage lessons from the medical sector, where AR applications have been extensively used for training, decision support, and scenario-based education (Chance, 2025). AR-based simulations in clinical training demonstrate the effectiveness of immersive learning in improving procedural accuracy and situational awareness. Research also highlights that structured AR training modules significantly enhance practitioner readiness and reduce error rates in high-stakes environments (Selvaskandan et al., 2024), offering a transferable model for government adoption. Similarly, AI-driven analytics in healthcare improve predictive capabilities and operational efficiency, providing valuable insights for public-sector adaptation. By adopting sector-specific best practices, governments can design targeted training programs, establish competency frameworks, and implement scenario-based exercises for civil servants interacting with immersive governance platforms.

9.3 Integrating AI Ethics into Institutional Practice

Organizational adaptation also entails embedding ethical considerations into institutional routines. Policies and procedures must align with AI ethics principles, covering issues such as bias mitigation, transparency, accountability, and citizen privacy (Marshall & Naff, 2024). Training modules should include ethics-focused scenarios that guide decision-makers in responsible deployment of AI–AR technologies. Furthermore, institutions must cultivate a culture of continuous learning and evaluation, ensuring that emerging risks are addressed proactively and that staff remain proficient in evolving technological and ethical standards.

Table 4. Institutional AI–AR readiness assessment dimensions

Dimension	Description	Indicator
Human Resources	Skills and expertise of staff to operate AI–AR systems	Number of trained personnel, competency scores
Infrastructure	Availability and quality of hardware, software, and networks	System uptime, device availability, network latency
Training and Capacity Building	Programs to develop immersive governance skills	Number of training sessions, participation rate
Regulatory and Ethical Alignment	Policies supporting ethical AI–AR adoption	Presence of AI ethics guidelines, compliance audits

In summary, institutional readiness and capacity building are critical determinants of successful AI–AR immersive governance. By aligning resources, training programs, and ethical frameworks with technical deployments, governments can ensure that citizens benefit from transparent, participatory, and responsible digital governance solutions.

10. FUTURE DIRECTIONS AND SMART CITY INTEGRATION

10.1 AI–AR, 6G, and Immersive Technologies for Smart Cities

The convergence of 6G networks, Artificial Intelligence (AI), and Augmented Reality (AR) is transforming urban governance and citizen engagement (Chataut et al., 2024). High-speed, low-latency 6G enables AI engines to perform real-time predictive modeling, behavioral analysis, and adaptive decision-making efficiently. AR overlays translate these insights into intuitive, context-aware visualizations, helping citizens understand public policies, urban planning, and service delivery. This combination forms the core of future smart city ecosystems, promoting transparency, participatory governance, and effective resource allocation.

Global trends in VR and AR, especially in mental health and education, demonstrate immersive experiences' potential for scalable citizen engagement (S. Gao et al., 2025). Interactive simulations allow citizens to explore policy scenarios, learn emergency procedures, and engage with civic initiatives safely and intuitively. Such applications exemplify how immersive technologies can support experiential learning, behavioral adaptation, and civic empowerment, extending beyond conventional communication channels.

10.2 Smart Transportation, Predictive OSH, and Citizen Digital Twins

Smart transportation represents a key area for AI–AR integration, optimizing traffic flows, enhancing pedestrian safety, and coordinating emergency responses (Obasi & Benson, 2025). AR-based signage and interactive route guidance improve situational awareness, while AI predicts hazards to create proactive, safer urban environments. Similarly, predictive Occupational Safety and Health (OSH) systems allow authorities to anticipate risks and mitigate accidents in public spaces, ensuring ethical responsibility in digital governance.

Citizen digital twins virtual representations of individuals' interactions within urban systems offer a participatory governance tool. By simulating policy impacts on behavior, authorities can test interventions, assess inclusivity, and refine urban planning before real-world implementation. Digital twins enable citizens to visualize outcomes, provide feedback, and co-create solutions with public institutions, reinforcing engagement, transparency, and accountability.

11. CONCLUSION

This study has explored the transformative potential of integrating Artificial Intelligence (AI) and Augmented Reality (AR) within public administration, emphasizing immersive governance as a next-generation paradigm. Across the chapters, the research traced the evolution from traditional e-government and smart governance toward immersive, citizen-centered frameworks, highlighting how AI serves as the cognitive engine and AR functions as an intuitive interface for engagement and transparency. By leveraging predictive modeling, automated evaluation, behavioral analysis, and context-aware AR visualizations, governments can transform decision-making from reactive management into proactive, intelligence-driven processes.

The integration of AI and AR has demonstrated tangible benefits in fostering citizen engagement, improving perceptions of safety, and enhancing transparency in policy communication. Case studies and cross-sector analogies from healthcare and occupational safety to sports analytics and urban planning illustrate how immersive technologies promote participatory governance and informed decision-making while mitigating risks related to bias, privacy, and digital overload. Furthermore, usability frameworks for Head-Mounted Displays (HMDs) and citizen-centric interface principles ensure that immersive systems remain inclusive, accessible, and capable of supporting equitable participation across diverse communities.

The journals referenced throughout this study provide a solid conceptual foundation for understanding the convergence of AI, AR, digital twins, IoT, and emerging communication networks. Collectively, these sources highlight the growing institutional need for adaptive governance models, scenario-driven evaluation, and ethical guidelines that align technological innovation with accountability, fairness, and long-term public value. These scholarly contributions also reinforce the argument that immersive governance will increasingly rely on multidisciplinary collaboration combining insights from public administration, computer science, behavioral studies, ethics, and urban policy.

Looking forward, AI and AR frameworks hold significant promise for shaping next-generation smart city ecosystems through real-time policy simulation, predictive safety management, and citizen digital twins that enable deeper civic engagement. As urban systems become more interconnected, future trends will increasingly involve autonomous decision-support agents, interoperable spatial platforms, multimodal public interfaces, and hyper-contextual public services that respond dynamically to citizen needs. Emerging technologies such as 6G networks, holographic communication, and advanced spatial analytics are expected to further accelerate this transformation, enabling ultra-low-latency public services and fully immersive civic environments. Governments may also adopt more resilient architectures that integrate edge intelligence, decentralized data governance, and cross-sector collaboration to maintain continuity during crises.

Looking ahead, immersive governance frameworks are likely to leverage digital twins to simulate complex urban, social, and policy scenarios in real time. The integration of multimodal XR interfaces will allow citizens to engage with data and simulations across multiple sensory channels, enhancing understanding, participation, and decision-making. Edge intelligence and distributed computing architectures will provide low-latency, context-aware decision support, while minimizing dependence on centralized infrastructures. Additionally, promoting interoperability and avoiding vendor lock-in will ensure governments can integrate diverse AI and AR systems flexibly, supporting sustainable and scalable public administration. These developments point toward a realistic and actionable path for future public governance that balances technological innovation with accessibility, resilience, and citizen-centric design.

Ultimately, this work affirms that immersive governance powered by the combined capabilities of AI and AR can create more transparent, engaging, and citizen-responsive public administration. The findings also suggest that sustained innovation, ethical vigilance, and institutional readiness will be essential as societies transition toward more immersive, data-driven, and future-oriented models of governance in the digital era. As these technologies continue to mature, governments that embrace experimentation, adopt adaptive regulatory frameworks, and invest in long-term capacity building will be best positioned to realize the full potential of immersive governance and deliver meaningful public value for decades to come.

REFERENCES

Aleva, T. K., Tabone, W., Dodou, D., & de Winter, J. C. F. (2024). Augmented reality for supporting the interaction between pedestrians and automated vehicles: An experimental outdoor study. *Frontiers in Robotics and AI*, *11*, 1324060. DOI: 10.3389/frobt.2024.1324060 PMID: 38352957

Alqutaibi, A. Y., Hamadallah, H. H., Oqbi, H. F., Almuzaini, S. A., & Borzangy, S. (2024). Current applications and future perspective of virtual reality in dental education and practice in Saudi Arabia: A scoping review. *The Saudi Dental Journal*, *36*(11), 1406–1416. DOI: 10.1016/j.sdentj.2024.09.007 PMID: 39619710

Anser, M. K., Nabi, A. A., Ahmad, I., Abro, M. M. Q., & Zaman, K. (2025). Advancing Mental Health Care: A Comprehensive Review of Digital Tools and Technologies for Enhancing Diagnosis, Treatment, and Wellness. *Health Care Science*, *4*(3), 163–178. DOI: 10.1002/hcs2.70018 PMID: 40563629

Baashar, Y., Alkawsi, G., Wan Ahmad, W. N., Alomari, M. A., Alhussian, H., & Tiong, S. K. (2023). Towards Wearable Augmented Reality in Healthcare: A Comparative Survey and Analysis of Head-Mounted Displays. *International Journal of Environmental Research and Public Health*, *20*(5), 3940. DOI: 10.3390/ijerph20053940 PMID: 36900951

Chance, E. A. (2025). The combined impact of AI and VR on interdisciplinary learning and patient safety in healthcare education: A narrative review. *BMC Medical Education*, *25*(1), 1039. DOI: 10.1186/s12909-025-07589-7 PMID: 40646457

Chataut, R., Nankya, M., & Akl, R. (2024). 6G Networks and the AI Revolution—Exploring Technologies, Applications, and Emerging Challenges. *Sensors (Basel)*, *24*(6), 1888. DOI: 10.3390/s24061888 PMID: 38544151

Elhanashi, A., Saponara, S., Zheng, Q., Almutairi, N., Singh, Y., Kuanar, S., Ali, F., Unal, O., & Faghani, S. (2025). AI-Powered Object Detection in Radiology: Current Models, Challenges, and Future Direction. *Journal of Imaging*, *11*(5), 141. DOI: 10.3390/jimaging11050141 PMID: 40422999

Gagandeep, V., Verma, J., Pradhan, K. B., & Singh, M. (2025). AI technologies in adaptive sports: Enhancing performance, health, and well-being. *Acta Psychologica*, *261*, 105879. DOI: 10.1016/j.actpsy.2025.105879 PMID: 41192399

Gao, S., Su, P., Wang, A., & Tao, Y. (2025). A Bibliometric Study of the Evidence About Applying Virtual Reality in Mental Health Care. *Journal of Multidisciplinary Healthcare*, *18*(0), 5213–5225. DOI: 10.2147/JMDH.S536946 PMID: 40900715

Gao, Y. (2025). The role of artificial intelligence in enhancing sports education and public health in higher education: Innovations in teaching models, evaluation systems, and personalized training. *Frontiers in Public Health, 13*, 1554911. DOI: 10.3389/fpubh.2025.1554911 PMID: 40371284

Glebova, E., Book, R., Su, Y., Perić, M., & Heller, J. (2023). Sports venue digital twin technology from a spectator virtual visiting perspective. *Frontiers in Sports and Active Living, 5*, 1289140. DOI: 10.3389/fspor.2023.1289140 PMID: 38116386

Lakshminarayanan, V., Ravikumar, A., Sriraman, H., Alla, S., & Chattu, V. K. (2023). Health Care Equity Through Intelligent Edge Computing and Augmented Reality/ Virtual Reality: A Systematic Review. *Journal of Multidisciplinary Healthcare, 16*(0), 2839–2859. DOI: 10.2147/JMDH.S419923 PMID: 37753339

Liu, J., Wang, X., & Zhang, J. (2025). Investigating Elderly Individuals' Acceptance of Artificial Intelligence (AI)-Powered Companion Robots: The Influence of Individual Characteristics. *Behavioral Sciences (Basel, Switzerland), 15*(5), 697. DOI: 10.3390/bs15050697 PMID: 40426474

Marino-Romero, J. A., Robina-Ramírez, R., Pavón-Pérez, J. A., & Roets, A. O. S. B. (2025). Enhancing happiness and well-being: AI-driven solutions for accessible, inclusive travel experiences for people with disabilities. *Disability and Rehabilitation. Assistive Technology, 20*(7), 2173–2184. DOI: 10.1080/17483107.2025.2488391 PMID: 40220310

Marshall, D. T., & Naff, D. B. (2024). The Ethics of Using Artificial Intelligence in Qualitative Research. *Journal of Empirical Research on Human Research Ethics; JERHRE, 19*(3), 92–102. DOI: 10.1177/15562646241262659 PMID: 38881315

Nandkumar, C., & Peternel, L. (2025). Enhancing supermarket robot interaction: An equitable multi-level LLM conversational interface for handling diverse customer intents. *Frontiers in Robotics and AI, 12*, 1576348. DOI: 10.3389/frobt.2025.1576348 PMID: 40365556

Obasi, I. C., & Benson, C. (2025). The Impact of Digitalization and Information and Communication Technology on the Nature and Organization of Work and the Emerging Challenges for Occupational Safety and Health. *International Journal of Environmental Research and Public Health, 22*(3), 362. DOI: 10.3390/ijerph22030362 PMID: 40238361

Selvaskandan, H., Gee, P. O., & Seethapathy, H. (2024). Technological Innovations to Improve Patient Engagement in Nephrology. *Advances in Kidney Disease and Health, 31*(1), 28–36. DOI: 10.1053/j.akdh.2023.11.001 PMID: 38403391

Wang, J., & Li, J. (2024). Artificial intelligence empowering public health education: Prospects and challenges. *Frontiers in Public Health*, *12*, 1389026. DOI: 10.3389/fpubh.2024.1389026 PMID: 39022411

Wei, R.-Z., Liu, X.-Y., & Lyu, P.-H. (2024). Bibliometrics of public administration research hotspots: Topic keywords, author keywords, keywords plus analysis. *Heliyon*, *10*(21), e39352. DOI: 10.1016/j.heliyon.2024.e39352 PMID: 39524883

Xu, C., Solomon, S. A., & Gao, W. (2023). Artificial intelligence-powered electronic skin. *Nature Machine Intelligence*, *5*(12), 1344–1355. DOI: 10.1038/s42256-023-00760-z PMID: 38370145

Zhang, P., Wang, Z., Wang, T., Liu, T., Wang, J., Gao, Y., & Li, W. (2025). Evaluating Augmented Reality Head-Mounted Devices in Healthcare: A Review of Hardware, Software, and Usability Approaches. *Medical Devices (Auckland, N.Z.)*, *18*(0), 427–445. DOI: 10.2147/MDER.S541187 PMID: 40873666

Chapter 10
Future Trends and Innovations in Digital Public Administration

Blaise Joseph
Saveetha School of Law, Saveetha Institute of Medical and Technical Sciences, India

J. Aadithya
https://orcid.org/0009-0002-6598-9350
Saveetha School of Law, Saveetha Institute of Medical and Technical Sciences, India

C. Devadharshini
https://orcid.org/0009-0006-6469-623X
Saveetha School of Law, Saveetha Institute of Medical and Technical Sciences, India

P. Selvakumar
https://orcid.org/0000-0002-3650-4548
Department of Science and Humanities, Nehru Institute of Technology, Coimbatore, India

S. Vignesh
https://orcid.org/0009-0002-0316-2155
Saveetha School of Law, Saveetha Institute of Medical and Technical Sciences, India

S. Giriprasad
https://orcid.org/0000-0002-7258-8056
SRM Institute of Science and Technology, India

ABSTRACT

The rise of Artificial Intelligence (AI)-powered governance marks a profound transformation in the way public services are delivered, managed, and experienced, ushering in a new era of efficiency, transparency, and citizen-centric administration. As governments worldwide face growing complexities—including rapidly expanding populations, socio-economic inequalities, climate challenges, and heightened expectations for accountability—AI has emerged as a strategic enabler capable of supporting smarter decision-making and seamless service delivery across the public sector. AI-powered governance leverages technologies such as machine learning,

DOI: 10.4018/979-8-3373-7804-6.ch010

natural language processing, predictive analytics, and autonomous systems to modernize public administration by automating bureaucratic operations, enhancing data-driven policymaking, and improving accessibility and responsiveness in citizen-facing services. For example, intelligent virtual assistants are increasingly deployed in municipal offices, healthcare facilities, welfare programs, and legal institutions to streamline case submissions.

THE RISE OF AI-POWERED GOVERNANCE: TRANSFORMING PUBLIC SERVICES

The rise of Artificial Intelligence (AI)-powered governance marks a profound transformation in the way public services are delivered, managed, and experienced, ushering in a new era of efficiency, transparency, and citizen-centric administration. As governments worldwide face growing complexities—including rapidly expanding populations, socio-economic inequalities, climate challenges, and heightened expectations for accountability—AI has emerged as a strategic enabler capable of supporting smarter decision-making and seamless service delivery across the public sector. AI-powered governance leverages technologies such as machine learning, natural language processing, predictive analytics, and autonomous systems to modernize public administration by automating bureaucratic operations, enhancing data-driven policymaking, and improving accessibility and responsiveness in citizen-facing services. For example, intelligent virtual assistants are increasingly deployed in municipal offices, healthcare facilities, welfare programs, and legal institutions to streamline case submissions, respond to queries in real time, and reduce administrative bottlenecks. By integrating AI with digital platforms, governments can deliver inclusive, multilingual, and around-the-clock services, significantly reduce service delays and operational costs while foster trust and satisfaction among diverse populations. A central driver behind the rapid rise of AI-powered governance is the unprecedented growth in data generated through digital public services, IoT-enabled urban infrastructures, and citizen engagement platforms. AI converts this vast data ecosystem into actionable insights that support evidence-based policymaking, allowing governments to detect patterns, forecast societal needs, and anticipate emerging risks before they escalate into crises.

Smart cities exemplify the integration of AI-driven public governance, where traffic optimization, energy management, waste collection, and environmental monitoring rely on intelligent automation to improve quality of life and sustainability performance. Similarly, AI strengthens social services by identifying vulnerable populations, tailoring subsidy distributions, and preventing fraud or misuse of public funds, thereby ensuring more equitable governance outcomes. In regulatory functions,

AI is transforming compliance monitoring through advanced anomaly detection to combat financial crime, tax evasion, and corruption—longstanding barriers to efficient governance. Moreover, AI is becoming a catalyst for hyper-personalized public policy and services. Instead of one-size-fits-all programs, governments can deploy recommendation systems that tailor resources to individual or community-level needs, improving the effectiveness of public investments. Education systems are increasingly integrating AI to support personalized learning pathways, optimize resource allocations, and improve student performance analytics. Healthcare systems are adopting AI-driven diagnostics, telemedicine platforms, and public health surveillance systems that enhance accessibility and reduce inequalities in care delivery. Law enforcement and judicial systems are experimenting with AI for case prioritization, digital evidence analysis, and crime pattern detection, which can expedite justice processes and reduce case backlogs. However, such interventions must be implemented responsibly to avoid reinforcing bias, violating privacy, or undermining civil liberties.

DIGITAL TRANSFORMATION IN GOVERNMENT: TRENDS AND OPPORTUNITIES

Digital transformation in government represents one of the most significant administrative evolutions of the 21st century, fundamentally reshaping how the public sector operates, delivers services, and engages with citizens. (Basu S. K. et al. 2026) As societies become increasingly digital and data-driven, governments worldwide are adopting advanced technologies—such as cloud computing, artificial intelligence (AI), the Internet of Things (IoT), blockchain, and data analytics—to modernize legacy systems, reduce administrative inefficiencies, and improve responsiveness in public service delivery. The shift towards digital-first governance reflects a broader objective: to create agile, transparent, resilient, and citizen-centered institutions capable of addressing emerging socio-economic challenges, from rapid urbanization and climate pressures to pandemics and shifting public expectations. This transformation emphasizes connected digital ecosystems where services are integrated, interoperable, and accessible anywhere, anytime, ensuring that governance aligns with the needs of modern digital societies. (Basu S. K. et al. 2026) A primary driver of digital transformation in government is the growing demand for convenience, inclusiveness, and efficiency. Citizens increasingly expect the same seamless digital interfaces from public services that they experience in the private sector—from online banking to e-commerce and mobile healthcare. As a result, governments are replacing manual, paper-based processes with automated and online service portals for everything from tax payments and permit applications to voting, welfare access, and healthcare appointments. These digital services significantly reduce waiting times, cut operational costs, and minimize bureaucratic complexity, enabling faster and more satisfying interactions with government institutions.

Beyond efficiency, digitalization also enhances transparency by making data publicly accessible, enabling open-government platforms where citizens can track budgets, legislation, and performance metrics in real time. (Bertot J. C. et al. 2016) Such transparency fosters trust and accountability, helping to rebuild confidence in public administration during a time of growing skepticism toward political institutions. Data has become a strategic asset in digital governance. With the proliferation of public digital platforms, governments now collect and process extensive data on population behavior, urban systems, and economic trends. Advanced analytics and AI convert this data into actionable insights that support evidence-based policymaking, enabling earlier risk detection, better resource allocation, and more targeted social programs. For example, predictive analytics can identify communities at risk of poverty or health crises, guide preventative interventions, and improve long-term outcomes. AI-enabled data processing also improves internal operations—automating records management, fraud detection, and policy compliance monitoring—allowing public sector workers to focus on higher-value tasks requiring human judgment. (Bertot J. C. et al. 2016) Moreover, digital identity systems and secure authentication technologies facilitate secure service access while protecting citizen privacy. Many nations now deploy national digital ID platforms, enabling one-stop login credentials for multiple public applications, strengthening efficiency and inclusion across all demographic groups. Emerging technologies are further expanding the scope of digital transformation initiatives. IoT-enabled smart city infrastructures enhance traffic management, waste collection, water distribution, and environmental monitoring, optimizing urban operations while reducing emissions and resource waste.

CITIZEN-CENTRIC DIGITAL PUBLIC ADMINISTRATION: A NEW ERA — 10,000 CHARACTERS

Citizen-centric digital public administration represents a fundamental shift in governance philosophy—one that prioritizes the needs, experiences, and empowerment of individuals at the core of public service design and delivery. (Bobro N. et al. 2025) As digital transformation accelerates across the public sector, the focus is moving away from internal bureaucracy and toward seamless, accessible, and personalized interactions between citizens and the state. This new governance paradigm embraces a holistic view of service ecosystems, recognizing citizens not as passive recipients of government services but as active partners, co-creators, and evaluators of public value. Digital technologies, including artificial intelligence

(AI), cloud-based platforms, data analytics, and mobile applications, are enabling governments to redesign services around the lived realities of diverse population groups, ensuring solutions are intuitive, inclusive, and responsive to real-time needs. By applying human-centered design principles and leveraging digital tools, citizen-centric administration promotes transparency, trust, and accountability while improving equity in access to essential public services. One of the defining features of this transformation is the seamless integration of services across government agencies. Historically, citizens needed to navigate fragmented service channels, redundant paperwork, and complex administrative structures to access benefits, register properties, pay taxes, or obtain certifications. (Bobro N. et al. 2025) Citizen-centric models simplify these interactions by consolidating multiple services into unified digital platforms—sometimes known as "single-window" or "one-stop" government portals. These modernized systems allow individuals to complete tasks online without repeated authentication or re-entering personal information, significantly reducing procedural burdens.

Mobile-first public service delivery further enhances accessibility for remote, rural, or physically disadvantaged populations, ensuring that essential functions such as healthcare appointments, food subsidy claims, or disaster relief requests can be managed conveniently from any location. (Burlacu S. et al. 2024) Chatbots and AI-powered virtual assistants provide 24/7 multilingual support, removing language and literacy barriers that historically limited citizen participation. Data-driven personalization plays a key role in the rise of citizen-centric public administration. By responsibly analyzing demographic trends, usage patterns, and feedback data, governments can tailor services to the unique circumstances of individuals and communities. Predictive analytics can help identify under-served populations and proactively deliver support before social problems escalate. For example, early childhood assistance programs can automatically notify eligible families, or healthcare systems can alert patients to preventive screenings based on health risk profiles. (Burlacu S. et al. 2024) Digital identity frameworks ensure secure authentication and smooth access to services while protecting privacy rights through encryption and consent-based data usage. Such capabilities foster greater efficiency and equity by directing resources where they are most needed and creating personalized service journeys aligned with citizen expectations. Citizen-centricity also reshapes democratic engagement by strengthening participatory governance.

BLOCKCHAIN TECHNOLOGY IN GOVERNMENT: ENHANCING TRANSPARENCY AND SECURITY

Blockchain technology is rapidly emerging as a transformative force in government operations, offering unprecedented opportunities to enhance transparency, security, data integrity, and public trust in governance systems. (Criado J. I. et al. 2021) Traditionally, government institutions have relied on centralized databases and bureaucratic administrative structures to manage records, regulate transactions, and deliver public services. Although functional, these approaches can introduce vulnerabilities such as data manipulation, corruption, inefficiencies, and cyber threats, especially as the volume of sensitive information grows. Blockchain—built on decentralized, cryptographically secure distributed ledger architecture—addresses these challenges by enabling tamper-resistant recordkeeping, immutable audit trails, and verifiable data transparency across multiple stakeholders. In this new paradigm, trust is embedded within the technology itself rather than placed solely in human institutions, marking a significant shift in how governments secure and validate their operations. As digital transformation accelerates in the public sector, blockchain is increasingly recognized as a foundational infrastructure for future governance systems—empowering more accountable, efficient, and resilient public administration. (Criado J. I. et al. 2021) One of the most powerful contributions of blockchain to government is its ability to create secure and transparent record management systems. Public registries such as land titles, business licenses, identity documents, and civil status records (births, marriages, deaths) are essential government functions but have historically been subject to errors, fraud, or unauthorized alterations. Blockchain offers immutable ledger capabilities that ensure records are permanent, traceable, and instantly verifiable. Unauthorized changes become infeasible, eliminating opportunities for corruption and document forgery while strengthening citizen confidence in public institutions. This is particularly valuable in countries with weak administrative infrastructure or histories of disputed property ownership. Blockchain-enabled land registries, for example, support clear property rights, reduce legal conflicts, and protect vulnerable populations from displacement by providing irrefutable proof of ownership stored on decentralized networks.

Additionally, through smart contracts—automated and self-executing agreements encoded on blockchain—governments can streamline licensing, certification, customs processing, and procurement procedures without reliance on intermediaries, dramatically reducing processing times and opportunities for bribery. (Dahiya R. et al. 2026) Blockchain also plays a critical role in improving transparency in public finance and supply chains. Government procurement is a major area vulnerable to fraud, bid rigging, and illegal financial flows due to opaque procedures and limited oversight. Blockchain-based procurement systems give all authorized participants—auditors, suppliers, and the public—real-time access to transaction records, contract terms, and supplier performance histories. This visibility reduces corruption by preventing hidden modifications or manipulated bidding processes. Likewise, blockchain enhances accountability in public spending by enabling tracking of budget allocations from initial disbursement to final expenditure, helping to detect financial misuse and ensure taxpayer resources are used effectively. (Dahiya R. et al. 2026) In public sector supply chains—such as pharmaceutical distribution, critical infrastructure materials, and humanitarian assistance—blockchain ensures provenance traceability and product authenticity. This is essential for protecting public health and safety, especially in the fight against counterfeit medicines or disaster-relief fraud.

THE ROLE OF DATA ANALYTICS IN DIGITAL PUBLIC ADMINISTRATION

Data analytics has become a cornerstone of digital public administration, reshaping how governments operate, make decisions, and deliver services to citizens. (Dorovskaya Y. et al. 2020) As public institutions digitize and generate increasing volumes of data—from IoT-enabled infrastructure to online citizen platforms—the ability to extract meaningful insights has emerged as a critical capability for enhancing governance effectiveness and public value. Data analytics empowers governments to transition from reactive, fragmented models of administration to proactive, intelligence-driven governance systems capable of anticipating societal needs, efficiently allocating resources, and improving service outcomes. In this new paradigm, data is not merely a byproduct of administrative operations but a strategic asset enabling evidence-based policymaking, real-time monitoring, and continuous performance improvement across sectors such as healthcare, transportation, education, taxation, environmental management, and public safety. One of the most significant contributions of data analytics to digital public administration is the enhancement of informed decision-making. Traditional policy development often relied on limited historical records, manual reporting, and subjective assessments, making long-term planning difficult and vulnerable to errors. (Dorovskaya Y. et al. 2020) With advanced analytics, governments can integrate diverse datasets—from demographic trends and mobility patterns to economic activity and public sentiments—to uncover systemic issues, predict future trends, and evaluate policy impacts before implementation. Predictive analytics enables early risk detection in areas such as disease outbreaks, infrastructure degradation, or crime hotspots, supporting more cost-effective preventative interventions.

For instance, health agencies can analyze medical records and environmental indicators to forecast disease spread, while urban planners can use traffic and sensor data to simulate mobility scenarios and reduce congestion. (Dunleavy P. et al. 2006) These capabilities help public officials address problems before they escalate, fostering resilient and adaptable governance. Operational efficiency is another vital benefit of data-driven digital public administration. Automating data collection and analysis reduces administrative burdens, accelerates service delivery, and minimizes human errors in routine tasks such as document verification, eligibility screening, and compliance monitoring. Public finance departments use analytics to detect anomalies in tax submissions, identify fraud risks, and optimize auditing efforts. Welfare programs can cross-reference datasets to ensure benefits reach eligible recipients, reducing waste and preventing duplication. Resource optimization becomes more precise in sectors like energy and water management, where consumption analytics inform sustainable operations and climate adaptation strategies. By enabling continuous performance evaluation through key indicators and benchmarking, data analytics supports accountability and improves service delivery outcomes across government agencies. Data analytics is also crucial in enhancing citizen-centric governance. By analyzing user behavior and feedback on digital platforms, governments can redesign services to better align with citizen needs and expectations. (Dunleavy P. et al. 2006) Personalized recommendations—such as automated notifications for renewals, subsidies, or healthcare screenings—reduce access barriers and create more inclusive service environments. Sentiment analytics derived from social media and feedback channels allow public institutions to understand community concerns in real time, improving civic engagement and public communication.

E-GOVERNANCE: BRINGING SERVICES TO YOUR FINGERTIPS

E-governance has rapidly emerged as a transformative paradigm in public administration, reshaping how governments interact with citizens and deliver essential services by leveraging digital technologies that place governance literally at people's fingertips. (Dzvinchuk D. et al. 2022) Driven by advancements in information and communication technologies (ICT), mobile connectivity, cloud platforms, artificial intelligence, and data analytics, e-governance aims to eliminate traditional bureaucratic complexities and create more efficient, transparent, and user-centric service ecosystems. (Dzvinchuk D. et al. 2022) At its core, e-governance represents the shift from hierarchical, paper-based administrations to seamless digital interfaces where citizens can access public services anytime, anywhere, reducing both the physical and socio-economic barriers to government access. Digital identity systems, electronic portals, and mobile applications are redefining public service delivery, enabling citizens to complete tasks such as applying for licenses, paying taxes, obtaining certificates, lodging complaints, and accessing welfare benefits without requiring physical visits to government offices. This shift not only enhances user convenience but also reduces administrative overheads and opportunities for corruption, as automation and traceable digital workflows ensure accountability in decision making. In developing nations, e-governance serves as a critical tool for reducing disparities in service accessibility, particularly for rural populations, through innovations such as mobile governance (m-governance), community digital centers, and localized service platforms supporting multiple regional languages.

Figure 1. Digital transformation trends

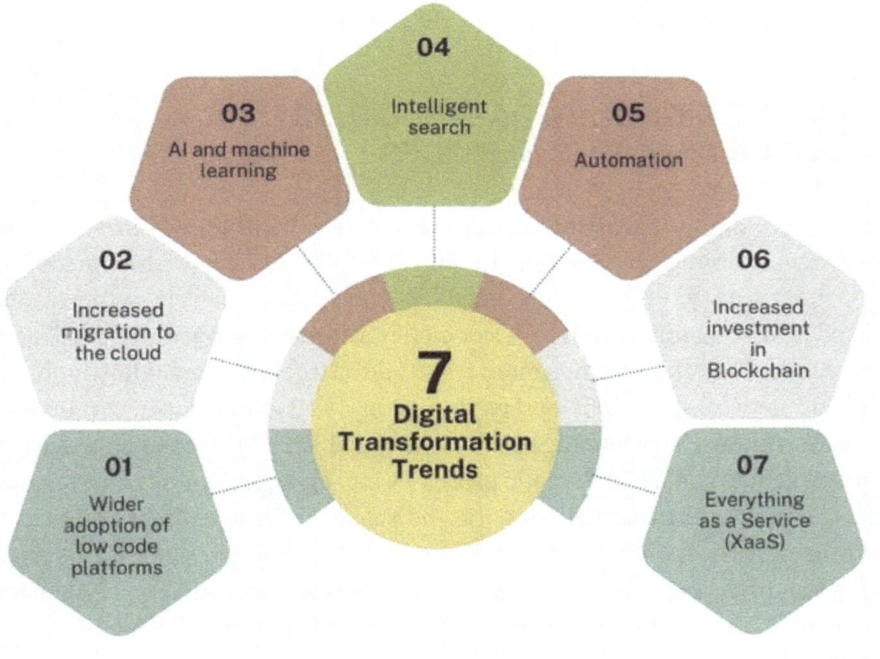

By integrating digital payment solutions and biometric authentication, governments are enabling direct benefit transfers that minimize intermediaries and fraud while improving the efficiency of welfare distribution. Furthermore, e-governance plays a vital role in fostering a transparent and participatory democracy. (Fannur F. et al. 2023) Interactive portals, open-data platforms, and civic engagement applications allow citizens to monitor government performance, provide feedback, and engage in decision-making processes. Such participatory mechanisms promote accountability, trust, and public involvement, strengthening democratic institutions. Governments are increasingly adopting data analytics and artificial intelligence to offer proactive governance, where citizen needs are anticipated rather than merely responded to. Predictive analytics can identify service bottlenecks, forecast demand for healthcare or education resources, and detect anomalies in fiscal operations. AI-enabled chatbots and virtual assistants simplify information access, helping citizens navigate services more efficiently without relying on physical administrative support. Blockchain technology is also becoming instrumental in ensuring data integrity, enhancing the security of public records, and reducing risks of manipulation or unauthorized access, especially in sensitive domains like land registration, identity management, and voting systems. (Fannur F. et al. 2023) These technological innovations collectively contribute to a modern governance model that values accessibility, transparency, efficiency, and resilience.

INNOVATIVE DIGITAL INFRASTRUCTURE FOR EFFICIENT PUBLIC SERVICES

Innovative digital infrastructure has become a critical foundation for modern governance, enabling governments to deliver public services with unprecedented levels of efficiency, reliability, accessibility, and citizen-centric responsiveness. (Fishenden & Thompson, 2013) As societies witness a growing dependence on digital ecosystems, the deployment of robust infrastructure—including high-speed broadband networks, secure cloud environments, scalable data centers, interoperable platforms, artificial intelligence systems, and smart IoT-enabled assets—has transformed traditional bureaucratic processes into agile, technology-driven service models. Digital infrastructure supports the seamless flow of information across government entities, allowing for real-time coordination and integrated decision-making that minimizes redundancy and accelerates service delivery. (Fishenden & Thompson, 2013) For instance, cloud-based government services reduce the need for manual record-keeping and physical paperwork, enabling citizens to access crucial services such as welfare applications, healthcare records, educational support, and utility systems from any location at any time. This shift not only increases public satisfaction by eliminating long wait times and physical visits to government offices but also enhances operational efficiency by reducing administrative burdens, enhancing resource utilization, and enabling automation-driven workflows. Interoperable platforms play a particularly significant role in breaking down data silos, ensuring that various government departments can securely share and reuse information to provide holistic and coordinated services.

Adopting open standards and unified digital frameworks, governments can streamline complex procedures—such as licensing, immigration, tax filing, and procurement—into intuitive and user-friendly services that align with the concept of a "single digital government." Moreover, innovative digital infrastructure strengthens security, resilience, and transparency in public services. (Gaie & Mehta, 2024) The protection of sensitive citizen data remains a top priority for governments, especially as digitization expands the scope and volume of information being processed and stored within public systems. Advanced encryption, multi-factor authentication, blockchain-based identity verification, and zero-trust cybersecurity models are now being integrated into government networks to combat risks related to cyberattacks, data breaches, fraud, and unauthorized access. Digital infrastructure that supports data governance frameworks and continuous monitoring further enhances accountability and compliance, ensuring that public institutions maintain the highest standards of trustworthiness in managing citizen data. Additionally, the adoption of distributed and resilient infrastructure—such as hybrid cloud architectures and decentralized communication systems—strengthens operational continuity during crises, including natural disasters, system failures, or sudden surges in service demand. (Gaie & Mehta, 2024) This resilience is essential for protecting mission-critical services like emergency response coordination, public transportation management, and digital healthcare systems that must remain operational even under extreme stress.

DIGITAL PUBLIC ADMINISTRATION: A KEY TO GOOD GOVERNANCE

Digital public administration has become a cornerstone of modern governance, enabling governments to operate more transparently, effectively, and responsively in an increasingly digital society. (Gupta A. K. et al. 2023) By leveraging advanced technologies such as artificial intelligence, big data analytics, cloud computing, blockchain, and the Internet of Things (IoT), digital public administration transforms traditional bureaucratic structures into agile, citizen-centered service ecosystems. Good governance emphasizes key principles including accountability, participation, transparency, efficiency, equity, and rule of law—all of which are enhanced through the digitization of administrative systems. Digital platforms allow governments to provide services more efficiently by automating routine tasks, centralizing information, and enabling faster decision-making processes. Citizens benefit from seamless access to public services—from applying for certificates, receiving social benefits, and accessing healthcare records to paying taxes or engaging in civic participation—

without the delays and complexities of paper-based systems. Additionally, digital identity solutions and interoperable platforms reduce redundant data submissions, improving user experiences and reducing administrative burdens. The ability to interact with government anytime and anywhere breaks geographic and socio-economic barriers, promoting more inclusive governance. (Gupta A. K. et al. 2023) Overall, digital public administration places citizens at the heart of governance and ensures that services reach them with speed, simplicity, and fairness. Transparency and accountability are significantly strengthened through digital governance initiatives. Governments can utilize information systems to provide real-time data on budgets, procurement activities, and policy outcomes, enabling citizens and oversight bodies to monitor how resources are allocated and spent. Open government data platforms democratize access to public information, fostering public trust and enabling informed participation in policy-making processes. Digital tracking and electronic workflows reduce opportunities for corruption by ensuring traceable transactions and minimizing human intervention in high-risk processes. Blockchain technology further enhances transparency and trust by creating immutable records of land ownership, financial disbursements, licenses, and other essential documents.

Accountability is reinforced through performance dashboards and citizen feedback mechanisms embedded in digital portals, enabling continuous assessment of administrative services. In this environment, governance becomes more ethical, predictable, and just—key elements of good governance. (Havale D. S. et al. 2026) Inclusivity and equity, two core principles of good governance, are also strengthened through digital public administration. Governments are increasingly adopting mobile-first service strategies, recognizing that many citizens, particularly in developing nations, rely heavily on mobile connectivity rather than desktop access. Multi-language interfaces, voice-enabled services, and accessibility tools support equitable access for individuals with disabilities, low digital literacy, or limited educational backgrounds. By leveraging geospatial analytics and citizen databases, governments can target programs to underserved populations more accurately, improving access to healthcare, education, social protection, and emergency relief. Direct benefit transfers and digital payments reduce leakages and ensure that subsidies reach the intended beneficiaries promptly and securely. (Havale D. S. et al. 2026) Digital inclusion policies that expand connectivity and provide digital literacy training help bridge the digital divide, ensuring that vulnerable populations are not excluded from digital transformation. Thus, digital public administration can play a transformative role in advancing social equality and enhancing the democratic participation of marginalized communities.

THE IMPACT OF DIGITALIZATION ON PUBLIC SERVICE DELIVERY

Digitalization has fundamentally transformed public service delivery across the world, reshaping how governments interact with citizens, manage internal operations, and pursue the goals of transparency, accountability, and inclusive development. (Jukić T. et al. 2019) Traditionally, public services were characterized by paperwork-intensive procedures, lengthy processing times, and limited accessibility, especially for geographically remote or marginalized groups. Digitalization replaces these outdated structures with innovative, technology-driven systems supported by artificial intelligence (AI), big data analytics, cloud computing, digital identity, automation, and mobile platforms. These technologies streamline administrative processes, enable seamless data exchange across agencies, and reduce human intervention, which in turn minimizes delays, human errors, and opportunities for corruption. Citizens can now conveniently access essential services—such as healthcare, licenses, tax payments, pensions, and welfare benefits—at any time through user-friendly digital portals, mobile applications, and virtual service centers. This shift has led to significant improvements in efficiency, service quality, and citizen satisfaction, enabling a more inclusive and citizen-centric public administration ecosystem. (Jukić T. et al. 2019) The impact of digitalization is particularly visible in developing nations, where mobile governance and digital payment solutions are bridging long-standing gaps in public service accessibility and socio-economic equity. One of the most transformative effects of digitalization is the enhancement of service transparency and accountability. E-governance platforms allow real-time tracking of applications, transactions, and public project progress, giving citizens greater visibility into government workflows.

Digital public dashboards and open data initiatives enable democratically empowered citizens, journalists, and civil society to analyze government performance, detect inefficiencies, and advocate for policy improvements. Blockchain technologies further enhance trust by securing records against tampering and guaranteeing traceable documentation. Through these innovations, digitalization fosters credibility and strengthens the social contract between the state and citizens. Importantly, automated auditing systems and electronic procurement platforms help reduce corruption by limiting discretionary power and ensuring fair, data-driven decision-making. (KruhloV. et al. 2023) Thus, digitized service delivery supports a governance environment where accountability is measurable and public trust is continuously reinforced. Digitalization has also enabled governments to transition from reactive to proactive service delivery. Predictive analytics and AI-driven decision support systems allow the public sector to anticipate citizen needs and respond before issues escalate—for example, predicting healthcare demands during outbreaks, identifying populations at risk of poverty, or forecasting traffic congestion to optimize transport policies. Digital twins and sensor-driven IoT infrastructure provide real-time insights into critical urban operations such as water distribution, waste management, and emergency response systems. (KruhloV. et al. 2023) These capabilities improve resource management and promote sustainability, particularly in fast-growing urban environments. Furthermore, automation and robotic process technologies help governments allocate skilled human resources toward complex decision-making tasks rather than repetitive administrative work. This results in higher productivity, better policy execution, and more agile public institutions capable of adapting to dynamic societal demands.

EMERGING TECHNOLOGIES IN DIGITAL PUBLIC ADMINISTRATION

Emerging technologies are playing a transformative role in the evolution of digital public administration, marking a new era of governance where efficiency, transparency, inclusivity, and responsiveness define service delivery. (Lenart R. et al. 2025) As governments shift from traditional bureaucratic models to technology-enhanced ecosystems, advanced tools such as artificial intelligence (AI), big data analytics, blockchain, cloud computing, robotic process automation (RPA), Internet of Things (IoT), digital identity solutions, and extended reality (XR) are increasingly embedded into public operations. AI and machine learning have become central to digital governance strategies, enabling automated decision-making, predictive analytics for policy formulation, enhanced public resource allocation, and personalized public services guided by citizen data insights. For instance, AI-powered chatbots and virtual assistants are now widely adopted for 24/7 service delivery, reducing administrative workloads while improving accessibility. (Lenart R. et al. 2025) Big data analytics supports evidence-based policymaking by aggregating and analyzing massive datasets from public platforms, IoT sensors, and administrative systems, allowing decision-makers to identify societal trends, forecast future needs, and respond proactively to emerging social challenges. Blockchain technology enhances trust and transparency in administrative processes by creating immutable, decentralized public records that protect data integrity and reduce corruption risks. Its applications span secure voting systems, transparent procurement processes, land registry modernization, and digital identity management.

Meanwhile, cloud computing provides the foundational infrastructure required to scale digital public services securely and cost-effectively, enabling inter-departmental data sharing and reducing the reliance on legacy systems that often limit government responsiveness. (Momen M. N. et al. 2023) Robotic Process Automation is reshaping internal administrative tasks, automating repetitive functions such as license processing, tax filing, and document verification, thereby accelerating turnaround times and freeing human resources for higher-value strategic roles. The IoT is generating real-time insights for smart city governance, where connected devices monitor traffic flows, energy consumption, public safety, sanitation, and environmental conditions. These insights enhance urban planning, sustainability initiatives, and emergency response systems. Emerging digital identity frameworks, powered by biometrics and cryptographic security, are enabling seamless access to public services through secure citizen authentication, while reducing identity fraud and administrative errors. Extended reality technologies—including augmented reality (AR), virtual reality (VR), and mixed reality (MR)—are introducing innovative methods for training public employees, enhancing citizen engagement, and offering immersive public information experiences. (Momen M. N. et al. 2023) The rise of digital twins—virtual replicas of physical public infrastructure—further supports simulation-driven planning, predictive maintenance, and enhanced disaster preparedness.

SUSTAINABLE DIGITAL PUBLIC ADMINISTRATION: A GLOBAL PERSPECTIVE

Sustainable Digital Public Administration (SDPA) has emerged as a critical paradigm in global governance, aligning digital transformation initiatives with environmental stewardship, social inclusion, and long-term economic resilience. Around the world, governments are integrating Information and Communication Technologies (ICTs), artificial intelligence (AI), big data, cloud computing, blockchain, and other digital innovations into administrative frameworks with the objective of transforming public service delivery while advancing sustainability goals. SDPA supports the principles of efficient resource utilization, reduced carbon footprint of public operations, improved governance transparency, and equitable access to services across diverse populations. (Nongkoo A. et al. 2023) By digitizing services such as permitting, tax administration, and public procurement, governments dramatically reduce paper consumption, travel needs for citizens, and infrastructure burdens associated with traditional bureaucratic models, thereby contributing to environmental conservation. At the same time, digital public platforms foster social sustainability by making public services more accessible to rural communities, individuals with disabilities, and marginalized groups, addressing socioeconomic disparities and strengthening citizen participation in governance systems. Globally, the adoption of SDPA differs across regions, influenced by technological maturity, governance capacity, political leadership, and socioeconomic context. (Nongkoo A. et al. 2023) Advanced digital nations such as Estonia, Denmark, Singapore, and South Korea serve as benchmarks showcasing how integrated digital ecosystems—from national digital identity systems to real-time open data portals—can support both sustainability and high administrative performance.

These countries leverage e-governance as a fundamental public infrastructure, enabling citizens to complete nearly all service interactions online, reducing emissions associated with physical mobility and processing. Meanwhile, developing nations in Africa, Asia, and Latin America are rapidly digitizing public administration through mobile-first strategies, fintech-enabled social assistance platforms, and smart governance solutions tailored to resource-constrained environments. (Pakhnenko O. et al. 2023) International cooperation and global standards, led by organizations such as the United Nations, World Bank, and OECD, provide frameworks for building inclusive sustainable digital ecosystems that support the Sustainable Development Goals (SDGs), with particular focus on SDG 16 (Peace, Justice, and Strong Institutions) and SDG 9 (Industry, Innovation, and Infrastructure). Sustainability in digital governance also hinges on responsible technology deployment. Many governments are now embracing green ICT policies that prioritize data center energy efficiency, low-carbon cloud services, and the use of renewable energy to power digital infrastructure. Circular economy principles are being incorporated into public procurement, ensuring responsible management of e-waste and longer lifecycle use of IT equipment. (Pakhnenko O. et al. 2023) Additionally, open data initiatives and transparency platforms empower civil society and the private sector to collaborate on solving environmental and social challenges, strengthening long-term sustainability. Ethical AI frameworks are increasingly guiding public sector innovation, ensuring that automated decision systems remain fair, transparent, and accountable, preventing discriminatory practices and bias amplification. Privacy-by-design principles, cybersecurity strategies, and stronger data governance models are also critical, securing public trust and safeguarding the integrity of digital administration.

DIGITAL PUBLIC ADMINISTRATION: A TOOL FOR CITIZEN ENGAGEMENT

Digital Public Administration (DPA) is increasingly recognized as one of the most powerful enablers of citizen engagement in contemporary governance. As societies evolve into data-driven digital ecosystems, the integration of digital technologies into public sector operations has fundamentally reshaped how citizens interact with government institutions. DPA expands democratic participation by providing citizens with more direct, convenient, and transparent avenues to voice their opinions, access information, and co-create public value. (Raghavan A. et al. 2025) Through online platforms, mobile applications, social media channels, e-consultations, e-participation portals, and digital feedback systems, citizens can now contribute to policymaking processes in real time, breaking the constraints of physical distance, bureaucratic complexity, and limited administrative capacity. These digital tools create more responsive, inclusive, and collaborative governance environments, allowing public institutions to understand societal needs better and formulate policies that reflect diverse community perspectives. As digital transformation accelerates globally, governments increasingly view citizen engagement not merely as a democratic ideal but as a strategic asset for improving public service quality, accountability, and trust. The rise of open government data has played a key role in reinforcing engagement within DPA frameworks. (Raghavan A. et al. 2025) By making datasets publicly accessible, governments empower civil society organizations, journalists, researchers, entrepreneurs, and ordinary citizens to scrutinize performance, detect inefficiencies, and propose innovative solutions to social challenges. Transparency becomes more than a political commitment—it becomes a digitally enforceable norm. Machine-readable open data combined with interactive dashboards enhances governmental accountability by enabling citizens to track expenditures, monitor emissions, evaluate public projects, and compare administrative performance across regions. Public agencies benefit from this transparency as well, because it strengthens legitimacy and encourages evidence-based policy corrections.

Artificial intelligence also enhances citizen engagement by powering intelligent public interfaces such as chatbots and virtual assistants that provide personalized support 24/7, simplifying access to essential services while reducing administrative burden. (Rajesh R. et al. 2026) These AI tools can analyze citizen feedback at scale, identify emerging concerns, and support proactive decision-making, thus transforming reactive governance into anticipatory governance. Social media has become a vital channel for public communication and participatory governance, enabling instant interaction between policymakers and the public. Governments employ platforms like X/Twitter, Facebook, YouTube, WhatsApp, and local digital forums to share crucial updates, combat misinformation, promote civic campaigns, and gather rapid public sentiment. (Rajesh R. et al. 2026) In crisis management scenarios—such as pandemics, natural disasters, or transportation disruptions—digital communication channels offer real-time updates that can save lives and maintain public order. Participatory budgeting tools, digital petition systems, and crowdsourcing platforms allow citizens to propose ideas, vote on spending priorities, and collaborate on community development. These digital modes of engagement broaden the reach of democracy beyond elections, enabling continuous citizen involvement in governance and fostering a sense of shared responsibility for public outcomes. Additionally, digital identity systems—such as India's Aadhaar, Estonia's eID, and EU Digital Identity Wallet—simplify and authenticate participation in online governance activities, ensuring secure access and verifiable civic engagement.

THE ROLE OF GOVTECH IN DIGITAL PUBLIC ADMINISTRATION

GovTech—short for Government Technology—has emerged as a pivotal force shaping the modernization of Digital Public Administration (DPA), transforming how governments design, deliver, and manage public services in the digital age. Representing both a technological movement and a global public sector innovation ecosystem, GovTech emphasizes the strategic adoption of advanced digital tools such as artificial intelligence (AI), cloud computing, blockchain, Internet of Things (IoT), robotic process automation (RPA), data analytics, and human-centered service design to enhance government efficiency, transparency, and citizen experience. (Satyanarayana P. et al. 2026) Unlike traditional e-government models that focused primarily on digitizing existing processes, GovTech advocates for comprehensive public sector transformation by rethinking administrative workflows, enabling integrated and interoperable public platforms, and fostering collaboration between governments, startups, academia, and civil society. Through GovTech initiatives, governments are transitioning into agile digital organizations capable of responding rapidly to emerging social, economic, and environmental challenges, while empowering citizens to participate more actively in governance. At its core, GovTech promotes citizen-centric public administration by placing user needs and societal value creation at the forefront of digital innovation. This shift replaces bureaucratic complexity with seamless digital service journeys that are intuitive, inclusive, and accessible anytime and anywhere. Digital identity systems, single-window service portals, and mobile-first public applications streamline interactions by enabling individuals to access multiple government services through unified authentication and interoperable platforms. GovTech also enables automation of administrative tasks through RPA and AI-driven decision systems, reducing delays, human errors, and operational costs in public service delivery. (Satyanarayana P. et al. 2026) Predictive analytics offers governments the ability to anticipate service demand and optimize resources, improving readiness for crises such as pandemics, natural disasters, and economic instability.

Meanwhile, blockchain ensures secure and tamper-proof public records, strengthening trust in sensitive functions such as land registration, digital voting, social welfare disbursement, and supply chain monitoring within government procurement. (Scupola A. et al. 2016) The global growth of GovTech is supported by innovation ecosystems in which government agencies collaborate with startups and technology enterprises to create scalable and cost-effective digital solutions. Countries across Europe, Asia, and the Americas have established GovTech accelerators, regulatory sandboxes, digital transformation departments, and national innovation labs to co-develop technologies tailored to public administration needs. These public-private partnerships enable rapid experimentation and deployment of emerging tools without overwhelming government infrastructure and budgets. GovTech marketplaces and open API frameworks support secure data exchange between agencies while allowing external innovators to create complementary services. (Scupola A. et al. 2016) This collaborative environment not only stimulates economic growth in local technology sectors but also enriches public service portfolios with creative and user-friendly solutions inspired by private-sector design approaches. GovTech also plays a crucial role in strengthening government accountability and transparency. Through open data platforms, real-time monitoring tools, and digital performance dashboards, citizens gain unprecedented visibility into public spending, program results, and policy outcomes.

DIGITAL IDENTITY AND AUTHENTICATION: A NEW FRONTIER

Digital identity and authentication technologies have emerged as a new frontier in the modernization of governance systems, financial services, healthcare access, and everyday digital interactions, playing a foundational role in enabling secure, trusted, and inclusive participation in the digital economy. As societies undergo rapid digital transformation, individuals increasingly rely on online services to access essential public functions, conduct financial transactions, study remotely, engage in e-commerce, and communicate across the globe. (Semenets-Orlova I. et al. 2022) This dependence on digital ecosystems necessitates robust mechanisms to verify identity, protect data integrity, and ensure privacy. Digital identity solutions—ranging from biometric-based authentication such as facial recognition and fingerprint scanning to cryptographically secured digital ID wallets—are redefining how people prove and manage their identity in both public and private sector applications. Governments and organizations around the world are building national digital identity infrastructures to support seamless online service access, reduce fraud, enhance administrative efficiency, and improve the citizen experience. These efforts are transforming not only the mechanics of authentication but also broader notions of identity ownership, trust, and governance. (Semenets-Orlova I. et al. 2022) The adoption of digital identity systems greatly accelerates service delivery in digital public administration by providing a secure and unified method for accessing government services. Traditional paper-based processes that once required multiple in-person visits and redundant verification steps can now be replaced with streamlined digital workflows. National programs such as India's Aadhaar, Estonia's eID, and Singapore's SingPass demonstrate the transformative potential of digital identity ecosystems in decreasing friction in service delivery, supporting electronic signatures, enabling secure tax filing, and facilitating transparent social welfare distribution. These systems contribute to stronger accountability and reduced corruption by ensuring that benefits reach the right recipients without leakage.

In addition, digital identity supports financial inclusion, particularly in emerging economies, by allowing unbanked and underbanked populations to securely participate in digital finance and access credit, savings, and insurance services. The interoperability of digital identity across sectors—from healthcare and education to transportation and telecommunications—lays the foundation for unified access to public and private services, ultimately creating a more connected and equitable society. (Storozhenko L. et al. 2024) Authentication technologies continue to evolve rapidly, shifting from knowledge-based systems such as passwords and PINs, which are highly vulnerable to breaches, toward multi-factor and biometric authentication methods that offer higher security and usability. Password fatigue and increased cyber threats have made traditional credentials insufficient for protecting sensitive digital interactions. Multi-factor authentication combines something users know, something they have, and something they are, significantly reducing the risk of unauthorized access. Biometrics—including iris scans, voice recognition, and behavioral patterns such as typing rhythms—add layers of verification that are uniquely tied to individuals and difficult to replicate. (Storozhenko L. et al. 2024) Passwordless authentication models are gaining momentum, offering both convenience and stronger security by using cryptographic keys stored on user devices. Meanwhile, decentralized identity frameworks leverage blockchain technology to support self-sovereign identity (SSI), empowering individuals to control their identity data and decide when and how their credentials are shared.

CYBERSECURITY IN DIGITAL PUBLIC ADMINISTRATION: CHALLENGES AND OPPORTUNITIES

The accelerating digital transformation of public administration has fundamentally reshaped how governments operate, deliver services, and interact with citizens. (Tate M. et al. 2018) As digital platforms, cloud-based infrastructures, artificial intelligence (AI), and the Internet of Things (IoT) increasingly underpin essential administrative functions—from identity management and taxation to public healthcare, elections, and national security—cybersecurity has emerged as a central pillar of a resilient and trustworthy digital public sector. However, with this rapid digitalization comes an expanded cyber-attack surface, heightened exposure to sophisticated cyber threats, and critical vulnerabilities that challenge the security, privacy, and integrity of public sector operations. Digital public administration systems are prime targets for cybercriminals, hacktivists, and state-sponsored actors due to the sensitive data they manage and the societal disruption that can result from breaches. Therefore, ensuring strong cybersecurity capabilities is not merely a technical necessity but a core governance imperative essential for protecting democratic institutions, maintaining citizen trust, and preserving national stability in an increasingly interconnected world. One of the most pressing challenges stems from the complex and legacy-laden IT infrastructures embedded within government agencies. Many public institutions operate outdated systems that lack sufficient security features and are incompatible with modern defense mechanisms, making them vulnerable to attacks such as ransomware, phishing, and zero-day exploits. Modernization is further hindered by bureaucratic procurement frameworks, budget constraints, and long development cycles that cannot keep pace with the rapidly evolving threat landscape. (Tate M. et al. 2018) Additionally, the fragmentation of government IT ecosystems—where data and responsibilities are distributed across multiple agencies—creates interoperability gaps and weak points that cyber attackers can exploit.

This complexity is exacerbated by a shortage of skilled cybersecurity professionals within the public sector, leading to reliance on third-party vendors and increasing supply chain risks. Consequently, digital public administration must confront the dual challenge of upgrading legacy infrastructures while building institutional capacity and expertise in cybersecurity governance. (Virali B. et al. 2026) Cyber threats targeting digital public administrations are growing not only in frequency but in sophistication and intent. Ransomware attacks have crippled municipal governments, shut down public services, and exposed sensitive personal data. State-sponsored cyber espionage campaigns aim to access classified government records or manipulate political processes, including election interference operations that threaten democratic sovereignty. Identity theft and large-scale data breaches undermine national digital identity infrastructures and compromise the confidentiality of citizens' information. Critical public utilities—such as water, power grids, transportation networks, and emergency services—are increasingly controlled through digital systems and IoT devices, making them susceptible to cyber-physical attacks with potentially catastrophic consequences. (Virali B et al. 2026) The emergence of AI-enabled threats, including deepfake-driven disinformation campaigns and automated cyberattacks, further challenge government security strategies, requiring proactive defense mechanisms capable of real-time threat detection and response.

CONCLUSION

The future of digital public administration is rapidly being shaped by groundbreaking technological innovations, evolving citizen expectations, and global societal challenges that demand more agile, transparent, and resilient governance systems. As governments continue to adopt emerging digital technologies—such as artificial intelligence (AI), blockchain, the Internet of Things (IoT), digital twins, and quantum computing—they are redefining how public services are designed, delivered, and evaluated. Digital public administration is shifting from a traditional bureaucratic model toward a data-driven, citizen-centered, and proactive governance paradigm capable of anticipating needs rather than merely responding to them. This transformation is accompanied by a strategic emphasis on interoperability, automation, cybersecurity, and inclusive access that ensures no person or community is left behind in the digital era. Over the coming decades, public administration will increasingly transition into a fully integrated digital ecosystem where administrative processes operate autonomously, services are accessible anytime through intuitive digital interfaces, and policy decisions are guided by real-time analytics and predictive insights generated from vast streams of public data. A dominant trend shaping this future is the widespread adoption of AI and machine learning across government sectors. AI-powered systems are enabling automation of repetitive administrative tasks, improving public sector productivity, and reducing compliance burdens for citizens and businesses. Intelligent virtual assistants are becoming primary interaction channels for public services, offering personalized and multilingual support that enhances accessibility. Predictive analytics allow governments to detect fraud, optimize resource allocation, forecast social needs, and implement preventive policies—for example, predicting disease outbreaks or identifying at-risk populations before issues escalate.

As AI moves into high-stakes governance domains such as justice, policing, and social welfare, ethical frameworks, algorithmic transparency, and human oversight will be essential to ensure fairness and accountability. The rise of explainable AI and responsible data governance will play a pivotal role in maintaining public trust in automated decision-making systems. Blockchain and decentralized technologies represent another transformative force in the future of digital public administration. Blockchain-based digital identity systems are expected to strengthen data ownership and verification, reduce identity fraud, and support secure cross-border public service delivery. Smart contracts will streamline administrative processes such as permits, benefits distribution, and procurement by eliminating intermediaries and improving traceability. Decentralization reduces single points of failure, making digital governance infrastructures more resilient to cyber threats and operational disruptions. As global digital identity interoperability grows, citizens may soon interact with governments across different countries using a unified identity layer, enabling international mobility in work, education, and healthcare. However, the integration of blockchain in the public sector must be guided by robust legal frameworks and standardization efforts to overcome scalability and regulatory challenges. The convergence between the physical and digital realms—enabled by IoT devices, robotic automation, and digital twins—will redefine public infrastructure management.

REFERENCES

Basu, S. K., Mandal, R., Kar, A., Patra, S., Sudheer, P., & Manjunath, T. C. (2026). The Internet of Things and Real-Time Process Monitoring. In Martínez-Falcó, J., Sánchez-García, E., & Marco-Lajara, B. (Eds.), *Navigating Digital Transformation Through Business Process Management* (pp. 303–334). IGI Global Scientific Publishing.

Bertot, J. C., Estevez, E., & Janowski, T. (2016, March). Digital public service innovation: Framework proposal. In *Proceedings of the 9th International Conference on Theory and Practice of Electronic Governance* (pp. 113-122). DOI: 10.1145/2910019.2910108

Bobro, N., Bielikov, V., Matveyeva, M., Salamakha, A., & Kharchun, V. (2025). Innovations in Public Administration and Management for Implementing Effective Strategies and Tools. *Salud. Ciencia y Tecnología-Serie de Conferencias*, *4*, 1483. DOI: 10.56294/sctconf20251483

Burlacu, S., Crețu, R. C., Potcovaru, A. M. B., & Călin, A. M. (2024). Integrative digital governance: The role of public administration in promoting sustainable development amid post-pandemic technological innovations. In *Proceedings of the International Conference on Business Excellence* (Vol. 18, No. 1, pp. 725-732). Sciendo. DOI: 10.2478/picbe-2024-0063

Criado, J. I., Dias, T. F., Sano, H., Rojas-Martín, F., Silvan, A., & Filho, A. I. (2021). Public innovation and living labs in action: A comparative analysis in post-new public management contexts. *International Journal of Public Administration*, *44*(6), 451–464. DOI: 10.1080/01900692.2020.1729181

Dahiya, R., Kaple, G., Anute, N., Sudheer, P., Selvakumar, P., Manjunath, T. C., & Sharma, M. (2026). AI Tools for Automating Data Collection and Analysis. In Vrba, J., & Huynh, T. (Eds.), *Revolutionizing Academic Research With AI and Augmented Reality* (pp. 459–486). IGI Global Scientific Publishing.

Dorovskaya, Y., Mokhorov, D., Snetkov, V., Semenova, K., & Tebryaev, A. (2020, September). The social consequences of innovations in public administration. [). IOP Publishing.]. *IOP Conference Series. Materials Science and Engineering*, *940*(1), 012044. DOI: 10.1088/1757-899X/940/1/012044

Dunleavy, P., Margetts, H., Bastow, S., & Tinkler, J. (2006). New public management is dead—Long live digital-era governance. *Journal of Public Administration: Research and Theory*, *16*(3), 467–494. DOI: 10.1093/jopart/mui057

Dzvinchuk, D., Borshch, H., Tsygylyk, N., Dobosh, Z., & Dziubynska, O. (2022). Public management for sustainable development: Current challenges and future trends. *Cuestiones Políticas*, *40*(73), 741–753. DOI: 10.46398/cuestpol.4073.42

Fannur, F., Sabaruddin, I., & Ramdhani, N. (2023). Innovative leadership approaches for enhancing digital governance and collaborative networks in public administration. *Journal Social Civilecial*, *1*(2), 84–99. DOI: 10.71435/610487

Fishenden, J., & Thompson, M. (2013). Digital government, open architecture, and innovation: Why public sector IT will never be the same again. *Journal of Public Administration: Research and Theory*, *23*(4), 977–1004. DOI: 10.1093/jopart/mus022

Gaie, C., & Mehta, M. (2024). Digital transformation of public services: introduction, current trends and future directions. In *Transforming Public Services—Combining Data and Algorithms to Fulfil Citizen's Expectations* (pp. 1–28). Springer Nature Switzerland. DOI: 10.1007/978-3-031-55575-6_1

Gupta, A. K., & Lamsal, B. P. (2023). From traditional to innovative public service: a review of paradigm shifts. *Вопросы государственного и муниципального управления*, (6), 137-156.

Havale, D. S., Patole, J., Anute, N., Rane, D. P., Shah, A. H., & Selvakumar, P. (2026). Digital Tools and Resources for Teaching Sustainability. In Hans, E., & Hans, A. (Eds.), *Harnessing E-Learning to Create a Sustainable Future* (pp. 45–74). IGI Global Scientific Publishing.

Jukić, T., Pevcin, P., Benčina, J., Dečman, M., & Vrbek, S. (2019). Collaborative innovation in public administration: Theoretical background and research trends of co-production and co-creation. *Administrative Sciences*, *9*(4), 90. DOI: 10.3390/admsci9040090

KRUHLOV, V., & TERESHCHENKO, D. (2023). Innovations in the system of public administration. *Вісник Національного технічного університету «ХПІ». Серія: Актуальні проблеми розвитку українського суспільства*, 74.

Lenart, R., & Chen, J. (2025). Integrating post-Schumpeterian perspectives with modern public sector trends. In *Handbook on Post-Schumpeterian Innovations* (pp. 273–285). Edward Elgar Publishing. DOI: 10.4337/9781035322510.00025

Momen, M. N., & Ferdous, J. (2023). Digital innovations in public administration and public service delivery. In *Governance in Bangladesh: Innovations in Delivery of Public Service* (pp. 31–44). Springer Nature Singapore. DOI: 10.1007/978-981-99-0424-2_3

Nongkoo, A., & Hamanee, S. (2023). Applying Government Innovations for Public Management and Public Service. *Ramkhamhaeng International Journal of Science and Technology*, *6*(1), 41–50.

Pakhnenko, O., & Kuan, Z. (2023). Ethics of digital innovation in public administration. *Business Ethics and Leadership*, *7*(1), 113–121. DOI: 10.21272/bel.7(1).113-121.2023

Raghavan, A., Demircioglu, M. A., & Orazgaliyev, S. (2025). Can VUCA events catalyze digital public sector innovations? Evidence from three digital innovation trends in Asia. *Journal of Open Innovation*, *11*(2), 100529. DOI: 10.1016/j.joitmc.2025.100529

Rajesh, R., Veena, S., Shanthini, A., & Deva Prasanna, D. S. J., Yasmeen, & Manjunath, T. C. (2026). AI for Predictive Sustainability in Healthcare. In C. Sheih, P. Upadhyay, M. Bhutani, V. Bandaru, & P. Dass (Eds.), *Responsible Innovation in Smart Healthcare: AI, IoT, and Ethical Sustainability Practices* (pp. 27-56). IGI Global Scientific Publishing.

Satyanarayana, P., Anute, N., Ghewari, A., Chahande, S., Sharma, A., & Manjunath, T. C. (2026). Interdisciplinary Applications of AI and AR in Research. In Vrba, J., & Huynh, T. (Eds.), *Revolutionizing Academic Research with AI and Augmented Reality* (pp. 283–310). IGI Global Scientific Publishing.

Scupola, A., & Zanfei, A. (2016). Governance and innovation in public sector services: The case of the digital library. *Government Information Quarterly*, *33*(2), 237–249. DOI: 10.1016/j.giq.2016.04.005

Semenets-Orlova, I., Shevchuk, R., Plish, B., Grydiushko, I., & Maistrenko, K. (2022). Innovative approaches to development of human potential in modern public administration. *Economic Affairs*, *67*(4s), 915–926.

Storozhenko, L., Olshanskyi, O., Stativka, N., Chernoivanenko, A., & Hordiienko, Y. (2024). Public Administration in the Context of Digital Transformation: Innovations and Challenges. *Revista de Cercetare si Interventie Sociala*, •••(85), 85. DOI: 10.33788/rcis.85.8

Tate, M., Bongiovanni, I., Kowalkiewicz, M., & Townson, P. (2018). Managing the "Fuzzy front end" of open digital service innovation in the public sector: A methodology. *International Journal of Information Management*, *39*, 186–198. DOI: 10.1016/j.ijinfomgt.2017.11.008

Virali, B. M., Jagtiani, J., Pathak, G. P., Satyanarayana, P., Selvakumar, P., & Manjunath, T. C. (2026). Problem Solving Skills. In K. Francis & K. Hendrickson (Eds.), *Public Sector Burnout and Wellness: Research and Experiences* (pp. 241-266). IGI Global Scientific Publishing.

Chapter 11
Impact of Augmented Reality on Visual, Experiential, and Collaborative Learning in Early Education

Pancham Singh
https://orcid.org/0009-0005-0435-7941
Department of Information Technology, Ajay Kumar Garg Engineering College, Ghaziabad, India

Pawan Kumar Goel
https://orcid.org/0000-0003-3601-102X
Department of Computer Science and Engineering, Raj Kumar Goel Institute of Technology, Ghaziabad, India

Ravindra Kumar Yadav
Department of Electronics and Communication and Engineering, Raj Kumar Goel Institute of Technology, Ghaziabad, India

ABSTRACT

The past few years have experienced a tremendous advancement in the area of educational technology. One of such technologies is Augmented Reality (AR) that has a possibility to be applied in classroom presences in preschool and primary education. Elementary level learners are young, and their response is in the form of young learners. AR is more suited to their learning, well to visuals, interaction, and physical interaction environment. This has introduced some visible changes in the way learning and teaching processes occur. This article summaries the available

DOI: 10.4018/979-8-3373-7804-6.ch011

studies on the use of AR in early education. The findings found out that the learners who engage AR tools in their learning process were better than those clung to the old ways of doing things. Since AR converts abstract concepts into graphics, younger minds find it easier to understand. These dynamic representations allow interest develops, concentration increases, involvement increases. AR has demonstrated beneficial outcomes in team and experiential learning.

1. INTRODUCTION

Augmented Reality (AR) is a technology which adds a virtual layer on top of the actual world, like images, text, 3D models, or animation, to the real-life setting of a user in real time. AR integrates, unlike Virtual Reality, which is a fully immersive virtual reality, virtual components with the real world, giving the user an opportunity to interact with both in real time (Azuma, 1997). AR can be often lived through such devices as smartphones, tablets, Augmented Reality glasses, and headsets. AR becomes quicker becoming a part and parcel of our lives. Shopping apps like Amazon have also offered a view-in-your-room service, which allows us to have a virtual placement of the products such as decor and furnishing in our houses with the camera of our phone. Others such as mobile games like Pokémon GO, Augmented Reality filters in social media. AR is an emerging technology that is applicable in numerous fields, but in terms of the sectors where it is high it is demanded that the government intervenes. Education and healthcare are undoubtedly the most important aspects of the matter to the growth and well-being of a nation. Our concern in this article was on AR in the education sector.

AR can be used in education, which will result in higher engagement and interactivity and an increase, enhanced practice in the real world. It has the potential to increase workplace productivity as well as offers real-time data visualization (Saidin et al., 2015). This is especially remarkable in its increasing applicability in the sphere of education. Research indicates that AR will help students become more curious, motivated, and understanding through transforming studying as an involving and practical process. In pre-school and physical education (PE), towards example, AR introduces such subjects of natural science as visualizing concepts by allowing children to see them, like animals, plants, or ecosystems, in a manner that is interactive and appealing to the eyes (Garzón, 2021). This is not only beneficial in assisting young learners in comprehending complex concepts in a much easier manner, but it also empowers teachers to have creative tools to gain attention and reinforce knowledge, which in the end positions schools as progressive places that encourage exploration, engagement, and permanent education outcomes.

AR is effective in enhancing memory, vocabulary, and creativity, as well as skills, environmental consciousness through embodied text, and children exhibiting greater understanding, faster understanding of material than conventional. AR modules are improved in primary settings. The types of AR may be differentiated into several according to the interaction mechanism. Marker-based AR applies to visual triggers that are preprogrammed like QR codes, fiducial markers, also known as particular 2D images, to position digital content in the physical space. In education, this modality is useful to change non-interactive educational resources into assets, including books and diagrams (YuLung Wu et al., 2015). Learners are able to scan a specified marker, access multimedia overlays or supplementary 3D models, which offer a high level of tracking sustainability and low entry barrier to incorporation of interactive media in the current curricula. Markerless AR uses Simultaneous Localization and Mapping (SLAM) technology and device sensors to read the geometry of the surrounding environment without necessarily being physical triggers.

This technology is capable of real-time detection of surfaces, enabling students to project and operate 3D simulations such as architectural models or planetary systems on any flat plane. Location-based AR combines Global Positioning System (GPS) information, accelerometers, and digital compasses to provide site-specific pedagogical stimuli (Sen et al., 2025). Unlike vision-based systems, this modality initiates digital overlays based on the learner's geographic location and orientation.

This type of AR is particularly effective for situated learning and field-based inquiries, where information related to historical events, geological formations, or simulated environmental conditions are overlaid onto physical features to enhance contextual immersion. AR also involves superimposition and recognition algorithms that partially or entirely replace the original perception of a physical object with an augmented digital representation (Garzón et al., 2017). In educational research, this approach is commonly used to provide "X-ray" views of complex structures, such as human organs or mechanical clockwork (Singh et al., 2024). By superimposing virtual schematics onto real objects, AR enables visualization of internal processes and hidden structural layers that are otherwise invisible to the naked eye, thereby supporting a deeper understanding of complex functional systems.

Figure 1. Use of AR in different fields

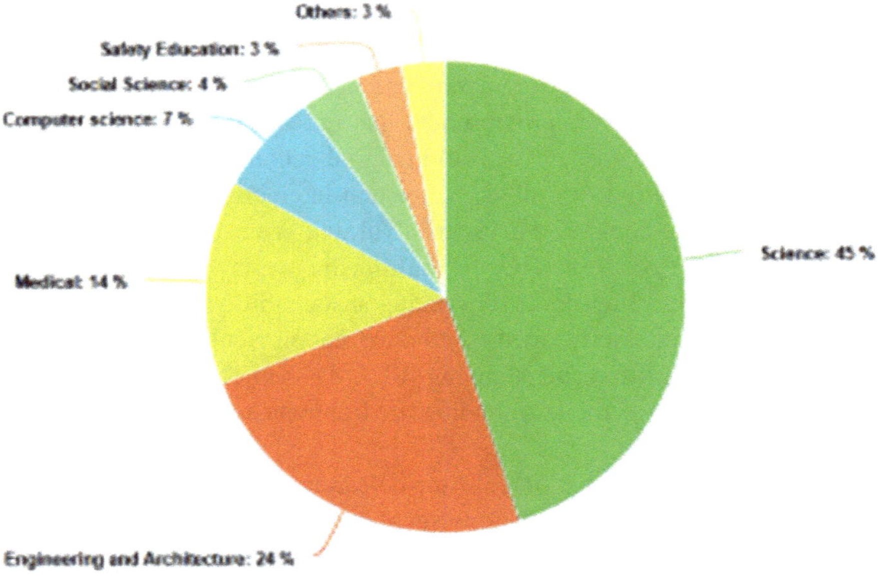

AR when used in conjunction with or in place of other traditional learning methods, has shown enormous promise for improving students' focus, knowledge acquisition, comprehension, and motivation (Preka & Rangoussi, 2019). A total of 63 studies were conducted. Based on the results, augmented reality emerged as a highly specialized and important tool that can enhance the teaching and learning of Natural Science and its related subjects. When discussing preschool and primary education, we must consider the perspectives of parents, teachers, and, of course, students. They all have a positive outlook on the application of this technology in the education field.

Then we learned from the research papers that students who use this technology have better learning outcomes than those who study through older methods. AR also effectively facilitates learning, scaffolding, and experiential learning, enabling students to communicate and interact with their peers and internet-based content. It helps teachers deliver high-quality content by using this technology (Kansal et al., 2023). If we are talking from the student's point of view, their perspective will start developing from childhood. Only if they have a certain perspective related to natural science to give them a great visualization (Fan et al., 2020). We can use this technology. Specifically, the AR allows the use of AR to provide. It becomes a reality and motivating because student acquires power and self-confidence when his or her knowledge increases. Others to be more inquisitive. Although it has its advantages, there are such problems as access and over-dependency on gadgets continue, but the beneficial effect of AR on cognitive and social development makes it an essential means to early inclusive education

2. LITERATURE REVIEW

A large number of studies are underway in the area of AR in education, and several studies have already been done, been overlaid over the physical world of the user. AR inserts digital information real-time and provides interactive and immersive experiences (Parmaxi & Demetriou, 2020). In learning, AR is being used to improve learning by superimposing the contextual data and to generate interactive simulations (Lai & Cheong, 2022). This literature review addresses the notion on how AR maximizes the user experience in learning places, where the special focus of attention is on engagement, motivation, learning achievement, and challenges.

(Kiourexidou et al., 2024), examines the connection between user experience (UX) and interface design influence educational AR performance. The researchers applied a mixed-method with a total of 93 respondents who participated with surveys conducted on AR perceptions and usability tests of Google Arts and Art Projector aspect of Culture with Eight Golden Rules of Schneiderman. Key findings show easy-to-use and perceived educational utility with significant positive correlations between the two, demographic differences (males and younger users more accepting to AR).

(Kumar et al., 2025), undertakes an in-depth examination of the way AR changes contemporary methods of education. The article examines the revolution of AR in learning methodologies through the development of hybrid education spaces in which digital aspects superimpose the real world. This paper explores the idea of how AR enhances student comprehension with the help of immersive experiences in education, especially in the subjects with heavy visualization (biology, chemistry, mathematics, geography).

In this research, (Balog & Pribeanu, 2010), studies the psychological factors which influence the intention to implement augmented reality teaching platforms (ARTP), particularly among students, on the effectiveness of enjoyment in technology acceptance. The research is empirical that shows that in education, ease of use is less relevant than intrinsic motivation (enjoyment) to AR acceptance, implicating that it should be more important to make AR learning experience engaging and fascinating than it should be just by making them user-friendly.

The study conducted by (Gill et al., 2023) shown that an AR educational game had a positive impact on motivation of the students in two sets of playing tests. The research discovered that digital game-based learning (DGBL) is most favored instead of the traditional, which promotes higher-order cognitive skills similar to critical thinking, communication, and collaboration. The AR game, developed using techniques of microlearning, less information density, and cognitive overload during the creation of a representative learning atmosphere. In particular, the study entailed the use of 68 subjects and a mixed-methods approach, which gives strong evidence of the capability of the technology to transform learning engineering by making the education more interesting and interactive.

(Chen et al., 2025), summarized that AR objects are visualized through 3D, which does not need the utilization of computers and other equipment. Interactive material may be used to get the learners involved and enhance their involvement in the learning process. AR possesses the potential by connecting the already known information about learners and the newly added skills and knowledge to improve memorization and offer naturalistic and experiential learning opportunities.

(Khan et al., 2019), presented an analysis of the possible advantages of augmented reality on instruction and education. AR applications help the learner to find intricate meaning. Quintero et al. (2019) suggested that the AR-enhanced environment supports self as well as leader-learner guided education, which facilitates holistic learning conditions that sustain students of various needs and styles of learning. Students can discover various ideas and computer-generated 3D models and interactive scenes.

(Mahadzir, 2013), described that anything that impedes quick visual access can now be easily viewed and handled with the help of augmented reality. This method is particularly interesting to study human bones, muscles, organs, and nerves. Recent developments underline the fact that AR is majorly used in the observation of objects.

(Clark et al., 2011), concentrated on how augmented reality allows the visualization and manipulation of objects that can otherwise be hard to see. AR can be embedded in digilogs, pop-up books, interactive games, flashcards, puzzles, and so forth. Spatial awareness software, coloring and handwriting apps, and the like are offering rich IT learning experiences.

(Fan et al., 2020), suggested that augmented reality (AR) would be applicable in a range of learning environments to offer both audio and visual support to support the diversity of learning requirements of disabled and struggling students. It is a learning tool that is interactive and stimulating and helpful in ensuring inclusivity of children with disabilities in education and aids in achieving the goal of education for all.

(Quintero et al., 2019), clarified that though these are evident in past research, they did not provide the explanation benefits. There are still a lot of issues with the implementation of AR applications. One of the poorest issues is the poor educational worth of AR applications. It describes the methods and strategies adopted by teachers in order to lead students in learning.

(Thangavel et al., 2025), stressed that it is necessary to develop pedagogical principles. It is essential to collaborate with teachers and researchers to make sure that augmented reality (AR) applications are properly made to promote learning. Through such collaboration, students, teachers, and parents will be given an opportunity to utilize AR to the fullest in the educational process. Another importance of the study is the need to design cost-effective classroom settings that will help the students in their more conceptual grasp of things and allow the teachers to present better explanations, which are more interactive and correct. Yet, realizing cost-effectiveness continues to be a major obstacle for developers. Hence, there is an urgent need for a pedagogical framework that maps AR-based learning applications to current learning theory and technology demands. Also, to ensure accessibility, AR technologies can be optimized so that they are smartphone-compatible. This would eliminate the need for additional hardware and enable a wider community of students and teachers to benefit from the learning advantages of AR.

3. METHODOLOGY

The proposed study will examine the effects of augmented reality (AR) on natural science education in preschool and primary school children. An extensive literature review was carried out, applying a critical or integrative literature review methodology. The two key areas of the review concerned questions: the first one is research with preschool or primary students, and the second is the challenges and advantages of AR in early education (Aydoğdu, 2022). The data gathering and the methodology are described how it was conducted. There was a combination of qualitative and quantitative in this study (Radu, 2014). The qualitative data were collected through surveys and interviews with parents and teachers to know their understanding, views, and experiences. Quantitative information would consist of test scores and student surveys to evaluate learning outcomes.

Figure 2. Workflow diagram of AR/VR

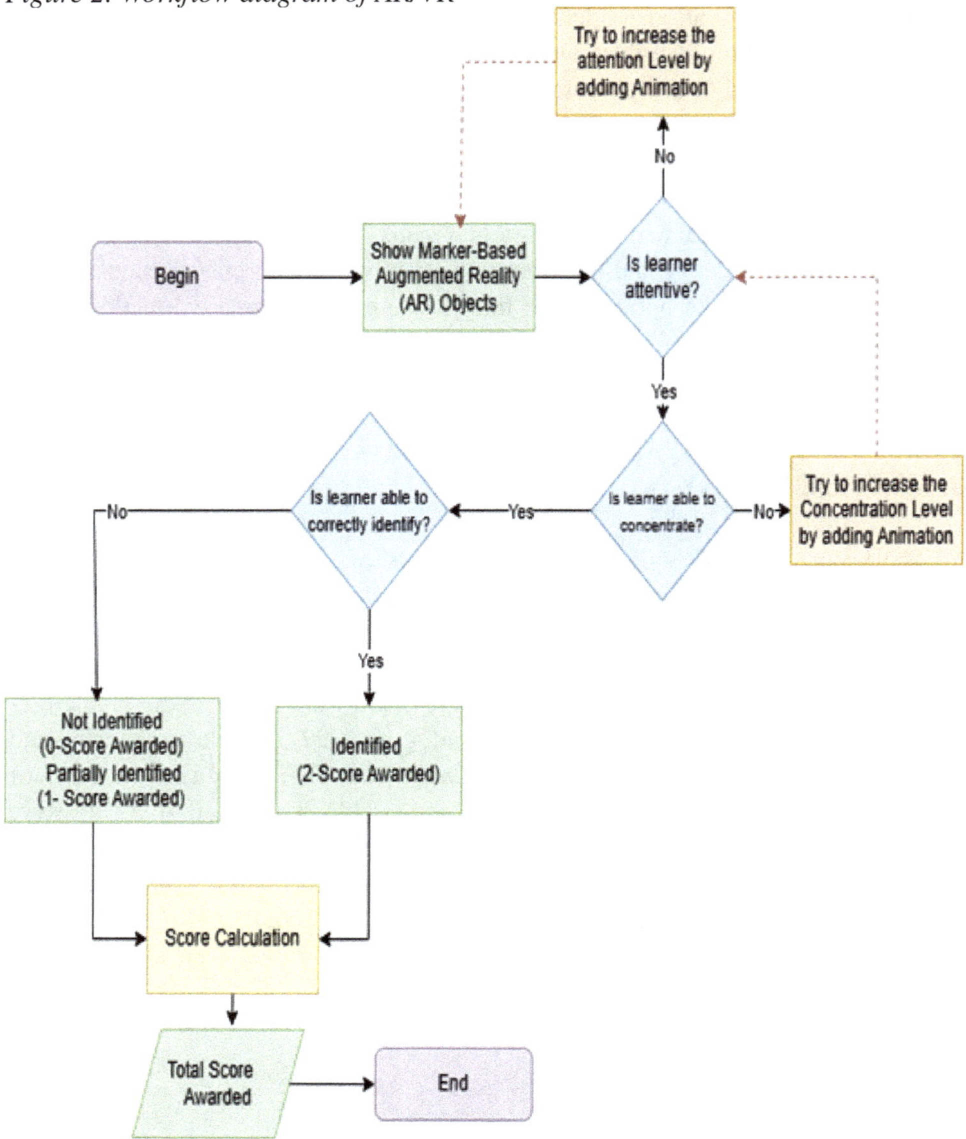

Primary school students and preschoolers were the target population of the study. Data were gathered in schools in urban and semi-urban schools. Participants included 30 students (by education level) and 5 to 10 teachers and parents that participated in interviews and offered feedback (Abrar et al., 2019). AR content was developed using the Unity platform, and it was the one that allowed the creation of interactive and graphical learning tools. This material included 3D visualization of animals and engaging games such as shape-matching and storytelling that are aimed at rendering science young child-friendly and appropriate education (Motahar et al., 2018). The study had a systematic procedure, beginning using a pre-test to gauge the engagement and knowledge of students prior to use of AR. Then, AR tools were incorporated in lessons between 2 and 4 weeks through tablets and smartphones as a normal aspect of classroom activities.

AR is a wonderful tool that will make the process of learning more exciting and purposeful. Instead of just reading, students may now see the 3D images, animations, and sounds that may appear when they are reading a book or watching a video just around them on a phone, tablet, or headset. Such a form of learning is particularly beneficial, since it captures the interest of students and makes them attentive (Sarosa et al., 2019). The diagram we are looking at indicates, step by step, the way AR can increase attention, concentration, and understanding in the classroom. The whole process begins when a student points his device at a marker of AR, which is a special printed image, which, in scanning, leads to a display on the screen of something in the form of an interaction, such as a model or animation. This brings the subject to life in an entertaining manner. But when the student is not interested right away, the system has no surrender. It attempts to do it once more with the use of sounds and animation, which tend to catch the attention of the student better (Bizami et al., 2023). In this manner, the learning system will remain flexible and changes to the requirement of the student at that time.

After the student begins paying attention, the next thing is to find out whether he is able to remain attentive. This is whereby the test of concentration is tested. Again, if the pupil is distracted, the machine pushes him again by animation and sound to help bring their focus back. This back-and-forward model demonstrates how AR can be interacted in real time and the learner, as well as not losing the interest (Lai & Cheong, 2022). In the event the student is attentive and focused, he or she proceeds to the identification phase, where they must be able to identify or react to the AR content. On their comprehension, they are granted a score. A student who fails to respond in any way scores 0, a student who understands partially scores 1, and a full answer is right, 2. The scores are used to determine the effectiveness of learning by the student, whether AR material is effective.

This whole process assists in making the process of learning more personal, responsive. AR is a process of establishing learning instead of merely presenting lessons in a one-fits-all manner. It enhances such aspects as attention span, concentrating capability, and recognition skills. It provides teachers and parents with helpful feedback as well, based on actual performance. In a nutshell, this AR-based method does not only teach; it supports, leads, and reacts to the student during the learning process (Cakir & Korkmaz, 2019). It creates a rich, hands-on, and conducive atmosphere in which the students feel more motivational and inquisitive. For play school, this type of learning experience can be significant to learners and many others. While it is more extensively applicable in special education, AR enhances the learning strategies of all students by improving and moving it closer to the interactive, creative, and fun.

4. RESULTS AND DISCUSSIONS

The role of natural sciences as one of the factors that may impact students regarding their perceptions and understanding of the natural world is great. It is significant to introduce the subjects to the children when they are young in attempts to help them establish a reasonable background in education. It can be greatly influenced by good teaching of natural sciences on scientific thinking, argumentative ability, and value of the nature of scientific knowledge (Thangavel et al., 2025). It also creates a desire and motivation to learn scientific-related careers.

It is one which contains abstract and complicated ideas, which may be difficult to the layman children without having any visual aid. This is especially so in primary education and early childhood. Studies have always indicated that AR is a useful tool in the intensification of teaching and getting acquainted with natural sciences.

Positive feedback has been received by the teachers, students, and the parents, and perceptions about the use of AR in science education. In these studies, students who were taught based on AR outperformed the other students taught using conventional teaching methods. Using AR led to increased motivation, involvement, and increased insight, which tend to result in a state of flow where the learners are engrossed with the learning.

The students got more concentrated, interested, and ambitious at what is being taught and also at the process of learning itself. Their academic performance enhanced, having equally high or higher scores than students in conventional classes (Balog & Pribeanu, 2010). In addition, AR has also rendered the learning process enjoyable and made students understand scientific ideas better, clearly.

In addition to the advantages that AR has on preschool and primary students, it is also a useful resource support to the teachers to present quality lessons. AR has one of its main advantages to teachers, will not need expensive or specialized equipment. Nevertheless, the importance is identified in the research of equipping the teachers with proper training and professional development courses to aid them to use AR and associated technologies empirically. Also, there is an evident necessity to produce and distribute AR educational resources that can be easily accessible to the masses

Although ample work has been done in AR research, a comparison of these studies indicates that most of them target secondary and tertiary levels of education (Turan et al., 2018). This implies an evident gap in empirical work on primary and particularly preschool level education, where little studies are available. Future research must also examine how student individual characteristics could influence the efficacy of AR-based learning interventions.

Figure 3. Methods used by the teachers in education

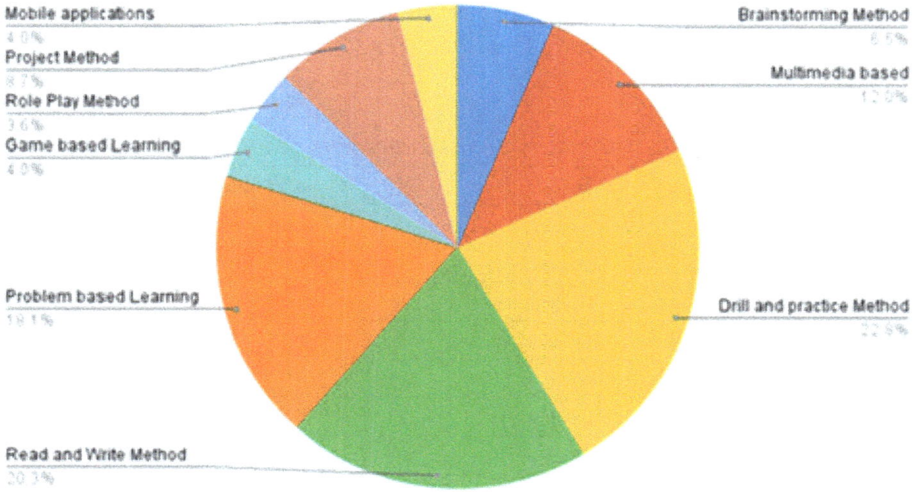

Figure 4. Limitation of existing mobile applications

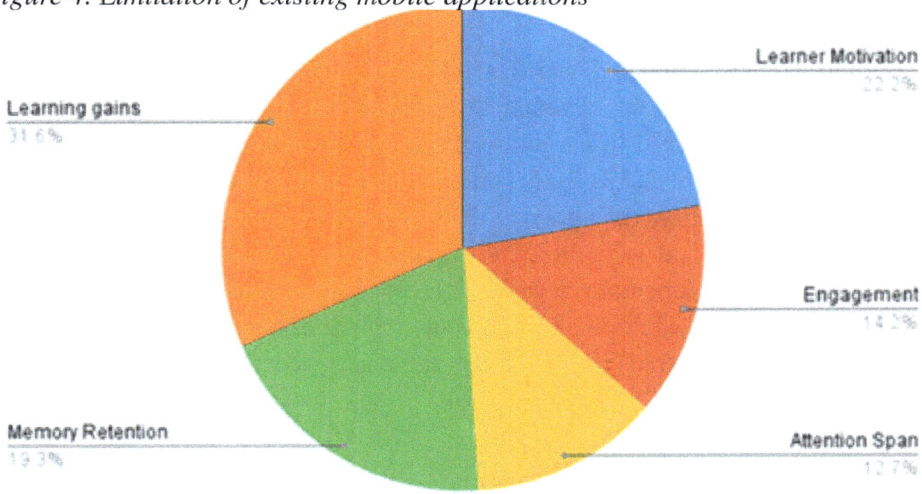

4.1. Educational Fields Utilizing AR Applications

In examining areas of education where augmented reality (AR) can be integrated, particularly in preschool and primary school (PPS) education, twelve key educational domains have been identified (labeled H1 to H12), as outlined in Table X (Edler & Kersten, 2021). Our analysis indicates that 39% of the reviewed studies focused on developing AR-based applications for teaching the English language, represented by category H1.

Table 1. Showing augmented reality applied currently in different studies

S No.	Types	No. of Studies	Percentage
H1	English Learning	10	14%
H2	Mathematics problem solving	8	11%
H3	Mother language learning	4	6%
H4	Native + English language Learning	4	6%
H5	Object recognition	3	4%
H6	Science and Technology	3	4%
H7	Astronomy education	2	3%
H8	Religious or spiritual education	2	3%
H9	Environmental science education	1	1%
H10	Moral and Values education	1	1%
H11	Literacy and reading comprehension	1	1%
H12	Music education	1	1%

Mathematics problem-solving (H2) and mother language learning (H3) have also been identified as lead fields in which AR applications have been applied. These two topics were addressed in ten and eight of the seventy-one examined studies, respectively (Mahadzir, 2013). Also, other educational areas involving AR were noted to include integrated English and indigenous language instruction, object recognition, science and technology, astronomy education, religious or spiritual education, and environmental science education. These areas are classified as H4 to H9 in the Table. In addition, AR has been applied in other domains, including moral and values education (H10), literacy and reading comprehension (H11), and music education (H12).

4.2. Technologies Used at Present

Three kinds of augmented reality (AR) technologies are found to be utilized in the making of AR applications: mark-based AR(M1), markless AR(M2), and map-based AR as mentioned in the table. Because it offers consistent tracking through static marks like cards, magazines, and QR codes, it is the most popular type of augmented reality. However, markless or map-based AR does not require marks. To ascertain a device position and location, it uses mobile device hardware, including camera, accelerometer, GPS and compasses. Field trips and game-based applications are its primary uses in outdoor education. Only one and three articles, respectively, reported map-based AR (M3) and markless AR(M2), whereas 85% of the reviewed articles employed the mark-based AR approach (shown as M1 in the table). Additionally, two articles that both mark-based and received 5% result.

Table 2. Showing studies on different technologies

NO.	CATEGORIES	FREQUENCY OF STUDIES	PERCENTAGE
M1	Mark-based	62	85%
M2	Markless	3	5%
M3	Map-based	1	1%
M4	Both mark-based and markless	12	3%
M5	Null	3	6%

Figure 5. Types of augmented reality used in PPS education

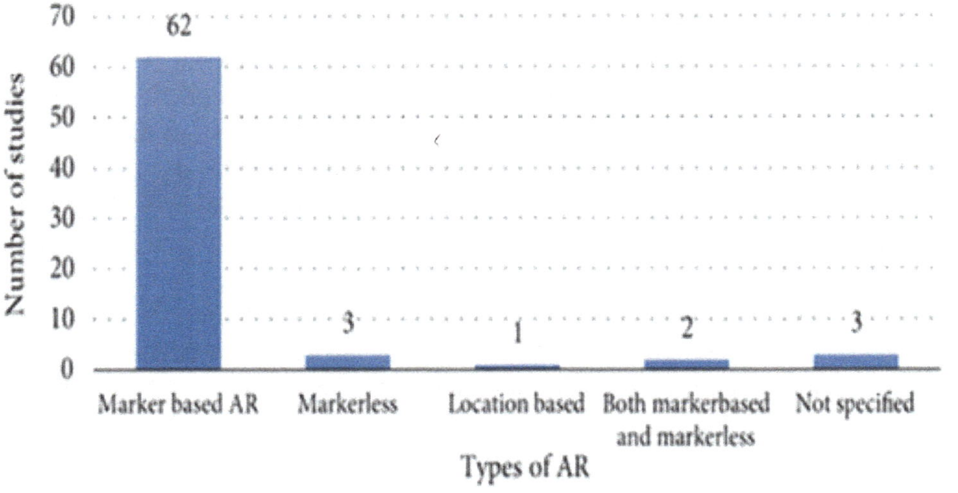

5. CONCLUSION

The project involves a systematic review on AR in school education. A set of appropriate articles was obtained from the Google Scholar database. Nine suggested research questions guide the study, which is concerned with investigating the use of AR technology, including its advantages, disadvantages, challenges, varieties, affordability, research studies, hardware and software utilized, and the exact educational areas where AR is utilized. Based on the analysis of these research questions and current AR models, some of the issues that were identified include usability, technology complexity, technical problems, information overload, and possible health consequences. Although traditional instruction still dominates, increasing evidence suggests that AR can be successfully blended with traditional methods to improve learning. Good examples are its use in English language learning, maths problem-solving, astronomy, social studies, environment science, and other subject-matter areas. This review can be of great use for researchers who want to know the role and capacity of augmented reality in education.

REFERENCES

Abrar, M. F., & Islam, Md. R., Hossain, Md. S., Islam, M. M., & Kabir, M. A. (2019). Augmented Reality in Education: A Study on Preschool Children, Parents, and Teachers in Bangladesh. In J. Y. C. Chen & G. Fragomeni (Eds.), *Virtual, Augmented and Mixed Reality. Applications and Case Studies* (Vol. 11575, pp. 217–229). Springer International Publishing. DOI: 10.1007/978-3-030-21565-1_14

Aydoğdu, F. (2022). Augmented reality for preschool children: An experience with educational contents. *British Journal of Educational Technology*, *53*(2), 326–348. DOI: 10.1111/bjet.13168

Azuma, R. T. (1997). A Survey of Augmented Reality. *Presence (Cambridge, Mass.)*, *6*(4), 355–385. DOI: 10.1162/pres.1997.6.4.355

Balog, A., & Pribeanu, C. (2010). The Role of Perceived Enjoyment in the Students' Acceptance of an Augmented Reality Teaching Platform: A Structural Equation Modelling Approach. *Studies in Informatics and Control*, *19*(3). Advance online publication. DOI: 10.24846/v19i3y201011

Bizami, N. A., Tasir, Z., & Kew, S. N. (2023). Innovative pedagogical principles and technological tools capabilities for immersive blended learning: A systematic literature review. *Education and Information Technologies*, *28*(2), 1373–1425. DOI: 10.1007/s10639-022-11243-w PMID: 35919874

Cakir, R., & Korkmaz, O. (2019). The effectiveness of augmented reality environments on individuals with special education needs. *Education and Information Technologies*, *24*(2), 1631–1659. DOI: 10.1007/s10639-018-9848-6

Chen, G., Wang, H., Liang, A., Oubibi, M., & Zhou, Y. (2025). From detached observer to immersive participant: An augmented reality-based experiential learning approach to promote academic performance and learning behaviors in science education. *Computers in Human Behavior Reports*, *19*, 100756. DOI: 10.1016/j.chbr.2025.100756

Clark, A., Dunser, A., & Grasset, R. (2011). An interactive augmented reality coloring book. *2011 10th IEEE International Symposium on Mixed and Augmented Reality*, 259–260. DOI: 10.1109/ISMAR.2011.6143487

Edler, D., & Kersten, T. P. (2021). Virtual and Augmented Reality in Spatial Visualization. *KN - Journal of Cartography and Geographic Information*, *71*(4), 221–222. DOI: 10.1007/s42489-021-00094-z

Fan, M., Antle, A. N., & Warren, J. L. (2020). Augmented Reality for Early Language Learning: A Systematic Review of Augmented Reality Application Design, Instructional Strategies, and Evaluation Outcomes. *Journal of Educational Computing Research, 58*(6), 1059–1100. DOI: 10.1177/0735633120927489

Garzón, J. (2021). An Overview of Twenty-Five Years of Augmented Reality in Education. *Multimodal Technologies and Interaction, 5*(7), 37. DOI: 10.3390/mti5070037

Garzón, J., Pavón, J., & Baldiris, S. (2017). Augmented Reality Applications for Education: Five Directions for Future Research. In De Paolis, L. T., Bourdot, P., & Mongelli, A. (Eds.), *Augmented Reality, Virtual Reality, and Computer Graphics* (Vol. 10324, pp. 402–414). Springer International Publishing., DOI: 10.1007/978-3-319-60922-5_31

Kansal, M., Singh, P., Shukla, S., & Srivastava, S. (2023). A Comparative Study of Machine Learning Models for House Price Prediction and Analysis in Smart Cities. In F. Ortiz-Rodríguez, S. Tiwari, P. Usoro Usip, & R. Palma (Eds.), *Electronic Governance with Emerging Technologies* (Vol. 1888, pp. 168–184). Springer Nature Switzerland. DOI: 10.1007/978-3-031-43940-7_14

Khan, T., Johnston, K., & Ophoff, J. (2019). The Impact of an Augmented Reality Application on Learning Motivation of Students. *Advances in Human-Computer Interaction, 2019*, 1–14. DOI: 10.1155/2019/7208494

Kiourexidou, M., Kanavos, A., Klouvidaki, M., & Antonopoulos, N. (2024). Exploring the Role of User Experience and Interface Design Communication in Augmented Reality for Education. *Multimodal Technologies and Interaction, 8*(6), 43. DOI: 10.3390/mti8060043

Kumar, A., Bhadauriya, A. S., Kaushik, A., & Singh, P. (2025). Augmented Reality (AR) and its impact on learning methodologies. *Journal of Advances in Science and Technology, 22*(2), 112–121. DOI: 10.29070/fmfvkc30

Lai, J. W., & Cheong, K. H. (2022). Educational Opportunities and Challenges in Augmented Reality: Featuring Implementations in Physics Education. *IEEE Access : Practical Innovations, Open Solutions, 10*, 43143–43158. DOI: 10.1109/ACCESS.2022.3166478

Mahadzir, N. N. N. (2013). The Use of Augmented Reality Pop-Up Book to Increase Motivation in English Language Learning For National Primary School. [IOSRJRME]. *IOSR Journal of Research & Method in Education, 1*(1), 26–38. DOI: 10.9790/7388-0112638

Motahar, T., Fatema, T., & Das, R. (2018). Bornomala AR-bengali learning experience using augmented reality. *Proceedings of the 20th International Conference on Human-Computer Interaction with Mobile Devices and Services Adjunct*, 182–188. DOI: 10.1145/3236112.3236138

Parmaxi, A., & Demetriou, A. A. (2020). Augmented reality in language learning: A state-of-the-art review of 2014–2019. *Journal of Computer Assisted Learning*, *36*(6), 861–875. DOI: 10.1111/jcal.12486

Preka, G., & Rangoussi, M. (2019). Augmented Reality and QR Codes for Teaching Music to Preschoolers and Kindergarteners: Educational Intervention and Evaluation: *Proceedings of the 11th International Conference on Computer Supported Education*, 113–123. DOI: 10.5220/0007682301130123

Quintero, J., Baldiris, S., Rubira, R., Cerón, J., & Velez, G. (2019). Augmented Reality in Educational Inclusion. A Systematic Review on the Last Decade. *Frontiers in Psychology*, *10*, 1835. DOI: 10.3389/fpsyg.2019.01835 PMID: 31456716

Radu, I. (2014). Augmented reality in education: A meta-review and cross-media analysis. *Personal and Ubiquitous Computing*, *18*(6), 1533–1543. DOI: 10.1007/s00779-013-0747-y

Saidin, N. F., Abd Halim, N. D., & Yahaya, N. (2015). A Review of Research on Augmented Reality in Education: Advantages and Applications. *International Education Studies*, *8*(13), 1. DOI: 10.5539/ies.v8n13p1

Sarosa, M., Chalim, A., Suhari, S., Sari, Z., & Hakim, H. B. (2019). Developing augmented reality based application for character education using unity with Vuforia SDK. *Journal of Physics: Conference Series*, *1375*(1), 012035. DOI: 10.1088/1742-6596/1375/1/012035

Sen, C., Yogi, K. K., & Singh, P. (2025). NVCED: Novel Deep Learning Model for Video Classification Enhanced by Temporal Feature Extraction. *2025 Artificial Intelligence and Smart Technologies for Sustainability Conference (AISTS)*, 1–6. DOI: 10.1109/AISTS66100.2025.11233141

Singh, P., Pahuja, N., Kansal, M., Gurung, S., Shukla, U., & Gupta, S. (2024). Enhancing Tourism Experiences and Preserving Cultural Heritage with AR and VR. *2024 2nd International Conference on Disruptive Technologies (ICDT)*, 225–231. DOI: 10.1109/ICDT61202.2024.10489490

Thangavel, S., K, Sharmila, & K, Sufina. (2025). Revolutionizing Education Through Augmented Reality (AR) and Virtual Reality (VR): Innovations, Challenges and Future Prospects. *Asian Journal of Interdisciplinary Research*, 1–28. DOI: 10.54392/ajir2511

Turan, Z., Meral, E., & Sahin, I. F. (2018). The impact of mobile augmented reality in geography education: Achievements, cognitive loads and views of university students. *Journal of Geography in Higher Education*, *42*(3), 427–441. DOI: 10.1080/03098265.2018.1455174

YuLung Wu. YuTien Wu, & ShuMey Yu. (2015). *An Augmented-Reality Interactive Card Game For Teaching Elementary School Students*. DOI: 10.5281/ZENODO.1110752

Chapter 12
Case Studies of AI-AR Applications in Urban Planning and Emergency Management

Defia Ulandari
https://orcid.org/0009-0002-2136-1633
Universitas Esa Unggul, Indonesia

Binastya Anggara Sekti
https://orcid.org/0000-0001-5489-4888
Universitas Esa Unggul, Indonesia

ABSTRACT

The convergence of Artificial Intelligence (AI) and Augmented Reality (AR) is reshaping the foundations of urban governance and emergency management toward more predictive, participatory, and sustainable models. This chapter explores the practical applications of AI-AR synergy through global case studies in Singapore, Japan, Barcelona, and Los Angeles, revealing how data analytics and immersive visualization strengthen decision-making and crisis response. Findings indicate that AI enables predictive modeling for urban and disaster management, while AR bridges human understanding through real-time visualization and public engagement. However, challenges related to ethics, privacy, and digital inequality persist, necessitating a human-centered governance framework. This study concludes that AI-AR integration can advance smart, resilient, and inclusive cities when guided by transparency, sustainability, and cross-sector collaboration.

DOI: 10.4018/979-8-3373-7804-6.ch012

CHAPTER 1 INTRODUCTION

The development of digital technologies in the last two decades has not only brought technical changes, but triggered a profound paradigm shift in urban governance and emergency management. In the midst of this transformation, *Artificial Intelligence* (AI) and *Augmented Reality* (AR) have emerged as synergistic forces that form the concept of smart *governance* that is data-driven, participatory, and adaptive (Garaus et al., 2025). However, this integration goes beyond just automation; it reflects the evolution towards *Human-Centered AI,* where the technology is designed to expand the cognitive capacity of humans in the face of the increasingly dynamic complexity of public spaces.

AI-AR synergy creates a new cognitive infrastructure for cities. AI acts as a "brain" that analyzes massive data for pattern detection and prediction, while AR serves as an intuitive interface that visualizes such data in *real-time* in the real world (Pike, 2025). In the *discourse of Critical Smart Cities*, this integration is seen as an attempt to transform cities into entities capable of "learning", but at the same time raises new challenges regarding who is in control of the digital narrative.

Figure 1. The rise of AI-AR synergy in smart governance

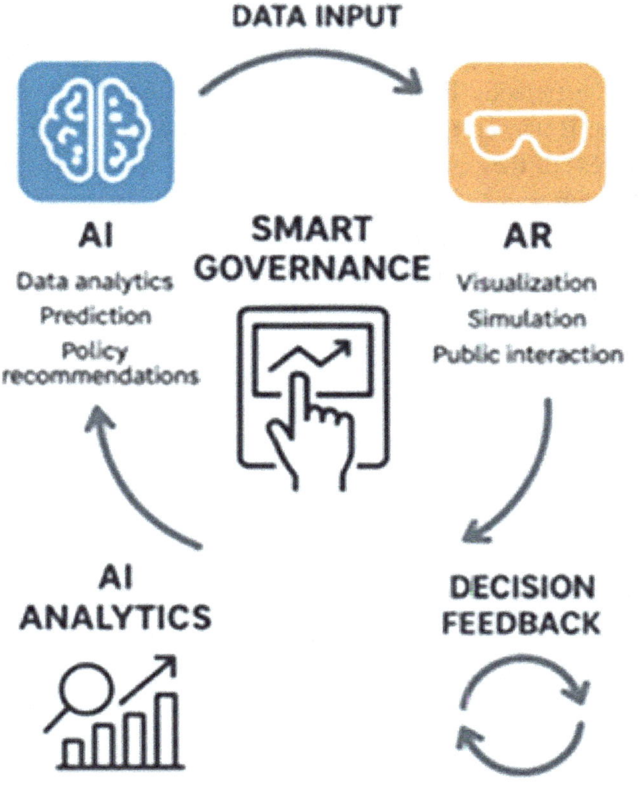

In the urban planning sector, AI-AR is the foundation for the *digital twin* ecosystem. Projects like *Virtual Singapore* show how AI-based 3D city models are used for traffic simulation and disaster risk mitigation in a transparent manner. This approach transforms urban planning from a static process to a more democratic collaborative dialogue, where citizens can visualize the impact of policies before they are implemented. This is in line with the findings (Garaus et al., 2025) that innovative digital experiences can improve public perception of institutional efficiency, as long as data integrity is maintained.

In the emergency management domain, this technology offers a more precise response. AI detects risks through environmental sensors, while AR provides critical visual guidance for officers in the field (Zaidi et al., 2025), reducing the potential for human error during crises. Nonetheless, the use of surveillance technology in crisis management often sparks debates about the balance between operational efficiency and citizen privacy.

Theoretically, this transition reflects the trend of Industry 4.0 that demands governments to not only be managers of resources, but also managers of digital ecosystems involving academia and the private sector. Research (Bghdadi & Zairul, 2024) confirms that enhanced visual and spatial literacy through AI-AR not only impacts technical efficiency, but also on user behavior and the intensity of community participation. However, as emphasized in the discussion of ethics in the next chapter, the success of these systems relies heavily on algorithmic transparency to avoid biases that can trigger social injustice.

Through global case studies in Singapore, Barcelona, Japan, and Los Angeles, this chapter will critically explore how AI-AR synergies are applied to build urban resilience. The main focus of this analysis is to map best practices, structural barriers, and policy directions to ensure that this digital transformation remains inclusive, sustainable, and human-centered.

CHAPTER 2 AI-AR INTEGRATION IN URBAN PLANNING: TOOLS AND TRANSFORMATIONS

Digital transformation has brought about a significant shift in the urban planning paradigm. If previously the planning process was carried out through a conventional approach that relied on static spatial data, now a new approach has emerged that is dynamic, predictive, and visually interactive thanks to the integration of Artificial Intelligence (AI) and Augmented Reality (AR) (Garaus et al., 2025). The combination of these two technologies creates a more responsive and participatory urban planning space, while strengthening the scientific basis for decision-making at the local government level.

2.1 AI-AR as a Cognitive Infrastructure for Cities

AI in the context of urban planning acts as a "brain" that processes big data from environmental sensors, transportation systems, to citizen participation platforms. Through techniques such as machine learning, this system can recognize traffic patterns, predict congestion, and optimize land use (Pierdicca et al., 2024). AR, on the other hand, acts as a cognitive interface that displays the results of such analysis into a 3D visual form on top of a map of a real city. Thus, planners can interact directly with the data through immersive simulations that facilitate the exploration of various development scenarios.

An example of this can be seen in the Virtual Singapore project, The project combines AI algorithms with AR interfaces to optimize energy management, transportation planning, and disaster mitigation. Technically, the effectiveness of the

Digital Twin system is highly dependent on global interoperability standards as set by the Open Geospatial Consortium (OGC). The use of OGC protocols such as the SensorThings API (STA) for *real-time integration of IoT sensor data*, CityGML for semantic 3D city modeling, as well as the OGC API - Features, ensures that various data streams from different vendors can communicate with each other without significant technical barriers (Luo et al., 2025).

2.2 Spatial Visualization and Public Participation

One of the biggest challenges in urban planning is the limited public participation due to the complexity of technical data. AI-AR integration answers these problems by presenting interactive spatial visualizations that can be accessed by ordinary people. With AR, citizens can view a simulation of the development plan directly at a physical location, while AI analyzes citizen input to adjust policies according to the needs of the community (Adawiyah et al., 2024).

As stated by (Bghdadi & Zairul, 2024), AI-AR-based visualization also serves as an educational tool that increases spatial and design literacy among the community. This is similar to an immersive architecture learning approach that allows participants to understand the relationship between space, function, and environment through hands-on experience. In the context of urban planning, this visualization not only enhances public understanding, but also builds a sense of ownership of the city's space.

Public involvement through this digital platform strengthens the concept of citizen-centered governance, where citizens are no longer policy objects, but active actors in the planning process. Technologies such as the developed DeepReality Framework (Pierdicca et al., 2024) demonstrate the open-source potential of AI-AR in supporting collaboration between governments, academics, and citizens in designing transparent and openly verifiable urban projects.

2.3 Sustainable Planning and Environmental Design

AI and AR also play an important role in achieving sustainable development goals. With predictive and visualization capabilities, urban planners can identify the environmental impact of a project before construction begins (Meto & Halilaj, 2025). For example, AI models can predict increased carbon emissions due to the construction of new buildings, and through AR the impact can be visualized in real-time on site.

This approach is in line with the concept of green urbanism, which emphasizes the integration between technology and sustainability. According to (Gao et al., 2023), the application of smart classrooms in science education provides inspiration for smart city design that is also educational and environmentally friendly. With AR, urban parks or public areas can be used as "open learning spaces" to introduce the concept of ecology and sustainability to the community.

Furthermore, AI assists urban planners in creating simulations of various climate scenarios to predict the effects of extreme weather changes on infrastructure (Zaidi et al., 2025). This allows for more adaptive decision-making to environmental crises, especially in big cities with high levels of pollution and urbanization such as Jakarta, Tokyo, and Barcelona.

2.4 Infrastructure and Transportation Optimization

Table 1. Comparison of traditional vs. AI-AR approaches in urban planning

Aspect	Conventional Approach	AI-AR Approach
Data	Relies on static, historical, and often siloed data (e.g., census reports, old maps, periodic surveys).	Utilizes dynamic, real-time, and predictive data (e.g., IoT sensors, live traffic feeds, AI-driven simulations).
Visualization	Static 2D blueprints, physical scale models, or non-interactive 3D renders.	Immersive, interactive 3D models. Augmented Reality (AR) overlays digital plans onto the real-world environment.
Public Participation	Passive and low-engagement methods (e.g., town hall meetings, reviewing complex technical documents).	Active and accessible engagement. Citizens can use AR to visualize proposed changes on-site and provide instant, geo-located feedback.
Efficiency	Slow, manual, and labor-intensive processes. Design revisions are time-consuming and costly.	Automated analysis (AI) and rapid, on-site validation (AR). AI enables generative design to explore thousands of options, reducing errors and speeding up iterations.

AI-AR integration is not only limited to conceptual planning, but also applied to infrastructure management and public transportation. AI-based systems can identify congestion and regulate traffic through machine learning algorithms, while AR helps operators visualize road conditions or utility networks in the field (Boone et al., 2024).

Barcelona is an important example in the application of this concept. The city uses AI-driven mobility systems integrated with AR to monitor traffic flow and support an eco-friendly transportation system. AI is used to analyze vehicle and emissions data, while AR displays interactive maps that allow operators to monitor critical areas directly (Garaus et al., 2025).

Although this technology offers high efficiency, its implementation in the field must be subject to strict data privacy regulations. In the territory of the European Union, for example, the use of IoT sensors and mobility monitoring cameras is required to comply with the General Data Protection Regulation (GDPR). The city government has a legal responsibility to conduct *a Data Protection Impact Assessment* (DPIA) to ensure that monitoring the movement of citizens does not violate the privacy rights of individuals. Its main policy challenge is to maintain transparency; citizens should be given access to clear information, for example through QR codes in public areas regarding the purpose of data collection and their rights to the data (Soriano-gonzalez et al., 2023).

2.5 Implementation Challenges: Infrastructure, Cost, and Ethics

Despite its great potential, the implementation of AI-AR in urban planning faces a number of obstacles. First, uneven digital infrastructure is one of the major challenges in the adoption of *smart city technology*, leading to an implementation gap between developed and developing countries (Hussain et al., 2025). Second, the cost of developing 3D models and AI-based predictive systems is quite high, requiring large investments from the government and the private sector. Third, ethical and privacy issues are a major concern, especially related to the collection of data on the location and behavior of citizens through AR devices (Semjonov et al., 2024).

In the context of design ethics, (Pike, 2025) emphasizes that immersive technology must always consider the human aspect so as not to reduce the social meaning of public spaces. Urban planning should still place people as the center, not just digital data objects. Therefore, a balanced policy is needed between technological innovation and the protection of citizens' rights.

In addition, the skills of the workforce are a crucial factor. Many government institutions still lack human resources with competencies in the fields of data analytics, AR design, and digital ethics. Initiatives at the higher education level, through the integration of technologies such as *the Internet of Things* (IoT), *Augmented Reality* (AR), and *Artificial Intelligence* (AI), can be a long-term solution to “produce superior graduates” who are tech-literate and ready to meet the needs of urban professionals (Soegoto et al., 2022).

CHAPTER 3 AI-AR IN EMERGENCY MANAGEMENT: ENHANCING REAL-TIME RESPONSE

Artificial Intelligence (AI) and Augmented Reality (AR) technologies are not only transforming urban planning, but are also becoming crucial elements in emergency management and disaster management. In recent decades, the increasing intensity of natural disasters, climate change, and the complexity of urbanization have demanded smarter and more responsive systems (Zaidi et al., 2025). AI functions as an analytical engine capable of predicting risks and processing data from environmental sensors, while AR allows for the visualization of crisis situations directly on the ground. The integration of the two strengthens the ability of governments and rescue teams to make fast, accurate, and data-driven decisions.

3.1 AI in Disaster Prediction and Early Detection

AI provides a strong analytical foundation for early warning systems. Through machine learning models and real-time data processing, AI systems can recognize geological, weather, and social patterns that indicate potential disasters such as floods, earthquakes, or wildfires (Boone et al., 2024). In the context of smart cities, data is collected from thousands of IoT sensors, cameras, and satellites, then processed to generate spatial risk predictions (Ellahi et al., 2025).

For example, a *Smart Monitoring System* (Gozuoglu, 2025) has been developed for power grids that integrates Edge AI and Augmented Reality (AR). This system is capable of *real-time* fault detection and predictive maintenance. With predictive analytics algorithms, AI can identify potential disruptions before system failures spread, while AR allows field technicians to visualize network data and AI-generated diagnoses directly on top of physical infrastructure.

In addition to disaster prediction, AI also helps in resource prioritization. By analyzing demographic and infrastructure data, AI can determine which regions are most vulnerable and need help first. (Kurni & Srinivasa, 2024) assert that IoET-based analytics capabilities can be adapted for emergency systems, where intelligent devices in the field communicate with each other to provide decentralized yet synchronous situational data.

3.2 AR as a Visualization Tool and Field Guide

In crisis situations, visualization is a vital aspect because it helps officers understand complex conditions quickly. AR brings digital information into the user's real view through smart glasses or portable device screens. This technology minimizes the need to move between interfaces and improves situational awareness (Rasheed et al., 2024). For example, rescuers can see the direction of evacuation, the position of the victim, or dangerous waterways directly on the disaster field through an AR digital overlay.

(Rasheed et al., 2024) highlight the potential of AI-driven AR glasses in real-time multilingual communication during cross-border humanitarian missions. In international relief operations, officers often face language constraints that slow down coordination. With AI support integrated in AR, the system can translate conversations and field commands instantly, ensuring there is no miscommunication in high-risk areas.

Another implementation can be seen in the Los Angeles Fire Department (LAFD) which developed the AI-AR Wildfire Command System, which is a monitoring platform based on drone data, satellite imagery, and risk maps visualized with AR (Zaidi et al., 2025). This system helps field commanders determine the priority of evacuation areas and the direction of winds that affect the spread of fires. The integration of temperature and humidity sensors allows the AI model to predict changes in fire intensity minutes before it reaches a tipping point.

3.3 AI-AR Collaboration in Rapid Decision Making

One of the main advantages of AI-AR synergy is the ability to create an interactive decision support system (DSS). The system combines real-time data, predictive analysis, and spatial visualization in a single platform (Pierdicca et al., 2024). For example, in earthquake simulations, AI can calculate potential structural damage based on geotechnical models, while AR displays its impact on a 3D map of the city directly to decision-makers.

(Pike, 2025) explains that this mixed reality concept creates a new form of "digital stage" where humans and technology interact in real-life scenarios. In the context of disaster management, this means that field leaders can "see the future" i.e. the results of disaster simulations before taking action. Such predictive systems can reduce strategic errors and accelerate the distribution of aid to locations that need it most.

Another example comes from Japan through the AR Disaster Simulation System, where the government uses a combination of AI-AR to train citizens to deal with earthquake and tsunami scenarios (Garaus et al., 2025). This system not only helps the public understand evacuation procedures, but also educates them about the risks of the surrounding environment. In the long term, this participatory education-based approach strengthens the city's social resilience to disasters.

3.4 Application in Public Space and Infrastructure

In addition to the emergency level, AI-AR technology is used in smart surveillance systems to detect potential security and public health risks. (Shah et al., 2022) highlight that during the COVID-19 pandemic, AI-AR was used to monitor crowds, evaluate physical distancing, and identify high-risk individuals based on movement patterns. In urban contexts, these systems can be adapted to detect potential fires, riots, or industrial incidents early.

(Zaidi et al., 2025) developed the concept of personalized fitness and posture assistant based on computer vision and AR. Although the focus is on individual health, the technology can be adapted for the monitoring of the body position of field officers to reduce fatigue and injuries during rescue operations. A similar approach was used in virtual training for emergency response teams, utilizing AI-VR-AR hybrid platforms to realistically simulate extreme conditions (Meto & Halilaj, 2025).

In the field of disaster logistics, AI-AR-based systems can optimize aid distribution routes by taking into account road conditions, traffic density, and population need levels. (Semjonov et al., 2024) adds that the efficiency of WebAssembly-based computing allows for fast data processing directly in the browser without the need for large servers, this is especially useful in field conditions with limited communication infrastructure.

3.5 Ethics, Data Security, and Community Engagement

Despite its potential, the use of AI-AR in emergency management poses ethical and social challenges. One of them is data privacy. Citizen location data, camera footage, and biometric information collected for disaster prediction systems can be misused if not managed with strict security policies in place (Ellahi et al., 2025). Therefore, any implementation must adhere to the principles of algorithmic transparency and protection of individual privacy.

(Bghdadi & Zairul, 2024) reminds that the success of immersive technology is not only determined by its technological sophistication, but also by its social acceptance. The community needs to be actively involved in the process of developing, training, and using the system so that technology can truly improve social resilience, not just technical efficiency. This principle is in line with the human-centered design approach that places humans at the center of digital interaction.

CHAPTER 4 TECHNICAL AND ETHICAL CHALLENGES

While the integration of Artificial Intelligence (AI) and Augmented Reality (AR) offers tremendous potential for urban planning and emergency management, its implementation is inseparable from a variety of technical, ethical, and social challenges. In the context of public governance, this challenge is not only a matter of technological efficiency, but also related to data security, social justice, algorithmic transparency, and digital infrastructure readiness (Ellahi et al., 2025). Without proper mitigation, the risk of data misuse and algorithmic bias can reduce public trust in smart technologies that are supposed to support the public interest.

4.1 Data Quality and Algorithm Accuracy

One of the biggest obstacles in the implementation of AI is inconsistent data quality. AI requires large amounts of data to train predictive models, but urban data is often incomplete, non-standardized, or comes from biased sources (Pierdicca et al., 2024). For example, faulty sensors or unupdated population data can result in erroneous predictions, potentially significantly affecting urban planning decisions or emergency responses.

Additionally, algorithmic bias is an important issue. When AI models are trained using unrepresentative data, predictive outcomes can reinforce social inequality. (Bghdadi & Zairul, 2024) emphasized that in the context of digital architecture education, design bias can result in non-inclusive visualizations. The same is true in urban planning: if training data only reflects a specific area, the AI-recommended policies may ignore the needs of marginalized areas.

To address this issue, it is recommended to use *explainable AI* (XAI) that allows practical *decision-makers* as *humans-in-the-loop* to understand and oversee algorithmic recommendations before making final decisions. That way, decision-makers remain in full control of the analytics process and can assess whether AI recommendations are relevant and ethical (Tschiatschek et al., 2024).

4.2 Data Security and Privacy

The privacy and data security aspects are of major concern in the implementation of AI-AR, especially since these systems often rely on spatial sensors, cameras, and user location data (Semjonov et al., 2024). In smart city management, information about residents' movements, mobility patterns, and household conditions can be recorded through IoT systems and projected in AR. If such data is leaked, the consequences concern not only individual privacy, but also national security.

(Ellahi et al., 2025) added that in the context of the halal supply chain, data security is a fundamental integrity issue. Similar principles can be applied to smart city governance, where information integrity is the cornerstone of public trust in digital policy. Therefore, every government that implements AI-AR must have a public data governance policy that includes transparent regulations on the storage, deletion, and access to information.

4.3 Limitations of Infrastructure and Digital Access

Another significant challenge is the inequality of digital infrastructure between regions. Not all cities have adequate internet connectivity, computing capacity, and sensor systems to support AI-AR technology (Hussain et al., 2025). As a result, the implementation of smart city systems is often only effective in metropolitan areas, while small cities or rural areas are lagging behind digital transformation.

In the study on the Internet of Educational Things (IoET), (Kurni & Srinivasa, 2024) highlights that digital access is not only a technological issue, but also human competence. This is also true in government: without adequate training, public servants find it difficult to operate AI-AR-based analytics and visualization systems. The lack of data-literate human resources causes many projects to fail to function optimally despite the advanced technology.

Increasing digital literacy and collaboration between institutions is an important step to overcome this problem. As suggested by (Boone et al., 2024), technology-based educational collaboration models can be an inspiration to train public employees to be adaptive to AI-AR-based systems, both in the context of urban management and emergency management.

4.4 Issues of Ethics, Transparency, and Public Trust

AI-AR poses a new ethical dilemma in public governance. One of them is the transparency of the algorithm whether the public has the right to know how the AI system generates certain decisions (Zaidi et al., 2025). In urban planning, AI may recommend evictions or relocations based on data analysis, but without transparency, such policies can lead to citizens' distrust of the government.

According to (Garaus et al., 2025), public acceptance of new technologies is highly dependent on user experience and perceptions of digital justice. When citizens feel engaged and understand the logic of the system, they tend to accept data-driven policies more openly. Therefore, governments need to adopt a digital ethics framework that ensures fairness, inclusivity, and accountability in every stage of AI-AR use.

(Pike, 2025) emphasizes that immersive technologies such as AR should not only be seen as functional tools, but also as spaces for social and cultural interaction. In a public context, AR visualization must be designed so as not to cause discrimination or manipulation of public perception. For example, the view of a policy simulation in AR should include socio-economic variables so that the results are not biased against certain groups.

4.5 Balance between Automation and Human Intervention

One of the philosophical questions that arises is: to what extent can decisions be left entirely to intelligent systems? AI has the ability to process data at scale and generate optimal recommendations, but the final decision in a public context must still be in the hands of humans (Meto & Halilaj, 2025). This is important because public policy considers not only technical efficiency, but also social, moral, and political values.

(Zhang & Miao, 2025) emphasized that learning based on immersive technology needs to be balanced with human judgment so that the decision-making process remains reflective. In urban planning, for example, AI systems may suggest the reduction of green areas for the sake of transportation efficiency, but humans must consider the ecological and psychological impact on citizens. Therefore, the human-in-the-loop approach is a key principle in the implementation of AI-AR in the public sector.

4.6 Sustainability and Social Impact Issues

In addition to technical and ethical aspects, sustainability is also an important challenge. The use of AI-AR requires large computing power and high energy consumption. A study by (Baek et al., 2025) shows that the new generation of DRAM devices is designed to improve computing energy efficiency, yet at the city scale, the energy load remains significant. Therefore, the government needs to ensure that digital transformation also supports the green computing agenda.

From a social perspective, this technology can widen the digital divide between groups of people who have access to technology and those who do not (Adawiyah et al., 2024). If not properly regulated, the use of AI-AR will only reinforce social inequality. Therefore, digital literacy programs and public access to AR platforms must be part of inclusive policies in every smart city project.

Table 2. Categories of AI-AR challenges and mitigation strategies

Technical / Ethical Challenge	Impact	Solution or Mitigation
Digital Divide & Infrastructure	Uneven adoption of technology between developed and developing nations, reinforcing existing socio-economic gaps.	Investment in robust ICT infrastructure and policies focused on digital inclusion to bridge the gap.
Workforce Skills Gap	Government institutions lack human resources competent in data analytics, AR design, and digital ethics, hindering effective implementation.	Integrate IoT, AR, and AI into higher education curricula to "produce excellent graduates" ready for modern urban challenges.
AI "Black Box" & Ethics	Risk of biased or opaque algorithmic decisions; loss of human control and public trust in critical urban planning processes.	Implement Explainable AI (XAI) and "Human-in-the-Loop" (HITL) frameworks to ensure transparency, accountability, and human oversight.
Data Privacy & Security	The vast amount of real-time data (from IoT sensors and AR) creates significant vulnerabilities for citizen surveillance or data breaches.	Employ privacy-by-design principles, strong encryption, and clear data governance policies that comply with regulations (e.g., GDPR).

CHAPTER 5 COMPARATIVE ANALYSIS OF GLOBAL CASE STUDIES

The implementation of the integration of *Artificial Intelligence* (AI) and *Augmented Reality* (AR) in various cities of the world not only demonstrates technological advancements, but also reflects how each political entity grapples with the ethical, infrastructure, and governance challenges that have been identified in Chapter 4. This section evaluates the four major cities of Singapore, Barcelona, Japan, and Los Angeles through the analytical lens of data sovereignty, participation models, and implementation gaps.

5.1 Singapore: Data Sovereignty and the Dilemma of Transparency in the Digital Twin

Singapore is a leader in the development of *the concept of urban digital twins* through the *Virtual Singapore* platform that integrates *real-time sensor data* for policy simulation. However, through the lens of data security (Chapter 4.2), the project faces major data sovereignty-related challenges and legislative barriers.

In contrast to cities that prioritize full openness, the Singapore government must balance the transparency of public simulations with the interests of strict national security. In an effort to mitigate national data security risks, Singapore adopted multi-layered security protocols, where access to sensitive data is restricted even though the visual interface is immersive for city planners. This suggests that the effectiveness of *digital twins* depends not only on technological sophistication, but also on the ability of regulators to navigate the boundaries between public information rights and the protection of the country's vital infrastructure.

5.2 Barcelona: The Advantages of Public Participation vs. a Top-Down Approach

Barcelona made an important contribution in showing how AI-AR can be used to strengthen *citizen engagement*. Through open data policies and the integration of AI sensors in public facilities such as bus stops, Barcelona is creating a more inclusive governance model compared to the *top-down* approach that often dominates other smart cities.

Explicit comparisons show that if the *top-down* model (as seen in Singapore) emphasizes more on cross-agency operational efficiency, the Barcelona model is more successful in building public trust by making citizens active actors in the urban design process. By using AR to visualize mobility and environmental data, Barcelona has succeeded in lowering the technical barriers that usually hinder public participation in public policy. This success confirms Chapter 4.4's argument that social acceptance of technology is highly dependent on perceptions of digital justice and active community engagement.

5.3 Japan: Social Resilience and Immersive Training Simulations

Japan's focus lies on the use of AI-AR to strengthen disaster preparedness through post-earthquake and fire evacuation simulation systems. An analysis of the Japanese model shows the use of technology to address the HR competency challenges discussed in Chapter 4.3. By combining AI predictions about fire spread with AR visualization for evacuation routes, Japan was able to practically increase people's risk literacy. This approach shifts the focus from just data analysis in the control room to field education that builds social resilience from the bottom up.

5.4 Los Angeles: Infrastructure Gaps and Research Gaps in Fire Management

A case study in Los Angeles reveals a significant *research gap* between the ambition of technology and the reality of implementation. Although the use of generative AI has been developed to predict the spread of wildfires in 2D and 3D models, journalistic or academic evidence that explicitly incorporates the results of such AI predictions into a visual AR interface for officers in the field is still very limited.

This gap is a direct reflection of the digital infrastructure challenges discussed in Chapter 4.3. Although the prediction algorithms are sophisticated, the implementation of AR for firefighters in remote areas faces major constraints related to internet connectivity, mobile device computing capacity, and the high cost of developing 3D models. Los Angeles is a clear example that the sophistication of AI algorithms will not be maximized without the support of physical infrastructure and AR hardware that are capable of operating in extreme conditions in the field.

BAB 6 COMPARATIVE ANALYSIS AND POLICY IMPLICATIONS

The application of Artificial Intelligence (AI) and Augmented Reality (AR) in urban planning and emergency management does not take place uniformly around the world. Cultural differences, technological capacity, legal frameworks, and societal readiness result in interesting variations to analyze. This section presents a comparative analysis of various case studies of Singapore, Japan, Barcelona, and Los Angeles and highlights the policy implications that emerge from the integration of AI-AR in public governance.

6.1 Comparison of Implementation Approaches

Structurally, the four cities have different approaches to adopting AI and AR. Singapore focuses on data-driven urban governance, Japan stands out in disaster resilience and simulation-based training, Barcelona emphasizes sustainability and citizen engagement, while Los Angeles prioritizes real-time risk management based on predictive analytics (Garaus et al., 2025).

In Singapore, the government plays a leading role through a top-down governance approach that emphasizes cross-agency coordination. Systems such as *Virtual Singapore* allow for cross-sector data integration with high security (Pierdicca et al., 2024). This model stands out in operational effectiveness, but it requires a large investment and mature digital infrastructure.

In contrast, Japan prioritizes an educational and social approach, with a focus on community resilience. AR technology is used to train people to deal with earthquakes and tsunamis, strengthening citizens' awareness and preparedness (Pike, 2025). This approach is based on bottom-up participation, where the community is the main subject, not just the recipient of information.

Barcelona represents a collaborative approach between the public, private, and academic sectors. Through its open data policy, the city invites innovators and researchers to contribute to the development of AI-AR systems (Semjonov et al., 2024). This approach allows for continuous innovation, but it also poses challenges in data coordination and standardization.

Meanwhile, Los Angeles uses a crisis intelligence-based approach, which relies on the integration of AI-AR for disaster monitoring and rapid decision-making (Zaidi et al., 2025). The city government is working with research institutions and the technology sector to build a predictive system that is able to map fire risk and guide evacuations in real-time.

6.2 Technology Dimension and System Maturity

From a technology maturity perspective, Singapore and Los Angeles are at a high model maturity stage with a complete digital infrastructure and national policy support. Japan is in the intermediate category, with a strong focus on community-based implementation, while Barcelona stands out more in inclusive policy experiments that combine sustainability and community engagement (Garaus et al., 2025).

Studies (Pierdicca et al., 2024) show that the maturity of AI-AR systems depends on three main factors Spatial and temporal data quality, Cross-sector integration rate, and Analytics-based decision-making capacity.

Singapore excels in all three because it has a *National Digital Twin* system with high-quality data. Los Angeles excels in the integration of disaster sensors and predictive AI analytics. In contrast, Japan stands out in the use of AR for risk education, and Barcelona in data openness and public engagement.

6.3 Impact on Governance and Citizen Participation

AI-AR integration not only strengthens technical efficiency, but also changes the relationship between government and society. (Garaus et al., 2025) emphasizes that this technology creates experience-based governance, where citizens can "see" the impact of policies directly through AR visualization. This increases trust and transparency in the governance process.

For example, in Barcelona, citizens can use AR applications to see how environmental policies will affect their area, resulting in increased participation (Bghdadi & Zairul, 2024). In the context of Singapore, citizens can also access simulated development plans through the Virtual Singapore platform to provide feedback.

However, this data-driven approach also raises concerns. Without strict privacy regulations, digital participation could turn into mass surveillance. (Garaus et al., 2025) assert that intelligent monitoring systems can open up the risk of data misuse if they are not accompanied by strong ethical oversight.

Thus, ethical data governance policies need to be an integral part of every smart city project. The government must ensure that AI-AR technology is used for citizen empowerment, not control.

6.4 Operational Efficiency and Urban Resilience

In terms of efficiency, all cities showed significant improvements in data-driven decision-making. In Los Angeles, AI-AR integration accelerated the coordination process between fire units by up to 40% (Zaidi et al., 2025). In Singapore, urban energy management has become more economical as AI systems can predict consumption based on weather conditions (Ellahi et al., 2025).

However, the most significant impact is seen on urban resilience. AI-AR allows governments to not only respond to disasters, but also anticipate and simulate potential risks (Rasheed et al., 2024). Thus, public policy is now moving from *a reactive governance* model to *predictive governance*, where decisions are made based on a proactive analysis of future possibilities.

This is in line with the view (Pike, 2025) that immersive technology creates a "digital interaction space" where humans can experience a reality that has not yet occurred to understand the consequences. In the context of public policy, these simulative capabilities help leaders make more comprehensive, evidence-based decisions.

6.5 Global Policy Implications

Based on a comparative analysis, several strategic policy implications can be formulated to ensure effective and ethical adoption of AI-AR in public governance:

1. Creation of a National Regulatory Framework for AI-AR

Countries need to adopt clear digital ethics and data protection regulations. This regulation should regulate the collection, storage and processing of public data in a transparent manner (Ellahi et al., 2025).

2. Application of Human-in-the-Loop Principles in Intelligent Systems

AI should not replace human decision-making, but rather support it (Zhang & Miao, 2025). Every system must have a human intervention mechanism to ensure a balance between efficiency and social value.

3. Improving Digital Literacy and Training of Public Apparatus

As suggested by (Kurni & Srinivasa, 2024), technology-based education needs to be expanded so that government employees can comprehend and manage AI-AR systems competently.

4. Strengthening Cross-Sector and International Collaboration

Collaboration between government, universities, and the private sector is the key to success. The Barcelona model based on data disclosure can be used as a reference to encourage local innovation (Semjonov et al., 2024).

5. Integration of Sustainability and Energy Efficiency Aspects

The use of AI-AR must be aligned with *green computing* and energy efficiency policies (Baek et al., 2025). Every city needs to ensure that its digital infrastructure does not add to the global carbon burden.

6. Implementation of Participatory and Inclusive Policies

The government needs to provide an interactive platform so that the public can understand, provide input, and participate in the AI-AR-based planning process (Adawiyah et al., 2024).

6.6 Reflections on Regional Differences

From cross-regional analysis, it can be concluded that AI-AR is not universal, its success is greatly influenced by the local context. Developed countries with high technological capacity, such as Singapore and the US, are putting AI-AR as part of national strategies. Meanwhile, countries with a social focus such as Japan emphasize aspects of education and community preparedness. On the other hand, European cities such as Barcelona prioritize ethics, transparency, and sustainability more in their digital policies (Bghdadi & Zairul, 2024).

This different approach actually enriches global insights. From this it can be seen that the success of AI-AR adoption is determined not only by the sophistication of the technology, but also by the policies, culture, and social structures that support it. In this regard, the experiences of those cities provide valuable lessons for developing countries to design relevant and contextual digital strategies.

CHAPTER 7 CONCLUSION

The integration between Artificial Intelligence (AI) and Augmented Reality (AR) has opened a new era in modern city governance, making governance systems more predictive, participatory, and resilient. Cross-country studies in Singapore, Japan, Barcelona, and Los Angeles show that AI-AR synergy not only serves as a technological innovation, but also as an instrument of social and institutional transformation towards a government that is more adaptive to urban dynamics (Garaus et al., 2025).

From a technical perspective, the application of AI-AR accelerates decision-making, improves resource efficiency, and creates a space for digital interaction between governments, citizens, and the environment (Pierdicca et al., 2024). Projects such as *Virtual Singapore* demonstrate how *digital twins* can predict development scenarios and public policy impacts through AR-based visualizations (Quek et al., 2023). A similar approach was implemented in Barcelona with a focus on sustainable mobility and citizen engagement through *AI-powered* smart mobility dashboards (Soriano-gonzalez et al., 2023).

In the context of emergency management, the combination of AI-AR has been shown to increase the effectiveness of responses to crises. In Japan, AR-based simulation systems are used for earthquake evacuation training (Tang, 2024), while in Los Angeles, generative AI technology is applied to predict the spread of wildfires in 2D and 3D models (Models & Learning, n.d.). This predictive approach helps speed up coordination, reduce the risk of human error, and save lives (Rasheed et al., 2024).

However, the success of AI-AR implementation also comes with multidimensional challenges. Issues of data security, individual privacy, and algorithmic bias are critical issues that require strong ethical governance (Semjonov et al., 2024). In addition, the digital divide between metropolitan and rural areas shows an imbalance in access to technological innovation (Hussain et al., 2025). This challenge is increasingly complex with a lack of human resources who have competence in data analysis and immersive visualization design (Soegoto et al., 2022).

From an ethical point of view, the *human-in-the-loop approach proposed by* (Tschiatschek et al., 2024) is important to ensure that AI-based decision-making still maintains human moral reflection. This is in line with the view (Zhang & Miao, 2025) that emphasizes the need for a balance between automation and empathy in immersive technology-based systems. In addition, the massive use of technology must consider environmental impacts as the high energy consumption of AI-AR computing demands *a more sustainable* green computing strategy (Baek et al., 2025).

The success of AI-AR implementation also depends on social acceptance. (Bghdadi & Zairul, 2024) emphasized that public participation is key for immersive technology to not only strengthen technical efficiency, but also deepen citizen engagement. In this context, AR visualization can serve as an educational medium and social dialogue that fosters collective awareness of city policies.

7.1 Strategic Recommendations for the Future

Based on the results of the study and comparative analysis, several strategic recommendations can be formulated to ensure effective, inclusive, and ethical adoption of AI-AR in public governance:

1. Build an AI-AR National Ethical Framework

Governments need to develop *an AI-AR Ethical Governance Framework* that governs the principles of algorithmic transparency, data privacy, and social responsibility in public decision-making (Tschiatschek et al., 2024).

2. Improving Digital Literacy and Human Resources Capacity

In line with (Soegoto et al., 2022), higher education institutions need to integrate AI, AR, and IoT into the public curriculum to produce government professionals who are data-literate and adaptive to technology.

3. Encouraging Multi-Sector Collaboration and Open Innovation

Models such as *DeepReality* (Pierdicca et al., 2024) prove that *open-source frameworks* accelerate innovation while increasing public transparency. The government, industry, and academia need to work together to build an open research ecosystem that supports the development of AI-AR based on local needs.

4. Integrating the principles of digital sustainability

The implementation of AI-AR must be aligned with green energy and power efficiency policies (Baek et al., 2025). Every city needs to measure the carbon impact of its digital systems and adopt low-emission solutions for data centers and cloud computing.

5. Increase Public Engagement through AR Visualization

The government needs to develop an interactive AR platform that allows the public to see the impact of public policies directly before they are implemented.

This approach not only increases transparency, but also strengthens the legitimacy of data-driven policies (Bghdadi & Zairul, 2024).

6. Maintaining a Balance between Automation and Human Values

AI-AR technology should not replace humans, but expand the capacity of humans to think and act more reflexively (Zhang & Miao, 2025). The government needs to ensure that every intelligent system has a human intervention mechanism as the final decision-maker.

7.2 Closing

Ultimately, the future of smart cities depends on how humans orchestrate the relationship between artificial intelligence and augmented reality. AI brings incredible analytical and predictive capabilities, while AR delivers visual experiences that reinforce empathy and social understanding (Pike, 2025). When the two are combined in public governance, not only efficiency is achieved, but also fairness, transparency, and sustainability.

By adopting the principles *of human-centered governance*, cross-sectoral collaboration, and digital ethics-based policies, AI-AR can be the foundation for future cities that are not only technologically intelligent, but also resilient, equitable, and empathetic to their citizens (Garaus et al., 2025).

REFERENCES

Adawiyah, S. R., Purwandari, B., Eitiveni, I., & Purwaningsih, E. H. (2024). The Influence of AI and AR Technology in Personalized Recommendations on Customer Usage Intention: A Case Study of Cosmetic Products on Shopee. *Applied Sciences (Basel, Switzerland)*, *14*(13), 5786. Advance online publication. DOI: 10.3390/app14135786

Baek, J.-H., Kim, J.-H., Sung, Y.-C., Jeong, J.-W., Park, J.-K., Oh, H.-K., Lee, B.-H., Ko, D.-W., Oh, T.-S., Hong, S.-G., Kwon, C.-K., Lim, D., Kim, M.-O., Bae, S.-J., Oh, T.-Y., & Hwang, S.-J. (2025). A 16Gb 12.7Gb/s/pin LPDDR5-Ultra-Pro DRAM with 4-Phase Self-Calibration and AC-Coupled Transceiver Equalization in a 5th-Generation 10nm DRAM Process. *Digest of Technical Papers - IEEE International Solid-State Circuits Conference*, *510–512*, 510–512. Advance online publication. DOI: 10.1109/ISSCC49661.2025.10904794

Bghdadi, M., & Zairul, M. (2024). A THEMATIC REVIEW ON ARTIFICIAL INTELLIGENCE (AI), VIRTUAL REALITY (VR), AND AUGMENTED REALITY (AR) IN ARCHITECTURE EDUCATION. *Alam Cipta*, *17*(2), 55–66. DOI: 10.47836/AC.17.2.PAPER06

Boone, R., Davis, R., Starnes, J., & Ghorashi, B. (2024). *Industry 4.0 Applications to Three Engineering Operations – A Learning Experience for Senior Engineering Students*. https://www.scopus.com/inward/record.uri?eid=2-s2.0-105004876072&partnerID=40&md5=0495f3a6687c31af1a06b5483d0510e1

Ellahi, R. M., Wood, L. C., Khan, M., & Bekhit, A. E.-D. A. (2025). Integrity Challenges in Halal Meat Supply Chain: Potential Industry 4.0 Technologies as Catalysts for Resolution. *Foods*, *14*(7), 1135. Advance online publication. DOI: 10.3390/foods14071135 PMID: 40238310

Gao, X., Wang, Y., & Cao, Z. (2023). Light Practical Smart Experiment Classroom and Smart Education Application Solutions in Popular Science Corner. In *Lecture Notes in Educational Technology: Vol. Part F1761* (pp. 223–225). DOI: 10.1007/978-981-99-6225-9_33

Garaus, M., Treiblmaier, H., Wagner, U., & Garaus, C. (2025). Innovating the experience economy: How novel technologies transform customer experiences. *Digital Business*, *5*(2), 100134. Advance online publication. DOI: 10.1016/j.digbus.2025.100134

Gozuoglu, A. (2025). *Smart Monitoring of Power Networks: Augmented Reality and Edge AI for Grid Resilience*.

Hussain, A., Rubab, [2]narjis, Tausif, [3]sumaira, Aslam, S., Iftikhar, A., Imran, M., & Nasir, A. (2025). Emerging Trends in Smart Cities: Technologies, Challenges, and Opportunities. *Journal of Computer Science and Technology Studies*, *9*, 1–16.

Kurni, M., & Srinivasa, K. G. (2024). *The Internet of Educational Things: Enhancing Students' Engagement and Learning Performance*. DOI: 10.1007/978-3-031-67387-0

Luo, J., Liu, P., Xu, W., Zhao, T., & Biljecki, F. (2025). A perception-powered urban digital twin to support human-centered urban planning and sustainable city development. *Cities (London, England)*, *156*, 105473. DOI: 10.1016/j.cities.2024.105473

Meto, A., & Halilaj, G. (2025). The Integration of Cone Beam Computed Tomography, Artificial Intelligence, Augmented Reality, and Virtual Reality in Dental Diagnostics, Surgical Planning, and Education: A Narrative Review. *Applied Sciences (Basel, Switzerland)*, *15*(11), 6308. Advance online publication. DOI: 10.3390/app15116308

Pierdicca, R., Tonetto, F., Paolanti, M., Mameli, M., Rosati, R., & Zingaretti, P. (2024). DeepReality: An open source framework to develop AI-based augmented reality applications. *Expert Systems with Applications*, *249*, 123530. Advance online publication. DOI: 10.1016/j.eswa.2024.123530

Pike, S. (2025). *AI, AR, AND VR IN THEATRE AND PERFORMANCE: Technology in the Present and Future of Live Creative Arts*. DOI: 10.4324/9781003521907

Quek, H. Y., Sielker, F., Akroyd, J., Bhave, A. N., von Richthofen, A., Herthogs, P., Yamu, C. van der L., Wan, L., Nochta, T., Burgess, G., Lim, M. Q., Mosbach, S., & Kraft, M. (2023). The conundrum in smart city governance: Interoperability and compatibility in an ever-growing ecosystem of digital twins. *Data & Policy*, *5*, e6. https://doi.org/DOI. DOI: 10.1017/dap.2023.1

Rasheed, Z., Ghwanmeh, S., & Almahadin, A. (2024). A Critical Review of AI-Driven AR Glasses for Realtime Multilingual Communication. *Advances in Science and Engineering Technology International Conferences, ASET*. DOI: 10.1109/ASET60340.2024.10708749

Semjonov, A., Bornholdt, H., Edinger, J., & Russo Russo, G. R. (2024). *Wasimoff: Distributed Computation Offloading Using WebAssembly in the Browser*. 203–208. DOI: 10.1109/PerComWorkshops59983.2024.10503392

Shah, I., Doshi, C., Patel, M., Tanwar, S., Hong, W.-C., & Sharma, R. (2022). A Comprehensive Review of the Technological Solutions to Analyse the Effects of Pandemic Outbreak on Human Lives. *Medicina (Lithuania)*, *58*(2). DOI: 10.3390/medicina58020311

Soegoto, E. S., Soegoto, H., Soegoto, D. S., & Soegoto, S. W. (2022). Indonesian Journal of Science & Technology A systematic Literature Review of Internet of Things for Higher Education. *Architecture and Implementation.*, *7*, 511–528.

Soriano-gonzalez, R., Perez-bernabeu, E., Ahsini, Y., Carracedo, P., Camacho, A., & Juan, A. A. (2023). *Analyzing Key Performance Indicators for Mobility Logistics in Smart and Sustainable Cities : A Case Study Centered on Barcelona*.

Tang, K. (2024). *Multi-Objective Evcuation Planning Model Considering Post-Earthquake Fire Spread : A Tokyo Case Study*.

Tschiatschek, S., Stamboliev, E., Schmude, T., Coeckelbergh, M., & Koesten, L. (2024). *Challenging the Human-in-the-loop in Algorithmic Decision-making*. https://doi.org//arXiv.2405.10706DOI: 10.48550

Zaidi, S. M. H., Bilal, M., Ashraf, S. N., Alharbi, A., Iqbal, R., & Zuberi, H. H. (2025). Review-Based AI-Driven Posture Correction and Personalized Fitness Assistant Using Computer Vision and Augmented Reality. *International Journal of E-Health and Medical Communications*, *16*(1), 1–25. Advance online publication. DOI: 10.4018/IJEHMC.381820

Zhang, Y., & Miao, Z. (2025). Enhancing EFL Learners' Engagement and Motivation Through Immersive Technologies: The Role of Artificial Intelligence, Augmented Reality, Virtual Reality, and Mobile Applications. *European Journal of Education*, *60*(2), e70128. Advance online publication. DOI: 10.1111/ejed.70128

Compilation of References

Abdillah, A., Widianingsih, I., Buchari, R. A., & Nurasa, H. (2024). Big data security & individual (psychological) resilience: A review of social media risks and lessons learned from Indonesia. *Array (New York, N.Y.)*, *21*, 100336. DOI: 10.1016/j.array.2024.100336

Abdullah, A. M. (2024). Protection of Privacy Rights Against Personal Data Collection by Generative AI Based on Conversations with Users. *Padjadjaran Law Review*, *12*(2), 145–156. DOI: 10.56895/plr.v12i2.1796

Abidin, F., & Tina, A. (2024).. . *Indonesia's Legal Policy on Protecting Personal Data from Artificial Intelligence Abuse.*, *07002*, 1–11.

Abrar, M. F., & Islam, Md. R., Hossain, Md. S., Islam, M. M., & Kabir, M. A. (2019). Augmented Reality in Education: A Study on Preschool Children, Parents, and Teachers in Bangladesh. In J. Y. C. Chen & G. Fragomeni (Eds.), *Virtual, Augmented and Mixed Reality. Applications and Case Studies* (Vol. 11575, pp. 217–229). Springer International Publishing. DOI: 10.1007/978-3-030-21565-1_14

Achiam, J., Adler, S., Agarwal, S., ... (2023). GPT-4 Technical Report. *arXiv preprint arXiv:2303.08774.*

Adawiyah, S. R., Purwandari, B., Eitiveni, I., & Purwaningsih, E. H. (2024). The Influence of AI and AR Technology in Personalized Recommendations on Customer Usage Intention: A Case Study of Cosmetic Products on Shopee. *Applied Sciences (Basel, Switzerland)*, *14*(13), 5786. Advance online publication. DOI: 10.3390/app14135786

Ahmad Tarikh, R. A. B. (2025). *COMPARATIVE ANALYSIS OF DATA PROTECTION LAW BETWEEN INDONESIA AND THE EUROPEAN UNION: A CASE REVIEW OF CAMBRIDGE ANALYTICA*. www.kominfo.go.id/content/detail/34906/pemeriksaan-dugaan-kebocoran-data-bpjs-kesehatan/0/berita_

Ainslie, S., Thompson, D., Maynard, S., & Ahmad, A. (2023). Cyber-threat intelligence for security decision-making: A review and research agenda for practice. *Computers & Security*, *132*, 103352. DOI: 10.1016/j.cose.2023.103352

Akbar, N., Kurnia Sitorus, H., Arifin, MY, & Nasution, P. (2025). Legal Protection of Consumer Personal Data in Digital Transactions. *Indonesian Law Journal, 2* (1).

Alaeifar, P., Pal, S., Jadidi, Z., Hussain, M., & Foo, E. (2024). Current approaches and future directions for Cyber Threat Intelligence sharing: A survey. *Journal of Information Security and Applications*, *83*, 103786. DOI: 10.1016/j.jisa.2024.103786

Al-Ansi, A. M., Garad, A., Jaboob, M., & Al-Ansi, A. (2024). Elevating e-government: Unleashing the power of AI and IoT for enhanced public services. *Heliyon*, *10*(23), e40591. DOI: 10.1016/j.heliyon.2024.e40591 PMID: 39654738

Aleva, T. K., Tabone, W., Dodou, D., & de Winter, J. C. F. (2024). Augmented reality for supporting the interaction between pedestrians and automated vehicles: An experimental outdoor study. *Frontiers in Robotics and AI*, *11*, 1324060. DOI: 10.3389/frobt.2024.1324060 PMID: 38352957

Ali, S., Abuhmed, T., & El-Sappagh, S.. (2023). XAI: Trustworthy artificial intelligence. *Information Fusion*, *99*, 101805. DOI: 10.1016/j.inffus.2023.101805

Almada, M. (2024). *Law & Compliance in AI Security & Data Protection.*

Almadani, M., Cahyani, A. A. D., & Khadafi, M. (2024). The Effect of Electronic-Based Government System (SPBE) Implementation on Performance Accountability in the Regional Secretariat of South Sulawesi Province. [Management of Apparatus Resources]. *MSDA Journal*, *12*(1), 96–132.

Almahmoud, Z., Yoo, P. D., Damiani, E., Choo, K. K. R., & Yeun, C. Y. (2025). Forecasting Cyber Threats: Future mitigation technologies. *Technological Forecasting and Social Change*, *210*, 123836. DOI: 10.1016/j.techfore.2024.123836

Al-Mhiqani, M. N., Alsboui, T., Al-Shehari, T., Abdulkareem, K., Ahmad, R., & Mohammed, M. A. (2024). Insider threat detection in cyber-physical systems: A systematic literature review. *Computers & Electrical Engineering*, *119*, 109489. DOI: 10.1016/j.compeleceng.2024.109489

Alpiah, S., Asbari, M., Saputri, I. A., & Adilya, N. R. (2024). Oversharing: The Urgency of Privacy in the Digital Age. [JISMA]. *Journal of Information Systems and Management*, *3*(1), 42–47. DOI: 10.4444/JISMA.V3I1.877

Alqutaibi, A. Y., Hamadallah, H. H., Oqbi, H. F., Almuzaini, S. A., & Borzangy, S. (2024). Current applications and future perspective of virtual reality in dental education and practice in Saudi Arabia: A scoping review. *The Saudi Dental Journal*, *36*(11), 1406–1416. DOI: 10.1016/j.sdentj.2024.09.007 PMID: 39619710

Alsharida, R. A., Al-rimy, B. A. S., Al-Emran, M., & Zainal, A. (2023). A systematic review of multiple perspectives on human behavior in cybersecurity. *Technology in Society*, *73*, 102258. DOI: 10.1016/j.techsoc.2023.102258

Amelia Azis, R., Olivia, F., & Arianto, H. (2023). REGULATORY IMPACT ASSESSMENT (RIA) IN POLICY FORMULATION. In *Regulatory Impact Assessment (RIA) In Policy Formulation Lex Jurnalica* (Vol. 20, Issue 1).

Angwin, J., Larson, J., Mattu, S., & Kirchner, L. (2016). Machine Bias: Software used to predict future criminals and its racial biases. In *Ethics of Data and Analytics*. Auerbach Publications.

Ansell, C., & Gash, A. (2008). Collaborative governance in theory and practice. *Journal of Public Administration: Research and Theory*, *18*(4), 543–571. DOI: 10.1093/jopart/mum032

Anser, M. K., Nabi, A. A., Ahmad, I., Abro, M. M. Q., & Zaman, K. (2025). Advancing Mental Health Care: A Comprehensive Review of Digital Tools and Technologies for Enhancing Diagnosis, Treatment, and Wellness. *Health Care Science*, *4*(3), 163–178. DOI: 10.1002/hcs2.70018 PMID: 40568629

APJII. (2025). *INTERNET PENETRATION SURVEY AND INTERNET USAGE BEHAVIOR 2025*.

Ardika, I. W. C. (2025). Legal Review of Personal Data Protection in the Digital Era: A Case Study of E-Commerce User Data Leaks. *Indonesian Journal of Law and Justice*, *2*(3), 11. DOI: 10.47134/ijlj.v2i3.3601

Arief, S. (2025). *Article 7 Regulatory Arrangements and Utilization of Artificial Intelligence (AI) in Realizing Personal Data Protection in Indo... 19% Overall Similarity*. 1–13.

Arif, M. (2025). *APJII General Arfizar Zulkarnaen, B.* INTERNET PENETRATION SURVEY AND INTERNET USAGE BEHAVIOR IN.

Arnstein, S. R. (1969). A ladder of citizen participation. *Journal of the American Institute of Planners*, *35*(4), 216–224. DOI: 10.1080/01944366908977225

Arrieta, A. B., Díaz-Rodríguez, N., & Del Ser, J.. (2020). Explainable artificial intelligence (XAI): Concepts and challenges. *Information Fusion*, *58*, 82–115. DOI: 10.1016/j.inffus.2019.12.012

Awadallah, O., Grolinger, K., & Sadhu, A. (2024). Remote collaborative framework for real-time structural condition assessment using Augmented Reality. *Advanced Engineering Informatics*, *62*, 102652. https://doi.org/https://doi.org/10.1016/j.aei.2024.102652. DOI: 10.1016/j.aei.2024.102652

Aydoğdu, F. (2022). Augmented reality for preschool children: An experience with educational contents. *British Journal of Educational Technology*, *53*(2), 326–348. DOI: 10.1111/bjet.13168

Azuma, R. T. (1997). A survey of augmented reality. *Presence (Cambridge, Mass.)*, *6*(4), 355–385. DOI: 10.1162/pres.1997.6.4.355

Baashar, Y., Alkawsi, G., Wan Ahmad, W. N., Alomari, M. A., Alhussian, H., & Tiong, S. K. (2023). Towards Wearable Augmented Reality in Healthcare: A Comparative Survey and Analysis of Head-Mounted Displays. *International Journal of Environmental Research and Public Health*, *20*(5), 3940. DOI: 10.3390/ijerph20053940 PMID: 36900951

Baek, J.-H., Kim, J.-H., Sung, Y.-C., Jeong, J.-W., Park, J.-K., Oh, H.-K., Lee, B.-H., Ko, D.-W., Oh, T.-S., Hong, S.-G., Kwon, C.-K., Lim, D., Kim, M.-O., Bae, S.-J., Oh, T.-Y., & Hwang, S.-J. (2025). A 16Gb 12.7Gb/s/pin LPDDR5-Ultra-Pro DRAM with 4-Phase Self-Calibration and AC-Coupled Transceiver Equalization in a 5th-Generation 10nm DRAM Process. *Digest of Technical Papers - IEEE International Solid-State Circuits Conference*, *510–512*, 510–512. Advance online publication. DOI: 10.1109/ISSCC49661.2025.10904794

Baheer, B. A., Lamas, D., & Sousa, S. (2020). A Systematic Literature Review on Existing Digital Government Architectures: State-of-the-Art, Challenges, and Prospects. In *Administrative Sciences* (Vol. 10, Issue 2, p. 25). DOI: 10.3390/admsci10020025

Balahur, A., & Turchi, M. (2014). Comparative experiments using supervised learning and machine translation for multilingual sentiment analysis. *Computer Speech & Language*, *28*(1), 56–75. DOI: 10.1016/j.csl.2013.03.004

Balog, A., & Pribeanu, C. (2010). The Role of Perceived Enjoyment in the Students' Acceptance of an Augmented Reality Teaching Platform: A Structural Equation Modelling Approach. *Studies in Informatics and Control*, *19*(3). Advance online publication. DOI: 10.24846/v19i3y201011

Bangor, A., Kortum, P. T., & Miller, J. T. (2008). Empirical evaluation of the system usability scale. *International Journal of Human-Computer Interaction*, *24*(6), 574–594. DOI: 10.1080/10447310802205776

Bastos, D., Fernández-Caballero, A., Pereira, A., & Rocha, N. P. (2022). Smart city applications to promote citizen participation in city management and governance: A systematic review. *Informatics (MDPI)*, *9*(4), 89. DOI: 10.3390/informatics9040089

Basu, S. K., Mandal, R., Kar, A., Patra, S., Sudheer, P., & Manjunath, T. C. (2026). The Internet of Things and Real-Time Process Monitoring. In Martínez-Falcó, J., Sánchez-García, E., & Marco-Lajara, B. (Eds.). *Navigating Digital Transformation Through Business Process Management* (pp. 303–334). IGI Global Scientific Publishing.

Bathaee, Y. (2018). The artificial intelligence black box and the failure of intent and causation. *Harvard Journal of Law & Technology*, *31*(2), 889.

Batty, M., Axhausen, K. W., Giannotti, F., Pozdnoukhov, A., Bazzani, A., Wachowicz, M., Ouzounis, G., & Portugali, Y. (2012). Smart cities of the future. *The European Physical Journal. Special Topics*, *214*(1), 481–518. DOI: 10.1140/epjst/e2012-01703-3

Batty, M., Hudson-Smith, A., Milton, R., & Crooks, A. (2019). *The computable city*. MIT Press.

Bennis, I., & Mouwafaq, S. (2025). Advancing AI-driven thematic analysis in qualitative research: a comparative study of nine generative models on Cutaneous Leishmaniasis data. BMC Medical Informatics and Decision Making, 25doi: PubMedDOI: 10.1186/s12911-025-02961-5

Bertot, J. C., Estevez, E., & Janowski, T. (2016, March). Digital public service innovation: Framework proposal. In *Proceedings of the 9th International Conference on Theory and Practice of Electronic Governance* (pp. 113-122). DOI: 10.1145/2910019.2910108

Bertot, J. C., Jaeger, P. T., & Grimes, J. M. (2016). Using ICTs to create a culture of transparency: E-government and social media as openness and anti-corruption tools for societies. *Government Information Quarterly*, *33*(2), 264–271. DOI: 10.1016/j.giq.2015.12.001

Bghdadi, M., & Zairul, M. (2024). A THEMATIC REVIEW ON ARTIFICIAL INTELLIGENCE (AI), VIRTUAL REALITY (VR), AND AUGMENTED REALITY (AR) IN ARCHITECTURE EDUCATION. *Alam Cipta*, *17*(2), 55–66. DOI: 10.47836/AC.17.2.PAPER06

Bhatnagar, S., & Singh, N. (2019). Assessing the impact of e-government: A study of projects in India. *Information Technologies and International Development, 15*, 1–17.

Biega, A. J., Potash, P., Daumé, H., Diaz, F., & Finck, M. (2020). Operationalizing the principles of the law of data minimization for personalization. *Proceedings of the 43rd ACM SIGIR International Conference on Research and Development in Information Retrieval*, 399–408.

Billinghurst, M., Clark, A., & Lee, G. (2015). A survey of augmented reality. *Foundations and Trends® in Human—Computer Interaction, 8*(2-3), 73-272.

Bizami, N. A., Tasir, Z., & Kew, S. N. (2023). Innovative pedagogical principles and technological tools capabilities for immersive blended learning: A systematic literature review. *Education and Information Technologies, 28*(2), 1373–1425. DOI: 10.1007/s10639-022-11243-w PMID: 35919874

Bobro, N., Bielikov, V., Matveyeva, M., Salamakha, A., & Kharchun, V. (2025). Innovations in Public Administration and Management for Implementing Effective Strategies and Tools. *Salud. Ciencia y Tecnología-Serie de Conferencias, 4*, 1483. DOI: 10.56294/sctconf20251483

Boone, R., Davis, R., Starnes, J., & Ghorashi, B. (2024). *Industry 4.0 Applications to Three Engineering Operations – A Learning Experience for Senior Engineering Students*. https://www.scopus.com/inward/record.uri?eid=2-s2.0-105004876072&partnerID=40&md5=0495f3a6687c31af1a06b5483d0510e1

Bork-Hüffer, T. (2017). Beyond Smart City. Singapore's "Smart Nation" strategy and the competition for model status. *Geographische Rundschau, 69*(7–8), 36–40.

Bosco G, Riccardi V, Sciarrone A, D'Amore R, Visvizi A. (2024). *AI-driven innovation in smart city governance: achieving human-centric and sustainable outcomes*. Transforming Government: People, Process and Policy. DOI: 10.1108/TG-04-2024-0096

Bostrom, N., & Yudkowsky, E. (2014). The ethics of artificial intelligence. In The Cambridge Handbook of Artificial Intelligence (pp. 316–334). DOI: 10.1017/CBO9781139046855.020

Bovaird, A. G., & Löffler, E. (2015). *Public Management and Governance*. DOI: 10.4324/9781315693279

Brabham, D. C. (2008). Crowdsourcing as a model for problem solving. *Convergence (London), 14*(1), 75–90. DOI: 10.1177/1354856507084420

Brabham, D. C. (2009). Crowdsourcing the public participation process for planning projects. *Planning Theory*, *8*(3), 242–262. DOI: 10.1177/1473095209104824

Brauneis, R., & Goodman, E. P. (2018). Algorithmic transparency for the smart city. *Yale Journal of Law & Technology*, *20*, 103.

Buçinca, Z., Malaya, M. B., & Gajos, K. Z. (2021). To trust or to think: cognitive forcing functions can reduce overreliance on AI in AI-assisted decision-making. Proceedings of the ACM on Human-computer Interaction, 5(CSCW1), 1-21.

Bunt, A., Lount, M., & Lauzon, C. (2012). Are explanations always important? *ACM International Conference on Intelligent User Interfaces*, 169–178.

Burlacu, S., Creţu, R. C., Potcovaru, A. M. B., & Călin, A. M. (2024). Integrative digital governance: The role of public administration in promoting sustainable development amid post-pandemic technological innovations. In *Proceedings of the International Conference on Business Excellence* (Vol. 18, No. 1, pp. 725-732). Sciendo. DOI: 10.2478/picbe-2024-0063

Busuioc, M. (2021). Accountability, control and power in data-driven public administration. *Public Administration Review*, *81*(5), 857–869. DOI: 10.1111/puar.13381 PMID: 34690372

Butcher, J., & Beridze, I. (2019). What is the state of artificial intelligence governance globally? *RUSI Journal*, *164*(5–6), 88–96. DOI: 10.1080/03071847.2019.1694260

Cakir, R., & Korkmaz, O. (2019). The effectiveness of augmented reality environments on individuals with special education needs. *Education and Information Technologies*, *24*(2), 1631–1659. DOI: 10.1007/s10639-018-9848-6

Calzada, I. (2019). Deciphering smart city citizenship: The techno-politics of data and urban co-operative platforms. *Revista Internacional de Estudios Vascos*, *63*(1–2), 42–81.

Cao, J., Lam, K.-Y., Lee, L.-H., Liu, X., Hui, P., & Su, X. (2023). Mobile augmented reality: User interfaces, frameworks, and intelligence. *ACM Computing Surveys*, *55*(9), 1–36. DOI: 10.1145/3557999

Capra, C. F. (2018). The Smart City and Its Citizens: Governance and Citizen Participation in Amsterdam Smart City. In I. Management Association (Ed.), E-Planning and Collaboration: Concepts, Methodologies, Tools, and Applications (pp. 321-341). IGI Global Scientific Publishing. https://doi.org/DOI: 10.4018/978-1-5225-5646-6.ch015

Carabantes, M. (2020). Black-box artificial intelligence: An epistemological and critical analysis. *AI & Society*, *35*(2), 309–317. DOI: 10.1007/s00146-019-00888-w

Chance, E. A. (2025). The combined impact of AI and VR on interdisciplinary learning and patient safety in healthcare education: A narrative review. *BMC Medical Education*, *25*(1), 1039. DOI: 10.1186/s12909-025-07589-7 PMID: 40646457

Chataut, R., Nankya, M., & Akl, R. (2024). 6G Networks and the AI Revolution—Exploring Technologies, Applications, and Emerging Challenges. *Sensors (Basel)*, *24*(6), 1888. DOI: 10.3390/s24061888 PMID: 38544151

Chatfield, A. T., & Reddick, C. G. (2018). A longitudinal cross-sector analysis of open data adoption by U.S. cities. *Government Information Quarterly*, *35*(4), 535–546. DOI: 10.1016/j.giq.2017.02.004

Chen, G., Wang, H., Liang, A., Oubibi, M., & Zhou, Y. (2025). From detached observer to immersive participant: An augmented reality-based experiential learning approach to promote academic performance and learning behaviors in science education. *Computers in Human Behavior Reports*, *19*, 100756. DOI: 10.1016/j.chbr.2025.100756

Chen, J. J. (2025). From Turing's conception of machine intelligence to the evolution of AI in early childhood education: Conceptual, empirical, and practical insights. *AI. Brain and Child*, *1*(1), 1. DOI: 10.1007/s44436-025-00002-6

Chen, M., Cao, Y., & Liang, Y. (2023). Determinants of open government data usage: Integrating trust theory and social cognitive theory. *Government Information Quarterly*, *40*(4), 101857. https://doi.org/https://doi.org/10.1016/j.giq.2023.101857. DOI: 10.1016/j.giq.2023.101857

Chen, S. Y., Kuo, H. Y., & Lee, C. (2020). Preparing society for automated vehicles. *Sustainability (Basel)*, *12*(19), 7844. DOI: 10.3390/su12197844

Chen, Y., & Chen, Z. (2024). Can e-government online services offer enhanced governance support? *Journal of Innovation & Knowledge*, *9*(3), 100526. DOI: 10.1016/j.jik.2024.100526

Chourabi, H., Nam, T., Walker, S., Gil-Garcia, J. R., Mellouli, S., Nahon, K., Pardo, T. A., & Scholl, H. J. (2012). Understanding smart cities: An integrative framework. In *Proceedings of the 45th Hawaii International Conference on System Sciences* (pp. 2289–2297). IEEE. DOI: 10.1109/HICSS.2012.615

Cihon, P., Maas, M. M., & Kemp, L. (2020). Fragmentation and the future. *Global Policy*, *11*(5), 545–556. DOI: 10.1111/1758-5899.12890

Cihon, P., Maas, M. M., & Kemp, L. (2020). Should artificial intelligence governance be centralized? Design lessons from history. *Proceedings of the AAAI/ACM Conference on AI, Ethics, and Society*, 228–234. DOI: 10.1145/3375627.3375857

Cindy Mutia Annur. (2022). *The Level of Personal Data Protection of Indonesian Citizens is Still Low. The Level of Personal Data Protection of Indonesian Citizens (2021).*

Clark, A., Dunser, A., & Grasset, R. (2011). An interactive augmented reality coloring book. *2011 10th IEEE International Symposium on Mixed and Augmented Reality*, 259–260. DOI: 10.1109/ISMAR.2011.6143487

Criado, J. I., Dias, T. F., Sano, H., Rojas-Martín, F., Silvan, A., & Filho, A. I. (2021). Public innovation and living labs in action: A comparative analysis in post-new public management contexts. *International Journal of Public Administration*, *44*(6), 451–464. DOI: 10.1080/01900692.2020.1729181

Cunneen, M., Mullins, M., & Murphy, F. (2019). Autonomous vehicles and embedded artificial intelligence. *Applied Artificial Intelligence*, *33*(8), 706–731. DOI: 10.1080/08839514.2019.1600301

D'Ignazio, C., & Klein, L. F. (2020). *Data feminism*. MIT Press. DOI: 10.7551/mitpress/11805.001.0001

Dafoe, A. (2018). *AI governance: A research agenda*. University of Oxford.

Dahiya, R., Kaple, G., Anute, N., Sudheer, P., Selvakumar, P., Manjunath, T. C., & Sharma, M. (2026). AI Tools for Automating Data Collection and Analysis. In Vrba, J., & Huynh, T. (Eds.), *Revolutionizing Academic Research With AI and Augmented Reality* (pp. 459–486). IGI Global Scientific Publishing.

Danry, V., Pataranutaporn, P., Mao, Y., & Maes, P. (2020). Wearable reasoner: Enhancing human rationality with an explainable AI assistant. *Augmented Humans International Conference*, 1–12.

De La Torre, F., Fang, C. M., & Huang, H.. (2024). LLMR: Real-time prompting of interactive worlds using large language models. *CHI Conference on Human Factors in Computing Systems*, 1–22. DOI: 10.1145/3613904.3642579

De Sousa, W. G., de Melo, E. R. P., Bermejo, P. H. D. S., Farias, R. A. S., & Gomes, A. O. (2019). How and where is artificial intelligence in the public sector going? A literature review and research agenda. *Government Information Quarterly*, *36*(4), 101392. DOI: 10.1016/j.giq.2019.07.004

Decker, M., Wegner, L., & Leicht-Scholten, C. (2025). Procedural fairness in algorithmic decision-making: The role of public engagement. *Ethics and Information Technology*, *27*(1), 1. DOI: 10.1007/s10676-024-09811-4

Dhanorkar, S., Wolf, C. T., & Qian, K.. (2021). Broadening XAI design across the AI lifecycle. *Designing Interactive Systems Conference*, 1591–1602.

Dinev, T., & Hart, P. (2006). An extended privacy calculus model for e-commerce transactions. *Information Systems Research*, *17*(1), 61–80. DOI: 10.1287/isre.1060.0080

Disemadi, H. S. (2021). The Importance of Special Regulations and the Utilization of Artificial Intelligence in Realizing Personal Data Protection in Indonesia. *Jurnal Wawasan Yuridika*, *5*(2), 177. DOI: 10.25072/jwy.v5i2.460

Do, T. L., Sanhae, K., Hwang, L., & Lee, S. (2024). Real-Time Spatial Mapping in Architectural Visualization: A Comparison among Mixed Reality Devices. In *Sensors* (Vol. 24, Issue 14, p. 4727). DOI: 10.3390/s24144727

Dogan, M. D., Gonzalez, E. J., Ahuja, K., et al. (2024). Augmented object intelligence with XR-objects.

Domi Dwi Kurniasandi, S. N. A. N. I. C. (2022). *REGULATIONS CONCERNING PERSONAL DATA PROTECTION IN THE USE OF E-COMMERCE SERVICES*. https://www.cnnindonesia.com/teknologi/20231231054937-192-1043657/daftar-dugaan-

Dorovskaya, Y., Mokhorov, D., Snetkov, V., Semenova, K., & Tebryaev, A. (2020, September). The social consequences of innovations in public administration. [). IOP Publishing.]. *IOP Conference Series. Materials Science and Engineering*, *940*(1), 012044. DOI: 10.1088/1757-899X/940/1/012044

Dunleavy, M., & Dede, C. (2014). Augmented reality teaching and learning. *Handbook of Research on Educational Communications and Technology*, 735–745.

Dunleavy, P., Margetts, H., Bastow, S., & Tinkler, J. (2006). New public management is dead—Long live digital-era governance. *Journal of Public Administration: Research and Theory*, *16*(3), 467–494. DOI: 10.1093/jopart/mui057

Dzvinchuk, D., Borshch, H., Tsygylyk, N., Dobosh, Z., & Dziubynska, O. (2022). Public management for sustainable development: Current challenges and future trends. *Cuestiones Políticas*, *40*(73), 741–753. DOI: 10.46398/cuestpol.4073.42

Edler, D., & Kersten, T. P. (2021). Virtual and Augmented Reality in Spatial Visualization. *KN - Journal of Cartography and Geographic Information*, *71*(4), 221–222. DOI: 10.1007/s42489-021-00094-z

Edy Susilo, M., Prayudi, P., & Yanu Florestiyanto, M. (2025). Oversharing Behavior of Gen Z on Social Media. *SHS Web of Conferences, 212*. DOI: 10.1051/shsconf/202521204022

Effendi, A. Y. (2019). Mobile Phone Addiction: Smartphone Use Among the Digital Generation of People with Disabilities in Indonesia. *2nd International Conference on Strategic and Global Studies (ICSGS 2018)*, 90–98.

Elhanashi, A., Saponara, S., Zheng, Q., Almutairi, N., Singh, Y., Kuanar, S., Ali, F., Unal, O., & Faghani, S. (2025). AI-Powered Object Detection in Radiology: Current Models, Challenges, and Future Direction. *Journal of Imaging*, *11*(5), 141. DOI: 10.3390/jimaging11050141 PMID: 40422999

Ellahi, R. M., Wood, L. C., Khan, M., & Bekhit, A. E.-D. A. (2025). Integrity Challenges in Halal Meat Supply Chain: Potential Industry 4.0 Technologies as Catalysts for Resolution. *Foods*, *14*(7), 1135. Advance online publication. DOI: 10.3390/foods14071135 PMID: 40238310

Engel, C., Linhardt, L., & Schubert, M. (2025). Code is law: How COMPAS affects the way the judiciary handles the risk of recidivism. *Artificial Intelligence and Law*, *33*(2), 383–404. DOI: 10.1007/s10506-024-09389-8

Equey, C., Priftis, A., Trabichet, J. P., & Hutzli, V. (2024). Designing a digital citizen-centered service. *Technological Forecasting and Social Change*, *202*, 123280. DOI: 10.1016/j.techfore.2024.123280

Eubanks, V. (2018). *Automating inequality: How high-tech tools profile, police and punish the poor*. St. Martin's Press.

Eubanks, V. (2018). *Automating inequality: How high-tech tools profile, police, and punish the poor*. St. Martin's Press.

European Union. (2016). *General Data Protection Regulation (GDPR)*. Official Journal of the European Union.

Fan, M., Antle, A. N., & Warren, J. L. (2020). Augmented Reality for Early Language Learning: A Systematic Review of Augmented Reality Application Design, Instructional Strategies, and Evaluation Outcomes. *Journal of Educational Computing Research*, *58*(6), 1059–1100. DOI: 10.1177/0735633120927489

Fannur, F., Sabaruddin, I., & Ramdhani, N. (2023). Innovative leadership approaches for enhancing digital governance and collaborative networks in public administration. *Journal Social Civilecial*, *1*(2), 84–99. DOI: 10.71435/610487

Felzmann, H., Villaronga, E. F., Lutz, C., & Tamò-Larrieux, A. (2019). Transparency you can trust. *Big Data & Society*, *6*(1), 2053951719860542. DOI: 10.1177/2053951719860542

Feretzakis, G., Vagena, E., Kalodanis, K., Peristera, P., Kalles, D., & Anastasiou, A. (2025). GDPR and Large Language Models: Technical and Legal Barriers. *Future Internet*, *17*(4), 151. Advance online publication. DOI: 10.3390/fi17040151

Festic, N., Büchi, M., & Latzer, M. (2021). Still there: Digital inequality and its evolution in the information society. *SCM Studies in Communication and Media*, *10*(3), 326–361. DOI: 10.5771/2192-4007-2021-3-326

Firlej, M., & Taeihagh, A. (2021). Regulating human control over autonomous systems. *Regulation & Governance*, *15*(4), 1071–1091. DOI: 10.1111/rego.12344

Fishenden, J., & Thompson, M. (2013). Digital government, open architecture, and innovation: Why public sector IT will never be the same again. *Journal of Public Administration: Research and Theory*, *23*(4), 977–1004. DOI: 10.1093/jopart/mus022

Floridi, L., Cowls, J., Beltrametti, M., Chatila, R., Chazerand, P., Dignum, V., Luetge, C., Madelin, R., Pagallo, U., Rossi, F., Schafer, B., Valcke, P., & Vayena, E. (2018). AI4People—An ethical framework for a good AI society. *Minds and Machines*, *28*(4), 689–707. DOI: 10.1007/s11023-018-9482-5

Floridi, L., Cowls, J., King, T. C., & Taddeo, M. (2020). How to Design AI for Social Good: Seven Essential Factors. *Science and Engineering Ethics*, *26*(3), 1771–1796. DOI: 10.1007/s11948-020-00213-5 PMID: 32246245

Fung, A. (2006). Varieties of participation in complex governance. *Public Administration Review*, *66*(s1), 66–75. DOI: 10.1111/j.1540-6210.2006.00667.x

Gagandeep, V., Verma, J., Pradhan, K. B., & Singh, M. (2025). AI technologies in adaptive sports: Enhancing performance, health, and well-being. *Acta Psychologica*, *261*, 105879. DOI: 10.1016/j.actpsy.2025.105879 PMID: 41192399

Gaie, C., & Mehta, M. (2024). Digital transformation of public services: introduction, current trends and future directions. In *Transforming Public Services—Combining Data and Algorithms to Fulfil Citizen's Expectations* (pp. 1–28). Springer Nature Switzerland. DOI: 10.1007/978-3-031-55575-6_1

Gangire, Y., Da Veiga, A., & Herselman, M. (2020). Information security behavior: Development of a measurement instrument based on self-determination theory. *International Symposium on Human Aspects of Information Security and Assurance*, 144–157. DOI: 10.1007/978-3-030-57404-8_12

Gao, X., Wang, Y., & Cao, Z. (2023). Light Practical Smart Experiment Classroom and Smart Education Application Solutions in Popular Science Corner. In *Lecture Notes in Educational Technology: Vol. Part F1761* (pp. 223–225). DOI: 10.1007/978-981-99-6225-9_33

Gao, S., Su, P., Wang, A., & Tao, Y. (2025). A Bibliometric Study of the Evidence About Applying Virtual Reality in Mental Health Care. *Journal of Multidisciplinary Healthcare, 18*(0), 5213–5225. DOI: 10.2147/JMDH.S536946 PMID: 40900715

Gao, Y. (2025). The role of artificial intelligence in enhancing sports education and public health in higher education: Innovations in teaching models, evaluation systems, and personalized training. *Frontiers in Public Health, 13*, 1554911. DOI: 10.3389/fpubh.2025.1554911 PMID: 40371284

Garaus, M., Treiblmaier, H., Wagner, U., & Garaus, C. (2025). Innovating the experience economy: How novel technologies transform customer experiences. *Digital Business, 5*(2), 100134. Advance online publication. DOI: 10.1016/j.digbus.2025.100134

Gari, N. (2025). *Car parking violation detection* [Data set]. Roboflow Universe. https://universe.roboflow.com/najlaa-gari-gywmx/car-parking-violation-detection/dataset/1

Garzón, J. (2021). An Overview of Twenty-Five Years of Augmented Reality in Education. *Multimodal Technologies and Interaction, 5*(7), 37. DOI: 10.3390/mti5070037

Garzón, J., Pavón, J., & Baldiris, S. (2017). Augmented Reality Applications for Education: Five Directions for Future Research. In De Paolis, L. T., Bourdot, P., & Mongelli, A. (Eds.), *Augmented Reality, Virtual Reality, and Computer Graphics* (Vol. 10324, pp. 402–414). Springer International Publishing., DOI: 10.1007/978-3-319-60922-5_31

Gasser, U., & Almeida, V. A. (2017). A layered model for AI governance. *IEEE Internet Computing, 21*(6), 58–62. DOI: 10.1109/MIC.2017.4180835

Gigerenzer, G. (2022). *How to Stay Smart in a Smart World: Why Human Intelligence Still Beats Algorithms*. MIT Press.

Gigerenzer, G. (2023). Psychological AI: Designing Algorithms Informed by Human Psychology. *Perspectives on Psychological Science*. Advance online publication. DOI: 10.1177/17456916231180597 PMID: 37522323

Gil-Garcia, J. R., Pardo, T. A., & Nam, T. (2016). What makes a city smart? Identifying core components and proposing an integrative framework. *Information Polity*, *21*(1), 61–87. DOI: 10.3233/IP-150354

Glebova, E., Book, R., Su, Y., Perić, M., & Heller, J. (2023). Sports venue digital twin technology from a spectator virtual visiting perspective. *Frontiers in Sports and Active Living*, *5*, 1289140. DOI: 10.3389/fspor.2023.1289140 PMID: 38116386

Goldsmith, S., & Crawford, S. (2014). *The responsive city: Engaging communities through data-smart governance*. Jossey-Bass.

Gomez, I., & Ilarri, S. (2024). Enriched traffic datasets for smart cities (Madrid): Integrating sensors, infrastructure, and weather data. *Data in Brief*, *57*, 110878. DOI: 10.1016/j.dib.2024.110878 PMID: 39309711

Goodchild, M. F. (2007). Citizens as sensors: The world of volunteered geography. *GeoJournal*, *69*(4), 211–221. DOI: 10.1007/s10708-007-9111-y

Goodman, B., & Flaxman, S. (2017). European Union regulations on algorithmic decision-making. *AI Magazine*, *38*(3), 50–57. DOI: 10.1609/aimag.v38i3.2741

Government of India. (2023). *Digital Personal Data Protection Act, 2023*. Ministry of Law and Justice.

Goyal, N. K. (2025). Security and privacy in IoT, fog, and blockchain networks. In Energy-Efficient Deep Learning Approaches in IoT, Fog, and Green Blockchain Revolution (pp. 371–398). IGI Global Scientific Publishing. DOI: 10.4018/979-8-3373-0300-0.ch015

Goyal, N. K. (2025). Weaponizing misinformation and cyberattacks on supply chains. In *Mass Media and Impact of Fake News on Supply Chains* (pp. 177–210). IGI Global Scientific Publishing., DOI: 10.4018/979-8-3373-2175-2.ch007

Goyal, N. K., Dandotiya, M., Kumari, M., Kaloria, S., & Anushya, A. (2025). AI-powered haptic devices for patient rehabilitation. In *Integrating AI With Haptic Systems for Smarter Healthcare Solutions* (pp. 143–170). IGI Global Scientific Publishing., DOI: 10.4018/979-8-3373-2307-7.ch007

Goyal, N. K., Dandotiya, M., Kumari, M., Sheikh, M. F., & Sharma, S. (2025). Emerging job roles leveraging artificial intelligence. In *Empowering Sustainable Performance and Competitive Advantage in Tourism* (pp. 89–126). IGI Global Scientific Publishing., DOI: 10.4018/979-8-3373-4546-8.ch004

Goyal, N. K., Dandotiya, M., Qurashi, J. A., Kumari, M., & Sharma, S. (2025). AI-driven predictive analytics for disease management. In *Utilizing AI of Medical Things for Healthcare Security and Sustainability* (pp. 231–276). IGI Global Scientific Publishing., DOI: 10.4018/979-8-3373-0690-2.ch008

Goyal, N. K., Kumari, M., Kushwah, V., Dandotiya, M., & Vijay, A. (2025). Evaluating blockchain security: Trade-offs in consensus mechanisms. *IET Conference Proceedings*, 2024(38),80–88. https://doi.org/DOI: 10.1049/icp.2025.0775

Gozuoglu, A. (2025). *Smart Monitoring of Power Networks: Augmented Reality and Edge AI for Grid Resilience.*

Graham, S. (2002). Bridging urban digital divides? *Urban Studies (Edinburgh, Scotland)*, *39*(1), 33–56. DOI: 10.1080/00420980220099050

Groumpos, P. P. (2010). Fuzzy Cognitive Maps: Basic Theories and Their Application to Complex Systems. In Glykas, M. (Ed.), *Fuzzy Cognitive Maps. Studies in Fuzziness and Soft Computing* (Vol. 247). Springer., DOI: 10.1007/978-3-642-03220-2_1

Gupta, A. K., & Lamsal, B. P. (2023). From traditional to innovative public service: a review of paradigm shifts. *Вопросы государственного и муниципального управления*, (6), 137-156.

Hamid, S., & Huda, M. N. (2025). Mapping the landscape of government data breaches (2006–2023). *Social Sciences & Humanities Open*, *11*, 101234. DOI: 10.1016/j.ssaho.2024.101234

Harrison, C., Eckman, B., Hamilton, R., Hartswick, P., Kalagnanam, J., Paraszczak, J., & Williams, P. (2010). Foundations for smarter cities. *IBM Journal of Research and Development*, *54*(4), 1–16. DOI: 10.1147/JRD.2010.2048257

Hartzog, W. (2021). What is privacy? That's the wrong question. *U.Chi. L. Rev.*, *88*, 1677.

Havale, D. S., Patole, J., Anute, N., Rane, D. P., Shah, A. H., & Selvakumar, P. (2026). Digital Tools and Resources for Teaching Sustainability. In Hans, E., & Hans, A. (Eds.), *Harnessing E-Learning to Create a Sustainable Future* (pp. 45–74). IGI Global Scientific Publishing.

Heeks, R. (2018). *Information and communication technology for development (ICT4D). Routledge Handbook of Development Management*. Routledge.

Helbing, D. (2019). Societal, economic, ethical and legal challenges of the digital revolution. In Towards Digital Enlightenment (pp. 47–72).

Hernández, J. L., García, R., Schonowski, J., Atlan, D., Chanson, G., & Ruohomäki, T. (2020). Interoperable Open Specifications Framework for the Implementation of Standardized Urban Platforms. In *Sensors* (Vol. 20, Issue 8, p. 2402). DOI: 10.3390/s20082402

Heyik, M. A., Erdoğan, M., & Romero-Martínez, J. M. (2025). AI-powered meta analysis of geospatial participatory platforms for ecosocial transition in urban design and planning. *Urban Governance*, *5*(4), 411–425. DOI: 10.1016/j.ugj.2025.09.006

Himan, A. (2025). *Urban Issues Dataset* [Data set]. Kaggle. https://www.kaggle.com/datasets/akinduhiman/urban-issues-dataset

Hitch, D. (2024). Artificial Intelligence Augmented Qualitative Analysis: The Way of the Future? [PubMed]. *Qualitative Health Research*, *34*. Advance online publication. DOI: 10.1177/10497323231217392

Hollands, R. G. (2008). Will the real smart city please stand up? *City (London, England)*, *12*(3), 303–320. DOI: 10.1080/13604810802479126

Huang, J., & Hu, Y. (2025). Systematic review of immersive VR in geography higher education. *Journal of Geography in Higher Education*, •••, 1–18.

Huebner, M., Meltzer, D. E., Ma, W., & Arrow, H. (2021). Correction: The Masters athlete in Olympic weightlifting: Training, lifestyle, health challenges, and gender differences. *PLoS One*, *16*(2), e0247110. DOI: 10.1371/journal.pone.0247110 PMID: 33566849

Huq, A. Z. (2019). Racial equity in algorithmic criminal justice. *Duke Law Journal*, *68*(6), 1043–1134.

Hussain, A., Rubab, [2]narjis, Tausif, [3]sumaira, Aslam, S., Iftikhar, A., Imran, M., & Nasir, A. (2025). Emerging Trends in Smart Cities: Technologies, Challenges, and Opportunities. *Journal of Computer Science and Technology Studies*, *9*, 1–16.

Ibáñez, M. B., & Delgado-Kloos, C. (2018). Augmented reality for STEM learning: A systematic review. *Computers & Education*, *123*, 109–123. DOI: 10.1016/j.compedu.2018.05.002

Ilaina, A. S. A., & Nugraha, I. F. (2025). Indonesia's Cybersecurity Capability Gap in Mitigating Cyberattacks on Digital Public Services 2020-2025. *Triwikrama: Journal of Social Sciences*, *8*(6), 141–150.

Ilo, C., DiVerdi, S., & Bowman, D. (2024). Goldilocks zoning: Gaze-aware VR notification placement. *ACM Symposium on Spatial User Interaction*, 1–12.

Imran, M., Castillo, C., Lucas, J., Meier, P., & Vieweg, S. (2020). AI for disaster response. *Proceedings of the International AAAI Conference on Web and Social Media, 14*(1), 357–366. DOI: 10.1145/2567948.2577034

Janssen, M., Brous, P., Estevez, E., Barbosa, L. S., & Janowski, T. (2020). Data governance for trustworthy AI. *Government Information Quarterly*, *37*(3), 101493. DOI: 10.1016/j.giq.2020.101493

Janssen, M., & Helbig, N. (2018). Innovating and changing the policy cycle. *Government Information Quarterly*, *35*(4), S99–S105. DOI: 10.1016/j.giq.2015.11.009

Janssen, M., & Kuk, G. (2016). The challenges and limits of big data algorithms in technocratic governance. *Government Information Quarterly*, *33*(3), 371–377. DOI: 10.1016/j.giq.2016.08.011

Janssen, M., & van den Hoven, J. (2015). Big and open linked data (BOLD) in government: A challenge to transparency and privacy? *Government Information Quarterly*, *32*(4), 363–368. DOI: 10.1016/j.giq.2015.11.007

Jefry, B., Gultom, E., & Yuanitasari, D. (2025). MISUSE OF CONSUMER PERSONAL DATA BY COMPANIES: A LEGAL STUDY FROM THE PERSPECTIVE OF CONSUMER PROTECTION LAW AND PERSONAL DATA PROTECTION LAW. *Indonesian Education Journal*, *6*(5), 1.

Jobin, A., Ienca, M., & Vayena, E. (2019). The global landscape of ethics guidelines. *Nature Machine Intelligence*, *1*(9), 389–399. DOI: 10.1038/s42256-019-0088-2

Judijanto, L., Saiful Basri, T., Madah Khulaili Harsya, R., Yuli Vandika, A., & Shandy Utama, A. (2024).. . *Legal Study of the Impact of Artificial Intelligence on Data Privacy Protection in Indonesian Cyber Law.*, *3*(02), 68–76. DOI: 10.58812/shh.v3.i02

Jukić, T., Pevcin, P., Benčina, J., Dečman, M., & Vrbek, S. (2019). Collaborative innovation in public administration: Theoretical background and research trends of co-production and co-creation. *Administrative Sciences*, *9*(4), 90. DOI: 10.3390/admsci9040090

Junaidi, & Rozlinda Mohamed Fadzil. (2024). The Importance of Legal Protection of Personal Data in E-Commerce Transactions Involving Artificial Intelligence. *Walisongo Law Journal (Walrev), 6* (2), 96–108. DOI: 10.21580/walrev.2024.6.2.25548

Jurafsky, D., & Martin, J. H. (2023). *Speech and language processing* (3rd ed.). Pearson., https://web.stanford.edu/~jurafsky/slp3/

Kansal, M., Singh, P., Shukla, S., & Srivastava, S. (2023). A Comparative Study of Machine Learning Models for House Price Prediction and Analysis in Smart Cities. In F. Ortiz-Rodríguez, S. Tiwari, P. Usoro Usip, & R. Palma (Eds.), *Electronic Governance with Emerging Technologies* (Vol. 1888, pp. 168–184). Springer Nature Switzerland. DOI: 10.1007/978-3-031-43940-7_14

Katadata Insight Center. (2021). *Status of Digital Literacy in Indonesia 2021. Ministry of Communication and Digital*. (undated). Accessed December 16, 2025, from https://www.komdigi.go.id/berita/siaran-pers/detail/imdi-2025-naik-ke-4453-indonesia-makin-cakap-digital

Kazimierczak, M., Habib, N., Chan, J. H., & Thanapattheerakul, T. (2024). Impact of AI on the Cyber Kill Chain: A Systematic Review. *Heliyon*, *10*(24), e40699. DOI: 10.1016/j.heliyon.2024.e40699 PMID: 39720055

Keykha, B., & Rezaie Kahkhajale, Z. (2024). Monitoring Postgraduate Students' Digital Literacy Based on Elements of the UNESCO Digital Literacy Competency Framework. *Academic Library and Information Research*, *58*(2), 47–60.

Khan, T., Johnston, K., & Ophoff, J. (2019). The Impact of an Augmented Reality Application on Learning Motivation of Students. *Advances in Human-Computer Interaction*, *2019*, 1–14. DOI: 10.1155/2019/7208494

Khetarpal, K., Riemer, M., & Rish, I. (2022). Towards Continual Reinforcement Learning. *Revista Perspectivas (Cochambamba)*, *75*, 1401–1476.

Kim, M., Suh, I., & Chung, Y. D. (2020). MARS: A multi-level array representation for simulation data. *Future Generation Computer Systems*, *111*, 419–434. https://doi.org/https://doi.org/10.1016/j.future.2019.11.010. DOI: 10.1016/j.future.2019.11.010

Kim, Y. (2014). *Convolutional neural networks for sentence classification. Proceedings of the 2014 Conference on Empirical Methods in Natural Language Processing (EMNLP)*, 1746–1751. DOI: 10.3115/v1/D14-1181

King, S. F., & Brown, P. (2007). *Fix my street or else: Using the Internet to voice local public service concerns*. In *Proceedings of the 1st International Conference on Theory and Practice of Electronic Governance (ICEGOV 2007)* (pp. 72–80). Association for Computing Machinery. DOI: 10.1145/1328057.1328076

Kingsto, J. (2017). *Using Artificial Intelligence to Support Compliance with the General Data Protection Regulation*.

Kiourexidou, M., Kanavos, A., Klouvidaki, M., & Antonopoulos, N. (2024). Exploring the Role of User Experience and Interface Design Communication in Augmented Reality for Education. *Multimodal Technologies and Interaction*, *8*(6), 43. DOI: 10.3390/mti8060043

Kirana, K. B., & Silalahi, W. (2025). Challenges of Artificial Intelligence (AI) Regulation from the Perspective of Personal Data Protection Law in Indonesia. *Cerdika: Indonesian Scientific Journal*, *5*(6), 1807–1817. DOI: 10.59141/cerdika.v5i6.2711

Kitchin, R. (2014). *The data revolution: Big data, open data, data infrastructures and their consequences*. SAGE Publications.

Kitchin, R. (2014). The Real-Time City? Big Data and Smart Urbanism. *GeoJournal*, *79*(1), 1–14. DOI: 10.1007/s10708-013-9516-8

Kitchin, R. (2021). Civil liberties or public good? Smart cities, surveillance, and privacy. *Journal of Urban Technology*, *28*(1–2), 3–19. DOI: 10.1080/10630732.2020.1781567

Kleinberg, J., Ludwig, J., Mullainathan, S., & Sunstein, C. R. (2018). Discrimination in the age of algorithms. *The Journal of Legal Analysis*, *10*, 113–174. DOI: 10.1093/jla/laz001

Krizhevsky, A., Sutskever, I., & Hinton, G. E. (2012). ImageNet classification with deep convolutional neural networks. *Advances in Neural Information Processing Systems*, *25*, 1097–1105. DOI: 10.1145/3065386

Kroll, J. A., Barocas, S., Felten, E. W., Reidenberg, J. R., Robinson, D. G., & Yu, H. (2016). Accountable algorithms. *University of Pennsylvania Law Review*, *165*, 633.

KRUHLOV, V., & TERESHCHENKO, D. (2023). Innovations in the system of public administration. *Вісник Національного технічного університету «ХПІ». Серія: Актуальні проблеми розвитку українського суспільства*, 74.

Kumar, A., Bhadauriya, A. S., Kaushik, A., & Singh, P. (2025). Augmented Reality (AR) and its impact on learning methodologies. *Journal of Advances in Science and Technology*, *22*(2), 112–121. DOI: 10.29070/fmfvkc30

Kurni, M., & Srinivasa, K. G. (2024). *The Internet of Educational Things: Enhancing Students' Engagement and Learning Performance*. DOI: 10.1007/978-3-031-67387-0

Kurnianingrum, T. P. (2020). The importance of protecting consumer personal data in the digital economy era. *Studies*, *25*(3), 197–216.

Lai, J. W., & Cheong, K. H. (2022). Educational Opportunities and Challenges in Augmented Reality: Featuring Implementations in Physics Education. *IEEE Access : Practical Innovations, Open Solutions*, *10*, 43143–43158. DOI: 10.1109/ACCESS.2022.3166478

Lakshminarayanan, V., Ravikumar, A., Sriraman, H., Alla, S., & Chattu, V. K. (2023). Health Care Equity Through Intelligent Edge Computing and Augmented Reality/Virtual Reality: A Systematic Review. *Journal of Multidisciplinary Healthcare*, *16*(0), 2839–2859. DOI: 10.2147/JMDH.S419923 PMID: 37753339

Laksito, J., Pratiwi, B., & Ariani, W. (2025). Harmonization of Data Privacy Frameworks in Artificial Intelligence: Comparative Insights from Asia and Europe. *Perkara: Journal of Law and Political Science*, *2*(4), 579–588. DOI: 10.51903/perkara.v2i4.2229

Latupeirissa, J. J., Dewi, N. L., Prayana, I. K., Srikandi, M. B., Ramadiansyah, S. A., & Pramana, I. B. (2024). Transforming Public Service Delivery: A Comprehensive Review of Digitization Initiatives. In *Sustainability* (Vol. 16, Issue 7, p. 2818). DOI: 10.3390/su16072818

Law, I. (2024). *European Union Artificial Intelligence Law. April.*

Lazcoz, G., & de Hert, P. (2023). Humans in GDPR and AIA governance of automated and algorithmic systems. A crucial prerequisite for preventing dereliction of responsibility. *Computer Law & Security Review*, *50*. Advance online publication. DOI: 10.1016/j.clsr.2023.105833

Lee, J., Wang, J., & Brown, E.. (2024). GazepointAR: Context-aware multimodal assistant for pronoun disambiguation in wearable AR. *CHI Conference on Human Factors in Computing Systems*, 1–20.

Leenes, R., & Lucivero, F. (2014). Laws on robots, laws by robots. *Law, Innovation and Technology*, *6*(2), 193–220. DOI: 10.5235/17579961.6.2.193

Leenes, R., Palmerini, E., Koops, B. J., Bertolini, A., Salvini, P., & Lucivero, F. (2017). Regulatory challenges of robotics. *Law, Innovation and Technology*, *9*(1), 1–44. DOI: 10.1080/17579961.2017.1304921

Lenart, R., & Chen, J. (2025). Integrating post-Schumpeterian perspectives with modern public sector trends. In *Handbook on Post-Schumpeterian Innovations* (pp. 273–285). Edward Elgar Publishing. DOI: 10.4337/9781035322510.00025

Liao, Q. V., Pribić, M., Han, J., ... (2021). Question-driven design for explainable AI UX. *arXiv preprint arXiv:2104.03483.*

Lim, J. (2024). *The Urgency of Personal Data Protection Related to Data Processing in the Form of Artificial Intelligence in Indonesia.*

Linders, D. (2012). From e-government to we-government. *Government Information Quarterly, 29*(4), 446–454. DOI: 10.1016/j.giq.2012.06.003

Li, R., Yuen, K. F., Wang, Y., & Lu, Y. (2025). System dynamics–based framework for modelling and assessing smart city resilience. A case study of Chengdu, China. *Sustainable Cities and Society, 107*, 107056. DOI: 10.1016/j.scs.2025.107056

Liu, B. (2012). Sentiment analysis and opinion mining. *Synthesis Lectures on Human Language Technologies, 5*(1), 1–167. DOI: 10.1007/978-3-031-02145-9

Liu, J., Wang, X., & Zhang, J. (2025). Investigating Elderly Individuals' Acceptance of Artificial Intelligence (AI)-Powered Companion Robots: The Influence of Individual Characteristics. *Behavioral Sciences (Basel, Switzerland), 15*(5), 697. DOI: 10.3390/bs15050697 PMID: 40426474

Li, W., & Zheng, X. (2024). Social Media Use and Attitudes Toward AI: The Mediating Roles of Perceived Fairness and AI Threat. *Human Behavior and Emerging Technologies, 2024*, 1–11. Advance online publication. DOI: 10.1155/2024/3448083

Lodge, M., & Wegrich, K. (2014). *The problem-solving capacity of the modern state. Governance challenges and administrative capacities.* Oxford University Press.

Luo, J., Liu, P., Xu, W., Zhao, T., & Biljecki, F. (2025). A perception-powered urban digital twin to support human-centered urban planning and sustainable city development. *Cities (London, England), 156*, 105473. DOI: 10.1016/j.cities.2024.105473

Lytvynova, S. H., & Semerikov, S. O. (2021). *Proceedings of the 4th International Workshop on Augmented Reality in Education.*

Maathuis, C., & Datcu, D. (2025). Transparency of AI-XR systems: Insights from experts. *IEEE AIxVR Conference*, 301–306.

Madon, S. (2020). Digital governance for development: A critical review of literature. *Information Polity, 25*(1), 5–20. DOI: 10.3233/IP-190146

Maeda, H., Sekimoto, Y., Seto, T., & Kashiyama, H. (2018). Road damage detection using deep neural networks. *IEEE International Conference on Systems, Man and Cybernetics*, 1–6. DOI: 10.48550/arXiv.1801.09454

Mahadzir, N. N. N. (2013). The Use of Augmented Reality Pop-Up Book to Increase Motivation in English Language Learning For National Primary School. [IOSRJRME]. *IOSR Journal of Research & Method in Education, 1*(1), 26–38. DOI: 10.9790/7388-0112638

Margetts, H., & Dunleavy, P. (2013). The second wave of digital-era governance: a quasi-paradigm for government on the Web. *Philosophical transactions of the royal society A: mathematical, physical and engineering sciences, 371*(1987), 20120382.

Marino-Romero, J. A., Robina-Ramírez, R., Pavón-Pérez, J. A., & Roets, A. O. S. B. (2025). Enhancing happiness and well-being: AI-driven solutions for accessible, inclusive travel experiences for people with disabilities. *Disability and Rehabilitation. Assistive Technology, 20*(7), 2173–2184. DOI: 10.1080/17483107.2025.2488391 PMID: 40220310

Marshall, D. T., & Naff, D. B. (2024). The Ethics of Using Artificial Intelligence in Qualitative Research. *Journal of Empirical Research on Human Research Ethics; JERHRE, 19*(3), 92–102. DOI: 10.1177/15562646241262659 PMID: 38881315

Maske, Y., Jakate, S., Thakare, C., & Lokhande, S. (2025). *Urban civic issues image dataset: Potholes and garbage (QR4Change)* (Version 2) [Data set]. Mendeley Data. DOI: 10.17632/zndzygc3p3.2

Mattioli, A., & Paternò, F. (2023). Mobile AR app for controlling smart home automations. *Proceedings of the ACM on Human–Computer Interaction*, 7(MHCI), 1–22.

Mattioli, A., & Paternò, F. (2023). *Towards explainable automations in smart homes using mobile AR*. IS-EUD Workshops.

McKinney, S. M., Sieniek, M., Godbole, V., Godwin, J., Antropova, N., Ashrafian, H., Back, T., Chesus, M., Corrado, G. S., Darzi, A., Etemadi, M., Garcia-Vicente, F., Gilbert, F. J., Halling-Brown, M., Hassabis, D., Jansen, S., Karthikesalingam, A., Kelly, C. J., King, D., & Shetty, S. (2020). International evaluation of an AI system for breast cancer screening. *Nature, 577*(7788), 89–94. DOI: 10.1038/s41586-019-1799-6 PMID: 31894144

Medhat, W., Hassan, A., & Korashy, H. (2014). Sentiment analysis algorithms and applications. *Ain Shams Engineering Journal, 5*(4), 1093–1113. DOI: 10.1016/j.asej.2014.04.011

Mehrabi, N., Morstatter, F., Saxena, N., Lerman, K., & Galstyan, A. (2021). A Survey on Bias and Fairness in Machine Learning. *ACM Computing Surveys, 54*(6), 1–35. Advance online publication. DOI: 10.1145/3457607

Meijer, A., Gil-Garcia, J. R., & Bolívar, M. P. R. (2016). Smart city research. Contextual conditions, governance models, and public value assessment. *Social Science Computer Review, 34*(6), 647–656. DOI: 10.1177/0894439315618890

Meijer, A., & Rodríguez Bolívar, M. P. R. (2016). Governing the smart city: A review of the literature on smart urban governance. *International Review of Administrative Sciences*, *82*(2), 392–408. DOI: 10.1177/0020852314564308

Méndez, J., Satkowski, M., & Rzayev, R. (2023). Explainability in hybrid user interfaces. *IEEE ISMAR-Adjunct*, 251–256.

Merchant, Z., Goetz, E. T., Cifuentes, L., Keeney-Kennicutt, W., & Davis, T. J. (2014). Effectiveness of virtual reality-based instruction: A meta-analysis. *Computers & Education*, *70*, 29–40. DOI: 10.1016/j.compedu.2013.07.033

Mersinas, K., & Bada, M. (2023). A behavior change approach to cybersecurity and the need for ethics. *International Conference on Cybersecurity, Situational Awareness and Social Media*, 107–129.

Meto, A., & Halilaj, G. (2025). The Integration of Cone Beam Computed Tomography, Artificial Intelligence, Augmented Reality, and Virtual Reality in Dental Diagnostics, Surgical Planning, and Education: A Narrative Review. *Applied Sciences (Basel, Switzerland)*, *15*(11), 6308. Advance online publication. DOI: 10.3390/app15116308

Mikropoulos, T. A., & Natsis, A. (2011). Educational virtual environments: A ten-year review of empirical research (1999–2009). *Computers & Education*, *56*(3), 769–780. DOI: 10.1016/j.compedu.2010.10.020

Milossi, M., Alexandropoulou-Egyptiadou, E., & Psannis, K. E. (2021). AI Ethics: Algorithmic Determinism or Self-Determination? A GDPR Approach. *IEEE Access : Practical Innovations, Open Solutions*, *9*, 58455–58466. DOI: 10.1109/ACCESS.2021.3072782

Ministry of Housing and Urban affairs. (2017). Swacchta – MoHUA: Citizen Grievance redressal platform under Swachh Bharat Mission (Urban). Govt. of India https://swachhbaharatmission.gov.in

Mishra, A. (2024). A Comprehensive Review of Artificial Intelligence and Machine Learning : Concepts, Trends, and Applications. *International Journal of Scientific Research in Science and Technology*, *11*(5), 126–142. DOI: 10.32628/IJSRST2411587

Mittelstadt, B. (2019). Principles alone cannot guarantee ethical AI. *Nature Machine Intelligence*, *1*(11), 501–507. DOI: 10.1038/s42256-019-0114-4

Mittelstadt, B. D., Allo, P., Taddeo, M., Wachter, S., & Floridi, L. (2016). The ethics of algorithms. *Big Data & Society*, *3*(2), 2053951716679679. DOI: 10.1177/2053951716679679

Moch, E., Oberdieck, T., Barenkamp, M., & Ritter, L. A. (2025). *KI-Anwendungen im Unternehmen – Effizienz steigern, Innovation fördern, Governance sichern.* Wirtschaftsinformatik & Management., DOI: 10.1365/s35764-025-00578-x

Momen, M. N., & Ferdous, J. (2023). Digital innovations in public administration and public service delivery. In *Governance in Bangladesh: Innovations in Delivery of Public Service* (pp. 31–44). Springer Nature Singapore. DOI: 10.1007/978-981-99-0424-2_3

Motahar, T., Fatema, T., & Das, R. (2018). Bornomala AR-bengali learning experience using augmented reality. *Proceedings of the 20th International Conference on Human-Computer Interaction with Mobile Devices and Services Adjunct*, 182–188. DOI: 10.1145/3236112.3236138

Motet Hansen, M., & Dahiya, B. (2025). Traffy Fondue: A smart city citizen engagement platform. *Frontiers in Sustainable Cities*, *7*, 1491621. DOI: 10.3389/frsc.2025.1491621

Motra, G. B., Sah, B. K., & Jha, P. (2021). Structural condition assessment and retrofitting of Shital Niwas building (presidential palace). *Progress in Disaster Science*, *10*, 100174. https://doi.org/https://doi.org/10.1016/j.pdisas.2021.100174. DOI: 10.1016/j.pdisas.2021.100174

Myrna Fitria, D. I. P. A. H. S. (n.d.). LEGAL PROTECTION AND RESPONSIBILITY FOR PERSONAL DATA INFORMATION LEAKS IN ELECTRONIC SYSTEM ORGANIZERS BASED ON A TRADE SECRET PERSPECTIVE. *Indonesian Scientific Journal, January* 2025 (1), 1–8. http://cerdika.publikasiindonesia.id/index.php/cerdika/index

Nabatchi, T., & Amsler, L. B. (2014). Direct public engagement in local government. *American Review of Public Administration*, *44*(4, suppl), 63S–88S. DOI: 10.1177/0275074013519702

Nadhifa, C. L., Irama, O. N., Lubis, A. S., & Harahap, J. P. R. (2025). CYBER RISK MANAGEMENT IN THE DIGITAL ERA: ANALYSIS OF MITIGATION STRATEGIES AND PREVENTIVE INNOVATIONS AGAINST CYBER CRIME IN INDONESIA. [MICJO]. *Indonesian Multidisciplinary Center Journal*, *2*(3), 2610–2619. DOI: 10.62567/micjo.v2i3.868

Nam, T., & Pardo, T. A. (2011). *Conceptualizing smart city with dimensions of technology, people and institutions*. In *Proceedings of the 12th Annual International Conference on Digital Government Research: Digital Government Innovation in Challenging Times*. (pp. 282–291). ACM. DOI: 10.1145/2037556.2037602

Nandkumar, C., & Peternel, L. (2025). Enhancing supermarket robot interaction: An equitable multi-level LLM conversational interface for handling diverse customer intents. *Frontiers in Robotics and AI*, *12*, 1576348. DOI: 10.3389/frobt.2025.1576348 PMID: 40365556

Newman, J., Mintrom, M., & Neill, D. O. (2022). *Digital technologies, artificial intelligence, and bureaucratic transformation. 136*(April 2021).

Nguyen, T. T., Tran, T. N. H., Do, T. H. M., Dinh, T. K. L., Nguyen, T. U. N., & Dang, T. M. K. (2024). Digital literacy, online safety behavior, and e-payment intention. *Journal of Open Innovation*, *10*(2), 100292. DOI: 10.1016/j.joitmc.2024.100292

Noble, S. U. (2018). *Algorithms of oppression: How search engines reinforce racism*. NYU Press. DOI: 10.18574/nyu/9781479833641.001.0001

Nongkoo, A., & Hamanee, S. (2023). Applying Government Innovations for Public Management and Public Service. *Ramkhamhaeng International Journal of Science and Technology*, *6*(1), 41–50.

Nordström, M. (2022). AI under great uncertainty: Implications and decision strategies for public policy. *AI & Society*, *37*(4), 1703–1714. DOI: 10.1007/s00146-021-01263-4 PMID: 34511737

Obasi, I. C., & Benson, C. (2025). The Impact of Digitalization and Information and Communication Technology on the Nature and Organization of Work and the Emerging Challenges for Occupational Safety and Health. *International Journal of Environmental Research and Public Health*, *22*(3), 362. DOI: 10.3390/ijerph22030362 PMID: 40238361

Obioha Val, O., Gbadebo, MO, Olaniyi, OO, Chinye, NC, & Balogun, AY (2025). Innovative regulation of open-source intelligence and AI deepfakes in managing public trust. *Michael Olayinka and Olaniyi, Oluwaseun Oladeji and Chinye, Noah Chukwufumnanya and Balogun, Adebayo Yusuf, Innovative Regulation of Open-Source Intelligence and AI Deepfakes in Managing Public Trust (January 30, 2025)*.

OECD. (2021). *The state of digital government*. OECD Publishing., DOI: 10.1787/4de9f5bb-

Offenhuber, D. (2014). Infrastructure legibility: A comparative analysis of open311-based citizen feedback systems. *Cambridge Journal of Regions, Economy and Society*, *8*(1), 93–112. DOI: 10.1093/cjres/rsu001

Oun, A., Hagerdorn, N., Scheideger, C., & Cheng, X. (2024). Mobile Devices or Head-Mounted Displays: A Comparative Review and Analysis of Augmented Reality in Healthcare. *IEEE Access : Practical Innovations, Open Solutions, 12*, 21825–21839. DOI: 10.1109/ACCESS.2024.3361833

Pagallo, U., Casanovas, P., & Madelin, R. (2019). The middle-out approach. *The Theory and Practice of Legislation*, *7*(1), 1–25. DOI: 10.1080/20508840.2019.1664543

Pakhnenko, O., & Kuan, Z. (2023). Ethics of digital innovation in public administration. *Business Ethics and Leadership*, *7*(1), 113–121. DOI: 10.21272/bel.7(1).113-121.2023

Pang, B., & Lee, L. (2008). Opinion mining and sentiment analysis. *Foundations and Trends in Information Retrieval*, *2*(1–2), 1–135. DOI: 10.1561/1500000011

Papp, G., & Lovaas, P. (2021). Assessing Cybersecurity Awareness of Small Institutions Using the Human Aspects of Information Security Questionnaire (HAIS-Q). *Intelligent Computing: Proceedings of the 2021 Computing Conference,* Volume 3, 933–948.

Parmaxi, A., & Demetriou, A. A. (2020). Augmented reality in language learning: A state-of-the-art review of 2014–2019. *Journal of Computer Assisted Learning*, *36*(6), 861–875. DOI: 10.1111/jcal.12486

Peixoto, T., & Fox, J. (2016). When does ICT-enabled citizen voice lead to responsiveness? *World Development*, *79*, 159–172.

Pierdicca, R., Tonetto, F., Paolanti, M., Mameli, M., Rosati, R., & Zingaretti, P. (2024). DeepReality: An open source framework to develop AI-based augmented reality applications. *Expert Systems with Applications*, *249*, 123530. Advance online publication. DOI: 10.1016/j.eswa.2024.123530

Pike, S. (2025). *AI, AR, AND VR IN THEATRE AND PERFORMANCE: Technology in the Present and Future of Live Creative Arts.* DOI: 10.4324/9781003521907

Ponto, K., Hartung, L., Zhao, Y., Sprecher, B., Tredinnick, R., & Banerjee, S. (2025). EasyVizAR: Supporting First Responders Through the Use of Collaborative Augmented Reality Tools. In *Applied Sciences* (Vol. 15, Issue 21, p. 11498). DOI: 10.3390/app152111498

Porumbescu, G. (2015). Does e-government enhance trust? *Public Administration Review*, *75*(4), 675–686.

Posetti, J., Aboulez, N., Bontcheva, K., Harrison, J., & Waisbord, S. (2020). *Online violence against women journalists. 'Online Violence against Women Journalists', edn*. UNESCO.

Prakash, D., & Karvonen, A. (2026). Institutional logics of the smart city and the emergence of new configurations of local governance. *Cities (London, England), 171*, 106727. DOI: 10.1016/j.cities.2025.106727

Preka, G., & Rangoussi, M. (2019). Augmented Reality and QR Codes for Teaching Music to Preschoolers and Kindergarteners: Educational Intervention and Evaluation: *Proceedings of the 11th International Conference on Computer Supported Education*, 113–123. DOI: 10.5220/0007682301130123

Priyadi, A., Trisno, A., Banjarnahor, H., & Sugianto, F. (2025). Building Digital Trust through Enforcement of Personal Data Protection Laws. In *Literacy Syntax* (Vol. 10, Issue 5).

Pujianto, A., Mulyati, A., & Novaria, R. (2018). UTILIZATION OF BIG DATA AND PROTECTION OF CONSUMER PRIVACY IN THE DIGITAL ECONOMY ERA. *Bijak Scientific Magazine, 15*(2), 127–137. DOI: 10.31334/bijak.v15i2.201

Quek, H. Y., Sielker, F., Akroyd, J., Bhave, A. N., von Richthofen, A., Herthogs, P., Yamu, C. van der L., Wan, L., Nochta, T., Burgess, G., Lim, M. Q., Mosbach, S., & Kraft, M. (2023). The conundrum in smart city governance: Interoperability and compatibility in an ever-growing ecosystem of digital twins. *Data & Policy, 5*, e6. https://doi.org/DOI. DOI: 10.1017/dap.2023.1

Quintero, J., Baldiris, S., Rubira, R., Cerón, J., & Velez, G. (2019). Augmented Reality in Educational Inclusion. A Systematic Review on the Last Decade. *Frontiers in Psychology, 10*, 1835. DOI: 10.3389/fpsyg.2019.01835 PMID: 31456716

Radu, I. (2014). Augmented reality in education: A meta-review and cross-media analysis. *Personal and Ubiquitous Computing, 18*(6), 1533–1543. DOI: 10.1007/s00779-013-0747-y

Raghavan, A., Demircioglu, M. A., & Orazgaliyev, S. (2025). Can VUCA events catalyze digital public sector innovations? Evidence from three digital innovation trends in Asia. *Journal of Open Innovation, 11*(2), 100529. DOI: 10.1016/j.joitmc.2025.100529

Rahwan, I. (2018). Society-in-the-loop. *Ethics and Information Technology, 20*(1), 5–14. DOI: 10.1007/s10676-017-9430-8

Rajagukguk, W., Heatubun, A., & Pane, M. (2023). Demographic and socioeconomic determinants of internet use in Indonesia. *ARPHA* Preprints, *4*, e109500.

Rajesh, R., Veena, S., Shanthini, A., & Deva Prasanna, D. S. J., Yasmeen, & Manjunath, T. C. (2026). AI for Predictive Sustainability in Healthcare. In C. Sheih, P. Upadhyay, M. Bhutani, V. Bandaru, & P. Dass (Eds.), *Responsible Innovation in Smart Healthcare: AI, IoT, and Ethical Sustainability Practices* (pp. 27-56). IGI Global Scientific Publishing.

Rakšnys, A. V. (2025). *THE USES OF ARTIFICIAL INTELLIGENCE IN THE PUBLIC SECTOR : CHALLENGES AND PROSPECTS. 24*(3).

Rasheed, Z., Ghwanmeh, S., & Almahadin, A. (2024). A Critical Review of AI-Driven AR Glasses for Realtime Multilingual Communication. *Advances in Science and Engineering Technology International Conferences, ASET*. DOI: 10.1109/ASET60340.2024.10708749

Ratti, C., & Claudel, M. (2016). *The city of tomorrow: Sensors, networks, hackers, and the future of urban life*. Yale University Press.

Revalina Annisa Antoine, NSFHHP (2025). *Misuse of Personal Data in Digital Transaction Technology in the Digital Banking Industry (Case Study of PT. Bank Syariah Indonesia).*

Ricciardi Celsi, L., & Zomaya, A. Y. (2025). Perspectives on Managing AI Ethics in the Digital Age. *Information (Basel)*, *16*(4), 318. DOI: 10.3390/info16040318

Rinaldo, & Puspitasari, D. (2024). Digital Risks in Developing Countries: Escalation of Cyber Threats in Indonesia (2020–2023). *Data: Journal of Information Systems and Management, 2* (3), 152–163. DOI: 10.61978/data.v2i3.697

Rocher, L., Hendrickx, J. M., & De Montjoye, Y.-A. (2019). Estimating re-identification success in incomplete datasets using generative models. *Nature Communications*, *10*(1), 3069. DOI: 10.1038/s41467-019-10933-3 PMID: 31337762

Rodrigues, R. (2020). Legal and human rights issues of AI: Gaps, challenges and vulnerabilities. *Journal of Responsible Technology*, *4*, 100005. DOI: 10.1016/j.jrt.2020.100005

Rohan, R., Pal, D., Hautamäki, J., Funilkul, S., Chutimaskul, W., & Thapliyal, H. (2023). A systematic literature review of cybersecurity scales assessing information security awareness. *Heliyon*, *9*(3), e14234. DOI: 10.1016/j.heliyon.2023.e14234 PMID: 36938452

Rosadi, S. D., Yuniarti, S., & Fauzi, R. (2022)... *PROTECTION OF DATA PRIVACY IN THE ERA OF ARTIFICIAL INTELLIGENCE IN THE FINANCIAL SECTOR.*, *1*(2), 353–366.

Rosado, D. G., Sánchez, L. E., Varela-Vaca, Á. J., Santos-Olmo, A., Gómez-López, M. T., Gasca, R. M., & Fernández-Medina, E. (2024). Security risk assessment and management for business process models. *Journal of Information Security and Applications*, *84*, 103829. DOI: 10.1016/j.jisa.2024.103829

Roziqin, A. (2025). *Analysis of Indonesian government policy on. 24* (1), 92–107. DOI: 10.1108/PAP-08-2020-0039

Roziqin, A., Fajrina, A. N., Sulistyaningsih, T., & Roziqin, A. (2022). *Development of e-Government in Indonesia: A bibliometric analysis.* DOI: 10.1080/09737766.2021.2007036

Roziqin, A., Kismartini, Fajrina, AN, Salahudin, & Sulistyaningsih, T. (2022). The Development of e-Government in Indonesia: A Bibliometric Analysis. *COLLNET Journal of Scientometrics and Information Management, 16* (1), 49–74.

Ruhlandt, R. W. S. (2018). The governance of smart cities. A systematic literature review. *Cities (London, England)*, *81*, 1–23. DOI: 10.1016/j.cities.2018.02.014

Rukanova, B., Tan, Y.-H., Slegt, M., Molenhuis, M., van Rijnsoever, B., Migeotte, J., Labare, M. L. M., Plecko, K., Caglayan, B., Shorten, G., van der Meij, O., & Post, S. (2021). Identifying the value of data analytics for government supervision: Insights from customs domain. *Government Information Quarterly*, *38*(1), 101496. DOI: 10.1016/j.giq.2020.101496

Sætra, H. S. (2020). Political harms of algorithmic governance. *Technology in Society*, *62*, 101283. PMID: 32536737

Sahu, C. K., Young, C., & Rai, R. (2021). AI in AR-assisted manufacturing: A review. *International Journal of Production Research*, *59*(16), 4903–4959. DOI: 10.1080/00207543.2020.1859636

Saidin, N. F., Abd Halim, N. D., & Yahaya, N. (2015). A Review of Research on Augmented Reality in Education: Advantages and Applications. *International Education Studies*, *8*(13), 1. DOI: 10.5539/ies.v8n13p1

Sanh, V., Debut, L., Chaumond, J., & Wolf, T. (2019). *DistilBERT, a distilled version of BERT: smaller, faster, cheaper and lighter*. arXiv. /arXiv.1910.01108DOI: 10.48550

Sarosa, M., Chalim, A., Suhari, S., Sari, Z., & Hakim, H. B. (2019). Developing augmented reality based application for character education using unity with Vuforia SDK. *Journal of Physics: Conference Series*, *1375*(1), 012035. DOI: 10.1088/1742-6596/1375/1/012035

Sarra, C. (2025). Artificial Intelligence in Decision-Making: A Consistency Test between the "EU AI Law" and the "General Data Protection Regulation.". *Athens Law Journal*, *11*(1), 45–62. DOI: 10.30958/ajl.11-1-3

Satyanarayana, P., Anute, N., Ghewari, A., Chahande, S., Sharma, A., & Manjunath, T. C. (2026). Interdisciplinary Applications of AI and AR in Research. In Vrba, J., & Huynh, T. (Eds.), *Revolutionizing Academic Research with AI and Augmented Reality* (pp. 283–310). IGI Global Scientific Publishing.

Schall, G., Mendez, E., Kruijff, E., Veas, E., Junghanns, S., Reitinger, B., & Schmalstieg, D. (2009). Handheld Augmented Reality for underground infrastructure visualization. *Personal and Ubiquitous Computing*, *13*(4), 281–291. DOI: 10.1007/s00779-008-0204-5

Schreiber, A. (2020). Privacy Blueprint: The Battle to Control the Design of New Technologies. By Woodrow Hartzog. [Cambridge, MA: Harvard University Press, 2018. x+ 366 pp. Hardcover £28.95. ISBN 978-06-74976-00-9. *The Cambridge Law Journal*, *79*(2), 377–380. DOI: 10.1017/S0008197320000355

Scupola, A., & Zanfei, A. (2016). Governance and innovation in public sector services: The case of the digital library. *Government Information Quarterly*, *33*(2), 237–249. DOI: 10.1016/j.giq.2016.04.005

Selvaskandan, H., Gee, P. O., & Seethapathy, H. (2024). Technological Innovations to Improve Patient Engagement in Nephrology. *Advances in Kidney Disease and Health*, *31*(1), 28–36. DOI: 10.1053/j.akdh.2023.11.001 PMID: 38403391

Semenets-Orlova, I., Shevchuk, R., Plish, B., Grydiushko, I., & Maistrenko, K. (2022). Innovative approaches to development of human potential in modern public administration. *Economic Affairs*, *67*(4s), 915–926.

Semjonov, A., Bornholdt, H., Edinger, J., & Russo Russo, G. R. (2024). *Wasimoff: Distributed Computation Offloading Using WebAssembly in the Browser*. 203–208. DOI: 10.1109/PerComWorkshops59983.2024.10503392

Sen, C., Yogi, K. K., & Singh, P. (2025). NVCED: Novel Deep Learning Model for Video Classification Enhanced by Temporal Feature Extraction. *2025 Artificial Intelligence and Smart Technologies for Sustainability Conference (AISTS)*, 1–6. DOI: 10.1109/AISTS66100.2025.11233141

Sen, A. (1999). *Development as freedom*. Oxford University Press.

Setiawan, HB, Fatma, &, & Najicha, U. (2022). PROTECTION OF PERSONAL DATA OF INDONESIAN CITIZENS RELATED TO DATA LEAKS. *Citizenship Journal, 6* (1).

Setiawan, H. B., & Najicha, F. U. (2022). Protection of Indonesian citizens' personal data regarding data leaks. *Journal of Citizenship*, *6*(1), 976–982.

Shah, I., Doshi, C., Patel, M., Tanwar, S., Hong, W.-C., & Sharma, R. (2022). A Comprehensive Review of the Technological Solutions to Analyse the Effects of Pandemic Outbreak on Human Lives. *Medicina (Lithuania), 58*(2). DOI: 10.3390/medicina58020311

Shayamunda, R., & Bhanye, J. (2024). Digital democracy in action: Impact of civic tech innovation on public service delivery. In G. Onyango & G. Karuri-Sebina (Eds.), *Digitalisation and public policy in Africa* (Studies in national governance and emerging technologies). Palgrave Macmillan. DOI: 10.1007/978-3-031-75079-3_8

Shin, B., Floch, J., Rask, M., Bæck, P., Edgar, C., Berditchevskaia, A., Mesure, P., & Branlat, M. (2024). A systematic analysis of digital tools for citizen participation. *Government Information Quarterly*, *101954*(3), 101954. DOI: 10.1016/j.giq.2024.101954

Shirazi, A., & Behzadan, A. H. (2015). Design and assessment of a mobile augmented reality-based information delivery tool for construction and civil engineering curriculum. *Journal of Professional Issues in Engineering Education and Practice*, *141*(3), 04014012. DOI: 10.1061/(ASCE)EI.1943-5541.0000229

Shrestha, A. K., Barthwal, A., Campbell, M., Shouli, A., Syed, S., Joshi, S., & Vassileva, J. (2024b). Navigating AI to address adolescent privacy concerns: An in-depth exploration and systematic review. *ArXiv Preprint ArXiv:2412.16369.*

Shrestha, A.K., Barthwal, A., Campbell, M., Shouli, A., Syed, S., Joshi, S., & Vassileva, J. (2024a). *Navigating AI to Uncover Adolescents' Privacy Concerns: An In-Depth Exploration and Systematic Review.*

Singh, P., Pahuja, N., Kansal, M., Gurung, S., Shukla, U., & Gupta, S. (2024). Enhancing Tourism Experiences and Preserving Cultural Heritage with AR and VR. *2024 2nd International Conference on Disruptive Technologies (ICDT)*, 225–231. DOI: 10.1109/ICDT61202.2024.10489490

Slater, M., & Wilbur, S. (1997). A framework for immersive virtual environments (FIVE): Presence in virtual environments. *Presence (Cambridge, Mass.)*, *6*(6), 603–616. DOI: 10.1162/pres.1997.6.6.603

Soegoto, E. S., Soegoto, H., Soegoto, D. S., & Soegoto, S. W. (2022). Indonesian Journal of Science & Technology A systematic Literature Review of Internet of Things for Higher Education. *Architecture and Implementation.*, *7*, 511–528.

Sonni, A. F., Mau, M., Akbar, M., & Putri, V. C. C. (2025). AI and Digital Literacy: Impact on Information Resilience in Indonesian Society. *Journalism and Media*, *6*(3), 100. DOI: 10.3390/journalmedia6030100

Soriano-gonzalez, R., Perez-bernabeu, E., Ahsini, Y., Carracedo, P., Camacho, A., & Juan, A. A. (2023). *Analyzing Key Performance Indicators for Mobility Logistics in Smart and Sustainable Cities : A Case Study Centered on Barcelona.*

Sri Wulandari, Y. (2025). ARTIFICIAL INTELLIGENCE AND DATA PROTECTION: A FAIR REGULATION ANALYSIS FOR THE INDONESIAN LEGAL SYSTEM. In *THE JURIS: Vol. IX* (Edition 1). http://ejournal.stih-awanglong.ac.id/index.php/juris

Srinidhi, S., Lu, E., & Rowe, A. (2024). XAIR: XR platform integrating LLMs with the physical world. *IEEE ISMAR*, 759–767.

Stahl, B. C., & Coeckelbergh, M. (2016). Ethics of healthcare robotics. *Robotics and Autonomous Systems*, *86*, 152–161. DOI: 10.1016/j.robot.2016.08.018

Stefanidi, Z., Margetis, G., Ntoa, S., & Papagiannakis, G. (2022). Real-Time Adaptation of Context-Aware Intelligent User Interfaces, for Enhanced Situational Awareness. *IEEE Access : Practical Innovations, Open Solutions*, *10*, 23367–23393. DOI: 10.1109/ACCESS.2022.3152743

Storozhenko, L., Olshanskyi, O., Stativka, N., Chernoivanenko, A., & Hordiienko, Y. (2024). Public Administration in the Context of Digital Transformation: Innovations and Challenges. *Revista de Cercetare si Interventie Sociala*, •••(85), 85. DOI: 10.33788/rcis.85.8

Suleymanoglu, B., Soycan, M., & Toth, C. (2024). 3D Road Boundary Extraction Based on Machine Learning Strategy Using LiDAR and Image-Derived MMS Point Clouds. In *Sensors* (Vol. 24, Issue 2, p. 503). DOI: 10.3390/s24020503

Sun, T. Q., & Medaglia, R. (2019). Mapping the challenges of artificial intelligence in the public sector. *Government Information Quarterly*, *36*(2), 368–383. DOI: 10.1016/j.giq.2018.09.008

Taeihagh, A., & Lim, H. S. M. (2019). Governing autonomous vehicles. *Transport Reviews*, *39*(1), 103–128. DOI: 10.1080/01441647.2018.1494640

Tang, K. (2024). *Multi-Objective Evcuation Planning Model Considering Post-Earthquake Fire Spread : A Tokyo Case Study.*

Tan, K. L., Lee, C. P., & Lim, K. M. (2023). A survey of sentiment analysis: Approaches, datasets and future research. *Applied Sciences (Basel, Switzerland)*, *13*(7), 4550. DOI: 10.3390/app13074550

Tate, M., Bongiovanni, I., Kowalkiewicz, M., & Townson, P. (2018). Managing the "Fuzzy front end" of open digital service innovation in the public sector: A methodology. *International Journal of Information Management*, *39*, 186–198. DOI: 10.1016/j.ijinfomgt.2017.11.008

Taylor, L. (2021). Public data governance: When openness and privacy collide. *Big Data & Society*, *8*(2), 1–13. DOI: 10.1177/20539517211042490

Thangavel, S., K, Sharmila, & K, Sufina. (2025). Revolutionizing Education Through Augmented Reality (AR) and Virtual Reality (VR): Innovations, Challenges and Future Prospects. *Asian Journal of Interdisciplinary Research*, 1–28. DOI: 10.54392/ajir2511

Tran, H. (2024). *Understanding user information behavior: An analysis of data protection measures on digital platforms.*

Trepte, S. (2021). A model of social media privacy: Privacy and communication in the context of social media affordances. *Communication Theory*, *31*(4), 549–570. DOI: 10.1093/ct/qtz035

Turan, Z., Meral, E., & Sahin, I. F. (2018). The impact of mobile augmented reality in geography education: Achievements, cognitive loads and views of university students. *Journal of Geography in Higher Education*, *42*(3), 427–441. DOI: 10.1080/03098265.2018.1455174

Ulnicane, I., Knight, W., Leach, T., Stahl, B. C., & Wanjiku, W. G. (2021). Framing governance for contested technologies. *Policy and Society*.

UNDP. (2023). *Human development report 2023–2024: Breaking the gridlock*. United Nations Development Programme.

United Nations. (2025). *World urbanization prospects: The 2025 revision*. United Nations Department of Economic and Social Affairs.

van Bekkum, M., & Borgesius, F. Z. (2021). Digital welfare fraud detection and the Dutch SyRI judgment. *European Journal of Social Security*, *23*(4), 323–340. DOI: 10.1177/13882627211031257

Van Binh, T., Minh, D. T., Linh, L. T. H., & Van Nhan, T. (2023). Location-based service information disclosure on social networking sites: The influence of privacy calculus, subjective norms, trust, and cultural differences. *Information Services & Use*, *43*(1), 39–62. DOI: 10.3233/ISU-230180

van Dijk, J. (2020). *The digital divide*. Polity Press.

Van Noordt, C., & Tangi, L. (2023). The dynamics of AI capability and its influence on public value creation in public administration. *Government Information Quarterly*, *40*(4), 101860. DOI: 10.1016/j.giq.2023.101860

van Winden, W., Oskam, I., van den Buuse, D., Schrama, W., & van Dijck, E.-J. (2016). *Organising smart city projects: Lessons from Amsterdam*. Amsterdam University of Applied Sciences.

Veale, M., & Brass, I. (2019). Administration by algorithm? In Karen Yeung & Martin Lodge (Eds.), *Algorithmic Regulation*. Oxford University Press. https://doi.org/10.1093/oso/9780198838494.003.0006.

Vieweg, S., Hughes, A. L., Starbird, K., & Palen, L. (2010). *Microblogging during two natural hazards events: What Twitter may contribute to situational awareness. Proceedings of the SIGCHI Conference on Human Factors in Computing Systems*, 1079-1088. DOI: 10.1145/1753326.1753486

Virali, B. M., Jagtiani, J., Pathak, G. P., Satyanarayana, P., Selvakumar, P., & Manjunath, T. C. (2026). Problem Solving Skills. In K. Francis & K. Hendrickson (Eds.), *Public Sector Burnout and Wellness: Research and Experiences* (pp. 241-266). IGI Global Scientific Publishing.

Visvizi, A., & Lytras, M. D. (2018). Rescaling and refocusing smart cities research: From mega cities to smart villages. *Journal of Science and Technology Policy Management*, *9*(2), 134–145. DOI: 10.1108/JSTPM-02-2018-0020

Wachter, S., Mittelstadt, B., & Russell, C. (2020). *WHY JUSTICE CAN'T BE AUTOMATED: BRIDGING THE GAP BETWEEN EU NON-DISCRIMINATION LAW AND AI*. 1–72.

Wachter, S., Mittelstadt, B., & Floridi, L. (2017). Why is a proper explanation of automated decision-making missing from the General Data Protection Regulation? *International Data Privacy Law*, *7*(2), 76–99. DOI: 10.1093/idpl/ipx005

Wang, J., & Li, J. (2024). Artificial intelligence empowering public health education: Prospects and challenges. *Frontiers in Public Health*, *12*, 1389026. DOI: 10.3389/fpubh.2024.1389026 PMID: 39022411

Wang, Y., Huang, X., Zhang, T., Jiang, B., & Wang, X. (2024). Impact of fiscal decentralization and local government competition on the supply of basic public services. *Heliyon*, *10*(4), e26511. DOI: 10.1016/j.heliyon.2024.e26511 PMID: 38420436

Wang, Z., Shi, Y., & Wang, Y.. (2024). G-VOILA: Gaze-facilitated information querying. *Proceedings of the ACM on Interactive, Mobile, Wearable and Ubiquitous Technologies*, *8*(2), 1–33.

Weber, M., Engert, M., Schaffer, N., Weking, J., & Krcmar, H. (2023). Organizational Capabilities for AI Implementation Coping with Inscrutability and Data Dependency in AI. *Information Systems Frontiers*, *25*(4), 1549–1569. DOI: 10.1007/s10796-022-10297-y

Wei, R.-Z., Liu, X.-Y., & Lyu, P.-H. (2024). Bibliometrics of public administration research hotspots: Topic keywords, author keywords, keywords plus analysis. *Heliyon*, *10*(21), e39352. DOI: 10.1016/j.heliyon.2024.e39352 PMID: 39524883

Wen, Y., Wu, L., He, S., Ng, N. H.-E., Teo, B. C., Looi, C. K., & Cai, Y. (2023). Integrating augmented reality into inquiry-based learning in science classrooms. *Educational Technology Research and Development*, *71*(4), 1631–1651. DOI: 10.1007/s11423-023-10235-y PMID: 37359487

Widijowati, D. (2023). *Improving Consumer Protection in Electronic Commerce Transactions* (Vol. 3, Issue 4).

Wirtz, B. W., Weyerer, J. C., & Geyer, C. (2019). Artificial intelligence and the public sector—Applications and challenges. *International Journal of Public Administration*, *42*(7), 596–615. DOI: 10.1080/01900692.2018.1498103

Wosny, M., & Hastings, J. (2024). Applying Large Language Models to Interpret Qualitative Interviews in Healthcare. [PubMed]. *Studies in Health Technology and Informatics*, *316*. Advance online publication. DOI: 10.3233/SHTI240530

Wu, S., Hou, L., Chen, H., & Zhang, G. (Kevin), Zou, Y., & Tushar, Q. (2023). Cognitive ergonomics-based Augmented Reality application for construction performance. *Automation in Construction, 149*, 104802. https://doi.org/https://doi.org/10.1016/j.autcon.2023.104802

Xu, C., Solomon, S. A., & Gao, W. (2023). Artificial intelligence-powered electronic skin. *Nature Machine Intelligence*, *5*(12), 1344–1355. DOI: 10.1038/s42256-023-00760-z PMID: 38370145

Young, M. M., Bullock, J. B., & Lecy, J. D. (2019). Artificial discretion: A framework for understanding the impact of artificial intelligence on public administration. *Perspectives on Public Management and Governance*, *2*(4), 301–313. DOI: 10.1093/ppmgov/gvz014

YuLung Wu. YuTien Wu, & ShuMey Yu. (2015). *An Augmented-Reality Interactive Card Game For Teaching Elementary School Students*. DOI: 10.5281/ZENODO.1110752

Zaidi, S. M. H., Bilal, M., Ashraf, S. N., Alharbi, A., Iqbal, R., & Zuberi, H. H. (2025). Review-Based AI-Driven Posture Correction and Personalized Fitness Assistant Using Computer Vision and Augmented Reality. *International Journal of E-Health and Medical Communications*, *16*(1), 1–25. Advance online publication. DOI: 10.4018/IJEHMC.381820

Zhang, D., Tan, W., Zelek, J., Ma, L., & Li, J. (2025). SLAM-TSM: Enhanced Indoor LiDAR SLAM With Total Station Measurements for Accurate Trajectory Estimation. *IEEE Transactions on Intelligent Transportation Systems*, *26*(2), 1743–1753. DOI: 10.1109/TITS.2024.3504487

Zhang, P., Wang, Z., Wang, T., Liu, T., Wang, J., Gao, Y., & Li, W. (2025). Evaluating Augmented Reality Head-Mounted Devices in Healthcare: A Review of Hardware, Software, and Usability Approaches. *Medical Devices (Auckland, N.Z.)*, *18*(0), 427–445. DOI: 10.2147/MDER.S541187 PMID: 40873666

Zhang, Y., & Miao, Z. (2025). Enhancing EFL Learners' Engagement and Motivation Through Immersive Technologies: The Role of Artificial Intelligence, Augmented Reality, Virtual Reality, and Mobile Applications. *European Journal of Education*, *60*(2), e70128. Advance online publication. DOI: 10.1111/ejed.70128

Zheng, Y., Capra, L., Wolfson, O., & Yang, H. (2014). Urban computing: Concepts, methodologies and applications. *ACM Transactions on Intelligent Systems and Technology*, *5*(3), 38. DOI: 10.1145/2629592

Zuboff, S. (2019). *The age of surveillance capitalism*. PublicAffairs.

Zuboff, S. (2019). *The age of surveillance capitalism. The fight for a human future at the new frontier of power*. PublicAffairs.

Züger, T., & Asghari, H. (2023). AI for the public. How public interest theory shifts the discourse on AI. *AI & Society*, *38*(2), 815–828. DOI: 10.1007/s00146-022-01480-5

About the Contributors

Jan Vrba, born in September 1990, holds EU and Czech citizenship. He resides in Czech Republic and Vietnam. Jan has been appointed Senior Full Professor ("Profesor Titular C") at Universidad Azteca, and he also earned a Ph.D. in Business Administration (Charisma University), D.B.A. in Human Resource Management, PhDr. in Political Science, and Master's Degrees in Big Data and Business Analytics. His career spans Vice-Dean and University Lecturer in the Czech Republic and Poland, Academic Expert in India, and Chief Innovation Officer in Malaysia. He leads international partnerships, global research management, and academic support in multicultural environments. Active in publishing as Deputy Editor-in-Chief and reviewer for peer-reviewed journals, he speaks at international conferences. Fluent in Czech, Slovak, and English. His research focuses on AI, public administration, and sustainability (SCOPUS/WOS indexed).

Thi Ngoc Quynh Huynh is an experienced educational consultant and lecturer based in Czechia, specializing in English language teaching and educational program development. She holds a Doctorate in Business Administration and a Master's degree from European institutions, as well as an MBA from Western Sydney University. Her career encompasses university lecturing, curriculum design, and leadership in language education, supported by multiple scholarships and academic awards that reflect her dedication to inspiring learners and advancing educational excellence.

Oldřich Hájek is a Czech academic, senator, and dean specializing in regional development and public administration. He holds advanced degrees in geography, public policy, and management, and presently serves as Dean at the Faculty of Administration and Economic Studies in Uherské Hradiště and as a senator in the Czech Parliament. His research focuses on territorial cohesion and regional policy, with publications in leading economic and geographical journals. Oldřich is also a passionate beekeeper.

***

A. Ranjithkumar is currently serving as an Assistant Professor of Political Science at the School of Law, Vel Tech University, Avadi, Chennai, Tamil Nadu. With a distinguished academic and professional career, he holds a Ph.D. in Politics and International Studies from Pondicherry University, a Master of Population Studies (MPS) from the International Institute for Population Sciences, Mumbai, and an M.A. in Development Administration from Gandhigram Rural Institute – Deemed University. He has also completed a Postgraduate Diploma in Industrial Relations and Labour Law (PGDIR & LL) from Pondicherry University and a B.P.Ed. from Vinayaka Missions University, Salem. Dr. Ranjithkumar has qualified the National Eligibility Test (NET) for Assistant Professor in Human Rights and Duties, Political Science, and Public Administration, conducted by the University Grants Commission (UGC), and was awarded the Dr. S. Radhakrishnan Postdoctoral Fellowship in Humanities and Social Sciences for the year 2014-15. His professional experience includes roles as an Assistant Professor at DLR Arts and Science College, Arcot, and Gandhigram Rural Institute, as well as research positions at Alagappa University, the National Law School of India University, and the Institute of Grassroots Governance. Dr. Ranjithkumar's research focuses on the Indian Political System, Local Government, Political Thought and Theories, Dalit Studies, and Development Administration. He has published over 35 research papers in leading journals and authored/edited 10 books on topics such as social justice, gender, and caste. He has received an International Travel Grant from the Indian Council of Social Science Research (ICSSR) to participate in the "Democratization and Autocratization: IPSA 75th Anniversary Conference" in Lisbon, Portugal, and Financial Assistance from ICSSR, Hyderabad, for organizing a National Conference on "Empowering Vulnerable Communities: Strategies for Inclusive Social Development." Dr. Ranjithkumar is an active member of professional bodies such as the International Political Science Association (IPSA) and the Indian Political Science Association, and he has organized over 10 international webinars and seminars. His areas of interest include Indian politics, local governance, Dalit studies, gender studies, and human rights.

Bartholomeus Dimanche Carl Beth is a computer science enthusiast with a strong interest in research and academic writing. His expertise lies in writing scientific journals and exploring topics related to technology, data systems, and innovation in computing. With a passion for continuous learning, he aims to contribute to the advancement of knowledge in the field of computer science through high-quality research and publications.

Devadharshini C is a third-year BBA LL.B. (Hons) student at the Saveetha School of Law, Saveetha Institute of Medical and Technical Sciences (SIMATS), Chennai, Tamil Nadu (600077). She has a keen academic interest in legal studies and business law, with a focus on understanding the intersection between law, commerce, and corporate governance. Her academic pursuits reflect a growing engagement with contemporary legal and business-related issues.

Angga Muhammad Galih is a dedicated professional with interests in information technology, digital systems, and applied computing. He has been involved in various academic and practical projects related to web-based application development, system analysis, and data management. His work emphasizes efficiency, reliability, and user-centered design in solving real-world problems. Angga demonstrates strong analytical skills and a collaborative mindset, enabling him to work effectively across technical and multidisciplinary environments. With a growing passion for technology-driven innovation, he continues to develop his expertise and contribute to the advancement of digital transformation in both academic and professional contexts.

Pawan Kumar Goel is a distinguished academician, researcher, and institutional leader with over two decades of experience in the field of Computer Science and Engineering. He is currently serving as an Associate Professor in the Department of Computer Science & Engineering at Raj Kumar Goel Institute of Technology, Ghaziabad, affiliated with Dr. A.P.J. Abdul Kalam Technical University, Lucknow. He holds a Ph.D. in Computer Science Engineering, M.Tech in CSE, and an MBA in Human Resource Management. He is UGC-NET qualified, has cleared GATE multiple times, and completed his B.Tech in Information Technology with distinction. In addition, he possesses numerous professional certifications in emerging technologies such as Artificial Intelligence, Blockchain, Cloud Computing, Cybersecurity, and Quantum Computing. Dr. Goel has made significant contributions to curriculum development, accreditation processes (NAAC and NBA), faculty mentoring, and institutional growth. He is a prolific author and editor with leading international publishers including IGI Global, Bentham Science, and Scientific International Publishing House. He has authored and edited several books and over 50 book chapters, and his research is widely published in Scopus and UGC-indexed journals. He has also presented his work at reputed IEEE international conferences. His research interests span AI and machine learning, cloud and edge computing, cybersecurity, Internet of Things, wireless sensor networks, and blockchain technology. He has filed multiple patents in areas such as smart agricultural drones, IoT-based health monitoring systems, and blockchain-integrated data management solutions. Dr. Goel has received several awards for academic excellence, including the International Achiever Award and Educator of the Year Award. He is an active member of professional bodies such as IEEE, ACM, CSI, and IFERP, and serves on editorial and review boards of various international journals. He is also the Institutional Ambassador for IFERP and SPOC for the Infosys Campus Connect Program. A dedicated educator, Dr. Goel teaches core computer science subjects and is known for his leadership, commitment, and passion for innovation in higher education.

Muhamad Rohisul Iman is a research assistant in the field of Informatics Engineering at Universitas Esa Unggul, Indonesia. His work focuses on artificial intelligence, digital ethics, and information systems, with active involvement in academic writing and technology-related research.

J. Aadithya is a third-year BBA LL.B. (Hons) student at the Saveetha School of Law, Saveetha Institute of Medical and Technical Sciences (SIMATS), Chennai, Tamil Nadu. His academic interests include legal studies and interdisciplinary approaches to law, with a focus on integrating legal principles with perspectives from business, social sciences, and public policy.

Shubham Jaiswal is a BTech Computer Science and Engineering student at Jaypee University of Engineering and Technology, Guna, India. He works on practical, problem-driven projects with real-world relevance. His academic interests include applied artificial intelligence, computer networks, distributed systems, and databases. He aims to contribute impactful research that bridges strong theoretical foundations and applied solutions.

Blaise Joseph is a Research Scholar at the Saveetha School of Law, Saveetha Institute of Medical and Technical Sciences (SIMATS), Chennai, Tamil Nadu. His academic interests lie in constitutional law, public law, and contemporary legal issues, with a strong emphasis on research-oriented and comparative public law studies. His work reflects a commitment to critical legal analysis and interdisciplinary perspectives in addressing evolving constitutional and public governance challenges.

Navin Kr. Goyal is an Associate Professor in the Department of Computer Engineering at Poornima Institute of Engineering & Technology, Jaipur, India. He holds a Ph.D. in Computer Engineering, with research focusing on ensemble machine learning approaches for fake review detection. With over two decades of experience in teaching, research, and academic administration, his areas of expertise include Artificial Intelligence, Machine Learning, Deep Learning, Web Technologies, and Information Security. Dr. Goyal has authored several peer-reviewed journal articles, conference papers, and international book chapters, and holds a published patent in Generative AI. He actively contributes to academic quality initiatives and international research collaborations.

Ryan Putra Laksana is a lecturer at the Faculty of Computer Science, Universitas Esa Unggul, Indonesia. He has extensive experience in teaching and research related to Information Technology, with a particular focus on the Internet of Things (IoT), project management, and other IT-related subjects. His academic interests include the development of intelligent systems, the integration of IoT in modern infrastructures, and the application of agile methodologies in IT project management. Ryan actively engages in research and collaborative projects aimed at advancing digital innovation and technology adoption in education and industry. His dedication to fostering technological literacy and developing practical IT solutions reflects his commitment to bridging the gap between academic research and real-world implementation.

Mohammad Jafar Loilatu is employed at Universitas Muhammadiyah Malang as a lecturer in the Department of Government Studies. Mohammad Jafar Loilatu is a doctoral student at the Department of Public Administration at the University of Gadjah Mada in Indonesia. Conducting research on the topics of urban mobility, urban governance, and public administration, looking for collaboration research on this topic, you can email me at jafarloilatu@umm.ac.id

Kunj Bihari Meena is a faculty member and researcher in Computer Science and Engineering at Jaypee University and Engineering Technology Guna. Dr. Meena has published multiple papers in reputed international journals and conferences, including SCI and Scopus-indexed publications. He has received Best Paper Awards for his research contributions and serves as a reviewer for prestigious SCI/Scopus journals and conferences. His areas of research include image processing, digital image forensics, deep learning, and blockchain.

Enrico Moch studied business administration at the University of Wismar and subsequently completed a degree in business law at Saarland University. Several years later, he completed a doctorate in economics on the topic of the influence of artificial intelligence on the world of work. His main job is as an administrative officer at the DLR Project Management Agency in the Society, Innovation and Technology division, where he is assigned to the AI Applications in Business department. In this role, he deals with the monitoring, evaluation and structuring of research and innovation projects in the context of digital technologies. Enrico Moch also works as a university lecturer at various institutions in Germany, including the Baden-Württemberg Cooperative State University Ravensburg. He also holds the position of Assistant Professor of Economics at the IICUT. He has been Academic

Director of the Herford-based GrandEdu Research School for several years. His research focuses on AI governance, technical data protection and the institutional governance of digital platforms. In terms of content, his work focuses on regulatory frameworks, governance structures and the economic impact of artificial intelligence and data-driven systems. Enrico Moch regularly publishes scientific articles, is involved in interdisciplinary book projects and is active in academic peer review. He is also active in knowledge transfer between academia and practice and hosts the podcast "GrandEdu Research School - On the trail of the economy!".

Shivam Nikhra is pursuing Bachelor of Technology (B.Tech.) in Computer Science and Engineering at Jaypee University of Engineering and Technology, Guna, India. He has a strong academic and research-oriented interest in Artificial Intelligence and Machine Learning, with particular emphasis on Natural Language Processing. His work is motivated by the practical and societal impact of intelligent systems and continues to develop his expertise through academic coursework, independent study, and applied projects in AI and ML.

Tobias Oberdieck is Managing Director of GrandEdu GmbH, a leading further education institution that specialises in preparing professionals for degrees such as the Bachelor Professional, Master Professional and Master of Business Administration (MBA). In his role at GrandEdu, he drives innovative educational strategies to actively support the recruitment of skilled labour in Germany. During his doctorate, Dr. Oberdieck worked as a research assistant at the Department of Business Administration and Economics at the Niederrhein University of Applied Sciences in Germany. During this time, he deepened his expertise in the areas of education management, labour market research and economic education models, which he now brings to his work at GrandEdu. His research focuses on the interface between continuing vocational training, academic education and the challenges of the modern labour market.

P. Selvakumar currently serves as an Associate Professor in the Department of Science and Humanities at Nehru Institute of Technology, Coimbatore, Tamil Nadu, India. With a teaching career spanning over a decade, he previously held positions as an Assistant Professor in the Department of Science and Humanities at various engineering colleges in Coimbatore from 2011 to 2023. Dr. P. Selvakumar's primary area of academic and research interest is phytochemistry, where he has made substantial contributions. His research credentials include 30 journal publications, 14 patents, and 25 conference papers. He has actively promoted faculty and student development by organizing 5 Faculty Development Programs (FDPs) and completing 3 NPTEL courses along with 60 Coursera certifications. His dedication to student success is evident in his role as a committed mentor, consistently guiding and supporting his students academically and personally. Recognized for his excellence in teaching, Dr. P. Selvakumar has received numerous accolades, including Best Teacher Awards. He is also an active member of MISTE (The Indian Society for Technical Education) and continues to play a vital role in both acade

Lars Arnold Ritter is a university lecturer and is currently doing his doctorate at the University of Library Studies and Information Technologies (ULSIT) in Sofia. In his dissertation, entitled Optimising the Organisation and Management of Information Processes for Increasing Motivation and Effectiveness of Adult Education, he is developing his own Learning Management System (LMS), which is geared towards efficiency, motivation and sustainability in adult education. He teaches academic work at several universities and combines academic expertise with practical advice.

Ali Roziqin is a Lecturer in the Department of Government Studies, Universitas Muhammadiyah Malang, Indonesia. He obtained his bachelor's degree from the Department of Public Administration at Universitas Diponegoro, Indonesia. He holds a Master of Public Administration from the Universitas Gadjah Mada, Indonesia. His research interests are in bureaucracy, public policy and administration, and public sector innovation. He has published papers in the reputable international journals like Sustainability (MDPI), Local Environment (Taylor and Francis), Tourism Critiques, Journal of Science and Technology Policy Management, Journal of the Knowledge Economy, Frontiers in Communication and Public Administration and Policy: An Asia-Pacific Journal and Public Administration Quarterly, as well as in the IGI Global

S. Giriprasad is an Assistant Professor in the Department of Electronics and Communication Engineering at SRM Institute of Science and Technology. His academic role involves teaching, research, and mentoring in the field of electronics and communication engineering, with an emphasis on advancing technical education and contributing to scholarly research in emerging areas of engineering and technology.

S. Vignesh is a second-year BBA LL.B. (Hons) student at the Saveetha School of Law, Saveetha Institute of Medical and Technical Sciences (SIMATS), Chennai, Tamil Nadu (600077). He is pursuing his undergraduate legal education with a particular interest in constitutional law, focusing on foundational principles, governance structures, and the evolving interpretation of constitutional frameworks in India.

Gusti Muhammad Sardana is a motivated individual with interests in information technology, digital systems, and applied computing. He has been involved in academic and practical activities related to software development, system analysis, and data management, with an emphasis on efficiency and usability. His work reflects strong analytical thinking and problem-solving skills in addressing real-world technical challenges. Gusti Muhammad Sardana is known for his adaptability and collaborative mindset, and he continues to develop his expertise in emerging technologies to support innovative digital solutions in academic and professional contexts.

Binastya Anggara Sekti has been a lecturer at the Faculty of Computer Science, Esa Unggul University, Jakarta, since 2016. He is actively involved in the Artificial Intelligence and Information Security Study Group. He holds a Bachelor's degree in Informatics Engineering from the Bandung Institute of Technology and a Master's degree in Information Systems Management from Trisakti University, Jakarta. Prior to entering academia, he accumulated over 25 years of professional experience as an IT practitioner in various companies across Jakarta. His work focused on developing data centers for internet service providers and delivering IT solutions for the manufacturing and oil & gas sectors. His research interests include artificial intelligence, cybersecurity, and the development of IT infrastructure.

Pancham Singh has been serving as an Assistant Professor in the Department of Information Technology at Ajay Kumar Garg Engineering College (AKGEC), Ghaziabad, since 2007. He has over 18 years of teaching experience, including both academic and industry exposure. He earned his B.Tech. in Computer Science and Engineering from UPTU, Lucknow, in 2005 and his M.Tech. in Information Technology from RTU, Kota, Rajasthan, in 2013. He is currently pursuing a PhD in CSE at the Netaji Subhas University of Technology (NSUT), New Delhi. Mr. Singh has authored and edited 5 books in the field of Computer Science. He has also presented and published more than 35 research papers in reputed journals and conferences. In addition, he holds over 45 national and international patents, including 6 design grants and 1 utility grant. His main research interests include Machine Learning, Deep Learning, the Internet of Things (IoT), and Software Engineering.

Sanjay Kumar Sinha is a well-known Academician, Administrator and is currently working as a Professor in the Department of Computer Engineering at Poornima Institute of Engineering & Technology (Poornima Group, Jaipur, Rajasthan). He has more than 23 years of teaching experience in the field of academics and administration and has held different positions in different institutions.

His research area was Big Data Analytics, and he also has an interest in Data Mining, Artificial Intelligence, Machine Learning, and Blockchain. He has published 31 research papers in IEEE, Springer, and Scopus-indexed journals, peer-reviewed journals. He has presented 12 Papers in National/International Conferences. He has written 06 Book Chapters, and 03 Patents Filed (two published). He has also served as an External Expert in various Research Development Committee, Subject Expert, Paper Setter & thesis evaluators in Colleges & Universities. He has actively participated in various Faculty Development Programs as well. He has attended 40 and more National/International Seminars/Workshops. Dr. Sinha has worked as NAAC Coordinator, NIRF Coordinator, IQAC Coordinator, Placement Officer & AISHE Coordinator at Kolhan University, Chaibasa, Jharkhand (a state govt. University). He is a life member of ACM, ISTE, and IEEE. He has successfully guided 01 PhD scholar and 09 PG Scholars (VGU, Jaipur), guiding 01 PhD. Candidate, Poornima University, Jaipur.

Tri Sulistyaningsih is a professor at the Department of Government Studies, Universitas Muhammadiyah Malang; now she is vice rector at Universitas Muhammadiyah Malang. Currently she publishes articles on specific issues such as public policy, urban governance, and local government. Email address: sulistyaningsih@umm.ac.id

Shreshtha Tudha is a BTech (Computer Science and Engineering) student at Jaypee University of Engineering and Technology, Guna, India. He has a strong interest in artificial intelligence and its real-world applications. Driven by curiosity and innovation, Shreshtha is focused on research in deep learning and intelligent systems.

Vipin Tyagi is a distinguished academician, researcher and author, currently serving as Dean (Academics and Research) at Jaypee University of Engineering and Technology in Guna, Madhya Pradesh. With a rich background in Computer Science, his expertise spans across Image Processing, Cyber Forensics and Speech Recognition. Prof. Tyagi has a prolific publication record, contributing significantly to his fields of interest. His scholarly work includes numerous journal articles, conference papers, and books. Some of his notable publications are in the areas of image forgery detection, image denoising and content-based image retrieval. He has authored and edited several books and papers in the field of Computer Science, such as "Digital Image Forgery Detection: Techniques, Challenges and Applications", "Predictive Computing and Information Security" and "Content-Based Image Retrieval: Ideas, Influences, and Current Trends" published by Springer Singapore. His book "Understanding Digital Image Processing" using MATLAB, published by

Taylor and Francis is highlighted by Mathworks. His scholarly work has earned him a respectable h-index and numerous citations in the academic community.

R.K. Yadav is a Professor and Head of the Electronics and Communication Engineering Department at RKGIT, Ghaziabad. He has more than 29 years of experience in teaching and research. His main areas of expertise include Microwave Engineering, Electromagnetic (EM) Waves, and Image Processing. He has published over 120 research papers in reputed national and international journals and conferences. He is also the author of a book on Microwave Engineering. Dr. Yadav is an active member of IEEE. He has successfully organized several international conferences in collaboration with IEEE and Elsevier. He also serves as an editor for a Springer journal and has worked as an editor for several books published by IGI Global, Nova Science Publishers, CRC Press, and others. He has guided 8 Ph.D. candidates in various research areas such as Microwave Engineering, Image Processing, and Integrated Circuits.

Muhammad Adi Zacky Zahran is a motivated individual with interests in information technology, digital systems, and applied computing. He has been involved in academic and practical activities related to software development, system analysis, and data management, with an emphasis on efficiency and usability. His work reflects strong analytical thinking and problem-solving abilities in addressing real-world technical challenges. Muhammad Adi Zacky Zahran is known for his adaptability and collaborative approach, and he continues to develop his expertise in emerging technologies to support innovative digital solutions in academic and professional contexts.

Index

www.ingramcontent.com/pod-product-compliance
Lightning Source LLC
LaVergne TN
LVHW081534300926
849161LV00006B/1429

* 9 7 9 8 3 3 7 3 7 8 0 4 6 *